Treating the Remarried Family

Treating the Remarried Family

Clifford J. Sager

Hollis Steer Brown • Helen Crohn

Tamara Engel

Evelyn Rodstein • Libby Walker

BRUNNER/MAZEL, *Publishers* • New York

Library of Congress Cataloging in Publication Data

Main entry under title:

Treating the remarried family.

   Bibliography: p.
   Includes index.
   1. Remarriage.   2. Marriage counseling.
3. Family life education.   I. Sager, Clifford J.,
1916–   .   [DNLM: 1. Family therapy. WM 430.5.F2
T784]
HQ 536.T63   1983   362.8'286   82-17811
ISBN 0-87630-323-8

Published by
BRUNNER/MAZEL, INC.
19 Union Square
New York, New York 10003

To the courageous families who worked with us to fulfill individual, marital and family life-cycle needs.

About the Authors

CLIFFORD J. SAGER, M.D.
  Director, Remarried Consultation Service and Director Family Psychiatry, Jewish Board of Family and Children's Services; Clinical Professor of Psychiatry, New York Hospital-Cornell Medical Center.

HOLLIS STEER BROWN, R.N.
  Associate Director, Remarried Consultation Service; Administrative Supervisor, Advanced Family Therapy Training Program, Jewish Board of Family and Children's Services.

HELEN CROHN, M.S.S., C.S.W.
  Supervisor, Madeline Borg Clinic and Advanced Family Therapy Training Program, Jewish Board of Family and Children's Services; Private Practice.

TAMARA ENGEL, M.S.W., C.S.W.
  Former Senior Social Worker, Jewish Board of Family and Children's Services; Private Practice.

EVELYN RODSTEIN, M.S.W., C.S.W.
  Supervisor, Advanced Family Therapy Training Program, Jewish Board of Family and Children's Services; Private Practice.

LIBBY WALKER, M.S.W., C.S.W.
  Supervisor, New York School for Psychoanalytic Psychotherapy; formerly Supervisor, Jewish Board of Family and Children's Services; Private Practice.

Contents

SECTION II. TREATMENT

Introduction

The remarried family is a new American family. Second marriages and stepchildren have existed at least since the beginning of recorded history, but only recently have those involved in remarried families come to constitute one-fifth of the population. Most remarriages now follow divorce, which has replaced the death of a spouse as the prevalent reason for dissolution of a first marriage. The remarried (Rem) family is a new family structure because the social conditions in which it exists differ from those of past centuries. While at the same time reflecting societal, legal, and religious changes that have already taken place, the existence of these families in such great numbers is creating new societal conditions and attitudes.

The remarried family has, in general, the same purposes and objectives as the intact, nuclear family. These are: *for the adults,* to provide a unique relationship of love, consideration, companionship, sexual gratification and, where desired, to have and care for mutual children; *for the children,* parenting and an environment in which to grow, individuate, and learn the culture and mores of the world about them. In Rem families some of the purposes and objectives for children are shared between the households of the two bioparents; one or more stepparents also are likely to be members of the co-parenting team. Children are brought up in two homes, often with appreciably different cultures and household rules.

We know, from their increasing appearance in our clinics, that many of these families are not functioning well. Many Rem families are in need of stepfamily life education, guidance, and therapeutic help. Recognizing that our therapeutic approaches, based largely on the structure, purposes, roles, myths, and values of the nuclear family, were inadequate when we began to treat and study Rem families, we set out to address a number of questions:

- Who are the people involved in these new family systems?
- What is the structure of the Rem family?
- In what ways do Rem families differ from intact families?
- What are the dimensions of the Rem family system?
- How do these systems operate for the well-being of the unit and the individual?
- How does the history of the people in Rem families help to shape their feelings and behavior?
- How can we devise ways to work more effectively in behalf of the Rem couple, the children, the former spouses, and *both* bioparents' new family constellations?
- How can we help prevent dysfunction in Rem families and short- and long-range adverse effects on children?
- Is there a positive potential that can enhance maturation, healthy values and fulfillment for children, as well as adults, in remarried situations? If so, how can we help to unleash and achieve this potential?

These are some of the questions we set out to examine six years ago. Because we are therapists working in a clinical setting, our first goal was to understand the structure, needs, and dynamics of Rem families, and that of the other spouse and his/her household, with the intent of increasing our therapeutic ability. At the same time, we hoped to develop a theory that would provide the substratum for our therapeutic and preventive endeavors. Much must still be done before remarriage and stepparenting will overcome the negative mythology that has surrounded them for centuries. First, however, the dynamics and processes of the stepfamily and the influences that shape it must be understood in order to develop a positive therapeutic approach. This book, like all such undertakings, is a work in progress.

The development of family therapy over the past 30 years and the evolution of a broadly based general systems approach that includes conceptualizing various levels of integration, all of which help determine behavior, form the theoretical basis from which we began our work. We are indebted to Scheflen (1981) for conceptualizing what we had been struggling towards—an approach to interdependent, cybernetically interacting levels within systems: biological, intrapsychic, interpersonal, familial, institutional, and societal. This integrated multisystems approach added to our understanding of the complex network so common to remarried families. It provides the most useful explanation for our observations made from various vantage points, as well as an effective rationale for therapeutic intervention. A wide range of interventions on different levels and with different subsystems becomes available when the therapist is comfortable with a multilevel conceptualization of the individual, family, and suprasystem.

THE REMARRIED CONSULTATION SERVICE

The Remarried Consultation Service was created in 1976 at what was then the Jewish Family Service of New York City. A survey of our cases had revealed a large number of family and marital units in which one or both adults had been previously married. Three-fifths of the adults were legally remarried; two-fifths lived together in a committed relationship with or without children from a previous marriage. The survey revealed the need for a unit to study the Rem phenomenon and to develop ways to improve our services to this group and to the other former spouse's family system upon whom they impinge.

The Remarried Consultation staff was composed of Clifford J. Sager, Director, Hollis Steer Brown, Associate Director, and a number of family and child therapists who worked in different local clinic offices of the agency. Each spent four days a week in his or her local clinic, seeing clients and serving as consultant on remarried situations to their colleagues. One-half of each therapist's caseload consisted of Rem cases. One day a week the staff met together to review cases, to have group supervision and live consultation interviews of families with the director and associate director of the service, to review the literature relevant to Rem, to build theory, to support one another, and to disseminate our findings to the rest of the agency's staff and to other professional colleagues. In 1978, the Jewish Family Service merged with the Jewish Board of Guardians to create the Jewish Board of Family and Children's Services; the merged agency continued the project. In September 1979, their task completed, the original staff, except for the director and associate director, went on to other duties, but remained together as a functioning group to write about their experiences and conclusions, particularly in this volume. The group included, in addition to Sager and Brown, Helen Crohn, Evelyn Rodstein and Elizabeth Walker. A new staff of experienced therapists came on in a training capacity to work with the director and associate director in the fall of 1979. Of these Ta-

mara Engel joined the book committee in December, 1980, Leila Perlmutter became the senior author of Chapter 13, which is also being published elsewhere, and Monica Hellman took prime responsibility for the
data collection and analysis that are presented.

THE CLINIC POPULATION

The Remarried Consultation Service staff of the agency during a four
and a half year period treated over 350 remarried families. Among them
they had 700 custodial or visiting children. In addition, many more families were seen in consultation.

The clinic patients were all residents of New York City. Affiliation to
one of the three major religious groups was claimed by 87%; of these
70% were Jewish, 16% Protestant, and 14% Catholic. Of the total number of families, 3% claimed other religions; the religion of 9% was unknown; 1% reported they had no religion.

The following data are based on 137 consecutive cases treated from
October 1979 through May 1981. The education levels of those in the
study were appreciably higher than the average for the Agency's clinics, as were the income levels. Five percent of the adult males had some
high school education, as did 9% of the women; 22% of men and 26% of
the women had completed high school; 13% of men and 21% of women
had some college; 28% of men and 25% of women had completed college;
27% of men and 19% of women had masters degrees; and 5% of men and
no women had doctorates.

In the vocational categories, 24% of men and 20% of women were in
unskilled work; 18.5% of men and 16.3% of women were skilled workers;
20% of men and 16.5% of women were in managerial positions; 27.5% of
men and 26% of women were professionals; no men were homemakers,
whereas 17.2% of the women were; men had 10% in other scattered categories, women 4%.

Income was classified in terms of total income of the biofather's
household and total income of the biomother's household. Thus, income
would include each spouse's income to that household if there were two,
as well as child support and alimony. Of the total, 8% of biofathers' income was at poverty level (1979 Labor Bureau definitions of 0 to $7,499
annually, including welfare), whereas 13% of biomothers' households
were in this category. At the low level ($7,500–$19,999 annually), there
were 37% of biofathers' and 34% of biomothers' households. In the middle income range ($20,000–$29,999), there were 22% of the biofathers'
households, and 27% of biomothers'. For the upper level ($30,000 and

above), there were 33% biofathers' households and 26% biomothers' households. It is of interest to note that, on the average, financial discrepancies between bioparents' households were not as great as might have been anticipated, although in any particular pair of bioparents' households there could be wide differences in total income levels.

The average number of years the Rem partners were remarried at time of application for service was 3.9; the average number of children in these Rem units was 2.1.

THE BOOK

The clinical work of the book is based on our experience with this population, as well as with some additional families seen in private practice by some of the staff. We are cautious about generalizing from this clinic population to Rem families who have not sought help or who come from other geographic, ethnic, religious and socioeconomic groups.

We believe that behavior is determined by many levels of interacting systems—from the microbiological to the ecological and societal. We focus in particular on three levels of interrelated systems in our understanding and therapeutic work: the family systems, the life cycles, and the intrapsychic (*systems-cycles-psyche*). It is important, however, to consider these three within the matrix of at least four other system levels: the biological, the peer group, the vocational or school, and the broader societal.

In remarried situations we concern ourselves with the Rem family and all those individuals and subsystems that have input to it, including former spouses and their households and children from prior marriages. All of these individuals and subsystems together are conceptualized as the Rem family suprasystem. The suprasystem reflects the history of the Rem family, as well as the current reality of those who have significant input into these complex families. This conceptualization reinforces the clinical need to make sure that all pertinent subsystems are seen in evaluation and possibly in treatment.

We recognize the importance of the traumatic steps that precede remarriage: dysfunctional couple (or death of spouse), separation, divorce, double single-parent households. How these stages have been handled is often an important determinant of the quality of the eventual Rem situation. However, in this volume we have devoted our major attention to the families of those who are legally remarried or living together in a committed relationship. The literature on the stages that precede remarriage is extensive; our knowledge of that literature and our own clinical experience with these stages are necessary to the understanding of remarried families and their suprasystems.

The Four Sections

Section I on *Structure and Theory* is composed of four chapters. Chapter 1 uses a single case to trace the sequential steps leading to the formation of a Rem family and its Rem family suprasystem. It illustrates the emotional wrench on all individuals at different points in the progression to Rem. Chapter 2 examines the differences in structure of nuclear and Rem families and the implications these structural differences have for individuals and subsystems of the family. Chapter 3 offers an integration of the individual, marital, and family life cycles and the purposes and needs of these three cycles. The concept of living out one's life cycle in two or more marital or family life cycles is advanced. Chapter 4 recognizes the primacy of the Rem couple in the new family. A comprehensive system of couple interaction within remarriage and methods for assessing the dynamics and quality of the interaction are discussed.

Section II includes basic tenets of *Treatment* for Rem families, individuals in Rem families, and other significant subsystems of the Rem suprasystem. The application of the theory developed in Section I is detailed and illustrated here. The first chapter in this section, Chapter 5, recognizes the importance of the therapist and deals with his or her emotional reactions in treating Rem cases, the pitfalls awaiting the therapist, and the need for a support system of colleagues. Chapters 6 and 7 present concepts and techniques, which are illustrated by the same case in both chapters. Chapter 6 develops methods of client engagement, evaluation, goal setting and treatment planning, while Chapter 7 elaborates on the middle and end phases of treatment. Modality choices and principles of whom to treat and when are discussed. Chapter 8 focuses on the marital couple subsystem in treatment, Chapter 9 deals with special aspects and problems of treating the prepubescent child, and Chapter 10 looks at the adolescent in Rem.

Section III on Special Issues of Remarriage features a series of short chapters that define and discuss common family situations as they are manifested in Rem families. Chapter 11 deals with ceremonies of passage that usually are regarded as joyous family events, but often are problematic in Rem families. Chapter 12 looks in depth at the remarried couple that is trying to decide whether to have a mutual child. Chapter 13 examines the wide variety of household sexual expressions that may occur within a remarried family due to the loosening of sexual bounda-

ries. Chapter 14 explores the strong emotions and motivations sur-
rounding the question of adopting one's stepchildren. Chapter 15 deals
with the problems created by a mentally ill Rem member, be it child,
partner, former spouse, or present spouse.

Section IV reviews our experiences and those of others in the area of
prevention. At the end of the book are a bibliography and appendices of
the various instruments referred to in the text.

We are at the beginning of a new era in family life that challenges our
concepts of tradition, possessiveness and the impermeable family boundaries. With a better understanding of the Rem family and its suprasystem we are in a position to support and foster creative childrearing and
adult relatedness in the more complex families of the emergent present
and the future. A new type of extended family is becoming available.
Our work has made us optimistic about the effective role the Rem family can have in fulfilling the developmental and life cycle needs of children and adults.

ACKNOWLEDGMENTS

We have worked together as a collaborative team for six years. *All*
authors have contributed to *all* the chapters. However, we do want to acknowledge that the case discussed in Chapters 6 and 7 was treated by
Tamara Engel and much of the discussion of the specific case originated
with her. She was also responsible for the basic work on several of the
chapters of Section III. Her ability as a writer is reflected throughout
the book. Leila Perlmutter was the major author of Chapter 13 on Loosened Sexual Boundaries. We are also grateful to Joseph G. Moore, Senior
Consultant, Child Welfare League of America, for his suggestions concerning Chapter 10 on adolescence.

Much is owed to Wanda Santaella and Elliot Zeisel, who left the service before we undertook writing this book. Their experiences and contributions are inextricably woven into the book, as are those of Joan Beir
who elected not to join the book team.

We are grateful to Sanford Sherman and Arthur Leader, formerly Director and Associate Director, respectively, of the Jewish Family Service, who gave their support and encouragement to the project, and to
Jerome Goldsmith, Executive Vice President of the merged Agency,
who continued that support and counsel. The Agency provided a hospitable matrix for the study and research. We are indebted to Judith Lang,
Associate Director of the Agency for reading the manuscript and giving
generously of her constructive criticism. We thank Bernard Mazel, our

publisher, for his faith in us, and Susan Barrows for her sensitive and knowledgeable editorial help.

Linda Garrett and Barbara Meyer were tireless as they retyped draft after draft after draft of each chapter as each of the authors left his/her imprint on it.

Permissions

Permission was granted by the American Psychiatric Association to reproduce the table that appeared in Ellen Berman and Harold Lief's article "Marital Therapy from a Psychiatric Perspective: An Overview," published in the *American Journal of Psychiatry,* 132(6):586, June 1975. Permission was granted by the Gardner Press, Inc. to reproduce three tables (1.1, 1.2 and 1.3) from *The Family Life Cycle* (1980) edited by Elizabeth Carter and Monica McGoldrick. These four tables are reproduced in Chapter 3.

C.J.S.
H.S.B.
H.C.
T.E.
E.R.
L.W.

SECTION I

Structure and Theory

CHAPTER 1

Formation of a Remarried Family—Evolution and Revolution

DEFINITIONS AND GUIDELINES

The remarried family is our focus. The term is used here to describe the second, reconstituted, blended or stepfamily. We previously have defined the remarried (Rem) family as a family that is created by the marriage (or living together in one domicile) of two partners, one or both of whom had been previously married and then divorced or widowed (Sager et al., 1981). There may or may not be children from prior marriages who visit or reside with them. The adult couple and the children comprise the Rem family system. This definition also allows for the inclusion of gay couples and their children from a prior marriage.

Additionally, there is a network of people and relationships created through the prior divorce and the formalization of the remarriage. These include the former spouses of one or both of the Rem adults (alive or dead), the families of origin of all the adults—the Rem couple and their former spouses, and the children of each of the adults. Grandparents, aunts, uncles, cousins, stepgrandparents belong here as well. Some of the Rem roles, such as stepparent, stepchild, and stepsibling, are not clearly defined by tradition or institutionalization. This network is similar to the extended family of a nuclear family, except that with the remarriage there are step, as well as blood and in-law ties; hence there is a need for a term other than "extended family." Bohannan (1971) uses the expression "divorce chains" to describe this network; we refer to this entourage as the "Rem suprasystem." The Rem suprasystem is impor-

3

tant because of its members' influence and input into the Rem family. The Rem family in this context is a subsystem of the Rem suprasystem. Thus, the suprasystem is made up of the network of the different individuals and functionally related people (subsystems) who impinge on Rem members. Some of these subsystems, such as the bioparent subsystem and the sibling-stepsibling subsystem, may cross two households. Each subsystem is at once a system in its own right and a subsystem in relation to the suprasystem. The suprasystem can be an important positive force, a strongly negative force, or a melange of contradictory forces, but it cannot be ignored. An understanding of the suprasystem and the power of some of its constituents as they affect the quality and viability of the Rem family can provide important leverage in the treatment of Rem. (See Figure 1.1.)

Each remarried family can be fully appreciated only in the context of its history and its antecedent family or families. It is *not* a reconstitution of its predecessor, the original nuclear family, although its members may expect it to provide the same love and mutual support and to

FIGURE 1.1
Schematic Drawing of Rem Family Suprasystem

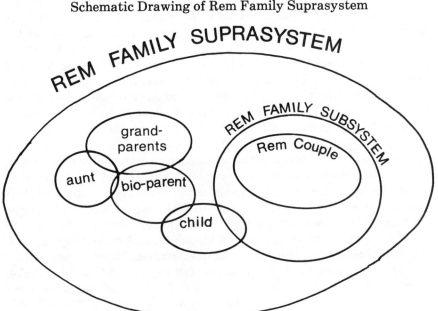

carry on the same parenting and childrearing tasks as the intact nuclear family. Similarly, using the nuclear family model as a road map or "ideal" does not work for Rem families. We support the view of Fast and Cain (1966) who suggest that Rem families be viewed as a structural variation of families. In this way their own distinct organizational point of view can be developed, separate from the normative pattern of the nuclear family. Unlike the nuclear family, a Rem family can assume many structural forms. This depends on whether one or both adult partners had been married before, whether either or both had children with previous spouses, whether their children are living with them and/or visiting, and whether or not they have mutual children. Walker and Messinger (1979) have clearly described 12 common structural types of Rem families, which are readily multiplied with the inclusion of additional variables.

A Rem couple has arrived at remarriage through a process of evolution and revolution, by planned changes as well as by the gradual accretion of unnoticed changes and by the sudden wrenching and far-reaching changes brought about by a spouse's death or by marital conflict, separation, and divorce. For the majority, changes are forced upon them. The children rarely play a knowledgeable or voluntary role in the decision-making process, either in the separation and divorce or the remarriage. They may be subject to damaging effects engendered by the fact that they cannot understand or control the adult actions that so deeply affect them.

For all concerned there is some degree of sadness and feeling of loss in the flood of change. Each step away from the original nuclear family and on into Rem is new for the adults and for the children and may create a loss of certitude, an increase of loyalty conflicts, heightened fears of abandonment and guilt, varying degrees of loss of contact with loved ones, financial problems, and a host of other stressful circumstances. At the same time, each step presents new challenges and tasks for all of the family members and requires new adaptations at systemic and individual levels.

We shall follow the Davidson-Hill-Olson families through three generations to see how a series of events lead to the formation of a Rem family and suprasystem. By reconstructing the intermediate critical steps, we can begin to appreciate how adults and children have been affected by each step and how the developing structure differs from the original, intact, nuclear family. Many far-reaching effects follow these structural changes, while at the same time the system tries to maintain the tasks and responsibilities of individual and family life cycles.

THE DAVIDSON-HILL-OLSON REM FAMILY SUPRASYSTEM

1) Formation of the Nuclear Family

Families of origin

Mary Hill, 20 when she married, is an only child, born into a tightly knit, lower-middle-class family in a small Northeastern city. Her father died of cancer when she was 15 and Mary's mother, unable to accept her anger at feeling abandoned, enshrined her husband and devoted herself to her child. She made no efforts to remarry. Mary had happy memories of her father, whom she loved dearly. Neither mother nor daughter had completed mourning; they incorporated Mr. Hill's existence into their enmeshed relationship with one another.

Joe Davidson, 22 when he married, is from the same city as Mary but from an upper-middle-class family. Joe had a distant relationship with his brother five years older. He remembered loud, "scary" arguments between his parents. When he was nine, ostensibly because of his father's alcoholism and a love affair, Joe's father left, and his parents divorced sometime later. Joe was terrified by his father's "desertion," as his mother termed it. After a short stay in a local guest house, Mr. Davidson took an apartment half a mile from his former home. Joe resisted his mother's need to build a closer dependence on him and resented her ubiquitous bitterness towards his father. He was angry with her and held her responsible for "driving Daddy away."

Mr. Davidson maintained regular visits with Joe and provided adequate financial support, but only perfunctory emotional support and closeness. Joe wanted more time and closeness with his father. Both he and his brother developed close peer relationships with friends, but not with one another. Joe's sports activities and friendships in high school and college became central in his cosmos. His paternal aunt and her husband became a second set of parents for him and it was to their house that his father often brought him for dinner. Over the years, Joe turned to them for support and approval. His relationship with them partially compensated for his parents' inability to nurture him.

Courtship

Mary and Joe knew one another casually in high school, but really discovered each other when Joe came home on visits from college where he was one of the "Big Men On Campus." Mary went to a local junior college, presumably for financial reasons, but also because she felt her mother needed her close by.

Unwittingly, Mary wanted a man who would take care of her, one like her idealized father. Joe was a familiar person to her, an updated image from the past. He carried himself with an air of maturity, competence and decisiveness that had pleased her when they courted. Joe loved Mary, who was beautiful, fun to be with, and made him feel important and wanted. He liked being in charge and enjoyed her helpless and child-like dependency.

Marriage

They started marriage as a parental (Joe)-childlike (Mary) partner-ship.* (See Figure 1.2.) As family responsibilities increased, Mary re-vealed greater competence and gradually took over leadership within their relationship. Mrs. Hill's closeness with Mary further minimized Joe's perceived role as husband and father. He increasingly surrendered

FIGURE 1.2
Davidson-Hill Nuclear Family at Time of Marriage

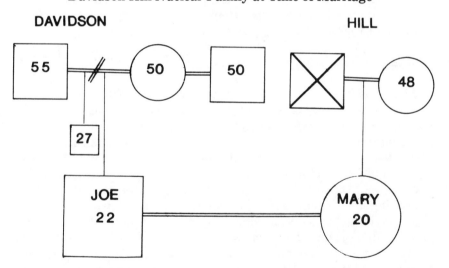

*See Chapter 4 for criteria for this typography of marriage.

authority to Mary and Mrs. Hill, a combined power with which he felt he
could not cope.

After eight years of marriage, the family was in severe trouble. Mary
and Joe now had two children, six-year-old Abner, named after Mary's
father, and four-year-old Sally, named after Joe's aunt.

Mrs. Hill was an important member of the family unit, visiting several times a week. She never developed a life of her own and thus had few
friends and interests. She worked only part-time and so was usually
available to babysit. Her presence grated on Joe; he felt he was always
dealing with her influence on Mary and that she had become the covert
value- and decision-maker in their home. He abdicated his family initiative and gradually became a morose, hostile, rebellious man.

Joe began to drink heavily, which led to more arguments with Mary.
He withdrew from the children and was erratic with them. They complained of too little time with him, and although he wanted to respond to
their needs, he seemed unable to do so. Mother and grandmother rallied
to "protect" the children from their father, who became inaccessible.
Joe blamed Mary and his mother-in-law's interference and influence for
the marital deterioration. Mary blamed Joe's drinking. No longer could
Joe maintain the hope that his marriage would be different from his parents'. After eight years of marriage and two years of repeated angry ad-
monishments from Mary to get out, Joe finally left. He had brushed
aside his aunt and uncle's suggestions that he get help with his drinking
problem or that he and Mary see a counselor together.

2) Separation and Divorce

Mary was frightened and bitter when Joe left. She felt deserted again,
as she had felt after her father's death. Mrs. Hill also reacted to Joe's
leaving as a second desertion, and within three weeks she moved into
her daughter's home. Mary was grateful for her mother's help, but uneasy about her close proximity. She felt further enmeshed and increasingly ambivalent about their relationship. She mused to herself, "If
only Joe could have been stronger he could have prevented all this from
happening, but he had to be weak like his father and drink instead."

The children had a strong support system in their mother and grandmother; this system, however, was hostile towards their father. The
children's own distant relationship with their father, as well as their
mother's and grandmother's anger towards Joe, sensitized them to go
along with the criticism of their father; thus their uneasiness and loyalty conflict intensified. They loved and needed their father but they felt
angry, guilty (especially Abner), deserted, and confused. They believed

their family had been destroyed and that they would never again be close to their father. Abner was seized by a vague sense of having lost his moorings. He was enuretic for several weeks and showed signs of incipient school avoidance. Sally became whiney and clung to her mother.

Joe was unhappy, too. To some extent he recognized how he appeared to be following his father's path: drinking, distancing from his children, blaming his wife. When Joe left home he stayed at the YMCA and for the first few days experienced a sense of relief and peace when he entered his room. Soon he began to feel depressed and lonely as he stared at the stark room. Its single bed and institutional tan walls began to get to him—a symbol of his emotionally isolated state. The one Van Gogh reproduction served only to emphasize the conformity to similar rooms of lonely men. He was tempted to return home, thought of the last dozen nights he had spent there, and went to a bar instead.

When the divorce was finalized a year later, Joe was living alone in a small but cheerful apartment he had decorated himself. He saw the children (now eight and six) regularly and, although he was still somewhat distant with them (they contributed somewhat to this interaction), he did try to plan activities that included occasional visits to the home of his mother (long since remarried) and his paternal aunt and uncle.

The children visited Joe with mixed feelings. Abner was more comfortable and relaxed than Sally, who seemed to be critical and resentful of her father. Both were suspicious of his distant interest in them and viewed him as the sole cause of the family disruption. Joe did not push, but he was consistent in keeping his appointments with them. He rarely spent time alone with either youngster.

Mary was consistently angry with Joe; she let him know this whenever he called or she saw him. She did not attempt to keep her feelings from the children who were very responsive to her emotional outbursts. Her world was shattered, and she was angry about returning to "the same relationship I had with my mother when I was an adolescent—except now I'm the mother of two, without a husband!"

Mrs. Hill increasingly took charge of her daughter's household and continued her denigrating comments about Joe. It was as if her anger at her own husband's "desertion" had now found an acceptable object on whom it could be discharged. She was oblivious to her contribution to the interactions within the family system. Mrs. Hill's contribution was only one of the multiple determinants—*if* Mary had reacted a little differently, or *if* Joe had reacted a little differently, the family system might have stabilized. But all three contributed to an unstable family system in which both marital partners' contractual terms and needs had been violated. The influence on the system of Joe's parents was less direct and not immediate, but the example they had set and their shaping of Joe had also been a significant determinant of the poor marital relationship.

The actual divorce was almost anticlimactic after the strong emotions and accusations of the first few months of separation. Divorce did not produce any dramatic, visible change in the family structure; Joe had secured his own apartment some months earlier. It did confirm that this family now lived in two households and that Joe and Mary were no longer man and wife.

Although they were no longer married, Joe and Mary's emotional divorce was far from complete; many ties, reinforced by telephone and personal contact, remained. For the children, the divorce did indicate with some finality that Daddy would not return home. (They never really understood why he had left and they experienced it as an abandonment of them.) They still held on to their desire and dream for reconciliation, but these were further from awareness now. Their dream was supported by the fact that the divorce had not made any apparent emotional or interactional change from the separation period. After the first few months of separation and Joe's definitive act of getting his own apartment, the separated family system had reached a steady state. The formal divorce apparently did not affect this equilibrium.

3) Post-divorce—Double Single-parent Household Stage

Mary now ostensibly headed the custodial single-parent household and Joe headed the visited single-parent household. Thus they were fully into the double single-parent household stage (see Figure 1.3). This stage had its onset when Joe established his own apartment. Although this stage can go on indefinitely, it most frequently changes when one or both former spouses remarry.

Dating

Joe dated several women after his divorce and swore to himself that he would "never marry and be controlled again." He was doing well in business and was rising rapidly in his company. But his life seemed empty; he felt depressed and continued to drink heavily. He met Barbara Olson, age 23, three years after his divorce. She was very attractive, had a good sense of herself, and related in a way that made Joe feel good about himself; she reassured him that he was lovable. Their brief period of romantic bonding soon suffered from a bitter battle concern-

FIGURE 1.3
Double Single-parent Stage

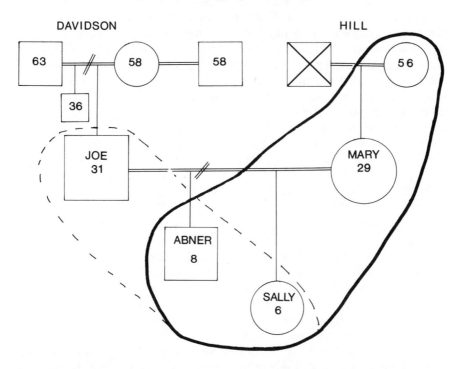

ing Joe's drinking. Barbara's ultimatum to Joe—"the booze or me"—closely coincided with a confrontation with the company president about his drinking. With medical help and his own determination, Joe was able to detoxify from alcohol and then became actively involved in Alcoholics Anonymous. After six months of sobriety, Barbara and Joe decided to marry four months hence, 19 months after their first date.

A few months prior to the approaching marriage, Joe became increasingly interested in his children, now 12 and 10. They were confused by their father's new involvement with them. They had made a reasonable adaptation to Joe's "duty" time with them. Although he had often tried, with the best of conscious intentions, he had done little more than arrange dinner and entertainment with them. He was unable to offer intimacy or availability to them in their ongoing process of "growing up." Although he had tried to hide his drinking problem from the children, he had not always been successful in doing so.

Abner and Sally

When Joe's behavior began to change, each child experienced increased conflict. The closer they felt to their father, the more ambivalent they were. They especially liked him now because he was not morose and irritable and was more "there" for them. However, they were uneasy and confused by the past hurts toward their mother, grandmother, and themselves. They had made their peace with a distant father and were wary of the changes in his behavior, but also they did want a full-time father like other children, as in their dim fond memories of him. They connected the change to his impending marriage. There was some increased closeness, but their wariness could be noted in Abner's expression to his sister, "I think Daddy loves us more now because he wants us to love Barbara." Edgy at first with Barbara, they remained somewhat suspicious and distant. Her role was not clear and the children sensed that things were in flux.

Joe

Without realizing it, Joe had reactivated his dream of the ideal life he could have had with Mary "if she had not changed." He wanted to roll back the years and replace a younger Barbara for Mary. Barbara would be the loving wife and good mother to his children without bringing a constant mother-in-law into their life. She would look up to him, be effective in her housewife and mother roles and always place him first as lover and husband. Joe's guilt for having divorced Mary and not giving more of himself to his children was eased by blaming the divorce on Mary because of her dependent relationship with her mother. His current behavior stemmed from an unconscious desire to wipe out the past 12 years and start over again with Barbara and his two "ready-made" children. He would not repeat his errors; this time he would remain in charge of his family and be benignly alert to any attempt of his new wife to take over. His plan was partly conscious, partly preconscious, and largely unconscious. He wanted to solidify his relationship with his children and see to it that his new wife would not supersede him in the children's affections. Unrealistically, he wanted Barbara to love the children as her own. This largely unconscious script motivated much of Joe's behavior with his new wife, his children, and his former wife.

Barbara

Barbara, a middle child, felt that her older brother and younger sister had received more attention and love from her parents. She was an executive trainee in the same company where Joe was an executive. She was impressed by his good looks, ability, strength and decisiveness at work, and his charm, wit and sexuality after work. She desired and believed that she was contracting for his undivided love and devotion. Joe emerged as a good and loving daddy for her; she had not fully understood the implications of Joe's expectation that she would become the "new mother" to two recalcitrant children of 12 and 10.

Barbara joined Joe in an unspoken fantasy that they would raise the children as if they were theirs, a type of folie-à-deux. Thus she readily agreed to his request not to have her own children with him. They would buy a house with two extra bedrooms because (in the unspoken and an unaware fantasy) the children would eventually live with them full-time, and Mary would magically disappear. Sally and Abner would love her immediately, and they would be a happy "normal" family.

Mary

Mary did some occasional dating, but she rarely saw a man more than a few times. The intense anger and pain from her experience with Joe prevented her from allowing herself to be vulnerable in a new relationship.

4) Remarriage

The Rem couple

Barbara and Joe married, each with an unexpressed contract (see Chapter 4), but united in their unconscious folie-à-deux based on Joe's fantasy. Barbara ignored the signs of Joe's characterological problems —his dependency and simultaneous need to believe he was in charge. He mistook her need for love and her compliance to his unconscious game plan as a childlike quality that would insure her dependence on him. Most of these behavioral determinants seemed to be operating beyond consciousness.

On the surface their expectations appeared to be complementary, although in actuality they were pseudomutual. Each had within him/herself the contradiction that would contribute to disrupting their seemingly harmonious system: Joe's impossible family life plan and Barbara's submersion of her own needs to have children and to be the prime object of Joe's love, despite the presence of two children and a former spouse towards whom he felt guilty and ambivalent.

The complex Rem suprasystem that was created with Joe's marriage to Barbara is schematized in Figure 1.4. Clearly, the Rem unit has a structure and multiple inputs from the suprasystem that would not exist in an intact family. The children are a subsystem in two homes. There

Figure 1.4
Olson-Davidson-Hill Family at Time of Remarriage

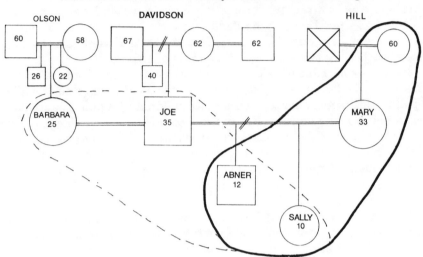

is a stepmother and a biofather who expects them to "come around," i.e., to choose his home as their primary residence, a distraught mother and grandmother who feel threatened, and a new set of stepgrandparents who do not know what their role should be. Joe's marriage to Barbara created a much greater impact on everyone than had the divorce after a year of separation. It restructured the suprasystem in a way that immediately affected all subsystems.

Rem household with children

Barbara had wanted a career when she married Joe and did not feel a need for children of her own. Prior to her marriage, she had thought she would fulfill her maternal needs through Joe's children, whom she had met and liked. Although Abner was moderately friendly and appeared to accept Barbara's limit-setting, Sally was quiet and withdrawn most of the time they were together. Although Barbara was nice to them, the children initially disliked and mistrusted her, and subconsciously blamed her for making their parents' reunion impossible. Barbara and Joe wanted the children to spend time with them and had chosen a house in an older part of town, a house sufficiently large for each child to have his or her own room. It had been Barbara's suggestion to purchase this house instead of a smaller one in a more fashionable section.

After a few visits from the children following the wedding, Barbara was hurt because the children wouldn't call her Mommy or Mom. She felt she was merely their father's wife, not their mother. Disappointed, she felt that all her efforts to make her and Joe's home their new home had been unappreciated.

Joe loved Barbara and his children, and he wanted them all to love each other. As tensions began to mount between the children and their stepmother, he found himself telling the children to love Barbara and to do as she wished. They became upset and felt their father cared more for her than for them. They sensed he was trying to manipulate them into making a choice between Barbara (i.e., him) and their mother, whose existence Joe and Barbara appeared to ignore. Sensing their father and stepmother's attitude, the children felt disloyal to their mother and grandmother whenever they experienced any positive feelings towards Barbara.

Barbara was terribly upset when she felt hostility from either child after she had had a good experience with them; she was irate when Sally would not wear her gift of new barrettes when she left to go home to her mother. She had no comprehension of what went into shaping their feelings. The children had asked neither for their father's remarriage nor for a new mother. Abner and Sally were unable to find an acceptable modus vivendi with their father and stepmother without causing too much conflict for their affection and loyalty to their mother. They felt angered by their father's and Barbara's demands for unconditional love and obedience. Even though they were prepared for the remarriage and had spent time with Barbara and their father, they were shaken by the actual event. Residual dreams of parental reunion were obliterated. Sally, in particular, experienced her father's loss *all over again* when he and Barbara left on their honeymoon. Abner felt uneasy and torn by divided loyalty.

After several months Barbara became increasingly confused and resentful. Joe, too, was confused and reactive since Barbara's relationship with the children did not follow his unconscious master design. He was unable to think through the effects of divided loyalty on the children: Barbara as loved stepmother-mother and he and Barbara as "loving parents" versus the children's biomother and grandmother.

5) Interaction Between the Rem Subsystems and the Other Parts of the Suprasystem

The maternal single-parent household subsystem

In their own enmeshed relationship, mother and grandmother had come to symbolize a merged concept of MOTHER for the children. Each was almost interchangeable for the other. On one level, Joe behaved with the children as though their biomother did not exist; on another level, he unconsciously appeased Mary and her mother so that they would allow the children to spend more time with Barbara and him; this facilitated his denial of their existence and relationship with Abner and Sally—an impossible cycle of contradictions!

The remarriage forced a restructuring of the relationship between the children's custodial single-parent system with their mother and grandmother and their new Rem family system with their father and Barbara. The visiting single-parent system that existed with Joe prior to his remarriage had aroused fewer loyalty conflicts and had allowed Abner and Sally to fantasize that their parents would reunite. Now, new requirements were made of the children by their father and Barbara and by their mother and grandmother. Demands on their time and loyalties (which had become stabilized over the years, even if these had not been optimal) had changed abruptly just prior to Joe's remarriage. The changing structure and goals in the Rem household led to a highly unstable system within each household and between households. Sally, with conflict, maintained a greater loyalty to the mother/grandmother axis; Abner was better able to cope with both axes but not without paying the price of distancing himself from everyone. His behavior was reminiscent of Joe's defensive maneuvers with his own divorced parents.

Despite her prior knowledge, Mary was panicked by Joe's remarriage, which crushed her fantasy of Joe's return and the reestablishment of the family which would live happily ever after. She felt as if a great steel door had clanged shut and locked her into a dull grey life with her mother and children, and she now believed (correctly) that Joe was trying to win the children away from her. Her anguish and depression were peppered by anger. She was forced to recognize that Barbara had replaced her as a wife and was also a threatened replacement as a mother to Abner and Sally.

Mary refused to speak to Barbara except to ask abruptly for Joe on the phone. She was envious of anything Barbara received from Joe; she regarded Barbara as the recipient of what was rightfully hers. She anticipated that Joe would pull further away after marriage and that she would have to fight to keep the children's affection. She feared they might prefer living in a "real family" with a married couple. Joe had abandoned her to her mother when they separated; now, in an unconscious reversal of generations, she tried to maneuver the children into playing the parent to her. Mary displaced much of her anger and frustration onto Abner, whom she identified with Joe, attacking him with hostile statements such as, "You and your father are alike—you really are his son!" On the other hand, Mary identified Sally with herself and her own mother as another vulnerable, exploited, abandoned female. She felt that the women were forced to cling together in defense against the males' desertions of them.

When the children returned from visits to the Rem household, Mary would pump them to find out how Barbara had looked and acted. She would also attempt to elicit other information, as she became increasingly bitter and angry. This made the children's reentry into Mary's household even more difficult. They (Abner particularly) felt that they were asked to betray their loyalty to their father; thus their mother's reactions alienated them further. Conversely, identifying with their mother, the children carried Mary's attitudes and messages to their Rem home, which made their entry there uneasy too. Unwittingly, they had become their mother's agents provocateurs. Their loyalties were divided among their mother, grandmother, father and stepmother. They loved their father and were eager to spend time with him, yet they felt guilty when they felt or showed positive response to Barbara, whom they did *not* accept as their mother, since they already had one!

Mary would often ask Joe for extra considerations beyond the letter of their divorce agreement, such as repairs to the house that was once theirs. Depending on how guilty he was feeling, Joe would either erratically volunteer to help or be angry with Mary's requests when, to himself, he predicted Barbara's displeasure with his actions. His actions or tone of voice to Mary on the phone began to be questioned by his wife, who resented his continuing involvement with Mary. He felt caught between the two women: "Each wants one hundred percent of me." He was unable to reconcile his unconscious residual feelings of caring and warmth for Mary and his guilt with his love for Barbara; nor could Barbara.

By the end of the first year Barbara saw the children no longer as individuals but rather as antagonistic agents of Mary's struggle with her for Joe. Barbara felt additional anguish and anger at Joe's provocative contributions to the deteriorating situations. She felt caught in a web spun by Joe and *his* family. Joe irritably blamed Barbara for the children's continued loyalty to their mother because she had not treated them lovingly enough. Barbara told Joe he had not really divorced Mary. Like a broken record, Joe kept telling Barbara he loved only her but had to communicate with Mary because of the kids; if he were friendly to Mary and helped her, she would cooperate more readily in plans for the children's visits. He desperately persisted in his enmeshed behavior as his dream of living happily ever after with his children and a docile Barbara seemed to evade fulfillment. The whirling tempo of cyclical events seemed to be increasing.

Mary's mother: Maternal grandmother

Mrs. Hill, the children's grandmother, also had considerable input to the new Rem system since she now lived with Mary and the children and was at home most days when the children returned from school. Still angry with Joe for the disruption of her daughter's marriage and for causing so much pain to herself, Mary, and the children, she repeatedly told her daughter, often within earshot of the children, that Joe was like all men—he would forget about Mary and the children now that he was remarried. She added fuel to Mary's anxiety and the children's feelings of insecurity.

Paternal grandparents

Joe's parents, themselves divorced, had a more distant but caring relationship with their son and grandchildren. Joe's mother sided with him but was mildly critical of his divorce and alcoholism. She identified him, in a love-hostile fashion, with her former husband. Usually accompanied by her second husband when she saw the grandchildren, she had welcomed the children's visits with Joe through the years. However, she only rarely invited the children to stay with them overnight, since she and her husband both worked and "you know how busy we are." She did not approve of Barbara at first, but had come to appreciate her "sobering" influence on her son.

Joe's father, Mr. Davidson, visited Joe's house and took the children out for grandfatherly treats. Wary of Barbara because of his own sexual impulses and desires for a younger woman, he defensively regarded her as a "gold digger" (sic) for marrying his successful son. He was bemused as he witnessed her desire to be loved by the children and their subsequent rejection of her. He was also somewhat hostile to his son, overemphasizing the similarity of his son's history to his own history of drinking, divorce, business success, and abdication of power at home. The parallel between his son's "negative" traits and his own made him anxious. He was particularly bothered by Joe's second attempt to build a more gratifying family life, something he had not attempted to do. At times when this hostility and bitterness burst through, he was puzzling to Joe. Joe's parents' attitudes and feelings were subtle but significant factors injected into the new family.

Stepgrandparents

Barbara's parents, the Olsons, had entered the scene in the roles of in-laws to Joe and stepgrandparents to Sally and Abner. Barbara displeased her parents when she had dated and then lived with Joe prior to marriage. Despite Joe's good income they were concerned about his drinking, his two children, and his age. The Olsons had been looking forward to grandchildren and were dismayed that their daughter had agreed to have no children of her own. They were unsuccessful at hiding their disapproval of the marriage, and their awkwardness was apparent during the few meetings with their stepgrandchildren. Abner and Sally were ill at ease with them too.

6) The Call for Professional Help

The time was five years post-separation, four years post-divorce, and 14 months since Joe's marriage to Barbara. Many of the forces that bear on this system erupted in mid-November, a week after parent-teacher conferences and a week before Thanksgiving, the harbinger of holiday and family gatherings.

At a school conference Mary heard from Abner's teacher that he was "a loner," that he seemed "troubled," and that he "never laughed." Mary, upset, immediately told her mother, who declared, "It's all Joe's fault." This depressed Mary even more. When Mary told Joe about the teacher's report, he was alarmed and said, "I'll have a talk with Abner," but he knew full well his difficulty in engaging Abner on any subject other than sports. When Joe mentioned Abner's report to Barbara, he was looking for comfort in the form of "an answer." Instead, she criticized Joe for not going to the parent-teacher conference: "Of course Abner would be depressed with such a disinterested father." Joe didn't want that response and felt defensive, since he had never felt the necessity to attend any school functions. He blamed Mary for not having invited him to the conference and both he and Barbara attacked her and Mrs. Hill, "the controlling bitches," for wanting to push Joe out of the picture. Barbara thought the "answer" was for Joe to stand up to Mary. Joe thought to himself, "If I had been able to stand up to Mary, I wouldn't have left her and you wouldn't be here today." Barbara was especially vulnerable at this point since she was experiencing additional job pressures and she had been fantasizing about "becoming pregnant as an out."

The Thursday evening prior to the children's weekend with their father and Barbara, Mary had dinner with several women friends from work. Mrs. Hill was feeling threatened since one of these women was a divorcee who was going to Weight Watchers in preparation for a "man hunt." Mrs. Hill preconsciously wondered if this woman would take Mary "hunting" with her. Grandma was in a "bad mood" that evening and did not pay attention when she helped the children pack their bags for the weekend. Instead, she haphazardly and unconsciously packed a dress that was too tight for Sally and jeans that were too short for Abner. (This was interesting on two counts: Mrs. Hill saw the children as if they were younger and packed clothes that were too small; she did not allow the children to choose and pack their own clothes.)

On Saturday morning, when Sally, in her typically whiney voice, complained to Barbara that her dress hurt under the arms, all hell broke loose. Barbara attacked Sally and yelled, "What does your mother do with all the money *we* send her!?" Joe, still drinking his morning coffee, felt like he had been attacked from behind. He heard Sally cry and immediately went to protect her. He asked Barbara, 'What the hell did you do?'' "What the hell did I do? What the hell don't *you* do!" was her vituperative retort. Abner began to cry and Joe thought, "If ever I need a drink it's now." He called his AA sponsor who urged professional help for Joe *and* his family. He discussed the suggestion with Barbara and she concurred.

Joe mentioned getting help to Mary who agreed since she too felt "desperate." At the time of Joe's original call for professional help he spoke of Abner's "isolation" in school and his unusual flood of tears during the weekend visit. Joe did say that he had been divorced and remarried, but he did not mention the frustration in his current marriage.

Joe, Barbara, Abner, Sally, Mary and Mrs. Hill attended the first session at the request of the therapist who explained the importance of including everyone involved with Abner.

DISCUSSION

Our knowledge of this Rem suprasystem began with Joe Davidson's initial telephone call to the agency. The family's chronicle illustrates the many steps and systemic changes involved as a nuclear family evolves into a Rem structure. A remarriage usually involves at least three family trees and cultures, as well as a history of loss and a struggle for fulfillment. This highlights the importance of taking a three-generational history and the need for understanding the effects of each structural change on the family system and on each person. This Rem suprasystem would have been even more complex if Barbara had been previously married and had brought with her a continuing tie with a former husband and biochildren. If this had been so, a change in ordinal position might then have occurred between the two sets of children. Or, if Mary had also remarried, this would have been an additional step which would have once again changed the suprasystem: Abner and Sally would then belong to both Rem households.

In the case as presented, the major points of transition and stress were:

1) The formation of the original nuclear family: the first marriage and the birth of Abner and then Sally.
2) Separation and Joe's move out, which had been preceded by:
   a) a failure to resolve conflicts;
   b) bitter fights over power and inclusion (Mary-Mrs. Hill-Joe);
   c) alcoholism;
   d) hostile withdrawal and the spouse's reaction to the withdrawal.
3) Divorce: the formalization of the end of the marriage and the old nuclear family.
4) Post-divorce: the double single-parent households that require parental interaction without additional disruption for the children.
5) Remarriage: undertaken in this case without a thinking through of needs, expectations and roles; this requires realignment once more between the Rem and single-parent household for the continuation of parenting and completion of emotional divorce between former spouses.

As we have seen, each of the periods of significant change en route to Rem is punctuated by a clear event that abruptly changes the structure of the family, with the possible exception of the more subtle effects of the legal divorce, which in this case reinforced structural changes already effected. Each of these definite punctuations is further marked by a period that may offer hope, distress, pain, elation, fear, love or relief that precedes and/or follows the action. There is usually some degree of sadness as one leaves one stage for another. For all concerned, major dislocations take place and new adaptations must be made. These are periods of severe stress which most people eventually handle well. For some it furthers their growth; for others it can be very destructive.

Divorce, the double single-parent household stage, and remarriage do not necessarily produce lasting negative effects on the involved adults and children. The 1980 United States Census figures report that five out of six divorced men remarry and three out of four divorced women remarry (*New York Times*, Nov. 5, 1981). Some have learned from their past marital experience how to work more effectively in a relationship. Others have learned to make a more suitable mate choice. After a period of some disruption, children of Rem families appear to do as well in general as do children from intact families. The quality of co-parenting and the age of the children at the time of the various nodal events are important factors in determining the likelihood of significant injury to the child (Wallerstein and Kelly, 1980). In the remarriage of one or both parents, children often find an additional parental figure who may effectively complement or supplement what cannot be secured from one or both bioparents. The entire process can be one of growth for children and adults—or it can be a disaster—or anything in between.

CHAPTER 2

Differences Between Nuclear and Remarried Families

Those who treat or live in Rem families are persistently confronted with the differences between nuclear and Rem families. Yet, it is the all too frequent denial of, confusion about, and lack of appreciation for the exact nature of these differences that cause additional stress for the Rem family and clinician. The Rem family is structurally different; it cannot replicate the lost intact nuclear family. To mitigate the effects of these inclinations and sort out this particular alchemistic dilemma, this chapter conceptualizes the differences between the ideally functioning nuclear family and the Rem family in terms of the following parameters:

1) Structure of the system.
2) Purpose of the system.
3) Tasks of the system.
4) Nature of the bonding of the system.
5) Factors influencing the adults in the system.
6) Factors influencing the children in the system.
7) Forces that impinge on the system.

1) STRUCTURE OF THE SYSTEM

Nuclear	*Rem*
a) Consists of two adults and one or more children who are progeny of the adults.	a) Consists of two adults and one or more children. Each child has been parented by only one of the adults.

23

Nuclear	*Rem*
b) Marital and parental tasks are exclusive to the marital dyad.	b) Marital and parental tasks are not exclusive to the Rem dyad. Parental tasks are shared with a previous spouse. Except when a widow marries a bachelor, at least three adults are involved, often four, and it is not impossible to have six (consider a third marriage for both spouses with the children from each former marriage).
c) Marital pair predates parental pair.	c) Parent-child unit predates marital pair. A buxom teenage girl reminded her stepmother, "I knew him first." Bonds between custodial parent and child are usually strong due to greater interdependence during the double single-parent stage. Therefore, it frequently is difficult for the new spouse to be accepted within the single-parent family system. The custodial parent and child may join forces to exclude the new spouse. The custodial parent may have a need to "divide and conquer" the spouse and children, which also prevents family consolidation.
d) Members belong to only one family system.	d) At least two members are part of another family system. In cases where there are more than two marriages and children from each marriage, several family systems may be represented.
e) A relatively closed system regarding inclusion of members. Its "membrane" is usually impermeable. Membership is clearly defined. Boundaries are biologically, legally, and geographically explicit.	e) A relatively open system regarding inclusion of members. Its "membrane" is semipermeable, e.g., visiting children. Membership is not clearly defined since there may not be a consensus about who is in the family, and some members may reside together in a "divided camp."

Nuclear	Rem
	Boundaries may be biologically, legally, and geographically blurred.
f) Significant others are usually experienced positively and seen as "family." If both adult partners have individuated from their family of origin, the input of significant others is less likely to contribute to system malfunction and instead be utilized positively. The potential for loyalty conflicts is not readily activated since there is only one mother and one father.	f) There is an increased number of significant others who may be experienced positively, negatively, or ambivalently, depending upon "whose side" they belong to.
	In-laws and former in-laws may have a strong influence on the Rem family system, especially if they played a large role in the single-parent phase. They may have been a sustaining support or a divisive presence. The adult may not have become emotionally divorced from his former spouse. This ongoing tie may disrupt the present system's consolidation. New significant others can be utilized positively or negatively, the most typical and potentially benevolent example being the third set of grandparents.
g) Husband and wife have symmetrical legal ties to their children. Siblings have legal ties to each other because they share the same parents. All nuclear family members are legally related to each other (Wald, 1981).	g) Legal ties are asymmetrical since the legal parent-child subsystem brings all prior legal rights and obligations into the new remarried family, but the stepparent-stepchild subsystem has no prior legal rights and obligations, nor does it acquire any at the time of remarriage. Stepsiblings do not share a legal tie.

2) PURPOSES OF THE SYSTEM

a) To establish a marital partnership where needs for companionship, emotional and sexual intimacy, financial support, and indi-	a) Same, but with the underpinning of the experience of failure (divorce) or loss (death of former spouse) which can affect the an-

Nuclear

viduation are met. Couple's "marriage contract" shows their uniqueness in their emphasis of various contract items.

b) Procreation is usually a goal; birth of child(ren) and the creation of a nurturing environment for them to grow physically, emotionally, and spiritually. In most instances, partners have congruent life-cycle goals which make it easier to resolve this issue.

Rem

ticipation of needs being met in the present relationship. Sometimes, added pressure to have a co-parent and provide a child with parental figures hastens the move into Rem.

b) Procreation is not always a purpose in Rem since the "instant family" exists in which childcare responsibilities and finances are shared, often ambivalently and unequally, by a divorced parental pair. This and the differences in life-cycle tasks, especially if one partner has a child, may cause the issue of a mutual child to be problematic (see Chapter 12).

3) TASKS OF THE SYSTEM

a) Consolidation of the marital system as it moves from courtship to a more reality-based bonding. Intrinsic to this is the couple's ability to establish clear boundaries between their dyad and others, e.g., family of origin and their child(ren).
b) Resolution of the individual life-cycle/marital-cycle conflicts of the partners. Both partners usually start out together at individual life-cycle stages that allow for the dovetailing of marital-cycle stages. Thus, there is greater congruence of each one's needs and age appropriateness for mastery.
c) Preparation for parental role after some resolution of individual life-cycle/marital-cycle conflicts. Before having children a transition period is possible where

a) Same. Boundaries between couple and external others are harder to achieve with the existence of former spouse(s), child(ren), and possibly grandparents who played an influential role during the double single-parent phase.
b) Same. In Rem, resolution may be more difficult, especially when partners are at different phases in their individual life cycle, with concomitant disruption in their marital life cycle. Sharp differences in significant areas may emerge unless resolution is achieved (see Chapter 3).

c) Same. In Rem it is more difficult since the couple is faced with an "instant family" where parental responsibilities may span the spectrum from total, erratic, or

Nuclear

ambivalence and practical realities can be worked through and available parent/parent and parent/child relationship models can be evaluated.

d) Shift from dyadic (adult/adult) to triadic (adult/adult/child) family structure. In almost all instances this comes about by the addition of one infant. Childrearing tasks, responsibilities, and attitudes are gradually evolved and assumed. The child accepts parenting from both adults.

Literature and classes on preparing for childbirth and parenting are popular. Greater participation of husband/father is encouraged during gestation; birth, postpartum, and thereafter.

e) To fulfill the intimacy needs of partners and provide a role model of intimacy for children.

Rem

infrequent care. Bioparent and stepparent models are largely unavailable, except for the myth of the "wicked stepparent." At the time of the remarriage, the child may need more attention than usual.

d) Shift from dyadic (adult/child) to triadic (adult/adult/child) family structure may include one child, or more, or the sum total of both spouses' children from previous marriages. Various characteristics of the children; age, sex, frequency of contact, standard of living, religion are considerations in becoming a family. Childrearing styles, especially around issues of limit-setting, may be and usually are areas of conflict for the adults and children. Some childrearing tasks and responsibilities may not be appropriate and/or acceptable to both partners. The child may not accept parenting from his stepparent.

e) Same, but task may be complicated by: (i) distancing maneuvers caused by the influence of introjection/projection cathexis of former spouse; (ii) loyalty conflict of parent vis-à-vis a new spouse and biological child (this is exacerbated when spouse and/or child desire exclusivity and compete for it); (iii) jealousy of new mate's former spouse; (iv) loyalty conflicts of child.

4) NATURE OF BONDING

a) Nuclear family's bond is intact, resilient, and members have not been scarred by the loss of

a) Bond may be less resilient since members bring with them the experience of "failure"/death

Nuclear

the family unit or one of its adult members.

b) Family milestones; birthdays, religious rites of passage, graduations, weddings, funerals etc.; are usually times that enhance family bonding.

c) Nuclear family is more likely to enjoy a sense of security because of their continuity, predictability, and traditions. This shared history strengthens the family's functioning as the individual's reference group. Each member has a sense of belonging.

d) Spontaneity is possible, as decisions about time, money and commitments are contained within the family.

Rem

and emotional scars from the loss. Fears of further loss may lead to an attenuated investment of affect in the bonding with spouse, children and stepchildren.

b) Milestones, rather than being experienced as occasions where bonding is enhanced, may instead heighten feelings of loss, sorrow, and divided loyalty. In Rem there can be chronic sorrow for the loss of the nuclear family, and family milestones, as well as the reentry and leave-taking of "visiting" children, are a reminder of this. Often this chronic sorrow is denied or given short shrift which creates a wedge in bonding possibilities (see Chapter 11).

c) Rem is less likely to enjoy a sense of security since history and traditions are inchoate. The different modus operandi of households may be experienced as culture shock, especially in relation to childrearing styles. Existential to the Rem experience, and not necessarily indicators of an unhealthy adjustment, are the questions "why?" and more potent "what if?" In the Rem family there is more of a need for what John Keats (1817) called "negative capability"—capability of being in uncertainties, mysteries and doubts without any irritable reaching after fact and reason.

d) Spontaneity may be difficult since issues of time, money, and commitments are shared elsewhere. Attempts at masterminding schedules, person priorities,

Nuclear

Rem

and family events drain energy
and lead to frustration.

e) Nuclear family is usually supported by extended families of
origin of partners, which height-
ens level of bonding.

e) Rem family is not always ac-
cepted/supported by extended
family members, which can impact negatively on bonding.

f) Emotional climate fosters the
capacity to tolerate ambivalence,
i.e., to recognize and tolerate loving and hostile feelings for the
same person. Hence, object constancy, where the person becomes as important as the function he performs, develops. With
the growth of object constancy
there is self-constancy and feelings of self-esteem.

f) The insecurity produced by the
structural changes that the Rem
family is heir to makes tolerating
ambivalence more difficult. For
example, the continuous financial
burden of child support can prevent the parent(s) from recognizing a child's own generous nature. Hence, object constancy
and the mutual appreciation and
esteem that resonate from it is
harder to achieve.

5) FACTORS INFLUENCING THE ADULTS IN THE SYSTEM

a) Either or both may be on the
rebound from a previous love relationship but this is not usually
so.

a) Either or both have been in a
terminated marriage. Partners of
the former married must face a
long series of conscious, preconscious and unconscious "tests."

b) There is relatively little or no
unfinished business that involves
contact with prior relationships.
What exists is not likely to remain highly cathected.

b) Often there is a continuing
contact with a former mate because of alimony, child support,
child visitation and ongoing
childcare arrangements. While
these contacts are essential,
some people use them as rational-
izations when they want to hold
on to a former spouse. Positive
but more often highly cathected
negative affect might continue,
disturbing the new marriage. In
the most problematic situations,
the equilibrium of the remarriage
may be maintained by partners
who share a pseudomutual hatred
for the "wicked ex-spouse." This

| *Nuclear* | *Rem* |

| | position is often a reaction formation against strong loving and sexual feelings for the former spouse. On the other hand, to attack the spouse's vulnerable areas about the previous marriage or mate is a common pursuit that usually has a negative effect on the current marriage. |

c) Individuals bring transferential influences based largely on parental introjections.

c) In addition to the influence of parental introjects there is also the influence of previous-mate introjects that compound and/or intensify projections on the new partner.

d) There is a desire and goal to be and remain a family. For both partners this is a "first" and they have not had any practice in the day-to-day living of married life. Thus more idealized expectations of marriage may prevail.

d) At least one partner has had the experience of the day-to-day living of married life. This may lead to more realistic expectations of marriage and a greater willigness to "work at" being married. This attitude may promote more dedication, flexibility, and willingness to be a married couple and family. Conversely, compulsive scrutiny of a mate's motivations and behavior of the denial of problems may be a negative manifestation.

e) Life cycle continues without interruption on one marital and one family life-cycle track.

e) Life cycle is lived out on two marital and family cycle tracks accompanied by degrees of conflict, confusion of responsibilities and guilt.

6) FACTORS INFLUENCING THE CHILDREN IN THE SYSTEM

a) Children are born into a family, grow up in it, cope with it, and imperceptively learn to introject aspects of both parents. A sense of identity comes from hav-

a) The nuclear family is defunct. The children are part of two family systems at two separate sites. There is mourning for the loss of the nuclear family, "the familiar

Nuclear	Rem
ing and belonging to a nuclear family and knowing what to expect from other family members. Laing (1971) describes this as "internalizing everyone's internalization."	way of earlier life," and the absent parent. Children had no say in the decision to break up the nuclear family or to choose stepparents. Often this causes helplessness, anger, guilt, noncooperation, divided loyalties, insecurity, identity diffusion, and lack of commitment to the Rem family unit.
b) Roots are stable: nuclear family, home, neighborhood, school, own and parents' friends and network.	b) Roots are likely to be disrupted or displaced. This tends to increase any proclivity towards anomie.
c) Ordinal sibling position is fixed and evolved with time. All are related by "blood" and usually show physical resemblance. Incest taboo is strong.	c) Stepsibling may enter de novo and alter ordinal positions. The biological parent's time and affection are shared with the new spouse, stepsibs and half-sibs if there is a mutual child. Roles towards stepsiblings are unclear. The incest taboo is not as strong. Multiple alliances are possible among Rem system members. Physical unlikeness may be obvious and may increase feelings of intrusion or isolation.
d) The presence of both parents in the home helps to place reality limits on oedipal fantasies and gratification.	d) In the double single-parent stage, parents often unknowingly gratify oedipal fantasies by assigning a quasi-husband or wife role to a child. The situation may also have played into promoting interdependence between parent and child. This makes a potent subsystem that can preclude consolidation of a functional Rem system.
e) The child may rebel against the system at times, but he or she maintains a sense of belonging and loyalty to the system. Age-appropriate rebellion is	e) The Rem family is a new system. If there has not been enough consolidation, an adolescent child may be extruded. One or both family systems may close ranks

Nuclear	*Rem*
a developmental need that the family can contain, albeit somewhat stressfully.	so that the child is not included in either household. More positively, Rem offers the opportunity for family systems to join ranks and have the adolescent participate in both households (see Chapter 10).
f) A child's role and function in the family system are experientially learned, shaped, and mastered as he grows and develops within the family. Changes in role assignments disquiet the system's steady state and are resisted.	f) Since Rem is a new beginning in the midst of life, the system is inchoate and the child's role and function are not yet internalized. This may provide an opportunity to change role assignment, but the uncertainty may raise the level of anxiety of all family members.
g) Loyalty to one *or* the other parent is not commonly demanded or put to the test. Therefore, potential loyalty conflict and guilt are minimized, usually within "normal" (oedipal) bounds.	g) Either or both bioparents may explicitly or implicitly demand singular loyalty. This is particularly so in the separation and early post-divorce stage, with an exacerbation likely at the time of remarriage. Even if not influenced by parents, the child may find internal reasons to feel guilty or to be partisan. The effects of divided loyalties on the new system are readily detected: hostility to the new relationship, negative comparison of stepparent to parent of same sex, anxiety and guilt if the child likes the stepparent, acting-out against the Rem parent, anger at recognition of Rem since the hope for reconciliation of the parents is now even more remote.
h) Child may harbor resentments against either or both parents for a variety of reasons.	h) Same as nuclear. There is special anger and resentment towards the parent who is seen as having broken up the nuclear family and "deserted" the child.

7) FORCES THAT IMPINGE ON THE SYSTEM

a) Children as Messengers

Nuclear	*Rem*
Children play parents off against one another; bioparents often talk to each other through the children. The child's role as messenger may reflect a positive or negative attitude of one parent towards the other. The child may act out for the parent with whom he identifies. Positive and negative identifications may be at play.	The impact on the system is multiplied in Rem because the parent(s) or stepparent may depend on the child to provide information about, or relay information to, the other system. A child may use the messenger role to gain favor with parental figures, to vent aggression ("a plague on both your houses"), or to divide the Rem couple and conquer the bioparent. One parent may use the child to "spy" on the other. Some children consciously and/or unconsciously slant information to be destructive/helpful to a parent's new relationship. This much "power" is not in the child's best interest (see Chapter 9).

b) Former Spouses

No former spouse but a previous lover may still be present in some capacity. If so, it may or may not be a serious disruptive force.	Former spouses are part of the Rem family suprasystem. Although they are not members of the Rem family, they may have great input and influence on the system. When couples have been married for many years and have had children together, their emotional divorce is rarely complete. Ex-spouses remain bound by positive feelings as well as the more commonly expressed negative ones. The expression of positive affect for a former spouse is often threatening to the new spouse.
	Ex-spouses can interject conflict, guilt, financial pressures,

Nuclear   *Rem*

and influence on children. Sometimes they are perceived as an
arm reaching from the past into
the present; "an unwanted guest
at the dinner table and in the
bedroom." Conversely, an increasing number of former
spouses are now able to collaborate in a mutually helpful way
that enhances rather than de-
tracts from each other's new
family systems.

c) Grandparents

Parents of the adults often have
their greatest impact on the nuclear family in the early years of
the marriage when the completion of the individuation of the
young adult is in process. As
grandparents, their role is usually an auxiliary one to that of the
child's parents. They have "the
pleasure without the hard work."

Grandparents are often pressed
into service or gladly volunteer
for childcare roles during the
double single-parent periods.
When the time for remarriage arrives, grandparents and child
may have developed a deep bond
that is hard to attenuate. It may
be difficult for grandparents to
accept a lesser role with the
child. At the time of Rem, new
sets of stepgrandparents may appear who can offer positive, negative, or neutral input to the Rem
suprasystem.

d) Siblings of Adults and Intimate Friends

Siblings and intimate friends of
the adults may play a significant
role and have input to the nuclear
family.

Siblings and intimate friends of
the adults may have played roles
similar to that of the grandparents and may continue to have a
significant input to the Rem family. Their effect on the system
may cause antagonism with the
new spouse if he does not feel fully accepted and respected. If the
new spouse does feel accepted,
this may be experienced as "an
enriched widening of the circle."

Nuclear	*Rem*
	Often friendships from the previous relationship become solidified or dissolved because of friends' antagonistic or partisan reactions to one of the partners. A friend who has a bipartisan reaction to a couple's breakup is hard to come by.

e) Forms of Communication

The medium for the message is most often face-to-face verbal and/or nonverbal communication. These contacts usually become part of the routine of daily living. Private conversations can take place unbeknown to other family members. When temporarily separated, telephone contact and letters are used.	Because of the physical distance of one parent, telephone and letters can be an important means of communication. These methods of contact may present problems since they are often experienced by adults and the child as: intrusions on the life space and routine of one household; an infringement on one's privacy since other family members may know of the contact; and bait for one's "curiosity" that can lead to entanglements. As one second wife said, "A rose is a rose is a rose in our home, but a telephone call from his ex is more than a telephone call." For some parents and children letters become very special.

f) Courts and Legal Process

a) Court system and legal contracts usually do not have an influence on family life. In the eyes of the court and legal process, marriage is seen as a partnership.	a) Court system and legal contracts that regulate alimony, child support, custody, visitation, etc., usually influence the Rem family. In the eyes of the court and legal process, divorcing and divorced couples are usually seen as adversaries; this stance can act against the resolution of differences. It is hoped that, with the advent of divorce mediation, this will change.

Nuclear	Rem
	In some families the real or imagined threat of "going back to court" provides more organized and orderly functioning. In the most severe instances that involve children, the court can actually provide a supervisory function.
b) Both bioparents have legal rights, duties and responsibilities to their children.	b) Noncustodial parents' rights, duties and responsibilities are often recodified by the courts. Stepparent and stepchild have no legal bond or responsibilities to one another.

g) Money

Money—its control, availability and use as a potent form of power —is a source of problems for many families. Over 51% of married mothers now contribute to the family income. Husbands or wives may contribute to their parent's or a sibling's support but this rarely becomes a source of serious marital problems or deprivation.	Money provides additional sources of problems for the Rem system. A remarried man who pays alimony and/or child support is often not in a position to enjoy his previous standard of living (nor are his former wife and children) or to consider having another child. Understandably, some new wives are unable to view the situation objectively and feel that whatever goes to the former spouse and children is taken away from her and her spouse. Husbands usually contribute to this destructive systemic dynamic. Often the system lacks the money to oil it properly. Conversely, a man who marries a woman who had been formerly married to a wealthier person can use this to demean himself or unjustifiably regard the affluence of his stepchildren's father as the reason for the children's preference for their biological father. Or, his own children cannot be given similar material

Nuclear	*Rem*
	things or have school and college choices open to them that his wife's children have. These are just a couple of examples of the real issues around money that must be dealt with in Rem.

Comparing and contrasting nuclear and Rem families inevitably lead to exaggerations in which the nuclear family is idealized and the Rem family appears as a situation so trouble filled that it is to be avoided. Neither polarized end is totally accurate. A more appropriate picture of family life is expressed in this Zen story.

A man is walking in the thick of the jungle and sees a crocodile at his feet. Terrified, he quickly climbs the nearest tree, and just when he begins to feel safe he notices a tiger overhead. He wonders out loud, "Tigers above me, crocodiles below me. . . ." Just then he notices a lush strawberry.

Such is the human journey: struggles, challenges, but just enough strawberries to make life worth living. Our experiences with Rem families indicate that the potential gratifications make the difficulties worthwhile.

CHAPTER 3

The Remarried Family
Life Cycle—The Concept
of Multiple Tracks

We usually think that if something is not one, it is more than one; if
it is not singular, it is plural. But in actual experience, our life is not
only plural but also singular. Each one of us is both dependent and
independent.

Suzuki, 1970, p. 25

... the task of the family is to create a resource, in the form of interpersonal enactments, that matches or meets a need. When the family performs this task, each member "grows itself up."

Terkelsen, 1980, p. 32

Far-reaching changes are being brought about in individual, marital,
and family systems cycles by the increasing incidence of divorce and
subsequent remarriage. As a consequence, individual life cycles are
often lived out over the course of two or more marriages. Husbands and
wives may be simultaneously bioparents and stepparents; children are
often raised in two households with the co-parenting efforts of two bioparents, one, two, or more stepparents, and assistance from a plethora
of biograndparents and stepgrandparents. We have found that concepts which originate from the life-cycle tasks and responsibilities for
intact marital and family systems may not provide relevant guidelines
for the newly made marriages and families of Rem or for the remaining
single-parent households. In fact, one of the keys to understanding Rem
from the individual, marital and family life-cycle framework is to appre-

ciate that, in addition to the disruption of these original cycles, there has been a *new* marital and family systems life cycle. On the systems level, this means that, with remarriage, there may be an "old" nuclear family life cycle continuing in some form, an "old" marital system life cycle which changes and may or may not become defunct with divorce, a new marital life cycle beginning with the remarriage, and a new Rem family life cycle which may begin at the same time. On the individual level, there is similar complexity, with each individual living his or her life cycle on multiple tracks. The task for the clinician is to be aware of the many simultaneous tracks on which the systems and their members are likely to be operating and to ascertain if needs are being met well enough in the different systems. The reality of the widespread existence of multiple tracks marks a sociological change that has many implications for present and future family life and childrearing practices. Children, in increasing numbers, are having some of their needs fulfilled in two or more family constellations, not just one.

In this chapter we shall discuss some of the life-cycle models which have contributed to our thinking about the Rem life cycle and the concept of multiple tracks. We shall then present a case that is charted to illustrate these developmental tracks for one individual. Finally, we shall examine the implications of using this framework in our clinical thinking and describe some Rem cases to show how the concept can be applied in clinical work.

INDIVIDUAL LIFE CYCLES

Life cycles, until recently, have been descriptive of an individual's development as he or she moved through life. The unit of attention had been the individual, with the focus on explicating those innate developmental processes which unfold according to the epigenetic principle (Erikson, 1968) at phase-specific times. In this construct, optimal development is sparked by the spiraling interaction of biological maturation (the unfolding of the innate ground plan) and good-enough responses from the environment to individual needs. Erikson has noted that, while such interaction varies from culture to culture, it must occur roughly at the proper rate and in the proper sequence which governs all epigenesis. Personality, then, can be said to develop "according to steps predetermined in the human organism's readiness to be driven toward, to be aware of, and to interact with a widening radius of significant individuals and institutions (1968, p. 93). The individual both responds to and evokes what he needs at each developmental step. It is hypothesized that failure to have needs met well enough in any phase leads to failure to master successfully the developmental tasks of that phase, with deficits and developmental arrests then occurring in that and subsequent phases. Failure in getting needs met can come from different factors, for instance: a poor "fit" between the individual and his environment (the interactional processes); physiological or psychological deficits within the individual; the inability of significant others to meet phase-specific needs; or different combinations of all these. With the disruption of divorce and remarriage, need attainment may be jeopardized.

Different researchers have concentrated their studies on various developmental stages and aspects of the individual life cycle. Freud (1905), with his formulations of psychosexual development, presented a personality theory in terms of the maturation of the drives. Others, including Anna Freud (1965), Spitz (1959, 1965), Erikson (1968), Winnicott (1965), Bowlby (1969, 1973, 1980), and Mahler and her colleagues (1975), have contributed enormously to our understanding of early development, some through extensive research with children. Some researchers, e.g., Levinson et al., (1974, 1978), Gould (1972, 1978), Scarf (1980), and Neugarten (1968), have focused on adult development by building on Erikson's (1968) view that development is a lifelong process, with the individual optimally reaching increasing levels of intrapsychic integration and interpersonal differentiation. Each has studied, identified, and elaborated normative phases in the life cycle of the adult. Levinson has concentrated his studies on men, Scarf on women, and Neugarten on those adults in their middle and later years. Neugarten (1968) suggests that for contemporary adults there is a diminution of the impact of biological maturation in development and suggests that age norms and age expectations, "the social clock," play a more significant part during the later years.

Individual life cycles unfold in a social systems setting; biology *and* society proscribe the developmental steps, as well as the tasks and responsibilities requiring mastery. The importance of the systems to which one belongs during life generally has been mentioned by these researchers in their studies, but they have not fleshed out the interaction between individuals and systems and have not focused on the transactional processes between them. Erikson, for example, is well aware of the complementarity and reciprocity between individual development and family development, but has not yet conceptualized it in systemic terms. As he noted: "It is as true to say that babies control and bring up their families as it is to say the converse. A family can bring up a baby only by being brought up by him. His growth consists of a series of challenges to them to serve his newly developing potentialities for social interaction" (1968, p. 96).

MARITAL AND FAMILY LIFE CYCLES

The application of systems theory and communications theory enables us to expand our unit of attention from the individual alone and his developmental processes to the interactional field. Our concern in this section is with the marital system and the family system. Not only is the life cycle of the individual played out in marital and family systems (family of origin, nuclear family, single-parent family, Rem family), but these systems themselves are not static. They have their own developmental processes and life cycles, with tasks and responsibilities to be mastered at phase-specific times, in order for system *and* individual needs to be met and for development to continue to unfold. From this perspective, when development falters or is disrupted, then the unit of attention is the interactional processes in the system, the hypothesis being that the current organizational development of the family or the family structure itself is deficient, and therefore failing to meet individual needs well enough. Optimally, in this model, individual, marital, and family life cycles are congruent, so that the greatest number of individual needs are met through family task fulfillment.

We may be closer to a working abstraction of reality if we can accept that "individual without family" and "family without individual" are both inadequate conceptualizations. We are both individual *and* family. If we can feel the correctness of this seemingly paradoxical formulation, we are closer to the next theoretical step on the developmental and therapeutic paths that are the most productive to explore.

We consider each unit of attention to be crucial for assessment and treatment. We conceptualize all Rem cases from a systemic and individual (life cycle and intrapsychic) point of view, and we also look at the interrelationship of these factors. We utilize our knowledge from all three areas to determine interventions, which are usually on a systemic level. We summarize these three areas or frames of reference as: systems-cycles-psyche.

Different researchers have been concentrating their studies on the marital and family system life cycles, although at this time there has been no systematic longitudinal research. Berman and Lief (1975), in their work with marital couples, found that critical stages in the marriages were intimately related to critical stages in the individual life cycle, and that issues which appeared to be purely individual or purely dyadic were often, in fact, the result of a complicated interaction between marital and individual crisis points (p. 585). They developed a table of the two life cycles—individual and marital—basing the individual stages of development on the work of Levinson and his associates (1974) and the marital stages on their own studies. Their chart is reproduced

TABLE 3.1
Individual and Marital Stages of Development

Item	Stage 1 (18–21 years)	Stage 2 (22–28 years)	Stage 3 (29–31 years)	Stage 4 (32–39 years)	Stage 5 (40–42 years)	Stage 6 (43–59 years)	Stage 7 (60 years and over)
Individual stage*	Pulling up roots	Provisional adulthood	Transition at age 30	Settling down	Mid-life transition	Middle adulthood	Older age
Individual task	Developing autonomy	Developing intimacy and occupational identification; "getting into the adult world"	Deciding about commitment to work and marriage	Deepening commitments; pursuing more long-range goals	Searching for "fit" between aspirations and environment	Restabilizing and reordering priorities	Dealing effectively with aging, illness, and death while retaining zest for life
Marital task	Shift from family of origin to new commitment	Provisional marital commitment	Commitment crisis; restlessness	Productivity: children, work, friends, and marriage	Summing up: success and failure are evaluated and future goals sought	Resolving conflicts and stabilizing the marriage for the long haul	Supporting and enhancing each other's struggle for productivity and fulfillment in face of the threats of aging
Marital conflict	Original family ties conflict with adaptation	Uncertainty about choice of marital partner; stress over parenthood	Doubts about choice come into sharp conflict; rates of growth may diverge if spouse has not successfully negotiated	Husband and wife have different and conflicting ways of achieving productivity	Husband and wife perceive "success" differently; conflict between individual success and remaining in the marriage	Conflicting rates and directions of emotional growth; concerns about losing youthfulness may lead to depression and/	Conflicts are generated by rekindled fears of desertion, loneliness, and sexual failure

		Intimacy	Power	Marital boundaries
	or acting out			
	stage 2 because of parental obligations	Fragile intimacy	Testing of power	Conflicts over in-laws
		Deepening but ambivalent intimacy	Establishment of patterns of conflict resolution	Friends and potential lovers; work versus family
		Increasing distance while partners make up their minds about each other	Sharp vying for power and dominance	Temporary disruptions including extramarital sex or reactive "fortress building"
		Marked increase in intimacy in "good" marriages; gradual distancing in "bad" marriages	Establishment of definite patterns of decision making and dominance	Nuclear family closes boundaries
		Tenuous intimacy as fantasies about others increase	Power in outside world is tested vis-à-vis power in the marriage	Disruption due to reevaluation; drive versus restabilization
		Intimacy is threatened by aging and by boredom vis-à-vis a secure and stable relationship; departure of children may increase or decrease intimacy	Conflicts often increase when children leave, and security appears threatened	Boundaries are usually fixed except in crises such as illness, death, job change, and sudden shift in role relationships
		Struggle to maintain intimacy in the face of eventual separation; in most marriages this dimension achieves a stable plateau	Survival fears stir up needs for control and dominance	Loss of family and friends leads to closing in of boundaries; physical environment is crucial in maintaining ties with the outside world

*From Levinson et al., 1974. Reprinted with permission from Berman, E. & Lief, H. Marital therapy from a psychiatric perspective: An overview. *American Journal of Psychiatry*, 132(6): 586, June 1975.

here (Table 3.1). Among the many possible variables, they selected what they felt to be the three issues that spawn marital conflict: intimacy, power, and inclusion/exclusion. They, like other marital and family therapists, view the marital couple as a system, and advocate a multilevel approach that takes into account both the individual and the interactional components in assessing and working with the dyad. Rhodes has elaborated a developmental approach to the life cycle of the family (1977) and then focused on potential crisis points and how these can be dealt with (1981).

Carter and McGoldrick (1980) present the view that the family itself has its own complex developmental processes and can be considered itself as a basic unit of emotional development. Their hypothesis, paralleling Erikson's for the individual, is that there are emotional tasks to be fulfilled by the system at each phase of its life cycle. These require a change of status and meaning for family members at each phase (p. 11). Terkelsen (1980), in the same volume, elaborates on Carter and McGoldrick's thesis, integrating individual developmental processes and family structure. He sees need attainment as the mainspring of human development (p. 32) and suggests that a family is "good enough" (Winnicott, 1965) to the extent that it matches specific elements of structure to specific needs. Change in the system occurs through the spiraling interaction between the emergence of a new primary need in one member and the resulting adaptation of the system to meet and integrate this need, thereby changing its entire structure in the process. Terkelsen identifies two levels of change: first order developments which arise from individual developmental needs, and which involve progressive increments of mastery, adaptation and integration into the system—a need to *do* something new; and second order developments, which require transformations of status and meaning or a need to *be* something new (p. 39). The latter developments may be either normative events in a family life cycle, e.g., marriage, birth, school, etc., or what Terkelsen calls paranormative events (those that abruptly change the family system), under which he includes marital separation, divorce, death or remarriage. His concept of the superstructure of the family life cycle from this point of view parallels Erikson's concept of the life cycle of the individual:

> The family life cycle corresponds in its broad overall shape to that of the individual life cycle. Specifically it is made up of a series of epochs, each epoch consisting of a "plateau" period and a "transition" period. The plateaus are extended periods of selective functional stability. Such changes as do occur are limited to changes evoked by first order developments. These are the times of change

by accretion. In contrast, transitional periods are characterized by structural unpredictability. The dominant theme is change by transformation, and it occurs in response to second order developments (Terkelsen, 1980, p. 40).

Carter and McGoldrick (1980) have developed a series of charts outlining the predictable stages of the family life cycle of the current middle-class American family. They include in their charts the stages of the life cycle, the emotional process of transition, including the key principles or "attitudes" which enable the family members to make the transition, and the second order changes in family status required before development can be resumed. They consider that the task of family members (and family therapy) is to identify and acknowledge the key principles or attitudes before moving on to the tasks which will lead to the reintegration and transformation of family structure. They, like us, consider the processes of marital separation, divorce, and then remarriage as dislocations in the family life cycle requiring additional restabilizing steps before ongoing development can be resumed. Since we have found their charts so helpful in clarifying our own thinking, we reproduce them here (Tables 3.2, 3.3, 3.4).

MULTIPLE TRACKS: INDIVIDUAL, MARITAL AND FAMILY SYSTEMS' LIFE CYCLES AND REMARRIAGE

The precursor to remarriage has been the disruption in all three life cycles; individual, marital and family (nuclear). The disruption has been an ongoing process, refuelled by each structural change brought about by the marital discord, physical separation, establishment of two single parent homes, and by the divorce. Subsequent dating and courtship of prospective Rem partners adds to the turbulence. Systems and individual needs may not be met well enough through this time, or are not addressed. The task of restructuring and reestablishing the systems so that needs can be met and development resumed is a difficult one.

With the remarriage, on the systems level, there is the creation of a new system, and an *addition* of new life cycle tracks: a remarriage life cycle, and, where there are children from a previous marriage, a Rem family life cycle. At the same time, again if there have been children from a previous marriage, the "old" nuclear family life cycle continues in some form, with the children needing parenting, contact with each bioparent, and other forms of support. Similarly, there commonly are remnants of affect and attachments between the former spouses in the

TABLE 3.2

The Stages of the Family Life Cycle

Family Life-Cycle Stage	Emotional Process of Transition: Key Principles	Second Order Changes in Family Status Required to Proceed Developmentally
1. Between families: The unattached young adult	Accepting parent offspring separation	a. Differentiation of self in relation to family of origin b. Development of intimate relationships c. Establishment of self in work
2. The joining of families through marriage: the newly married couple	Commitment to new system	a. Formation of marital system b. Realignment of relationships with extended families and friends to include spouse
3. The family with young children	Accepting new members into the system	a. Adjusting marital system to make space for child(ren) b. Taking on parenting roles c. Realignment of relationships with extended family to include parenting and grandparenting roles.
4. The family with adolescents	Increasing flexibility of family boundaries to include children's independence	a. Shifting of parent-child relationships to permit adolescent to move in and out of system b. Refocus on mid-life marital and career issues c. Beginning shift toward concerns for older generation
5. Launching children and moving on	Accepting a multitude of exits from and entries into the family system	a. Renegotiation of marital system as a dyad b. Development of adult to adult relationships between grown children and their parents c. Realignment of relationships to include in-laws and grandchildren d. Dealing with disabilities and death of parents (grandparents)
6. The family in later life	Accepting the shifting of generational roles	a. Maintaining own and/or couple functioning and interests in face of physiological decline; exploration of new familial and social role options b. Support for a more central role for middle generation c. Making room in the system for the wisdom and experience of the elderly; supporting the older generation without overfunctioning for them d. Dealing with loss of spouse, siblings and other peers and preparation for own death. Life review and integration

Reprinted with permission from Carter, E. A. & McGoldrick, M. (Eds.), *The Family Life Cycle.* New York: Gardner Press, 1980.

46

TABLE 3.3

Dislocations of the Family Life Cycle, Requiring Additional Steps to Restabilize and Proceed Developmentally

Phase	Emotional Process of Transition Prerequisite Attitude	Developmental Issues
DIVORCE		
1. The decision to divorce	Acceptance of inability to resolve marital tensions sufficiently to continue relationship	Acceptance of one's own part in failure of the marriage
2. Planning the break-up of the system	Supporting viable arrangements for all parts of the system	a. Working cooperatively on problems of custody, visitation, finances b. Dealing with extended family about the divorce
3. Separation	A) Willingness to continue cooperative coparental relationship B) Work on resolution of attachment to spouse	a. Mourning loss of intact family b. Restructuring marital and parent-child relationships; adaptation to living apart c. Realignment of relationships with extended family; staying connected with spouse's extended family
4. The divorce	More work on emotional divorce: overcoming hurt anger, guilt, etc.	a. Mourning loss of intact family: giving up fantasies of reunion b. Retrieval of hopes, dreams, expectations from the marriage c. Staying connected with extended families
POST-DIVORCE FAMILY		
A. Single-parent family	Willingness to maintain parental contact with ex-spouse and support contact of children and his family	a. Making flexible visitation arrangements with ex-spouse and his family b. Rebuilding own social network
B. Single-parent (noncustodial)	Willingness to maintain parental contact with ex-spouse and support custodial parent's relationship with children	a. Finding ways to continue effective parenting relationship with children b. Rebuilding own social network

Reprinted with permission from Carter, E. A. & McGoldrick, M. (Eds.), *The Family Life Cycle.* New York: Gardner Press, 1980.

TABLE 3.4
Remarried Family Formation: A Developmental Outline*

Steps	Prerequisite Attitude	Developmental Issues
1. Entering the new relationship	Recovery from loss of first marriage (adequate "emotional divorce")	Recommitment to marriage and to forming a family with readiness to deal with the complexity and ambiguity
2. Conceptualizing and planning new marriage and family	Accepting one's own fears and those of new spouse and children about remarriage and forming a stepfamily Accepting need for time and patience for adjustment to complexity and ambiguity of: 1. Multiple new roles 2. Boundaries: space, time, membership and authority 3. Affective issues: guilt, loyalty conflicts, desire for mutuality, unresolvable past hurts	a. Work on openness in the new relationships to avoid pseudomutuality b. Plan for maintenance of cooperative co-parental relationships with ex-spouses c. Plan to help children deal with fears, loyalty conflicts and membership in two systems d. Realignment of relationships with extended family to include new spouse and children e. Plan maintenance of connections for children with extended family of ex-spouse(s)
3. Remarriage and reconstitution of family	Final resolution of attachment to previous spouse and ideal of "intact" family; Acceptance of a different model of family with permeable boundaries	a. Restructuring family boundaries to allow for inclusion of new spouse—stepparent b. Realignment of relationships throughout subsystems to permit interweaving of several systems c. Making room for relationships of all children with biological (noncustodial) parents, grandparents, and other extended family. d. Sharing memories and histories to enhance stepfamily integration

*Variation on a developmental schema presented by Ransom *et al.* (1979)
Reprinted with permission from Carter, E. A. & McGoldrick, M. (Eds.), *The Family Life Cycle.* New York: Gardner Press, 1980.

"old," technically defunct, marital system life cycle. If there has not been sufficient emotional divorce, this continuing cycle can impede the development in the new marital life cycle. On the individual level, adults and children are living out their individual life cycles on multiple tracks.

Rem Marital Life Cycle

The Rem marital life cycle begins with the marriage of the new spouses. If the emotional divorce from the former partner(s) is complete enough, there can be a full commitment to the new marriage and a deepening intimacy. Consolidation of the Rem couple is important. Both spouses should be aware of and try to fulfill one's own and one another's romantic, love, sexual and companionship needs. If there are no children from previous marriages, or the children are now adults, it is easier for the spouses to consolidate and become a marital pair with congruent marital cycle needs. The same needs apply to such a couple as apply to any marital system (see Table 3.1). When there are children who require attention and time, or where an overly dependent emotional relationship exists between bioparent and child, the consolidation of the marital dyad becomes more difficult. The child may strive, often with the unconscious cooperation of his bioparent, to exclude the new spouse and stepparent from the system, thus contributing to forces that are disruptive to the new marital cycle.

Rem Family Life Cycle

The Rem family life cycle begins with the new commitment of the adult partners where there are children from a previous marriage, or with the birth of a mutual child to the Rem couple where there are no children from past relationships. As with the Rem marital life cycle, the Rem family life cycle is more complicated than the nuclear family life cycle, although the basic needs of the members and purposes of the family to care, protect and support are the same. Different is the disruption all members have suffered in the separation and divorce processes. Both adults and children bring to Rem a particular vulnerability and anticipation that this new system, too, will bring more loss. As Carter and McGoldrick (1980, p. 266) note:

> It is our experience that this is one of the most difficult transitions for families to negotiate. This is because of the wish for premature closure to end the ambiguity and pain, and because of the likelihood that the previous stage (mourning a death or working out the emo-

tional complexities of a divorce) has been inadequately dealt with, and will, in any case, be emotionally reactivated. Much therapeutic effort must be directed toward educating families about the built-in complexities of the process, so that they can work toward establishing a viable open system that will permit restoration of the developmental processes for their life-cycle phases.

The transformation of structure required in order for needs to be met —individual needs of the adults, couple needs, parenting needs, and the developmental needs of the children (usually now in two households)— can take time to accomplish and complex negotiations to effect. (See case example in Chapters 6 and 7.)

Table 3.5 illustrates multiple marital and family life cycle tracks of Rem. It is an extrapolation from Berman and Lief's chart (Table 3.1) and those of Carter and McGoldrick (Tables 3.2, 3.3, 3.4) and follows the life cycle of "Amy Greenson" as she separates from her family of origin, marries, has children, separates, divorces, lives as a single parent, and then remarries and begins a new family life cycle. It illustrates clearly the way in which previous and new marital and family cycles are current and overlap, and how additional life-cycle tracks are added to her life, rather than old ones merely being replaced. The table can be read vertically for a longitudinal view of the different life cycles—individual, marital and family—and horizontally for a cross-sectional view.

CLINICAL IMPLICATIONS: CONCORDANCE AND CONFLICT OF MULTIPLE TRACKS

When treating Rem families, it is important to appreciate the multiple tracks which Rem members and their subsystems are on at any point in time, and to determine if, how, and where needs are being met. Commonly, in Rem there may be congruence or conflict between life cycles. We need to assess from the framework of the family life cycle(s) the marital life cycle(s), as well as the individual life cycles for each adult and child.

The life cycles of the Rem partners may not be congruent when it comes down to the work and responsibilities required by their marital or family system's life-cycle purposes and needs. Consciously verbalized statements regarding intentions are not always accurate or fulfilled. Motivations are determined by factors beyond awareness that are then manifested as subtle behavior or feelings that ultimately can produce dysfunction in the marital or Rem family system.

The marital cycle of each spouse and the congruence of both adult

TABLE 3.5

The Individual, Marital and Family Life Cycle in Rem

Age	Individual Life Cycle	Marital Life Cycle	Family Life Cycle
18–21	Pulls up roots. Develops autonomy. (Amy M. moves out of family's home and attends college in another city.)	Shift from family of origin to new emotional commitment. (Amy meets George G. and they begin to date exclusively.)	During college, Amy still financially dependent on her family of origin; her old room is kept for her at home.
22–28	Provisional adulthood. Develops occupational identification. (Amy graduates and works as a teacher; shares apartment and then lives alone.)	Provisional marital commitment; stress over parenthood. (Amy and George engaged when Amy is 23; marry at 24.)	Self-sufficient vis-à-vis family of origin; her room at home is converted to study.
29–31	Transition at age 30; decides about commitment to work and marriage.	Commitment crisis. (Married six years, George is questioning the relationship. They receive marital counseling.)	Pressure from her family to stay together and have children; her father retires.
32–39	Settling down, deepening commitments. (Amy feels committed to George and desires children; she stops working with first child.)	Productivity: children, friends, work for George. (Their daughters are born when Amy is 32 and 34.)	Family with young children: need to accept new members, take on parenting roles.
40–42	Midlife transition; searching for fit between aspirations and environment. (Amy questions homemaker role, is restless and dissatisfied. After an impetuous sexual misadventure she avoids dating.)	Couple is summing up: success and failure evaluated. (Amy and George again receive counseling; George has affair; decision to separate is made when children are six and eight years old.)	Post-separation family: two households are set up. Amy returns to live with her parents; there is a resurgence of dependence on her family of origin as she returns to the job market. She has custody of children, who visit father. Grandparents very involved with children while Amy works and begins to date.

(continued)

51

TABLE 3.5 *(continued)*
The Individual, Marital and Family Life Cycle in Rem

Age	Individual Life Cycle	Marital Life Cycle	Family Life Cycle
43–45	Middle adulthood: restabilizing and reordering priorities; struggle to reestablish autonomy from her family of origin, dealing with work advancement. (Now begins to desire a loving relationship with a man.)	Continuing co-parenting relationship although marriage is dissolved. Beginning to date. Testing out new ways of relating to men.	Double single parent stage: Girls are now 11 and 9 and are part of both parents' households.
45–50	Tasks of middle adulthood continue. Emotional divorce from George sufficiently complete for her to contemplate idea of marriage again. (Difficulty allowing herself to trust again as love relationship develops.) Remarries to fulfill coupling needs. Simultaneously continues co-parenting of her children with first husband while taking on co-parenting role with second husband.	MARRIAGE #1 Need to co-parent the girls through their adolescence. Dealing with ex-husband on issues around the girls such as dating and their desire to visit father less often. MARRIAGE #2 (a) Entering new relationship with Steve. (b) Planning and conceptualizing new marriage. (c) Remarriage. (d) Making new commitment.	OLD FAMILY Allowing adolescent children to individuate. Launching children and moving on. REM FAMILY Restructuring family to include new spouse and stepson (age 10) who lives with Rem couple. Providing a nurturing environment to prepubescent child. Dealing with Steve's ex-wife.

Age					
			(e) Commitment crisis: questioning choice. (f) Resolving conflicts and stabilizing remarriage.		Family with adolescent child. (Cycle repeats what Amy experienced with her girls.) Launching child and moving on.
50–59	Looking ahead to enjoy the later years. Dealing with her own aging process.	Co-parenting relationship is less important. Establish a workable relationship with George around their adult children.	(g) Supporting and enjoying friends and activities as children begin to leave home.	Dealing with aging and illness of her parents.	Relating to her children's spouses and children.
59+		Little contact with George except for milestone events of children and grandchildren.	(h) Continuing support; retirement, pursuit of interests, individually and together with Steve.		Relating to stepson's spouse and children.

53

partners' life cycles determine the quality of the marital and family cycles. Children may be included by marital partners to the extent that adults allow them to expand the dyad to triadic systems (family). Problems result if the couple excludes the children and do not follow through on appropriate *family system cycle needs* for them.

The "new" family often involves adults in life-cycle stages that had not been available in the first marriage or the repetition of childrearing phases with stepchildren, as well as with the couple's mutual children. Thus, the multiple life-cycle tracks which Rem families and individuals experience may make life more complex by adding layers of existence, roles, and responsibilities. These can be enriching and fulfilling as the new tracks supplement the older and meet needs that were not met in the first marriage and family or that had been met for a time and then were lost.

CASE VIGNETTES

Concordance of Individual, Marital and Family Life Cycles

Mrs. Gill, a woman of 36, lived with her 12- and 10-year-old children. Her former husband, who lived across the country, showed little interest in his children. She met and eventually married a bachelor of 45, Mr. Walden. The couple had many common interests and they fit together well emotionally. Mr. Walden had known that, in addition to his attraction to and compatibility with Mrs. Gill, he wanted a "ready-made family"; he did not want infant children. Mrs. Gill needed a father surrogate for her children, as well as a husband for herself with whom to share her life.

After two and a half years of marriage and with the consent of the children and their biofather, Mr. Walden adopted the two children. The older child was preparing to leave for college, both had done well at school, at home, and with their peers, and the adults were in a good long-term bonding phase of marriage. The children saw their biofather briefly when he was in the East. In this instance, the individual and marital cycle needs of both adults fit well, and the needs for childcare in the family cycle and the children's needs for a father surrogate who was loving and firm were also met.

Conflict in Individual, Marital and Family Systems Life Cycles

A divorced woman in a somewhat similar situation, Mrs. Bohegian, with children six and 10 years old, married a bachelor six years her senior, Mr. Soroyan. He, too, claimed he wanted a "ready-made family." The marriage went well until the woman gradually realized that her husband had no interest in supplying any guidance or parenting to her children. He apparently vacillated between identifying with her two sons as their buddy and being envious of the time and attention his wife gave to them. At the same time, he did not want to have a child with his wife. Mrs. Soroyan began to feel increasingly that she had three competing male children on her hands.

On examination, it became clear that Mr. Soroyan, although well into the chronological age for parental responsibility, was not emotionally at that stage but related to his wife as his mother surrogate. Thus his life cycle and marital cycle needs differed from those of his wife. Also, he was unable to fulfill a parenting role when it was needed at a crucial stage in the family system's life cycle, even though this had been included in their premarital "contract" discussions.

This marriage, despite a year of treatment, did not last because the family system was unable to satisfy the appropriate life-cycle needs of its members. Mrs. Soroyan wanted a more equal partner; Mr. Soroyan, as became clear when the relationship of his own parents and his relationship to them was reviewed, was a kindly, childlike man who had been in search of a mother-wife. Mr. and Mrs. Soroyan's final three months of therapy were spent in facing their need to separate, to work out an amiable separation, and to deal with the feelings of the children and Mrs. Soroyan's anger and disappointment. Her husband continued in individual treatment after the separation and divorce; mother and children were seen together for two additional months; Mrs. Soroyan was also seen individually.

Conflict Between Marital and Family Systems Life Cycles

Mr. Lovitt, a noncustodial father, requested treatment with his children because of his concern that his former wife, who had been remarried for three years, and her second husband were neglecting the children. We were successful in having the children's mother and her husband come in for the first session. When they were seen all together and in different subsystems over four evaluation sessions, the story unfolded that, contrary to our expectations, this was not an irate former husband making charges because of his own ego needs or hostility to his former spouse. The Rem couple, Mr. and Mrs. Fast (the new husband was 12 years older than his present wife and had been widowed around the time his two grown children were leaving home) were continuing in their stage of short-term love bonding. They were so involved in fulfilling their romantic needs with one another that neither was inclined to give

more than casual concern, time, or affection to the 13- and 15-year-
old children residing with them.

Mr. Fast had seen his first wife through a long terminal illness,
had brought up his children, and now wanted "something for myself." Mrs. Fast, who had been a devoted mother but had felt unloved by her former husband, Mr. Lovitt, now too wanted to "enjoy life," travel extensively, and share "the good life" with her
husband. If this had been a first marriage, the children might have
been better able to handle being relegated to second place by the
parents' united front bonding. Instead, having gone through the
disruption of separation, divorce, and remarriage, and then the experience of emotional "desertion" by their mother and displacement by their stepfather, they felt lost and unloved until their biofather more actively began to fill the gap. The two children acted
out delinquently, both did poorly at school, and the younger child
was whiny and depressed. Mr. Lovitt had become concerned about
their deterioration, and the children's discussion reaffirmed the reality of his concerns. This intensified when the older child became
involved with marihuana, amphetamines, and barbiturates.

The biofather offered to take custody of the children (he had not
remarried but had been living with a woman in a committed relationship for two years). The children liked and got along well with
his partner. The father's partner now joined the sessions too.

It became clear that under the circumstances it would be better
for the children to be based in their father's home. This fit in well
with mother and stepfather's needs, but mother was not willing to
give up formal custody because she felt that to do so would reflect
badly on her. The therapist pointed out that once children reach
adolescence many custodial switches are made informally without
returning to the court for approval. This suggestion worked out
well because the children and adults were all willing to make the
change and mother did not feel censured by having a court "order" a
change in custody. Visitation agreements were then worked out.
The next few sessions were spent with the children and their mother
dealing with feelings about the custody change, and then with the
children, their father, and his partner working out ground rules
and role clarification. The mother felt she was doing what was best
for the children and herself.

In this case, Mr. and Mrs. Fast (mother and stepfather) were
perfectly compatible in where they were in their own life cycles and
in their marital system's cycle. These two cycles were not compatible with the family system's life cycle needs for the children—their
mother was willing to relinquish prime family cycle functions and
take a secondary role in childrearing. She was able to give up control when she was reassured that her children would be well taken
care of by their father. Mr. Fast had played through his childrear-

ing life-cycle stage and now wanted to enjoy what he had missed romantically. The biofather's ability to avoid arousing his former wife's guilt (perhaps because he had coped well with his own guilt about having initiated the divorce), to not insist on legal custody, and to control his hostile feelings contributed to a good resolution of the situation.

Conflict between Individual and Marital System's Life Cycle Needs

Mr. Cooper, with adolescent, visiting children, married a younger woman who had never been married. Having had children in a previous marriage, he did not want "to go through all that again" and now wanted reciprocal love and a playmate. Mrs. Cooper agreed to forgo having children. As time progressed, she recognized that her husband's children did not satisfy her need for a child and, as her friends were having babies, she now tried to convince her husband to have a child with her. He became angry because "she entered the marriage with her eyes open" and now wanted to alter their contract.

COMMON REM PARTNERSHIPS AS RELATED
TO SYSTEM LIFE CYCLES

1) Rem Partner with New Spouse, No Children

Both partners may want romantic love, intimacy, privacy of time with the other. Problems ensue, however: a) if one partner has already achieved in his or her life work and the other partner is still taking on challenges and striving for recognition and fulfillment; or b) if one mate does not want children, while the other mate has an overpowering desire for children. Their life cycle needs are not concordant with the marital system cycle needs of both.

2) Rem Partner with Noncustodial Children, New Spouse with No Children, Mutual Child a Yes/No Possibility

Each spouse now has his/her own life cycle; the Rem partner has a vestigial marital system life cycle and a new marital system life cycle. Because there are children from the prior marriage, he or she has an "old" family system life cycle and may well have a "new" family system life cycle if the Rem couple have children together. New spouse, who had not been married before, does not have a vestigial marital life cycle. The first partner's vestigial marital system life cycle may possible interfere with new marriage.

3) Rem Partner with Custodial Children; New Spouse Also Has Children

Children's needs may have to be met by two biological parents in two households. Each bioparent is providing a parental surrogate who can serve as a co-parent and who imparts a different culture and personality with which to cope, plus the possibility for alternative identifications and modi operandi. Family life-cycle stages required for childcare and childrearing may interfere with marital life cycle, e.g., desire for privacy and fulfillment of the need for the marital pair to be alone during the short-term bonding stage. There may be a lack of desire to be a responsible parent or parent surrogate for children and to work out an appropriate role with children. A stepparent may be competitive with his partner's child. The bioparent may be overly involved with his child and dilatory in helping the child to individuate. The child's individual life-cycle need to reestablish his former nuclear family (because this is the way he knows) may make the child an active obstructionist. He or she may in this respect carry out the wishes of the other bioparent. The expectations of the child may be unrealistic.

Conceptualizing remarriage for adults and children in terms of the individual, marital, and family life cycles helps to make sense in ordering the phenomena we observe in remarriage situations. It clarifies the etiology of some of the clinical manifestations that require attention in treatment. The concept of simultaneous multiple tracks on which one can live out one's life cycle has immediate clinical application and will play an important role in our later discussions of assessment and treatment.

CHAPTER 4

The Remarried Couple

The Rem couple is pivotal to the joining of the Rem family. The stronger the marital pair, the more likely the success of the Rem family subsystem. While many issues are common to both Rem and first-married couples, there are some unique aspects for the Rem couple that may make for a different type of marital experience, either enhancing their bond or creating marital discord. This chapter discusses the needs of the Rem couple as a subsystem of the Rem family; it separates the partners' relationship from additional persons and issues in the family system. We focus on the couple, keeping in mind that the remainder of the Rem family suprasystem is in the picture, although not brought into sharp focus here.

Motivation to remarry will be dealt with. The *marital contract* concept will be used as a framework for understanding the marital problems demonstrated by Rem couples. Seven major typologies of styles of relating in marriage, which can apply to all couples, will be described, and some comments will be made about which types are more likely to adapt well to Rem. The use of the contracts and the typologies, along with other approaches to treatment, will be discussed in Chapter 8.

MOTIVATIONS TO REMARRY

Widowhood usually is not a volitionally created state. Divorce is. It is an act on the part of one or both spouses to terminate a marriage and to seek a better life. To seek a better life may or may not include a new partner, but for most formerly married persons it does. About 83% of divorced men do remarry and 75% of women—both the ones who blew the whistle on the previous marriage and the ones who were left.

Many of the motivations to marry a second (or third) time are similar to those that move people to marry the first time. People, for the most part, elect to live with a mate of the opposite sex whom they initially love in order to bear and raise children, to seek emotional and financial security, and to build a support and living system around themselves. We will focus here on those motivations that are more particular for the person who remarries and for the never-before-married person who selects a divorced or widowed mate who may or may not have children.

Seagrave (1980) did an extensive review of the literature of the married, the separated, and the divorced in relation to their mental health. He found that studies done in the United States and Great Britain demonstrated that the divorced utilize mental health services at a rate four to five times as great as the rate married persons do. He further found that the divorced population is an extremely high-risk group for psychiatric hospitalization and outpatient psychiatric treatment. Surveys of psychiatric care provided by general practitioners indicate that the divorced and separated are also overrepresented among the population of general medical service users. In his conclusion, Seagrave states (1980, p. 195):

> Data reviewed in this article clearly indicate that severe marital discord, separation and divorce are related to emotional unrest, help-seeking behavior, and the utilization of mental health services. Whether marital discord and divorce are etiologically related to more severe psychiatric conditions such as affective disease and psychotic disorder is less clear. The admission data for psychiatric facilities are suggestive of such a relationship. Similarly, there is evidence linking unipolar depressive disorders with marital discord, although the available evidence doesn't allow one to differentiate whether marital discord plays an etiologic role.

Seagrave's findings suggest that many adults who had been married have such a strong need to have a unique mating relationship that they tend to be emotionally disturbed if they are not so connected. Do only the emotionally disturbed divorce? There may be a slightly higher rate of "basic" emotional disturbance among those who divorce or who have been divorced, but there is no evidence to support this. In fact, it is perhaps evidence of mental health to leave a marriage that is rife with disharmony rather than to stay when efforts to improve the situation have failed.

What does appear to hold, in many instances, is that the pain of separating and not being connected to a mate causes extreme disequilibrium. We can hypothesize that the need for a mate as a stabilizing self-selfobject to help maintain a sense of self-cohesion in the face of the threat of self-disintegration (Kohut, 1977) may be a determining factor. A large number of formerly married persons may experience the loss of the partner (the needed self-selfobject) as a threat to themselves, leading to a state of disintegration, with the accompanying states of rage, fragmentation, and/or depression. They may fear being alone, feel abandoned, fail to take care of their own person and living quarters, or go to irrational extremes to get back their former mate. The vacuum left by a departed mate can be devastating—as it also can be for the person who has elected to leave.

The cliché that a woman who cooks a good dinner for a divorced man has a head start in the courting competition also holds for the man who shows concern and an ability to set limits for a divorced woman's children, or who will remove her, if only temporarily, from the overburdening routine of job, home, and childcare. We find the promise of a caring and loving relationship to be the prime motivation for remarriage.

Other motivations flow from utopian dreams. The recently divorced mate was a horror—this one will be loving, kind, considerate, understanding, sexually giving (or have a lower or higher level of desire). The new mate will have all the pluses where the prior partner had minuses. The new mate will be the perfect loving person.

Motivations to remarry may include the desire to have a family. To be a parent to some one else's children may not only be acceptable but desirable. Young children may be frightening or burdensome, whereas once they walk, talk, go to school, or "can be reasoned with" their company is desired. Both men and women believe this or sometimes adopt the ready-made family outlook (cuckoo's nest syndrome) as a rationalization because of their intense desire to win over the potential spouse—who they sense wants this. Others, quite unconsciously, see the bioparent as a strong and able person who will also be their parent-spouse.

Someone with adolescent or older children is often motivated to seek out an appreciably younger mate—someone whom they can teach and guide (see "parental partner" later in this chapter), and whose freshness and discovery of the world will revitalize them. This was almost solely a male motivation in the recent past; now that an increasing number of women have money and power, however, we find the youthful qualities of a younger spouse to be a motivation for second marriages among older women, too. Still for others, the second marriage becomes an opportunity to fulfill what they had not done or had up to now—different lifestyle, work, fun.

Another group can be characterized as seeking to escape the parental home. For example, a younger, never-married woman may marry an older man with children to resolve her dependency on her parents. The older person is seen as a "good" parental figure who will fulfill deep emotional needs in a socially acceptable fashion and will provide prestige, financial security, and power.

Of interest is a small group of men and women who are widowed or have a chronically ill hospitalized spouse. They remarry or live together in a committed relationship with someone else, recognizing their need for connubial life, and possibly seeking to provide a parental surrogate for children. If their original marital relationship had been a good one and they were deeply in love they may, masochistically, choose a spouse who could not possibly be a suitable partner. The dynamic involved is a variation of the incomplete divorce and avoidance of mourning. In these instances the person remains "loyal" to his first love by deliberately (unconsciously and sometimes even consciously) marrying someone whom he recognizes he can never love. The commonplace rationalization is "if I work at it, I can love him/her enough. I know it will work out OK." It doesn't, and adds to the list of unsuccessful remarriages.

Short-term and Long-term Bonding

The demand that the marital relationship provide continued peak experiences is, of course, not consistent with what we know of short- and long-term bonding patterns (Tiger and Fox, 1971). Seeking the emotional rush and high of short-term bonding excitation may produce the syndrome of multiple sequential marriages or love affairs—another significant motivation for Rem. As the "being in love" of short-term bonding ends, some people find the quieter pleasure of long-term bonding dull and look for another "fix."

Domestic peace, financial security, help with childcare, getting out of the "meat auction block" of singles weekends, bars and clubs, and the desire for reliable companionship and protection from loneliness—all are reasonable motivations. These determinants may make some people uneasy when they are aware of them as major motivations because they believe that by accepting a mate for any of these reasons they may be compromising their own values.

Love in all of its polymorphous manifestations remains the greatest motivating force for marriage—the desire and need to be with that unique person, to share with him or her, to experience the pleasures and excitement of strong sexual arousal and gratification. Love, even in the midst of our materialistic culture, remains the prime matchmaker. Hope springs eternal—most who have been divorced do remarry!

MARITAL SUCCESS

Marital success can be measured in terms of the subjective and objective criteria that determine how the purposes and responsibilities of the marital system have been carried out (Lewis, Beavers, Gossett, and Phillips, 1976).

Opinions in the literature conflict about whether second marriages are more successful than first ones. No definitive longitudinal research using a random nonclinical population has been done. Researchers who address themselves to this issue include Monahan (1952), Glenn and Weaver (1977), Bernard (1971), and Bitterman (1968). Monahan found that remarriages for the widowed were likely to endure without divorce as well as did first marriages. This study was published in 1952 before the divorce explosion. For divorced persons, the likelihood of another divorce increases with each divorce and subsequent remarriage experience. Glenn and Weaver found no substantial differences between the marital happiness of first- and second-time couples, even when the first marriage had ended in divorce. Bernard also concluded that most people are as successful in their remarriages as in their first marriages. Bitterman noted that the majority of her remarried clients moved into their second marriages as impulsively as they had their first.

Several factors appear to contribute to the success of the second marriage. One factor is an optimum period of time between relationships; if remarriage occurs too soon, or the new relationship begins while the emerging partner-to-be is still with his first spouse, it is more likely that the old relationship will impede heavily on the new. If the single period is lengthy, and particularly if children are involved, it is more likely to be difficult to incorporate the new spouse into the parent-child dyad, hence paving the way for marital dysfunction. We concur with Hunt and Hunt (1977) that the optimum period for remarriage is three to five years after the initial separation. This allows time for the emotional divorce to proceed, to recover from ego injury and despair, and to experience a variety of relationships without clutching, out of fear or loneliness, onto the first person who comes along. It allows time to reevaluate oneself and one's relationships. Those spouses who between marriages receive therapy that deals with the kinds of relationships they form would be less likely to fall into the same patterns which were problematic the first time. Also, we hypothesize that certain types of marital interaction (to be explained below) bode more positively for marital success. About 65% of the formerly marrieds show greater maturity and a more healthy marital interaction in second marriages (Sager, 1981).

When we talk about "the" remarried couple, we do not refer to a simple dyadic relationship. Each adult carries into the developing dyadic system a plethora of attachments and obligations. Table 4.1 demonstrates that if we take into consideration gender, whether each partner was previously married, and whether or not there are custodial, and/or noncustodial children, there are 24 possible configurations of Rem couples. Different combinations of variables can produce different problems. If one adds other variables, such as the previous marriage ending by divorce or death and whether or not there is a joint child from the present relationship, the possible combinations of marital pairing are progressively greater than 24. For instance, the single woman who weds a formerly married man with or without children has expectations different from those of a previously married woman. The single spouse is unlikely to anticipate the degree to which his mate's former relationship will influence the current marriage. This spouse may expect romance and exclusivity in the relationship while the divorced spouse may expect solidity, security and a full family life. For example:

The Princes were a young professional couple married about a year. Mrs. Prince, in her late twenties, had led an active single life until she met Mr. Prince, who was divorced and the father of two school-aged children who lived with his ex-wife. They requested help for marital problems and the threatening dissolution of the relationship.* Mr. Prince complained that his wife resented his children and the time he spent with them on weekends, as well as the "generous" child support he gives to his former wife. Mrs. Prince stated that he constantly was talking to his ex-wife on the telephone, sometimes several times a day. She felt there was no time to be alone with him and that he was beginning to renege on the promises he had made during their engagement. She resented not spending the holidays with her parents, because *his* parents wanted to see *his* children. She expressed the feeling that his ex-wife was part of their family, and she wished he would get rid of all reminders of her existence which "invaded" their home.

During the engagement Mrs. Prince had erroneously thought that after the marriage she would be treated as "Number One" by Mr. Prince, or at least on a par with his children. Now she felt she was playing second fiddle. Mr. Prince felt justified regarding his attention to his children and was resentful that his wife was unable to deal with this in a "sufficiently mature manner," by taking a more "motherly" attitude.

---

*These partners formed rational (Mr. Prince)-romantic (Mrs. Prince) couple. These behavior profiles will be defined later in this chapter.

TABLE 4.1

Possible Rem Spouse and Children Combinations

	Woman Previously Single	Woman Divorced or Widowed No Children	Woman Divorced or Widowed Custodial	Woman Divorced or Widowed Noncustodial	Woman Divorced or Widowed, Both Custodial and Noncustodial
Man previously single	N.A.	1	2	3	4
Man previously divorced or widowed no children.	5	6	7	8	9
Man previously divorced or widowed custodial children.	10	11	12	13	14
Man divorced or widowed non-custodial children.	15	16	17	18	19
Man divorced or widowed both custodial and non-custodial children.	20	21	22	23	24

Unspoken assumptions and expectations of both spouses, when played out after marriage, led to great conflict. Each reacted as if a marriage contract (his or her own) had been agreed upon and its terms had then been violated by the other.

THE TWO SPOUSES' MARRIAGE CONTRACTS

We have found that the concept of individual marital contracts and the typology of intimate relationships developed by Sager (1976, 1977) are useful in Rem to pinpoint the problem areas in the new marriage and to provide a framework to assess the similarities, differences, growth, and regression between the first and second marriage.

The marriage contract and the typologies of marital relationships were developed to provide a framework for understanding the complexities of any marital pair. Here we have highlighted those aspects of the contract and the typologies which help us to understand and organize the complexities of the Rem pair and to make sense of what seems at times like "sound and fury, signifying nothing."

When we speak of a "contract," with which a couple entered the remarriage, we do not refer to a legal document or written agreement between the partners. However, some Rem couples do draw up prenuptial agreements that usually have to do with the dispersal of funds after divorce or death. Others draw up agreements regarding personal rights and the sharing of responsibilities, duties, and expenses, reflecting their current philosophy regarding their relationship as a couple. These are fine as far as they go, but they do not deal directly with emotional needs. The marital contract as used here means:

> ... the individual's expressed and unexpressed, conscious and unconscious, concepts of his obligations within the marital relationship and the benefits he expects to derive from marriage in general, and his spouse in particular. But what must be emphasized above all is the reciprocal aspect of the contract: what each partner expects to give, and what he expects to receive from his spouse *in exchange* is crucial to this concept. Contracts deal with every conceivable aspect of family life: relationships with friends, achievements, power, sex, leisure time, money, children, etc. (Sager et al., 1971, p. 312)

To this we can add relationships to stepchildren, former spouses, former in-laws, territoriality of homes, and a host of other factors peculiar to remarriage situations. A Rem partner perforce has to accept the actual existence of a Rem family suprasystem and to learn to deal with its subsystems. Its presence cannot be ignored.

Each spouse's individual contract is based on conscious, preconscious, and unconscious needs and wishes and each one acts *as if* the contract he or she holds has been agreed upon by the mate. Much of each partner's "contract" is not verbalized; it may even be beyond awareness. While the individual may be more or less aware of his or her own needs, he/she is usually unaware of many of the "terms" of the spouse's contract. Each one assumes that by attempting to fulfill the partner's needs as *he* or *she* perceives them, he/she will assure that his/her own needs will be met in exchange. When this does not happen, each mate may feel disenchanted, rageful, depressed, dissatisfied, or restless.

If clinicians will keep the notion of the "contract" in mind, they then can try to cull out each spouse's expectations and obligations of the other. They will be interested in finding out to what extent there is congruence, complementarity, or conflict between the two sets of "wants and givens." For Rem couples, clinicians should take note of the current contract, as well as the contract each had with the former spouse and how these have or have not changed. Typically, the conscious, verbalized expectations of the remarriage and the new partner often are the opposite of the perceptions of the first marriage partner. It is hoped that individuals have learned from the experience of previous marriages, have matured, or are in a different place in the life cycle. They may have different needs now, perhaps fewer are predicated upon inappropriate or unrealistic determinants.

There are three areas in which the *terms* of the contract are developed: 1) the expectations of marriage; 2) expectations based on biological and intrapsychic needs; and 3) parameters which are the external foci of problems rooted in areas 1 and 2. (See Appendix A for the Reminder List for Marriage Contracts for each of the three categories).

1) Expectations of the Marriage

This area relates to each person's purposes and goals in relation to the institution of marriage itself and what he/she is willing to contribute to the marriage. The most common expectations of marriage, as related to remarriage are:

   a) A mate who will be loyal, devoted and exclusive. The possibility of the kind of relationship one had as a child and lost, or wished for as a child. A relationship that is very like the one with the first mate when "things were good," or a relationship that will give what the first mate didn't, or a qualitatively different relationship. Romantic love and intimacy.

b) Help in dealing with, caring for, and disciplining the children.

c) Companionship and insurance against loneliness. A reprieve from the world of the formerly married and/or the single parent.

d) Marriage as a goal in itself. That one will live happily ever after once married. This is much less likely to be a conscious expectation of the remarried.

e) A panacea for the chaos and strife in one's life. To be rescued from responsibilities and burdens. To return to the "order" and "certitude" of marriage and the two-parent family.

f) A relationship till "death do us part." There may be a grim determination or pressure to maintain the marriage this time.

g) **Sanctioned and** readily available sex. Escape from the pressures of dating. Sex which is legitimate in the eyes of the children and an example of the values the parent wishes to transmit.

h) To have a child with the new mate.

i) A relationship that emphasizes parenting and family as well as marital life.

j) The possible inclusion of children, former friends, ex-in-laws, etc.

k) A home and economic unit, either sharing everything or keeping possessions and resources separated. Financial help.

l) A social unit which lends purpose to one's life.

m) To have an immediate, ready-made family.

n) To be taken care of by a strong mother or father figure.

o) To prove one's desirability and superiority as a spouse to one's former mate.

p) To rescue an apparently struggling person and perhaps his or her children.

2) Intrapsychic and Biological Needs

These parameters are based on the needs that arise from within the individual spouse rather than from within the marriage as a system in category 1. These individual parameters are important because it is here that the mate is expected to fulfill the needs of the spouse more directly, as contrasted to in the first category where the expectations were of the marriage itself. However, these areas overlap. The reciprocal nature of the contracts are especially important here: "I will give X and in return I expect Y." Some of the most common determinants are:

a) *Adaptations and ties to one's own children.* Does one recognize the need to alter an overclose bond with a child that developed during single-parent stage? Can one's new mate be understanding and helpful in moving towards a more individuating process? Does the new mate react by feeling excluded, jealous, angry?

b) *Ties to ex-spouse.* Is there an effective emotional divorce? Is one aware of residual feelings of affection, hostility or revenge towards the ex-mate which affect the relationship with the current spouse? Does one do provocative things to triangulate ex and current spouse? What is one's "contract" regarding the ex-spouse? What is one's understanding of what one wants regarding the new mate's feelings toward and conduct with his/her former spouse?

c) *Independence-dependence.* The individual's ability to function for himself or his need to combine with a mate to feel complete. For remarriage, one's ability to function independently may have been greatly enhanced by the formerly married or single-parent household stage, yet this may or may not be maintained in the new relationship.

d) *Activity-passivity.* The individual's desire and ability to take action to bring about what he or she wants. Again, this may have been enhanced by the necessities of single household stage, and greater activity may be sustained into the second relationship or lost when becoming part of a couple; i.e., "Now that I'm married, I will let him take over."

e) *Closeness-distance.* The closeness or exposure of feelings, thoughts, and acts to one's mate. Communication problems are often related to the ability or inability to tolerate closeness. How much distance and time alone does each mate need? Is there a reaction in this marriage which relates to the past—for example, a fear of risking too much closeness again, or a demand for closeness which wasn't present in the first marriage? Do either mate's children and their needs come between the two spouses?

f) *Use-abuse of power.* How much power and control does each one need? Can the individual have power, use power unambivalently and without anxiety? How is the need for power different or similar to the need in the first marriage? Outside forces are more likely to be influential; e.g., if one has a mate whose children have a bioparent and who pays towards their support, how does this affect the child's relationship with the other bioparent and stepparent?

g) *Dominance-submission.* What is the pattern of domination and submission? Do they alternate in a seesaw pattern? Are decisions made jointly? Is there an easy shift back and forth regarding decisions, responsibilities, duties? Does sexual behavior parallel or differ from general behavior?

h) *Guilt.* Does guilt influence behavior towards the former spouse, children, parents, or ex-in-laws. Do religious beliefs affect or color what one wants to give in the new marriage? Is one judgmental of the new spouse? Is it implied that he or she is too unfeeling or irresponsible in regard to his/her children, ex-spouse, etc.?

i) *Roles.* What does each partner expect to be his/her role as stepparent or parent to visiting or custodial children? What does each

spouse expect from the other in this regard? How does one expect
and desire co-parenting to work for the two bioparents and the
stepparents?

j) *Fear of loneliness or abandonment.* To what extent does the fear of
another loss or abandonment play into this marriage, into the
mate choice, into the interaction, into the feeling of love and need
for the partner?

k) *Need to possess and control.* To what extent does one have to possess and control his mate to feel secure? Is this a repetition of the
former relationship or not?

l) *Level of anxiety.* How anxious is each mate and how is anxiety
shown or defended against? How does each mate deal with the
other's anxiety? How does the anxiety relate to remarriage issues
such as fear of another failure, repetition of old patterns, fear that
the new mate will show evidence of acting like the former mate?

m) *Mechanisms of defense.* Which are characteristic defenses of each
mate with the other and how do they affect each other?

n) *Gender identity.* How secure is each mate in being a man or a woman, and how defensive and aggressive is each in affirming, denying, or being confused about gender? Is remarriage to affirm
gender identity?

o) *Characteristics desired in one's sex partner.* These include gender,
personality, physical appearance, expressiveness, achievement
level, giving and receiving love, tenderness, ability to function,
and many other parameters. May consciously or unconsciously
relate to the characteristics of the first mate (and/or parents). The
move from a heterosexual to a homosexual relationship would be
pertinent here also.

p) *Acceptance of self and other.* Does each partner have the ability to
love oneself as well as the other? Is the person or the function
he/she performs valued? Is love equated with vulnerability? Did
the partner "love" the first time and now equates love with
danger?

q) *Cognitive style.* The way in which a mate takes information in,
processes it, arrives at decisions, and communicates the process
and conclusions to the spouse. Intelligence and conceptualization
levels. Is the new mate's cognitive style like his/her new partner's?
Is there a positive complementarity?

3) External Foci of Marital Problems

These are the presenting complaints and may *appear* to be the core of
the marital problem; however they usually are the external manifestations of problems that are rooted in the first two major areas.

a) *Communication.* To what extent is the couple open with one another? Can the couple talk with, listen to, and understand each other? Can decisions be reached by talking over disagreements? Are quid pro quos arrived at?

b) *Lifestyle.* Are the spouses' lifestyles similar or are there differences which lead to arguing and comparison with the former marriage and family? Is the present pair better matched in this area or more adaptable? Are there cultural similarities and differences?

c) *Families of origin.* Does one partner resent the other's family or the mate's involvement with them? Does this grow out of the family's resentment of the new mate replacing the old? Did grandparents take a major role with grandchildren before remarriage? Is that position now usurped?

d) *Relations with ex-spouse and ex-in-laws.* How involved is each mate with the former spouse and former in-laws? How does this affect the current relationship?

e) *Childrearing.* Does the couple agree on how to raise the children, how much authority to exercise, how much leniency? Does the spouse without children need education about their development, needs, etc.? Are differences in this area really reflections of criticism of mate's behavior towards him/her?

f) *Relationship with children.* How does each relate to the other's and own children, both living-in and visiting? Are there alliances by blood ties? Are there noticeable prejudices? What role does the stepparent have—responsibilities, type of relationship, authority with stepchildren, etc.?

g) *Family myths.* A myth is an unrealistic evaluation by family members of the quality of their functions or state of being. Do partners collaborate in the maintenance of myths, for example, that the Rem family is perfect and harmonious?

h) *Money.* How is it controlled? Is it kept separate or combined? Does one partner feel cheated or in competition to meet the level of former spouse? How are resources from present and former marriages, as well as inherited money and property, allocated in wills? Does one spouse resent supporting the other's children or contributing to child support or alimony payments? Do adult children suspect new spouse or mutual child of "stealing" their inheritance?

i) *Family milestones and holidays.* What are expectations regarding who in the Rem and other bioparent's household will attend children's celebrations—birthdays, graduations, bar mitzvahs, confirmations, weddings? How are children expected to spend holidays, summers, etc.?

j) *Sexuality.* Attitudes and predilections may differ in frequency, forms of pleasuring, fidelity, initiation, openness with children about sexuality, etc. Is there an awareness of feelings regarding household incest, acting-out, or counterphobic actions? How is this dealt with by the adults and with the children? Is one partner compared unfavorably with former spouse? Does this block pleasure? Does present pair develop similar sexual difficulties as in previous relationship?

k) *Values.* Is there general agreement on priorities such as money, culture, ethics, relations with others, religion, use of time together and with others? Are the values so different as not to be tolerated? Can they adapt and be considerate of each other's place in the life cycle? How will differences of values and culture between two bioparent households be handled? Will they be left to chance? Will there be parent discussions, with or without children?

l) *Friends.* What is the attitude toward the other's friends? Can each tolerate the other's friends from the former relationship? Do all friends have to be joint or can each have individual friends? How much time should be for friends and how much time should be for couple activities?

m) *Roles.* What tasks and responsibilities are expected of each partner? Are they gender-determined or flexible? Is there an attempt to make the partner take the same role as former spouse? What is the evolving definition of the stepparent role?

n) *Interests.* Are they shared or not? Is one partner more interested in children than the other? Are differences respected or resented?

o) *Social Class.* Is there a difference in social class which creates problems? Religion? Children, especially, may suffer from socioeconomic differences, particularly if there is a marked difference between the two bioparents' standard of living, cultural level, and attitudes about and availability of money.

These three categories and the specific subjects in the reminder list are meant to be just that—a reminder list for the therapist and patients to think about and consider. Many items may not be applicable for a specific couple; some couples may think of other items not included on the list.

SOURCES OF CONTRACTUAL DIFFICULTIES

For Rem couples the primary source of contractual difficulties is usually two extremely incongruent contracts or two contracts which are based on unrealistic expectations of the remarriage. In the latter, one spouse may fulfill his or her obligations, but his or her own needs remain unfulfilled because the partner does not have the capacity to fulfill them or the expectations are based on an idealization that no relationship could realistically fulfill. In the former, the expectations of each do not jell; there is too much dissonance.

AWARENESS OF THE CONTRACT

There are three levels of contractual awareness for each individual: 1) conscious verbalized; 2) conscious but not verbalized; and 3) unconscious or beyond awareness. The conscious (level 1) includes what each states to the other in clearly understandable language. It then may be heard and received, screened out, or distorted by the other partner. In the conscious but not verbalized (level 2), the mate *thinks about* his expectations, plans, beliefs and fantasies but does not share them with the mate, sometimes out of fear, shame, or anger or for manipulative purposes. Level 3 comprises desires and needs which are more or less beyond the awareness of the individual. Aspects of the psychological needs are more likely to fit in here. Here, too, we often find contradictory and unrealistic desires within the same person. This is very common in parameters of power, closeness-distance, activity-passivity, and gender identity conflicts.

Contracts are not static. They change with time, with changes in needs, expectations, or role demands of the partners, or with the entry of a new force into the marital system. Often, in Rem, the new force may relate to the other person's former spouse or children entering, leaving, or creating change in the system:

In Mr. Arthur's second marriage, he made certain to choose a spouse with a career. His first wife had been very homebound and tied to their little daughters. The second Mrs. Arthur had a solid professional career and he liked that. But as she neared 37, she felt pressure to have a baby "now or never" and persuaded her husband to reluctantly agree. After delivery, she felt a personal commitment to stay home with the baby for several years. Mr. Arthur felt pressured about money and became depressed. For him, the contract had been changed, much against his wishes. Although he had reluctantly agreed to the change, it took time and therapeutic help for him to readjust his sights and to enjoy his child as his *and* his wife's, and to discontinue his destructive behavior.

As each person moves along in his/her own life cycle, this too may produce contractual changes that may be unilateral or are not brought to awareness and hence are potentially dysfunctional for the couple or family.

THE INTERACTIONAL CONTRACT

The two separate contracts find their expression in the interactional contract or script. This contract may be comprised of elements from both of the individual contracts, or it may be very different from what either person expected.

The interactional contract is *not* what the clinician tries to help the couple arrive at in therapy. It is largely *not* verbalized. It is the *operational* rules of the game in which each mate is trying to achieve the needs expressed in his or her individual contract. These individual contracts help the clinician and the couple to understand the ingredients that form the interactional contract, which is then made explicit. The interactional contract "provides the interactional field in which each struggles with the other to achieve fulfillment of his own individual contract, including all the realistic, unrealistic and ambivalent clauses that it contains. It is the place where each tries to achieve his own objectives and force the other to behave in accordance with his design of the marriage" (Sager, 1976, p. 28).

Unique for each couple, the interactional contract evolves from each person's most basic wishes and strivings and also from his/her individual defenses. It may have both positive and negative elements. Therefore, what may be evoked in one relationship may or may not occur in another.

During the process of each person's effort to write or think about his/her individual contract, the therapist learns the elements of the interactional contract and can then help the couple visualize the interactional contract that is in operation, with the idea of using this consciousness to work toward a new single contract. This will be discussed more fully in Chapter 8. The interactional contract, which is not the same as the single contract, is likely to change as a result of the resolution of the individual contracts and the therapist's direct efforts to improve the quality of interaction.

BEHAVIORAL PROFILES

Certain styles of behaving or adapting are often characteristically found grouped together for an individual. Sager has summarized these in a shorthand called behavioral profiles (1976, pp. 103–132). How one's behavioral profile fits or interacts with that of the mate is a useful way to think about some possible marital and Rem pairings.

By taking the sum of the parameters in Category 2 of the marital contract, "the biological and intrapsychic determinants of behavior," and adding the behavior that occurs as a result of these and the defensive mechanisms employed by each partner, seven behavioral profiles emerge that describe significant different behavioral approaches of each partner to the other. The behavioral profiles, although similar in some ways to Berne's Parent, Adult, Child designations (Berne, 1961) are modes which do not change as rapidly.

The behavioral profile refers to the prevalent way one mate relates to the other at any particular time. There is fluidity and change in immediate situations, but usually if we take an overall look for a period of time, we can identify a pattern. Sometimes, over time, with a partner who initially seemed very different from the first mate, a similar behavioral profile may emerge. This indicates that there may have been distortion in the original perception of the new mate or that as the relationship evolved there was a real change in the major thrust or adaptation of the partner's behavior. This can occur because partner "A" behaves transferentially in a way to elicit in his new partner "B" countertransferential reactions similar to the behavior A had elicited from his partner in his first marriage.

The following discussion summarizes the seven major behavioral profiles; for a more complete discussion the reader should refer to Sager, 1976, pp. 108–63. In addition, based on our theoretical knowledge and clinical impressions of Rem, partnership types and combinations which seem to function more successfully in Rem will be noted.

Equal Partners

Equal partners want equality for themselves *and* the partner. They tend to be cooperative and independent. They are capable of sustained intimacy without clinging and are able to share or assume decision making and to allow the mate to do the same. Equal partners give and accept love. An equal partner is relatively free of infantile needs which must be fulfilled immediately; further, he/she does not expect to have his/her lovability depend on how well he/she fulfills the infantile needs of the mate. At appropriate times the equal partner can be parental or childlike but is not "stuck" in either position.

Equal partner combinations can be highly adaptive for Rem. An equal partner would be able to share his mate as need be with children and others. Personal satisfaction would not come only through the mate. There would be flexibility in roles as required by Rem and respect of differences in such areas as childrearing, values, and lifestyles. Love and commitment would not be founded on a fear of loss or abandonment. An equal partner could take the necessary time to work through a steprelationship with his mate's children while tolerating not receiving immediate reciprocal affection.

Amy, an artist, divorced her husband after 15 years of marriage and two children. She had been a young bride who for many years accepted a childlike-parental relationship with her husband. As she matured she resented and struggled against her husband's need to keep her in a dependent position. She gradually gained confidence in her abilities. Marital conflict grew in direct ratio to her trying to establish a more equal relationship. She finally moved for a divorce, but had to accept a poor financial arrangement. With some child support money she went to work and became a successful art dealer.

Three years after divorce she met Gene, an architect, who had been divorced two years and had two children, 17 and 19 years old. Amy and Gene each wanted a love relationship, felt sure of whom they were and not only accepted but wanted to foster each other's independence and their interdependence. Her children, now in high school, lived with her. She and Gene spent an increasing amount of time together but maintained their own residences.

After one and a half years Gene and Amy moved into an apartment together that was large enough for them, her children and an extra bedroom-study for when his children stayed over. One year later they married because they liked the idea of the extra commitment. They each enjoyed one another's children, but appreciated they were not the bioparent and over a period of time worked out a relationship of mutual respect and understanding with each other's children. They enjoyed being with whichever children were at home but also enjoyed doing many things as a couple and traveling together. Household and vacation expenses were shared roughly in proportion to each one's income without the need to keep a strict ledger accounting.

Amy's former husband, Amy, and Gene often spoke together about Amy's children's needs and problems—a three-way co-parenting situation (Amy's husband had not remarried). Gene's former wife did not want to discuss her children with Amy so that a three-way co-parenting relationship did not exist there. However, Gene's children often discussed their feelings and problems with Amy by themselves, as well as with their father or with Amy and Gene together.

Each spouse brought friends to their relationship; some stayed, some did not. They found some new ones together and each had a few friends who were essentially his/her own. They joined one another at the other's professional gatherings when appropriate but if busy with one's own work each felt free to go to events alone without feeling injured or the other partner's feeling suspicious or threatened. They were intimate together and open; clouds in the sky were usually talked about before they became storms. Sex was excellent for each but at times one or the other was not turned on for a week or two, sometimes for no apparent reason. They learned these periods passed after a short time and active sex was resumed.

Romantic Partner

The romantic partner is dependent on his mate. He or she feels "incomplete" without his partner. Sentiment and anniversaries are important, such as the date of first kiss, etc. He/she is likely to be possessive and controlling, even when appearing otherwise. He/she is vulnerable if his partner refuses to play a romantic role. The partner must be a soul mate with similar values and reactions. Great value is placed on the intensity of love and the passion of sex as a measure of the success of the relationship.

Two romantic partners can be very successful as a couple. However, in Rem, the children may be left "parentless," to raise themselves, or may be subtly excluded from the home as adults are preoccupied with their togetherness. A romantic partner in combination with an equal partner may create problems in Rem if the romantic partner pushes for a great deal of togetherness and exclusivity. The mate's involvement with children of a former marriage, with an ex-spouse, with friends, and with a career developed before the marriage can be extremely threatening.

When Cindy and John Staller were dating, Cindy's eight-year-old daughter was kept in the background by the grandmother, who lived in the same building as John. Grandmother had also been the primary caretaker since Cindy's separation and since Cindy moved back in with her mother three years earlier. John liked the intensity of his and Cindy's relationship and enjoyed the occasional times Cindy's daughter was included in their dates. After the marriage, however, he began to feel pushed away by Cindy, who actually had an extremely close relationship, bordering on the symbiotic, with the girl. He reacted with rage. Criticism and frequent arguments between John and Cindy ensued. He felt cheated and tricked by Cindy's keeping her daughter in the background prior to marriage.

John felt that he had contracted for an exclusive romantic love relationship with Cindy and now they were a threesome with him as
the odd wheel.

Parental Partner

A parental partner relates to the mate as if to a child. Behavior may
range from very controlling and authoritative to mildly patronizing. It
may be benign, rewarding, or harsh, punitive and authoritarian. There
is a need to dominate the mate to assure the parental partner that he/she
is needed and therefore "loved." Torvald in Ibsen's "The Doll's House"
is the prototype, as the early Nora is the prototypic childlike partner.
Particularly relevant for Rem is one subtype of the parental partner
known as the "rescuer" who frequently teams up with a "save-me"
type. This is a relatively unstable and transient contractual relationship
that often begins to crumble after the rescue is over. In Rem, we often
see rescuers saving their partner from a former spouse, from poor economic circumstances, or from "problem" children. The relationship will
continue as long as the rescued person remains loyal and accepts his or
her needing to be in a rescued position, and as long as the rescuer continues to rescue. However, after being rescued the rescued partner is often
in need of another way of relating. Gratefulness does not replace love for
very long.

Other types of parental partners can function well in Rem, particularly if they act as a benevolent parent to the mate and the children; there
can be highly positive grounding provided for the family as long as the
parental partner is not challenged by the mate or children in terms of
authority and control, or as long as there is no threat of abandonment.
Rem parental partners may function well with their mates, but function
poorly with preadolescent and adolescent children when they try to
grasp authority too quickly and/or flaunt their relationship with the bioparent.

Mrs. Gould and her two adolescent sons from her former marriage
functioned fairly smoothly, with the older son taking a father-sur-
rogate role, until Mrs. Gould began living with her current man
friend, Mr. Small. He had raised his own two children in a highly
disciplined manner and sought to straighten out her children,
whom he found too "fresh" to their mother and too independent.
Mrs. Gould was pleased with his taking over the boys and the
household, and in his tendency to lead the relationship; her sons
balked at his criticism and what they saw to be excessive punitive-
ness. Repeated quarrels and attempts to discipline the boys put

their mother in conflict, caused her husband to accuse her of being too soft, and had the effect of prematurely pushing the boys out of the home.

Childlike Partner

This is the counterpart of the parental partner. The childlike partner wants to be taken care of, guided, and disciplined. In exchange he/she will support the mate's feeling of being an adult authority. Often the childlike partner controls the relationship by his/her power to threaten to leave.

A subtype of the childlike partner is the "save-me" partner who feels threatened by a hostile world and needs the rescuer partner in order to cope; in Rem it would more typically be the female partner who is unable to cope with disciplining the children, lawsuits from a former spouse, financial stress, and so on. We also see the male partner who is overwhelmed and is in need of the female protector as homemaker, childrearer, and stabilizer.

In Rem, the childlike partner can function well as long as the mate will take the complementary role, does not demand as equal partnership, and does not want parenting himself. The childlike partner seems to run into the most difficulty when she begins to compete with her stepchildren for care and attention. The childlike partner finds the presence of these children threatening to her position with the new spouse and she is unable to meet the children's need for her to parent them. Childlike-childlike partnership combinations, the "sandbox marriage," can function over a short range but are unstable for the long run. Crises develop and each then wants the other to be the parent, but neither accepts the parental role.

Rational Partner

The rational partner tries to establish a reasoned, logical, well-ordered relationship with responsibilities of partners well defined. He/she forms a close and emotionally dependent relationship. He/she cannot admit emotions influence behavior and is often more dependent than he appears. Underneath the rational partner's logic, there are genuine feelings of closeness and affection for the mate, as compared to the parallel partner, who is out of touch emotionally with the spouse. The rational partner's sense of order can be positive in Rem, but he/she may also find the chaos and complexity difficult to take. We often see that such partners have not had children themselves, and are completely confused and at odds with their stepchildren's responses to their approach. The mate too may subvert and criticize the rational partner, yet at the same time heap responsibility on him or her. The rational partner often acts as a steadying sail for a more volatile partner, while the latter serves as his or her emotion expressor whom he/she can gently censure for going too far or being too enthusiastic when anxiety rises.

Companionate Partner

The companionate partner seeks to ward off loneliness and to establish a relationship which need not include romantic love or passion, but does include thoughtfulness, loyalty, and kindness given to and desired from the partner. The companionate partner wants married life but may be afraid to love again. When uniqueness or love is requested of him, there can be problems. Often the companionate will carefully work out the financial agreements and other arrangements of a second marriage. Problems arise at times from a tendency to live with too many reminders of an idealized past love-marriage or to make comparisons to a former mate. Often having started as a marriage of convenience and accommodation, it can blossom into a very gratifying relationship for both partners. Similarity of partners' values and acceptance of partners' ties to their own children are important. Older couples who have adult children often present problems dealing with the allocation of current parental funds, as well as designations in wills. At times the couple's attachment to each other and their annoyance with children who are more concerned with their inheritance than their parent's happiness and security push the couple closer together. Residual oedipal-like factors in older children also complicate their reaction to a parent who remarries.

Parallel Partner

The parallel partner interacts with his mate to avoid an intimate relationship. He desires distance and emotional space and maintains all the forms of an intimate home but emotionally is not close. The partners' lives run parallel, rather than intertwined. His or her need to maintain distance usually stems from a fear of becoming merged with and controlled by the partner. In remarriage where children are involved and the demands of the complex interrelationships call for more than superficial involvement, the parallel partner may constantly feel invaded by the rest of the family. A woman parallel partner may resent the demands of being a stepmother to her mate's children, and fear that doing so would take over her life. She will tend to remain distant but does those things in good form that have to be done. The male parallel partner may dump his children on his wife, with the desire to pursue "his own thing." One mate may change his behavior over time, eliciting parallel functioning from the other:

> Sue, who had aspirations to be a writer, married Charles, a fairly successful novelist, who was a mentor to her and 15 years her senior. He had three sons from his former marriage in his custody; she had been married previously with no children. She threw herself into the "mother bit," especially with the two younger boys, ages nine and 11, who had been allowed to run free and "didn't even know how to brush their teeth." She took over the care of the boys and allowed Charles to pursue his writing. She did this intensively for three years but with a great deal of resentment piling up.
>
> Finally, she felt that her life was being thrown away, and that her career had stopped. She acted out her discontent by having several affairs and pressuring Charles into having an open marriage. When the younger boy was 12, she withdrew from them both, feeling they were now old enough to manage on their own. She began to pursue her career, and established herself in the household as a friendly roommate, with little contact with the others emotionally or physically. While Charles was disturbed by her lack of involvement with the children, and protested mildly, he could see her point of view, as he really wished to pursue his own work. The parallel emotional and living arrangement they set up suited him well and he too continued to immerse himself in his work. Their home ran smoothly for the most part; the children were sent off to boarding schools.

The marriage contract concept, along with the interactional contract and behavioral profiles, is helpful in understanding couple dynamics and suggesting points and approaches for therapeutic intervention. It is important to consolidate the couple relationship if the Rem family is to begin to be able to cope with its family tasks. In therapy this consolidation is often the first area for therapeutic work and the quickest way to lessen or end chaos in the family.

SECTION II

Treatment

CHAPTER 5

The Therapist

We feel it appropriate to focus first on the therapist in our discussion of treatment because he/she is an instrument of treatment and the designer of the therapeutic program.

The potential for counterproductive emotional and cognitive reactions in therapists varies with the general vulnerability of the therapist and with the amount of stimulation the therapeutic situation provides to the therapist's emotional and value systems. Working with Rem families provides a tremendous amount of such stimulation, possibly more than most other treatment situations. Strong feelings within the therapist are likely to be touched off because the Rem suprasystem cast of characters provides a rich panoply of personalities, behavior, changing alliances, and values. There is bound to be something in even the less complex case that will cause sympathetic chords to vibrate in the therapist. When the therapist recognizes these reactions in time, they become clues that can be turned to therapeutic advantage. When not recognized, they may produce the opposite effect.

The therapist who has had training and experience in individual, group, marital and family modalities is at an advantage when working with Rem. Knowledge of and experience in using a variety of theoretical approaches are also most helpful. Those we have found to be most useful are a *system approach* to understanding family dynamics, *psychoanalytic theory* to help one understand individual dynamics and their reciprocal relationship with family dynamics, and *learning theory* with its therapeutic application, behavior therapy. Techniques of behavior therapy, judiciously applied, can bypass much working-through and contribute to shortening the treatment process.

We add to this the conviction that a therapist must have had sufficient experiences in life to have gained some wisdom and compassionate understanding of human frailties so that acts and thoughts of patients or clients that do not coincide with his/her own are not judged as reprehensible, pathological, or pathogenic. A therapist's ego gratifications should not depend solely on his relationships with his patients; rather, these should come from a satisfying personal life and other interests. The therapist who works alone must have some means to review his work with colleagues. Not to do so ultimately affects the quality of practice and can lead to frustration and depression, or, conversely, to a defensive grandiosity.

As we discuss these issues, we will focus particularly on the therapist's reactions to the impact of Rem and how this can affect treatment. Countertransference, a specifically defined term in classical psychoanalysis, has been redefined in so many ways that we are loathe to use it for this type of family work. All emotional reactions by the therapist, or defenses against them are not necessarily countertransferential. To be clear, we shall define the term so we can employ it in this book as a shorthand (Sager, 1967). By countertransference we refer to those reactions in a therapist to his individual or collective patients (system) which impede the establishment or attainment of appropriate therapeutic goals. We divide these reactions into three groups: those set off by clients' values; those engendered by the intensity and quality of emotional stimulation; and those based on the therapist's being maneuvered into responding to the patient's (including their system's) transferential reactions to elicit the patient's (system's) unconscious need to have the therapist react that particular way. "System's transferential reaction" refers to the phenomenon of the system's giving the therapist a role assignment, e.g., as a grandparent, an outside authority, or even as one of those in the family system. It includes the system's resistance to having that role and reaction assignment changed because the system then will have to change. This type of response (system transference, therapist countertransference) is analogous to the infantile neurosis transference of the analysand that elicits the "expected" countertransference from the analyst.

VALUE ISSUES

The therapist may have values that differ from those that have made it possible for some Rem adults to divorce, remarry, live with someone without legal sanction, accept alimony and not work, accept alimony and live with another partner, give what the therapist may consider to be inadequate child support (financial and/or emotional), be "sexually promiscuous," or believe that their children can be brought up as well, if not better, in two households than in the old nuclear family household. Such values, actions, and feelings may touch off emotional reactions that relate to actual experiences in the therapist's life, or to those he has feared will happen or has not dared to risk because of guilt, anxiety, superego constraints, or cultural considerations. Some therapists may have an underlying concern that their mate might act as a particular Rem family member has.

These value issues may affect unmarried, once married, and remarried therapists. For the unmarried and the once married, the Rem situation can stimulate fears of what might happen or what they might fear to do. Often such fears become defensively expressed as value judgments that bind the anxiety. To illustrate:

Mr. A was a 55-year-old supervising therapist whose own marriage had been troubled and conflictual for many years. In working with a Rem couple composed of a man who had left his wife to marry a younger woman, the therapist found himself secretly relishing the couple's problems. "He deserved what he got," thought Mr. A. This judgment served to bind the anxiety he felt when contemplating leaving his own wife. He had often fantasized about it but felt it would be morally wrong.

Ms. S, an unmarried therapist who grew up in a Rem household tended to overidentify with an adolescent boy whose biofather died and whose mother remarried. This was similar to her own history, where she had experienced the remarriage of her mother as an abandonment. She tended to overprotect the boy, to shield him from his "rejecting" mother and stepfather.

Ms. E, a therapist who was divorced and remarried, found herself angered and turned off by the circumstances of a couple's affair which had led to their remarriage because this closely resembled the circumstances of the dissolution of her own first marriage. The therapist felt secretly that the couple deserved their current problems as retribution for their deceitfulness.

Mr. G was a 40-year-old therapist who had been married for 15 years. He had strong religious convictions that divorce was a sin and occurred when couples did not try hard enough. He found himself viewing Rem couples as morally lazy and as having severe personality problems "because their marriages had failed." His diagnostic labels reflected his feelings that they were mentally sick and/or depraved in some fashion.

Mrs. K, a therapist who had just married, found herself siding with Mr. T's second wife, who very much wanted to have a child. Mr. T opposed having a child as he had three children from his first marriage. The therapist was projecting her own intense desire for a child on to Mrs. T, experiencing Mr. T as depriving and Mrs. T as his victim.

All therapists can be vulnerable to the myth that Rem families must resemble nuclear families. Even when knowing better intellectually, they may react judgmentally to the differences and set up goals accordingly. Moral judgments are made about couples being disturbed because they are "two-time losers," "don't stick it out and make it work," or are selfish, uncaring, and hedonistic parents. Other judgments include: Stepparents must be wicked; grandparents are controlling; stepchildren become competitors, troublemakers and opportunistic; parent/child relationships formed during the double single-parent stage are symbiotic. These cliches, which may be veiled by diagnostic labels, do not address the complexity and dynamics of the system and persons involved.

EMOTIONAL INTENSITY

The complexity of the Rem system, the sense of despair and loss, the disorganization, and the family emergencies may suck in the therapist and spill over into his personal life.

During the first year of the Rem team, we studied the literature on separation, divorce, the formerly married, and remarriage and carried a heavy caseload of Rem families. We found ourselves feeling constantly drained and depleted. We were amazed by the amount of anxiety and pain we encountered in the families, and alarmed by the level of reactivity and chaos we witnessed. We felt helpless, depressed and paralyzed in the face of what appeared to be constantly erupting crises, and our feelings of helplessness refueled our despair. Discussion of our own reactions in weekly team conferences led to the discovery that our feelings were spilling over into our personal lives. Every person in one way or another had placed his/her individual personal relationship decisions on hold, because he or she was afraid to move either towards or away from any further involvement or commitment.

Mr. N, a single therapist in his late twenties, was living with his woman friend at the time he began working with Rem families. His constant exposure to broken marriages and painful abandonment caused him to magnify minor faults within his own relationship. He worried that any small problem might cause a breakup five years from now. He began badgering his friend for guarantees that problems would work out. His abandonment fears were heightened by the many abandoned women and men he worked with and he kept putting off the commitment to wed. His fantasies of "happily ever after," necessary for his romantic bonding, were being destroyed by what he saw in his work.

Dr. R, a once married, now divorced therapist in her forties, found herself hesitant to make a commitment to the man she had been seeing exclusively for the past two years. Her constant exposure to Rem problems that mirrored her own anxieties caused her to fear taking the leap of faith required to embark on another marriage. She found herself frequently testing her lover to see in what ways he was similar to or better or worse than her ex-husband.

Ms. G, a remarried therapist whose marriage was tenuous, found the exposure to problematic remarriages so painful that she responded with massive denial to her own situation. She found herself unable to make a decision about her marriage, to face the steady decay within it, and to decide it could not be reversed or to work to improve it.

Misdiagnosis

Often the intensity of the responses we found in Rem families led us to believe that members were highly disturbed and overreacting symptomatically. In reality these individuals were having an appropriate response to their chaotic and disturbing Rem suprasystem situation. This was especially evident in children's responses to parental separation and remarriage. It is important to appreciate how the stress of a family system's loss or change can produce extreme pathological behavior in a person who may be relatively healthy when free of such stress.

Wendy, a four-year-old girl, was brought to the clinic by her mother and stepfather for bizzare behavior including bedwetting, temper tantrums, defecating on the floor and then telling her stepfather, "This is for you." She had a hallucinatory experience when faced with a physical fight between her mother and biofather. At intake she was diagnosed as potentially psychotic. However, as treatment modulated the Rem family dynamics, Wendy resumed her behavior as a normal girl. Earlier behavior was in response to an unusually stressful experience.

Therapists, faced with the extreme chaos of these systems, tend to misdiagnose the behavior involved. This is detrimental to the family members, who also view their chaos in a self-denigrating way. The families need the therapists' reassurance (if true) that the chaos can be a temporary step towards unification of the Rem unit, rather than a continuing downward spiral toward further disintegration.

Our work (Crohn, Sager, Rodstein, Brown, Walker, and Beir, 1981; Chapter 9 of this volume), as well as Wallerstein and Kelly's (1974, 1976, 1980) studies of responses of children to separation, can be helpful in understanding children's responses to the stress of divorce and remarriage. As our understanding of the myths of remarriage and the differences between nuclear and Rem families has increased, we have been able to evaluate and differentiate between individual aberrant behavior and the stress reactions produced by the Rem family and Rem suprasystem.

MANIFESTATIONS OF COUNTERTRANSFERENCE

Countertransference responses occur when patients and/or their systems enmesh the therapist who reacts the way individuals or the system set him up to react; when this occurs anxiety is avoided and change is shortcircuited. In our work together we have begun to identify specific areas of vulnerability for each Rem therapist. Our countertransference responses are often complicated by the influence of our own emotional responses to the realistic intensity and despair of the Rem family system. We are not just pulled into the system; often we share some of the counterproductive and guilt-provoking beliefs of our clients. The intense demands for help, often with impossible goals, evoke powerful responses in the therapist.

Unrealistic Goals

Many Rem couples marry with the hope that this marriage will right all previous relationship disappointments, including both parental and past marital failures. They believe that this time their marriage contract and expectations, even though unrealistic and magical, will be fulfilled. Other family members, too, may unrealistically expect unmet needs from the former family to be gratified. They come seeking help to fulfill unrealistic expectations and have unattainable goals for therapy. Such goals are often based on a vision of making the Rem family over into the model of an intact, nuclear family—the so-called "reconstituted" family. The premise of the reconstituted family is false because a different cast of characters cannot reproduce the script of other times, other people. The model for the "reconstituted" family is usually an idealized one that has never existed; it ignores the powerful forces of the Rem suprasystem, e.g., the roles and current input of former spouses, children who know their bioparents, the two new spouses who come with their own culture and history of past attachments, and biograndparents who may have an influential role.

Despite knowing better intellectually and theoretically, the therapist can easily be drawn into accepting the impossible goals of the family. At times this may be based on identification with the family and denial that other goals must be found. For some therapists the source of this countertransferential reaction may be the anxiety of not being able to face the disappointment and anger of those clients whose expectations cannot be met. Falling in with the family's goals, the therapist is dragged down with them into feeling hopeless and disillusioned, and thus misses the opportunity to help the family establish more realistic goals. When a therapist is unable to truly accept the idea that Rem families can carry out the family tasks and purposes required for adults and children, he or she will remain in this morass; worse still, he or she may become judgmental, hostile, and rejecting of the family.

Unrealistic goals are often buttressed by a pseudomutual process where there is a tendency towards denial of history, ambivalence, and conflict.

Mrs. G, a widow with girls age 10 and 13, married Mr. F, a widower with a boy age 12 and a girl of 16. Both Mr. F and Mrs. G had hopes of providing their children with the missing parent they needed and of sharing a romance similar to the early years of their first marriages. The children also wanted to see their parents happy but had ambivalent feelings of mistrust, loyalty ties to their dead parents, and fears of losing their share of attention and special place in the larger unit.

Mr. F expected things to run "as smoothly as mayonnaise on bread." Instead, their new household was fraught with tensions, anger, and fights. He blamed the new Mrs. F and began to wish for an escape; his expectations had not worked out, nor had hers. Neither adult had expected that they would have meaningful conflicts as a result of the marriage.

Their expectations for a happy family as the Brady Bunch were being severely thwarted. However, they were afraid to face their feelings of disappointment since they associated this with failure. Rather than deal openly with the conflicts and their unmet expectations, they suppressed them and refused to discuss issues or face their existence. Every time a child would complain they would cut him or her off with authoritarian commands, "Act loving to each other like a family should." The children were frightened by the tension and worried about the pseudomutual demands made of them.

Reluctantly the family came to the agency for help. They told the therapist that their goal was to be a happy, harmonious family. The therapist accepted their goal. He set about to help members get along lovingly with each other. Whenever the therapist did bring up potential conflict areas, the family's defense of denial cut it off. The family remained silent, refused to deal with the issue, and shortly began to miss appointments. The therapist, sucked into the system's denial defense, stopped trying to open issues. Instead, he advocated a series of tasks that were designed to help the family care more for each other.

A more experienced Rem therapist would not have accepted the family's goals but would have suggested more limited ones. He might even have joined the resistance and assigned a "make nice to each other" task and when it failed used that to help the family see that the subsystems do not have to love one another. At that point the therapist might have been able to move the Rem unit to arrive at more meaningful goals.

The family was not able to complete any of the tasks assigned and dropped out of therapy six weeks later. Their negative experience in therapy probably served to reinforce their sense of failure. If the therapist had been aware of the false expectations around remarriage, he might have been able to break through the family's denial and validate the reality of genuine problems. The therapist inadvertently convinced them he could not help them, felt defeated and was relieved to have them discontinue.

Polymorphism of Denial

Denial is manifested, as a countertransferential reaction, in many ways. Rem families tend to deny their conflicts and disappointments. Denial can be manifested in several ways. Rem couples are afraid of conflict; it evokes fears of a second failure, which would then be experienced as proof of their inadequacy. This denial is often reinforced by those who cannot tolerate conflict and difference and have to deny their existence. Divorce had been the solution in the past marriage, and they see divorce again as the alternative when there is disappointment or conflict, since they often lack appropriate coping behaviors, such as self-assertion, negotiation, quid pro quo, ordering priorities, compromise ability, and the seeking of professional help.

Pseudomutuality

Besides these common nonpathological responses, if the Rem family is a pseudomutual one there is a united front and an even stronger tendency to deny differences and disappointments. Parents are likely to focus their problems on a child who becomes scapegoated. The therapist may sense the material is forbidden, join the denial, and also displace the conflict onto the child. The therapist may be unable to tolerate differences or anger or to be confident in confronting issues. The therapist is then sucked into the system and encourages the scapegoating and pseudomutuality.

In one Rem case it was only after the child was placed in a residential program that the couple was able to approach their long hidden marital conflicts. The week after the child was placed and the case was transferred, the therapist received a phone call. The stepfather, who had previously blamed all trouble on the stepson, wanted a divorce. The therapist had been taken in by the family's focus on the child. The couple had presented a unified front against the child and the child's behavior was sufficiently aberrant for the therapist to join the system's focus on the boy only. Within the framework of this understanding of the situation, placement had appeared to be the most appropriate goal.

Denial of history

Therapists may also collude with the family in their denial of the importance of history as relevant to the current problem in order to create the illusion of an intact family. They may be ashamed of their past and fearful of the therapist having the same value judgment of them that they have of themselves. Thus, they may keep former spouses and relationships a secret. The clue often will be the therapist's recognition that something incongruous is going on, or an awareness of his or her own reluctance to ask pertinent questions. It is much like the spouse, engaged in an extramarital relationship, who leaves signs about for his mate, but the mate, wishing to deny, doesn't "see" the obvious. In Rem situations we can't sit back and wait for self-disclosure. If we suspect that a patient or subsystem is uneasy about disclosing something before others, we have to use our clinical judgment (not our own defensive system) to determine whether to pursue the matter with other family members present or to see an individual or subsystem separately.

Mrs. J came in because her four-year-old boy, Ralph, had tantrums, which were directed primarily at his mother, who seemed overprotective. Mr. J, a lawyer, was constantly working and seemed to take little interest in his son.

In the history-taking process, Mrs. J left out that she had been raised by her mother and a stepfather who had been sexually involved with her. She felt ashamed and had unresolved feelings of anger towards him. Mr. J, a Catholic, concurred in this denial as a divorce in the family was not seen as respectable.

It was only midway through treatment that Mrs. J was able to verbalize feelings about her stepfather. The therapist was able to help her connect this to her keeping Mr. J away from their son. Mr. J, when his wife let him into the family system, became a more responsive father and Ralph's behavior problems eventually disappeared.

Another case presented a different basis for denying history:

Mr. and Mrs. W came in with the stated problems of secondary erectile dysfunction and Mrs. W's desire to become pregnant. Sex therapy was initiated after an exploration of the couple's satisfactory marital interaction and a mutual desire to have a child.

When sex therapy did not prove effective, the therapist belatedly began to ask questions about Mr. W's former marriage. Initially the subject had been avoided and the therapist had colluded with this. Mr. W had difficulty talking about his former marriage, as it brought up pain about his children, whom he had not seen for seven years. Mrs. W felt threatened, as it aroused her jealousy that his first wife had been able to have children and she had none. Her husband then began to talk about his guilt and fear of having more children whom he might have to leave some day. He felt he did not deserve to have children. His guilt and sense of unworthiness were the focus of several sessions. His potency was restored. The couple now could address the issues of their trust in the relationship and the impact of children in a meaningful way.

Denial of marital ambivalence

Therapists are often quite careful to help the children in Rem families preserve their positive images of both bioparents. Therapists usually can counter a parent's tendency to produce images of self or others as the all-good custodial parent, the all-bad stepparent, or the all-bad other bioparent. Black and white polarization can produce devastating results in preventing a child to develop a neutralized internalization of the parent as a human being.

However, a divorced spouse is often able to enlist many therapists in a partisan alliance against the non-present ex-spouse as a marital partner. The therapist may collude to preserve an image of the ex-spouse as all-bad and the new partner as all-good. This reaction serves to bind the anxiety about a ghost of the last marriage in the new relationship, and about the new partner choice. It may reassure the new partner, but not for long.

If the therapist goes along with the splitting maneuver, he may prevent the partner from dealing with the ambivalent feelings he has for his former spouse (Peck, 1974). It is important for the client to realize and for the therapist to validate that in addition to the negatives there were good times and loving feelings in the past relationship and that a mourning reaction to this loss is appropriate.

The consequence of the therapist's not helping someone to separate appropriately from the former partner may be a wild attempt to deny the validity of the past relationship. True emotional divorce becomes impossible. The new partner senses the dishonesty and feels more insecure. A person who has not separated or accepted the positive from the past marriage is not likely to be able to allow his or her children to do so; thus it becomes more difficult for the children to accept the Rem couple. From the life-cycle perspective, the old marriage cycle continues as the Rem cycle begins (see Chapter 3).

Therapists may feel anxious about exploring the positives of a first marriage with the Rem couple, and may collude with the client's denial and anxiety about loyalty issues. Here, the use of the genogram can be helpful. In the process of finding out the factual information of the first marriage, the therapist can also ask what the pluses were for the client in the relationship, before things began to go down hill. If the question is threatening to the present spouse, then that anxiety can be explored, and the couple can be helped to talk with one another about their fears. If it is clear that the client needs more help to facilitate mourning, then an individual session can be arranged for this purpose. It is important, however, to explore the feelings conjointly, so the new spouse does not feel excluded prematurely.

How these issues are handled is, of course, affected by the therapist's life experiences. Divorced therapists who have not resolved their own ambivalence about their former spouses may have difficulty allowing clients to resolve theirs.

Mr. Norman, a person who saw only black and white, brought his 15-year-old daughter Miriam for consultation because of her "wild behavior." He claimed she was taking after her Bohemian mother, a dancer who had left when Miriam was eight. Mr. N and his second wife, a mildly compulsive legal secretary, spent time at home berating Miriam for her transgression of household regulations. Both feared Miriam would follow in her biomother's footsteps.

From Mr. N's description, his first wife sounded like a lazy, callous, irresponsible woman and the therapist could not imagine what Mr. N could have loved about her. He secretly felt that Mr. N's second wife was a more compatible choice. Miriam spent sessions fighting provocatively with her father about her behavior. Any mention of her biomother brought anger and outrage that flooded the session.

However, when listening to Mr. N and Miriam fight, the therapist began to see an almost sensual enjoyment in Mr. N. The therapist suddenly realized that Mr. N was still very much attracted to Miriam's mother and he was still hurting from her abandonment.

The therapist held several individual sessions with Mr. N where he was able to get in touch with his mourning for his former wife. He missed her spontaneity and creativity. He was able to see how Miriam's resemblance was setting off old feelings. He became less angry and more accepting of his daughter.

Mrs. N sensed the change in her husband and began to feel threatened. She worried that she was not enough for her husband and that he still loved his first wife. She began to bear down on Miriam for her nonconforming behavior and to take up Mr. N's old position of the critical father.

In a couple session Mr. N was able to reaffirm his love for his second wife. Although there had been some special parts of his relationship with his first wife that could not be denied, he expressed that he was now committed to his second wife. He accepted her for who she was and appreciated her differences and valued them. He did not want or expect her to be different.

Denial of the suprasystem

Rem couples may deny the importance of the Rem suprasystem, refusing to discuss or involve ex-spouses, grandparents, steprelations, children, and other significant persons. Some try to cut off family members who remind them of or have been a part of painful relationships. Members of the former nuclear suprafamily may harbor mutual angry feelings or disappointments. Others want to blot out parts of their lives and obligations because they feel it would contaminate the present. If the family is ashamed of the "failure of divorce," they may hesitate to mention important members of their former family system. Many, filled with the idea that the past must be discarded, require some educational understanding to recognize when it may be important to involve other suprafamily members.

If the therapist is pulled into the system's denial of the suprasystem, he or she may end up participating in a collusion not to utilize the involvement of significant others. However, therapists also may have their own agenda in not considering or working with the Rem suprasystem; it is often seen as too complicated and something that is not usually done. Therapists may not be trained in handling large numbers of people and family networks. There are confusions and frustrations inherent in therapeutically dealing with ex-in-laws, spouses and semi-involved members of the suprasystem. It is often time-consuming and expensive. There may be long distance telephone calls and coordinating work with other therapists who may have members of the suprasystem in treatment with them. There are many realistic troublesome reasons for the therapist to avoid this type of work.

But clinical practice affirms the importance of including the Rem suprasystem in order to bring about change. True to systems theory, when a family feels threatened by change, forces will join together to counteract it. The more significant the change, the more powerful the forces activated to withstand it. In some situations, extreme criticism and stress will be placed on the therapist. Rem team support is essential to review assessment and strategy, discharge induced and/or personal countertransferential reactions and refuel, in order to follow through on the treatment plan rather than buckle under to the pressure of the Rem suprasystem resistance.

At the urging of his father, Mark Mandel, age 15, applied for treatment because of a difficult relationship with his mother with whom he had lived continuously since his parent's divorce when he was three years old. Mr. Mandel married a year later. Mother/son arguments had exacerbated when older brother Eugene, age 18, left for college five months previously. Mark's mother, seen individually, appeared quite disturbed. Despite complaints of financial duress, she had never worked nor planned to and there was evidence that she was becoming increasingly more delusional.

Mark's father, a substantial wage earner, was more available. Topology of the first marriage had been Mr. M. as paternalistic parent partner to his childlike wife partner.

During the first phase of treatment, father and son were seen for joint sessions and the older brother was included when he was in town. Biweekly telephone contact was maintained with Mark's mother. In joint sessions, Mark's suicidal ideation and his father's guilt, manifested by his extreme permissiveness with the children, was highlighted. Mr. M was helped to be more responsive to his children and to see the value of limit-setting. Father and son, for the first time, had something to argue about and Mark's depression lifted and he became less isolated.

In the next phase of treatment, telephone contact continued with Mark's mother who had begun to send the therapist reading material on various aspects of environmental pollution. The therapist scanned this material enough to discuss it briefly with her. Sessions expanded to include Mark's brother Eugene, who was home from college for the summer, and Mr. M's second wife and their nine-year-old daughter. The consolidation of the Rem family unit now became the focus.

As early as April, Mr. M told Mark that he wanted him to work over the summer. He would be willing to help him find employment, but he would not continue Mark's rather generous allowance during the summer. Mark responded to this "demand by my cheap old man" with the depression and suicidal ideation that had been present in early contacts. Rather than continuing his efforts to avoid loyalty battles, he joined with his mother's "hatred" of his father. She quite typically made a frantic midday call to Mr. M's office to warn him that his son might kill himself. Mark's older brother Eugene, who boasted of "great individuation" since he was away from home, was almost as frantic as his mother. Mr. M, who was a novice in setting limits, was nervous and his present wife and daughter were of little support. They wondered outloud to him, "Maybe Mark is really sick; after all, he has a crazy mother." This only made Mr. M feel guilty and ready to retract what he felt was in his son's best interest. Mr. M, quite atypically, telephoned to let the therapist know his dilemma. Mark's mother called too to lambast the therapist, to warn her of impending doom, and to threaten her with her plan to report her "incompetency, insensitivity, and inordinate gall," to the directors of the agency.

The Rem team was available to support the therapist at this time, to help assess the degree of Mark's depression (which was more pseudo-depression), and to validate the therapist's understanding of the workings of the Rem suprasystem. As a result, the director of the agency was alerted to the call. The therapist was able to support and encourage Mr. M's stand and give Mark feedback that she thought he could meet the challenge of summer employment. Within two days Mark got a job and was able to keep it for the entire summer. An added plus was that he met his first girlfriend where he worked. In subsequent treatment Mark's mother no longer wanted to talk with the therapist, no longer sent her reading material, and no longer threatened to report her to the powers that be. Although she dropped out of treatment, she was most helpful by no longer sabotaging her children's gains.

It would have been easy for the therapist to be overwhelmed by this massive resistance if she were not aware of her own feelings and supported by the rest of the service, her immediate supervisor, and the director of the agency.

Denial of intimacy/distance conflict

Therapists need to avoid denying the need for emotional distance or difference/separateness that is common in Rem. The historical development of a Rem family makes it particularly vulnerable to pseudo-closeness. Care must be taken not to reinforce the myth of instant love. The therapist cannot go along with the family's attempt to deny the difference between bioparent and stepparent by calling the stepparent "your mother" or "your father" when addressing the child. Rem adults have a need to want to create an instant warm relationship between stepparents and stepchildren. It alleviates the family's anxiety about their awkwardness with each other and gives them an illusion of being a happy "regular family."

Premature intimacy within step relationships exacerbates guilt and loyalty conflict and foments fears that have become associated with closeness: fears of loss, pain and abandonment. When a therapist helps bring a Rem unit towards greater closeness, he must be aware of the fears that occur as bonds tighten.

Mr. Greene sought treatment because of his nine-year-old daughter, Claire, who was involved in an embattled relationship with his second wife, Naomi, whom he had recently married. The family admitted to no problems other than the constant fighting between the two of them. Mr. G's first wife had died in an automobile accident four years earlier. Neither Mr. G nor Claire had mourned her death, but instead retreated into silent withdrawal and spoke of how they were alone together.

The therapist saw that the stepmother was a warm person who wanted to care for Claire, and that Claire had a need for a warm mothering figure. Mrs. G felt that loving her stepdaughter would please her new husband and would help to bury the ghost of his dead wife. The therapist became enmeshed in the family's need to see them relate warmly and during the first six sessions worked to foster harmony. After these sessions the family felt a honeymoon-sense of calm and wished to end treatment.

Two weeks later there was a desperate call from Mr. G. He reported that Claire had ripped some of Mrs. Greene's clothing after a fight with him. The fight had centered around Mr. G's telling Claire that he was going to give his wife an expensive piece of jew-

elry he had originally given to her mother. Claire claimed he had
told her some time ago that he was saving her mother's jewelry for
her. It was obvious that this situation was made to order to pull
the trigger of an already loaded gun. When the therapist explored
the situation, he found that premature intimacy had been threatening for Claire and Mrs. G. Mr. G had many guilt feelings about
remarrying and was unable to tolerate any closeness between the
two. He displaced this guilt by exacerbating conflict between his
wife and daughter. How he handled the jewelry situation was an
example of how he promoted divisiveness when he was in conflict
over his "loyalty" to his dead wife.

With this new knowledge the therapist changed strategy. He
saw Mr. G alone and with his daughter to do grief work around the
death of the first Mrs. G. These sessions brought father and
daughter closer in a more appropriate way than before. More secure in her father's love, Claire was able to let her stepmother into
the system. In family sessions the therapist validated how hard it
was for Mrs. G to break into the family and how initially she and
Claire, quite naturally, felt like competitors but were now seeing
they need not be. The therapist validated their need for and the
normality of distance. This took the pressure off Mrs. G to come in
and be a supermom. She stopped trying to curry favor with Claire.
In couple sessions Mr. and Mrs. G worked out her feelings of playing second fiddle to a dead woman. Mr. G worked through his guilt
over remarrying and the divisiveness he had been fostering between Claire and Mrs. G. The former was able to become a child
and the latter a stepmother.

In a follow-up interview a year later, the family reported greater
harmony. Mrs. G and Claire had a friendly, warm relationship and
Mr. and Mrs. G were more secure with each other.

In this case the therapist had allowed feelings of sentimentality to interfere with his ordinarily good clinical judgment and had fostered a
temporary flight into health instead of dealing with the source of overt
problems. The following case illustrates other possible pitfalls into
which an experienced therapist may stumble. The therapist at first did
not work effectively because personal reactions blunted her usual acumen.

The Lawrence family came in because of conflicts between the
13-year-old boy and his stepfather that had degenerated into physical fights. The whole family, especially the biomother and the
young adult sister, insisted on seeing the family's problem as the
boy's inability to relate with his new stepfather. In remarrying,
Mrs. L had hoped to give her son a "better father" and would con-

tinually push the two together and berate both of them when conflicts arose.

The stepfather had moved towards his stepson with an intensity that seemed inappropriate. He wanted love, affection and respect from the boy and responded in an enraged manner to what he considered the youth's withholding of these feelings. He also wished for similar closeness with his stepdaughter who responded by remaining distant and, when pressed too hard, becoming angry.

The therapist was initially horrified by both the emotional and physical violence. She responded to the family's overt request for peace and ignored the covert request that they all love each other "like a regular family."

As the therapist moved to end the fighting, the family responded with a deep depression, withdrawal and lack of relatedness. The fighting had served to cover over feelings of loss generated by their internal view that the remarriage meant they had to slam the door on all past life and all that had been dear to them. This was most apparent in the stepfather, who was able to get in touch with his feelings of guilt and sorrow about leaving his wife and three children. He realized that he had been trying to extract a compensatory pound of flesh in his relationship with his wife's children.

The family was able to talk about and mourn together the loss of their previous families, which created a temporary period of harmony and greater closeness. This closeness was broken up by the daughter and stepfather having a fight which resulted in physical violence. The fight seemed to be caused by unconscious incest fears that had been previously defended against by the fighting and withdrawal in the family system. The therapist's push for closeness prematurely dissolved the boundaries and created a crisis.

With this awareness the therapist was able to work more slowly and effectively by reestablishing step-by-step more achievable goals for the family. She recognized that with this family she had to help surface each member's fears and responses towards each other before they could find their own level of intimacy. After members had mourned the loss of old relationships, expressed their anxiety about new ones, validated the positive potential of their Rem family, and felt more secure in their boundaries, closeness became possible.

Denial of movitation for Rem

All too often children are told by their remarrying parent that the marriage is for the children's benefit. The parent is deceptive (consciously or unconsciously) to the children about his or her own needs. If

the therapist believes that it is appropriate for adults to divorce and remarry for their own needs and can be nonjudgmental in helping parents
deal with their responsibilities to their children, the therapist then will
be better able to avoid being drawn into the client's self-deception.

Abandonment

Loss and abandonment are prime issues for children and adults in
Rem. The therapist's own abandonment anxieties may be triggered in
working with Rem families. It can be difficult for a therapist to deal
with the numerous unwanted, orphaned, or abandoned children of Rem
who end up in his/her office. These children experience a great deal of
pain over their parents' divorce or remarriage which may have resulted
in serious dislocation and loss for them. The therapist may be drawn into wanting to be the good-enough parent for these children. To do this
hinders the child's working-through feelings of loss, anger, and disappointment with his or her own parents. For the therapist to become rescuer results in overidentification with the child against the bioparent. It
can also result in joining with the child in his/her displacement of angry
feelings onto the stepparent.

John was an attractive, waif-like child of 13 brought to the agency because of his disruptive behavior at home and school. He and
his mother had lived alone since his parents' divorce when he was
four. John's biofather was an alcoholic who had moved south and
rarely saw his son. John and his mother had developed an over-
sexually cathected relationship during the double single-parent
stage.
Mrs. Singer, John's mother, had remarried six months prior to
coming to the clinic. John had responded with hostile verbal attacks towards his stepfather. Mr. Singer was a rigid, nonverbal
man. Mrs. Singer was fluttery and seductive. She was convinced
that the problem lay in her husband's unresponsiveness to her
"poor abandoned son." She would cry about how disappointed she
was because she had married him to provide a father for John. In
response to John's provocations, the stepfather would finally
break down and hit him. Mrs. S would not protect her son during
the abuse but later would seductively offer John comfort, further
enraging her husband.
The therapist, whose own father had died when he was 12, felt
sorry for fatherless John. He was taken aback by John's lost waif
appearance and the stepfather's gruff manner. The therapist took
John's side in a righteous manner. This only served to alienate Mr.
S and reinforce John's displacement of his anger at his mother for

remarrying. Mrs. S colluded with this, as it allowed her to keep her son's support and be protected from his anger. It also served as a weapon over her new husband; she could make him feel guilty about abusing her only child.

When the therapist brought the case to the team for supervision, he was asked to role play John while another staff member became the therapist. Part of a troubling session was played out. In a few minutes it became apparent to the therapist that he had been drawn into the system by his own abandonment anxieties and the family's need to enmesh him into a system where the myth of the wicked stepfather was rampant, along with the corollary of the preservation of the overly close bond between mother and son.

The therapist volunteered to the other team members how sorry he felt for John, particularly because of his own experiences with his mother and stepfather. The group helped the therapist clarify the highly cathected connections. It is this ambience of openness, without obsessive psychologizing about one another's motivations, that makes these conferences so valuable.

The therapist was able to redirect treatment. He began to work with John around expressing his feelings about "sharing" his mother with her husband. In mother-son sessions he facilitated separation and encouraged mourning for his father. In family sessions he pointed out how Mrs. S subtly encouraged fighting between John and Mrs. S.

Couple sessions were held to consolidate the marital relationship and encourage Mrs. S to stop undermining her husband as a stepparent. Mrs. S admitted she married her husband because of his sexiness, love for her, and her belief that he would never abandon her. She was able to get a perspective on her distrust of men and her anger at her first abandonment. She let Mr. S into the family and began to take a firm but loving stance with John. John, after some initial rage at his mother, began to quiet down and become involved with peers and extracurricular sports. He and Mr. S developed a friendly but not close relationship. Mr. S, feeling cared about and supported by his wife, felt better, was able to have respect for John and the two began to spend some time together.

Children who have been abandoned often use abandonment as a threat: "If I can't have so and so here, I'll go live with Daddy!" or "I'll leave therapy" (a blow intended for the solar plexus of the parent or therapist). If the therapist accepts the child's threat without understanding its motivation or does not challenge the threat and its meaning, there is strong indication that the therapist has become anxious and immobilized. Chaos in the system and in treatment takes over. The therapist may experience fear and back off or become over authoritative. The child is left with the feeling that no one cares enough about him to either go after him or take him on.

Abandonment has been the only problem-solving method many Rem families have perceived as being available to them. When faced with conflict, these families' initial response may be to leave treatment, to leave each other, or to extrude a child. The therapist cannot support abandonment as a solution! When the anxiety evoked by abandonment threats within the system affects the therapist too, it is particularly important for him/her to assay his/her reactions in order to remain (or return to being) calm and firm in the face of this panic. The immediate task then becomes to defuse the threat and help the family learn alternative means of together working out the real issues.

Control

When the therapist is faced with chaos, ambiguity and disequilibrium in families, he or she may attempt to allay anxiety by becoming overcontrolling (as do some harried parents and stepparents) or by taking impulsive therapeutic action. He may rush too soon to try to impose order. He is likely to despair when the chaos does not right itself quickly in response to interventions and may consciously or unconsciously dismiss the family. The slightest gain or plateau in treatment can easily be used as an excuse for the therapist to terminate treatment.

Therapists and family members with strong needs for control or order may have difficulty with the looser structure and the shared and often ambiguous roles of the Rem family. When therapists feel overwhelmed with this chaos, they may become judgmental and punitive towards the family or depressed at their own lack of effectiveness. This is mirrored by the family's own feelings of shame and helplessness about not being able to create the perfect harmonious family of their dreams. The family and therapist emit messages to each other that there is something wrong and bad about the family and/or the therapist. When this occurs the therapist begins unconsciously to resent the family because they make him feel helpless, ineffective and impotent.

Mr. and Mrs. Hill came to the clinic because Mrs. Hill's 11-year-old daughter, Jill, was showing trichotillomania (hair-plucking). Mr. H, a verbally violent, abusive stepfather, was critical of Jill. Mrs. H was a moderately obese woman who overprotected Jill and would subtly counter Mr. H's authority and keep Jill allied with her against him.

The therapist felt overwhelmed in dealing with many members of the suprasystem, including stepsiblings, in-laws, and a particularly difficult grandmother. He was upset by Mr. H's lack of warm feelings towards his stepdaughter.

After much hard work, he was able to help Mrs. H join with her husband and form a parenting team. Mr. H felt less cut out of the system and no longer needed to hit his way into it. The therapist, after negotiating with all members of the Rem suprasystem, found a placement for Jill at a special day school for disturbed youngsters.

At this point, with the milieu of the school and the cessation of violence in the home, the therapist began to rationalize reasons for closing the case. During a team meeting, he realized that the chaos in the family, the amount of time and energy the case required, and the countertransference feelings of anger that were engendered were causing him to deny the family's need for continued treatment. Original reasonable goals had not been met and were being abandoned unilaterally by the therapist.

Therapists working in Rem need experience in accepting and working with the "normal" amount of chaos and disorganization that a new system composed of entrenched subsystems may well produce.

ORGANIZATIONAL STRUCTURES AND THE REM THERAPIST

Traditional clinic structures do not provide sufficient supports for the therapist faced with the issues raised in the process of treating Rem families. As we have just described, no matter how great the level of experience the therapist is bringing to bear, these issues can be fraught with anxiety and overload. Here we shall discuss ways that mental health service organizations can provide supports for their staff therapists working with Rem families without totally redesigning their clinic services. We shall explore such alternatives as special support groups, special training, the uses of co-therapy, multiple impact therapy, consultation, time-limited and caseload-limited services. Each of these service designs can alleviate the potential stress on the therapist and facilitate the treatment of Rem systems.

Support Groups

The emotional intensity and complexity of Rem dynamics and the constant wear and tear on the therapist working with these systems confirms the need for a supportive and trusting group of colleagues where intellectual learning can be integrated with peer support, supervision, and case consultation, and help in handling countertransference. Over a period of time group members become knowledgeable about one another's countertransference vulnerabilities, strengths, weaknesses, and therapeutic skills. Team consultation provides support, exploration, and gentle probing into these sensitive areas, and direction for each therapist to improve his work. The leadership of the group is key: It is crucial that the group be experienced as a facilitating and growth-enhancing environment where differences are respected, since different group members have different ways of using themselves, their theories, and techniques.

We discovered that the team or staff approach provided other special advantages both to team members and to our Rem family population. Therapists are encouraged through the continuing support of their colleagues to extend invitations to all relevant Rem suprasystem members, rather than settling for seeing only the presenting subsystem. When potentially dangerous situations are present, such as violence, suicide, household sexual abuse, or extrusion, the team is always available for consultation to both the therapist and family. Team members are also available for support in the form of co-therapy or multiple impact family therapy at a point of crisis. Over a period of time, team members become familiar with one another's caseloads, and after a brief presentation are able to step in quickly to ask a clarifying question or to offer a suggestion.

In consultation with other clinical facilities we have sometimes found that the need for a support group is masked by requests for more didactic knowledge. For example, a large community clinic requested a staff course on the structure and treatment of remarried families. The staff member who was to teach the course did an initial needs assessment and found that the clinic staff members were very sophisticated in terms of their skills and knowledge about Rem situations. What was lacking was an effective support system. Each worker reported directly to the head of the clinic for supervision and each felt secretly ashamed about his/her emotional responses and fears of incompetence with these families. Staff members kept these feelings to themselves. The course provided a safe outlet for therapists to share their feelings. They began to relate in a supportive way towards each other around practice and conceptual issues. With the director's approval our consultant then helped the clinic staff develop its own in-house support group.

If team support is not available, there are other alternatives, such as time-limited assignments. Wallerstein (1976) has spoken about the burn-out her research therapists experienced in working solely with newly divorced families. We agree with her recommendations that there should be time-limited assignments for these therapists and that some-one contemplating or currently experiencing divorce should not work on a related service. Therapists whose personal lives are still in a state of pain or crisis in relation to divorce and Rem issues should avoid working with these families. Those who have passed through these crises may bring a deeper understanding to their Rem work, although they will al-ways have to be alert to negative countertransference reactions. It is recommended also that Rem cases make up no more than 50% of a ther-apist's clinical practice.

Peer group supervision is especially valuable. Those who are in pri-vate practice or do not have a support group available where they work should participate regularly in a privately organized peer group. Such groups are indispensable to curtail therapeutic grandiosity, to check countertransference reactions, and to avoid the development of blind spots or the deterioration of one's practice techniques, concepts, and acumen. Such groups have to develop a sense of group security and con-fidentiality so that members can be open about their work and feelings.

Co-therapy

As a general rule we prefer not to use or recommend co-therapy for economic reasons because it approximately doubles the cost of treat-ment in clinic, agency, or private practice. We do advocate its use for training purposes to help a less experienced therapist feel comfortable; after a short time the more experienced therapist then retires as thera-pist and may become supervisor.

There are, however, a number of frequent exceptions to this guide-line. Sometimes it is important for a male or female therapist to join ses-sions for their authority or sensitivity as a man or woman or because a patient can more readily accept new ideas from someone of the same or different gender.

Co-therapy does provide an invaluable and even necessary treatment tool when the suprasystem presents complex situations, such as intense subsystem antagonism. For example, a therapist had worked for 11 months with a single parent and her seven-year-old daughter and had become identified as the mother's therapist. A co-therapist was needed in order to reach out and develop a connection to the child's remarried father and stepmother. After the connection was made and two sessions were held with all present, it was then possible for the original therapist alone to conduct the few additional conjoint sessions that were neces-sary with the mother, father, stepmother, and daughter.

Co-therapy is useful when there is a strong conflict between subunits,

usually ex-spouses, adolescent-parent or parent-grandparent, or when
the suprasystem involves more than six or seven members. It can help
the Rem therapist gain better control and order when working with particularly chaotic families. Consider this co-therapy situation:

> In a Rem suprasystem where the divorced couple had both re-
> married but still expressed consistent "hatred" for each other and
> were in the throes of a court battle, both Rem couples were given
> the opportunity to meet with a separate therapist before planning
> a co-therapy-led suprasystem meeting. The presenting problem
> was their 12-year-old son, who was expressing suicidal ideas.
> When the initial therapist found out from the biomother that she
> was "not even on speaking terms" with her former husband, the
> therapist secured her permission to have another therapist call
> and talk to her former husband about coming in with his new wife
> to discuss the child's problems. Each subsystem would have its
> own therapist. When the co-therapist called the boy's biofather,
> his immediate response was to ask if the therapist would also be
> seeing his former wife. The therapist responded that there would
> be *two* therapists and that the session would stay focused on how
> the adults in the two households could best help his son; other is-
> sues between him and his ex-wife would be ruled out of order.

Therapist: I would like to meet with you and your wife first and
then possibly at a later date there could be a meeting with
you, your wife and myself, and your former wife, her husband
and their therapist also. We would stay with the agenda of
how best to help your son.

Mr. W: Are you there to take my side?

Th: Well, I suggest working this way in the hope that it doesn't
come to that. I will try to make your viewpoint clear if you
have trouble getting it across. As you know, anger makes us
somewhat inarticulate at times.

Mr. W: But will you be in my corner?

Th: Yes—in yours and your son's.

Mr. W: Good. I'm glad to hear that. Then I'll come. You know we
have another date in Court next Tuesday. We're adversaries.

Th: I'm aware of that. At such time that there's a joint meeting, I
and my co-therapist will insist that your antagonism towards each other be put on the back burner while we stay focused on working to help your son.

Mr. W: (Sarcastically) Good luck! When do we meet?

The session that followed came off well. The skill of the two therapists made it possible to keep to the agenda. Lowering the anxiety of

both parents about their anticipated confrontation was done by strictly keeping them to the single subject.

It is easy for co-therapists to be drawn into counterproductive activity if they are not on guard against partisanship for "their" subsystem. It is important that therapists respect one another and are not competitive. Pre and post session discussions, if necessary with another colleague or the staff team, help to decathect the most difficult co-therapy relationships.

Family members often respond well to co-therapists. Co-therapy allows children who have grown up in one-parent families to begin to have the experience of "two-parent" households. Their abandonment fears are alleviated when they have two therapists. Seeing two therapists work together, negotiate their differences, and express their individuality can be used as role modeling for two-parent households, or, even at times, for living in two households with different rules and cultures.

Often the family itself will give clues that it needs a co-therapist. Some of these are: legitimate (non-manipulative) necessity for several sessions a week, requests for home visits, school or court interventions, conflicting loyalties of children, conflicting loyalties of adults, and the assumption of a co-therapist role by a family member which interferes with attaining therapeutic goals. The therapist, if not defensive or grandiose, may well feel relieved to respond to the clue by arranging for a co-therapist.

The experienced Rem family therapist frequently can achieve similar results to co-therapy through separate or split sessions with different subsystems of the Rem suprasystem. With subsystem meetings the therapist can help validate the history and experiences of subsystems and help them resolve problems within themselves. This facilitates an eventual consolidation between all of the parts of the Rem suprasystem. The therapist can handle divided loyalties, family secrets, mourning issues, and drives toward separation with judiciously used subunit treatment. The objective is to form a trusting alliance with each subsystem and to delineate all members' feelings around a problem. The therapist must be prepared, however, not to take umbrage if someone is suspicious of his acts or intent. This approach may enable different members of the subunits to gain perspective about the issue without worrying about what might be overstimulation from conflicting members of other units. The therapist can then bring everyone in the system together for a meeting. By this time members have alliances with the therapist, are less volatile about touchy issues, and usually can make effective use of the Rem suprasystem sessions.

By splitting a session the therapist can see one subsystem for part of a session, then another subsystem for the second part, and then bring everyone together for a third part. Some members of our team feel the therapist is wise to separately establish a personal connection with each bioparent or conflicting subunit. The therapist will then have less trouble with conflicts in Rem suprasystem meetings and the therapeutic role will be more easily understood and respected.

Treatment of the Rem suprasystem can be compared to three-dimensional chess, while subsystem treatment can be seen as separate validation of each dimension. There are layers of history, family ties, myths, culture, life-cycle stages, and complicated bondings that often must be dealt with and respected in order to complete unfinished business and be rejoined into one working unit. Subsystem and Rem suprasystem conceptualization and therapy are the ultimate expression of this model.

Multiple Impact Family Therapy

In some instances we have found it useful to use an adaptation of MacGregor's multiple impact family therapy (MIFT) (MacGregor, Ritchie, Serrano, and Schuster, 1964). MacGregor and his team conceived this modality of brief intensive treatment in 1956 in their work with adolescents and their families who had to travel long distances to get to the clinic. A therapist was assigned to each subsection and/or individual in the family. When all family members and therapists met in the larger sessions the professional assigned to each unit then spoke for and modeled more adaptive behavior for that unit. Although our families are usually within a short distance from our facilities, we have found it useful to adopt this model because of the difficulty some subunits of the Rem suprafamily have in productively communicating and working towards a common goal.

We assign a therapist to each of the several subsystems of the Rem suprasystem. Therapists serve as adjunct temporary negotiators and role models for the subsystem. This is a highly effective method especially in emergencies or consultations but because of the expense involved it cannot be continued for long. It is valuable in establishing family contact and familiarity with a number of staff members, so that families that return episodically for help can usually find a staff member whom they know from the past.

Mrs. Heller called the Agency because of her concern about her 14-year-old daughter, Sandra. She had been found using soft drugs, and spent all her time with 18-year-old Glen. Sandra's father had remarried and his new wife had recently had a baby girl. Sandra refused to have anything to do with her half-sister.

Consultation provided us with the information that Sandra was symbiotically tied to Glen in a Romeo and Juliet passion bond. Glen lived pretty much on the streets after being kicked out of his home by an angry stepfather. His passive, alcoholic mother hardly noticed his absence. When Mrs. H made an attempt to separate her daughter from Glen, Sandra made a suicide attempt and Glen became enraged and threatened Mrs. H.

As this system was in an explosive emergency situation, we asked all relevant members of both families to come in. Therapists were assigned to the following subsystems: Glen/Sandra, Mrs. H and her 10-year-old son; Mr. H and his new wife and baby; Glen's stepfather and mother. Each subsystem unit met with its therapist and clarified needs and fears. Then there was a large meeting with all subsystem units and each therapist. The director of the service was the coordinating therapist for the large meeting. The therapists helped their units to work out their conflicts with other units. These suprasystem sessions were held six times. A total of five therapists met with this suprasystem and its subsystems.

The therapeutic process is too lengthy to cover here. The end results were that Sandra, an extruded child, was placed in a group home because neither parent was able to provide adequate emotional nurturing for her. Glen became enrolled in a vocational training program. His mother and stepfather were able to assume a greater degree of responsibility for him, especially the stepfather, who had previously wished to deny his existence. The adult units carried on as before with Mr. and Mrs. H and baby as a new, competent triad. Mrs. H (Sandra's mother) and her younger son had a miserable home situation but Mrs. H did not want help. Glen's stepfather and mother went on their way. Our major focus had to remain with preventing the self-destructive behavior of Glen and Sandra.

FIGURE 5.1
Heller-Frank Families Connected by Their Adolescents' Love Pact.
Dotted Lines Indicate Subsystems Worked With.

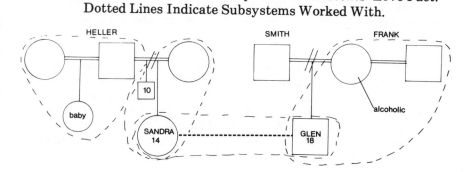

The use of MIFT enabled us to work quickly and effectively with every relevant member of the subsystem. We were thus able to reestablish equilibrium in a crisis. We were also able to monitor the ripple effect of change through the system that occurred with the removal of Sandra to a group home. The group home gave Sandra an alternative home with concerned people to whom she could relate. The potential of another crisis was defused as she made other attachments and did not have to be precociously mature. At follow-up three years later Sandra was preparing to go to college. She had done well academically. Her age-appropriate relationships were with male and female peers. Glen finished training school and was employed as a highly skilled worker in the same industry as his father. As an attractive young man he was "playing the field"; he felt he was not ready yet for another serious love commitment.

Facility Structure

A prime need in mental health facilities for treating Rem families is flexibility in intake procedures, techniques, use of modalities, and theoretical approach. The therapist must be able to move in and out of different parts of the system; to do this requires appropriate training and flexibility on the part of the therapist, as well as administrative cooperation. Various treatment modalities may have to be used concurrently or serially, including family suprasystem therapy, couple, child, individual, and group forms of treatment, and education. Psychotropic medication may also be required, as well as residential facilities (particularly for the extruded preadolescent and adolescent). Rem therapists should be well versed in the basics of family, child and individual treatment in order to be optimally effective. If they are not conversant with a range of modalities, they should know when to refer parts of the subsystems to other professionals for special diagnostic and/or therapeutic services.

In the following case a therapist from another service requested a consultation. When presenting the case at the Remarriage Consultation staff conference she stated she was uneasy about the outcome of her interventions.

Mrs. Kolb brought her 10-year-old son to the clinic because of his provocative, defiant behavior towards her and her live-in male friend. Mrs. K was a withdrawn woman, who scapegoated her son Douglas to avoid dealing with her difficulties with George, her friend. The therapist rigidly adhered to family sessions without adequately assessing Douglas' degree of disturbance. Douglas had such severely internalized conflicts of long duration and such poor ego integration that he did not improve as Mrs. K became more reasonable and gentle. Family sessions evoked primitive feelings in him that flooded his weak defenses and fragile ego. The therapist, aware of Douglas' restlessness and loosening of associations in sessions, finally brought the family in for consultation with the Remarriage Consultation Service staff.

The team advised immediate individual assessment of Douglas, with the professional who did the assessment being prepared to have time to see him in individual child therapy, and separate sessions for the couple. They thought Douglas needed a safe relationship in which he could build up his defenses and work out conflicts. It was felt that in six months to a year Douglas might be sufficiently integrated to benefit from family sessions.

In retrospect, a more detailed history and examination would have revealed Douglas' and his mother's pathology and need for a different therapeutic approach. The therapist and her supervisor were too intent on utilizing a particular modality that led them to blur their usual diagnostic acumen. Fortunately, therapist and supervisor were concerned and secure enough to ask for help.

Any pragmatic clinician reading this chapter must at this point be asking, "Where do they find the time?" Time, length of interviews, number of sessions, amount of telephone work required, and resultant actual cost of treatment in Rem situations are crucial issues for family and staff. Clinic structures, third-party payment, and government regulations are still geared for individual treatment and often do not meet the necessities of family or Rem treatment. We have found that initial family sessions often require an hour and a half. Conflicting subsystems, ex-spouses, adolescents who need individual as well as family time may require two sessions a week or an extended session when people are seen sequentially in subsystems. If the therapist does not feel he or she has the latitude to take this time he or she may feel overwhelmed and discouraged. When mental health facilities, regulatory and funding agencies do not give recognition for the amount of extra work that goes into treating a Rem family, staff becomes resentful and can perceive of work in this area as an unrewarding burden.

Realistically, public clinic funding and private practice fees cannot cover the cost of ideal treatment. It is our experience that the support of the organization, the refueling available from a supportive group of colleagues, and the satisfaction gained from learning the concepts and methods of treating Rem families and seeing them work can contribute to the incentive for staff and administration to find the necessary time.

The great amount of time we put in on our early cases was for purposes of learning Rem structure and dynamics and to develop treatment techniques and methodology. What we ultimately arrived at is a system of therapy that usually calls for one therapist; however, that therapist does require the support of his colleagues who see similar types of families. The more diverse the professional theoretical and experience backgrounds of the team, the more exciting and rewarding will the team effort be for all concerned, staff and patients.

CHAPTER 6

Beginning Treatment: Evaluation and Engagement Phase

Most Rem couples who come to treatment are reminded of their previous failed marriage and are fearful that this marriage will turn into the painful nightmare of another divorce experience. This creates a particular vulnerability which can leave members reluctant to admit problems and to ask for help, or to sustain treatment once it is begun. The level of anxiety at the first session can be extremely high. It is incumbent on the therapist to be sensitive to this vulnerability—it is so easy to lose the Rem family at this time. The clinic population of Rem contains a large proportion of fragile systems with low levels of cohesiveness, resilience, and trust in their capacity to survive intact. Instead of having been a system that functioned well at one time and then began to malfunction, a significant segment of Rem couples and families has not been able to consolidate into a viable functioning unit, except perhaps for a brief honeymoon period. Others have done well for years but then began to falter over internal contradictions such as disparities in individual life-cycle needs or other changed conditions. We shall put emphasis on those factors that are unique to Rem families; we understand that these families and couples are also subject to the same stresses as are nuclear families.

The therapist treating remarried families must keep several levels in mind:

A. *Family Systems Frame:* The purposes the symptom serves in (1) the Rem suprasystem, (2) the different subsystems, and (3) the individual.

115

B. *Life-Cycle Frame:*
   1) The life-cycle needs of the Rem suprasystem.
   2) The life-cycle needs of the different subsystems: the Rem family, the Rem couple, the bioparents, the single-parent family, the sibling-stepsibling unit, etc.
   3) The life-cycle needs of the individuals.
C. *Intrapsychic Frame:* The intrapsychic needs, based on an understanding of where each person is in his or her intrapsychic world.
D. *Societal Frame:* Cultural, socioeconomic, religious, ethnic, gender roles, and relations.
E. *Biological:* Genetic, biochemical, medical, physiological.

In this chapter we shall describe how we translate this construct into our practice with Rem from the very first telephone call through the remainder of the evaluation period. This period can take as much as three to five meetings of one to one-and-a-half hours. During this time we begin to establish and agree upon mutual goals with all of the Rem and relevant suprasystem members, set fees with them, and determine our ongoing treatment plan. We consider this phase to be a cooperative venture of exploration and discovery in which all family members are actively involved. Goals are set for what each individual might want to achieve, both for himself and for the family.

We will use the clinical case of the Stein/Miller suprasystem as a paradigm for engagement and assessment methodology. In Chapter 7 we will see the Stein/Miller suprasystem engaged in the middle and termination phases of therapy and follow-up.

GOALS FOR THE EVALUATION PERIOD

1) To develop a working alliance and connection with every member of the Rem suprasystem who is involved in the problem(s).
2) To establish with all of the members what their separate perceptions of the problem(s) are and explore those areas in depth, so we can achieve a good beginning understanding of what the troubles are and their duration.
3) To begin to establish treatment goals with each family member for:
   a) oneself;
   b) one's subsystem(s): the Rem subsystem, the bioparent household subsystem, etc.;
   c) the Rem suprasystem.
4) To set the fees with the consideration that it might be appropriate

for each subsystem to make a financial contribution to the treatment.
5) To generate a tentative hypothesis about the dysfunction—within the Rem suprasystem and the specific Rem subsystem and other bioparent subsystem, as well as the individual.
6) To develop the direction and treatment plan with the family, and establish a treatment contract for the ongoing work.

INVOLVING THE REM FAMILY AND SIGNIFICANT MEMBERS OF ITS SUPRASYSTEM

Our optimal goal is to include the Rem family and *all* the relevant suprafamily members from the beginning. If one ignores significant suprasystem members, for instance a bioparent or grandparent who has high input into the presenting problem, then sooner or later either that "significant other" will try to sabotage treatment or there will be a failure to resolve the problems in the Rem subsystem. Once therapy has begun, it is more difficult to include members, for instance a former spouse, since the therapist is likely to be identified as being partisan to the Rem family and viewed with suspicion or hostility by others in the suprasystem.

However, these principles are applied flexibly and with sensitivity. It is wise to avoid battles with family members, and we settle graciously for less than the optimal if we will otherwise lose the family. The guiding slogan might be: Cast as wide a net as necessary, but don't lose the lead fish, or there may not be another opportunity. We do not, however, give up easily. We use our ingenuity, time, and energy to work towards arranging for everyone to be seen at least once during this evaluation phase. We have alternative pathways to follow. We may do lengthy telephone work with the caller; have an in-person interview with the initiator of treatment; or meet with a subsystem first in order to achieve our goal.

The First Telephone Call

Treatment begins with the first telephone call. Our goals for this stage vary, depending on the nature of the presenting problem or symptoms and the nature of the Rem suprasystem. If the call comes from a Rem couple and they are requesting marital therapy for themselves, we make the appointment for both spouses and finish the call. Where a child is identified as "the problem," our optimal goal is to have all of the parenting adults, whether they be bioparents, stepparents, grandparents or stepgrandparents, as well as the other children, present for the first meeting. We achieve this by introducing the caller to the concept of the Rem suprasystem. We find out who is in the overall family, who and where each bioparent is, and how much contact the child has with each. If the caller is not one of the bioparents, then we want to know his or her relationship to the child and to each of the child's bioparents. We remind the caller that the child has two bioparents and that each is important and needed by the child. We ask about others in the Rem suprasystem, including visiting and living-in children, stepchildren, half-siblings, grandparents and significant others. We ask if the bioparents/stepparents have discussed with one another the child's problems, and who knows of the call for help. We may do a thumbnail genogram for ourselves at this point so we can order the information.

With this beginning understanding of the compositon and nature of the Rem suprasystem and its problem, we then proceed to introduce the caller to the idea of including all the parental figures as well as the children in the evaluation. We often get a negative response. However, once it is explained, clients are often willing to cooperate. Where there is hesitation and there clearly continues to be much dissension in the Rem suprasystem, especially between the two household subsystems, we listen to the concern and try to point out that since the child is in the middle and does live in both families, it is in the best interests of the child for the adults to work together. Here we may underscore that it will be the parenting and stepparenting issues that will be addressed in the first session, rather than the former spouses' complaints against each other. We make sure to adhere to this statement in the session, setting limits and halting discussions of other than parenting matters.

Where our caller is opposed to the inclusion of others, has not told the other parent of the interest in treatment, or identifies the other bioparent as "anti-therapy," we might use the following technique. We move them away from a blaming, critical approach to one that emphasizes cooperation. We rehearse with our caller what he or she can say and how he/she might say it. Most often when individuals have been guided in this way, they can, despite their anxiety, follow through, or they can then see that they, themselves, do not want to include the other parent.

If the caller is unsuccessful in getting the former spouse to agree to come in, we then ask permission to call directly. We explain why we are calling, our concern for their child, and why we consider his or her presence invaluable. Our goal is to bypass the anger, hostility, and fear of the spouses at this time.

Illustrative Case

The Stein-Miller family is a relatively uncomplicated middle-class Rem suprasystem. The dialogue is lightly edited to maintain anonymity and grammatical clarity without affecting significant content or the context in which it occurred. Ms. Stein first contacted the agency by telephone.

Ms. Stein: I was referred to you by my daughter's school. Deirdra's teacher called me in and told me that Deirdra is a loner; she doesn't have a best friend in the class and she seems to be off in her own space a lot. While I was there I spoke to Liza's teachers and they said she's "moody." The girls are both very bright but . . . but they may have problems.

Therapist: You called the right place.

Ms. Stein: I work. Your office is four blocks from my house. They said you have evening hours so I don't have an excuse.

Therapist: And you do sound concerned. First, I need some specific information about your family. Does the girl's father know of your call?

Ms. Stein: No, we have been divorced for a while.

Therapist: How long?

Ms. Stein: Almost five years.

Therapist: Have you remarried?

Ms. Stein: No, but I went back to using my maiden name.

Therapist: Is he remarried?

Ms. Stein: Yes. He and his wife lived together for some time and they got married about three months ago.

Therapist: And where does he live?

Ms. Stein: Across town.

Therapist: How often do the girls see him?

Ms. Stein: It's hard to say. The divorce agreement says one thing, but in reality it's less. About every other weekend, I'd say, on the average.

Therapist: Could you give me the ages of your daughters?

Ms. Stein: Deirdra was ten last month and Liza will be six next month.

Therapist: And are there any other family members involved with the girls?

Ms. Stein: Do you mean grandparents?

Therapist: Yes.

Ms. Stein: Not really. My parents live in Florida and always have. We usually see them twice a year. Their father's parents are quite old and live in a nursing home.

Therapist: Thank you. I have a clearer picture of your situation and the important people in your daughters' lives. You did say their father does not know of your plan to call us?

Ms. Stein: Right. We don't have much to say to each other about the girls and when we do, we argue. I'm the custodial parent. I see no need to tell him.

Therapist: It sounds like your talks with him about the girls have been upsetting for you.

Ms. Stein: (with anger) You better believe it.

Therapist: From my experience with divorced couples with children I think I have some idea of what you may be feeling.

Ms. Stein: (calmer) I hope so.

Therapist: And what I have found to be helpful when children of a divorce and a remarriage are having difficulty is for the parents, stepparents, and children to attend at least the first meeting.

Ms. Stein: You have to be joking.

Therapist: I can understand your reaction, but I am serious.

Ms. Stein: I can't consider that. Charles and I would be arguing with each other and his wife would join him.

Therapist: I would not let that happen.

Ms. Stein: Hmmm.

Therapist: Our purpose is to understand what is and what has happened in the family that leaves the girls unhappy now. There are three adults in their lives who care about them and could help improve the situation.

Ms. Stein: (More willing to consider the idea once the therapist assured her she would be protected.) It sounds interesting, but how on earth would I get him to come in? I don't think I like the idea.

Therapist: What don't you like about it?

Ms. Stein: I'm afraid I'll get the third degree.

Therapist: What would the third degree be about?

Ms. Stein: A hard time. He would want to know what's going on, why I hadn't told him, what kind of place I called and on and on.

Therapist: Do you think you could answer those questions?

Ms. Stein: Yes, but I don't want to be criticized by him. He has no right. I'm the one doing all the hard work.

Therapist: If you anticipate criticism, I can understand your hesitation. How willing would you be to try to ask him to come in?

Ms. Stein: Do I have a choice?

Therapist: Of course.

Ms. Stein: Where should I begin?

Therapist: You know him and how he is. Any thoughts on how to approach him?

Ms. Stein: Well he's their father. I could tell him I spoke to the girls' teachers and they think they have problems, so they referred me to the Jewish Board of Family and Children's Services, and I spoke to a therapist there and the therapist said that in divorced and remarried families they like to see everyone involved with the girls at the first meeting.

Therapist: How does that sound to you?

Ms. Stein: It's the truth. I can try it.

Therapist: Fine. If you have any further questions or if their father does, you can get back to me.

Ms. Stein: OK. Wish me luck.

Therapist: Good luck . . . but one more thing. Let's talk about how you can prepare the girls.

Ms. Stein: Oh. I didn't think about that. I'll just tell them that . . . that . . . what should I say?

Therapist: How about the truth?

Ms. Stein: (quizzically) That their teachers said they seemed troubled and we are all worried and want to find a solution?

Therapist: (Somewhat uncomfortable with the use of the word solution but decides to let it ride and register it in terms of her understanding of Ms. Stein.)

Appointment set. Fee structure discussed.

Next day—Call from Mr. Miller

Mr. Miller: I'm Mr. Miller. My wife, I mean ex-wife, spoke to you yesterday about my girls.

Therapist: Yes.

Mr. Miller: I just want to check this out. You want *all* of us, me, my wife, Karen, and the girls at the first meeting?

Therapist: Yes, I can appreciate your shock but that is what I urged. (Similar explanation that was given to Ms. Stein is given to Mr. Miller.)

Mr. Miller: Yes, that is what Karen said. My wife is a little anxious; she suggested I call and check this out. Besides, that time is not convenient for me. I'm an architect and I teach on Monday evenings. Any other time would be fine.

Therapist: Thursday at 7:00 is open the following week.

Mr. Miller: That's fine with me.

Therapist: (Therapist thinks Rem scheduling is never easy—there's always a hitch.) Will you call Ms. Stein and see if that is OK with her?

Discussion

Ms. Stein was eventually willing to contact her former husband. If she had been adamantly opposed to contacting him, the therapist might have considered:

1) meeting with her alone to explore her opposition;
2) meeting with her and the girls to engage her/them;
3) contacting the ex-husband herself with the permission of Ms. Stein.

Notice that Ms. Stein anticipates the session turning into a battle, and when the therapist assures her that she, the therapist, will not let that happen, Ms. Stein is more willing to consider the idea. It is important for the therapist to anticipate this anxiety and be able to communicate that she can control the session. This telephone contact with Ms. Stein and then Mr. Miller demonstrates the outreach Rem work requires when the therapist is serious about seeing the Rem suprasystem. Often it is the therapist's reluctance to get involved in this process that defeats this approach.

INITIAL MEETINGS: EVALUATION PERIOD

Prior to the meeting, the therapist makes sure there are enough chairs and sufficient space for everyone. For the children there are two or three sets of family puppet dolls, enough to include the possible combinations of bioparents, stepparents and children. Also available are age-appropriate play material, paper, crayons, dolls, trucks, cars, soldiers, etc.

The task of the therapist in this initial meeting is to help the family members feel welcome, to begin to develop a working alliance with each, and to begin the process of establishing a "safe," facilitating therapeutic environment. Family members are helped to express their feelings about being present and are asked what they see as the problems, both for themselves and for their families. Where there is a scapegoated child, the therapist may relabel the behavior by directing the attention to the positive purpose and function it may be serving in the Rem supra-system. At the same time, the therapist is thinking diagnostically and formulating a tentative hypothesis about the purpose of the presenting problem(s) for the Rem suprasystem, the subsystems and the individual. Also, life-cycle and intrapsychic aspects are being considered for every member.

Illustration

The family arrived in separate subsystems—first Mr. and Mrs. Miller and then Ms. Stein and the children. In the waiting room Mr. and Mrs. Miller were seated together, the girls were in the toy area, and Ms. Stein was standing with a magazine.

The therapist introduced herself to each person individually, beginning with Ms. Stein, moving to the Rem couple, and then to Deirdra and Liza. They were all invited into the office. There was a circular seating arrangement. Ms. Stein sat next to the therapist with Liza at her side, then Deirdra, then Mr. Miller, then Mrs. Miller at the other side of the therapist.

The therapist immediately took charge of the session.

Therapist: I know a little about your situation and I want to hear more. But first how do each of you feel about being here tonight?

Deirdra: It feels funny to be here in the same room with mommy, daddy, and Marlene. I'm nervous but I'm not happy at school and mommy said this could help.

Therapist: (Cognizant that Deirdra and not a parent answered first.) So you're nervous but hopeful things will be better for you?

Deirdra: Yes.

Mrs. Miller: I'm also a little nervous about being all together but I'm glad because I've noticed that the girls, especially Deirdra, seem to be angry and reluctant to help around the house when we are together. I mentioned this to Charles.

Mr. Miller: She did but I didn't take her seriously. Sometimes I think she's too critical of the girls but if the school refers us I think it's time to look and see what's wrong.

Ms. Stein: (Angrily) I've mentioned the girls had problems to you too, but you never listen to me.

Mr. Miller: (Looks aghast—moves chair ever so slightly close to the corner) (Angrily) You never said a word to me.

Therapist: Ms. Stein, Mr. Miller, let me stop you right now! I said I would

not let either of you fight with each other. That will not get us any-
where and in fact it might make you—all of us—feel more helpless
about improving things.

Everyone: (Calm, silence; everyone is breathing regularly again)

Therapist: I gather that in some way Deirdra and Liza's problems in
school served the purpose of getting us all together to look at what
is happening in the families. So far we haven't heard from Liza
(Liza sat quietly and did not want to play with the puppets or draw
a picture). Liza, I'm wondering if you could tell us how you feel
about being here?

Deirdra: She's shy.

Therapist: (Notices that Deirdra speaks for her sister and the parents allow it.)

Liza: Like Deirdra said.

Therapist: Could you say it in your own words?

Liza: No.

Therapist: Not yet.

Liza: (Smile)

Therapist: Now, I would like to ask each of you what you see as the problem or problems?

Deirdra: I'd be happier if I had a best friend in school.

Therapist: (Again noticing Deirdra and not the parents began.) I know
you would. This is a hard question: Is there anything that is happening or happened in the family that makes it hard for you to
have a good time in school?

Deirdra: (Sheepishly) I'm sad. I hope this doesn't hurt your feelings,
Marlene, but I would like my parents to be together.

Ms. Stein: (Disgusted) I have gone over this with her a hundred and one
times. I told her that that would not happen. I point out other families where there is a divorce but she still brings this up. It's so frustrating.

Therapist: So what you've tried is not working.

Ms. Stein: Right.

Mr. Miller: Deirdra and Liza occasionally mention this to me, too. I give
them the same explanation but since I got married and they were
flower girls at the wedding they stopped.

Ms. Stein: (To Mr. Miller) I didn't know they talk about this with you.

Mr. Miller: They had.

Therapist: What Deirdra and Liza are probably doing is trying to deal
with their sadness about their parents' divorce. All children, and
even children who are fond of their stepparent, have to deal with
this loss. The parents do as well, but it seems that so far the chil-

dren and you (to Mr. Miller and Ms. Stein) haven't found a satisfactory way to do this.

Ms. Stein and Mr. Miller: (Shake heads in acknowledgment.)

Mr. Miller: I don't think I see enough of the children.

Ms. Stein: I agree!

Mr. Miller: Since I've been with Marlene I see them more. She helps me with the girls. But I would like to see them more. I have a very busy schedule. I have to travel and make site visits and I teach. But I want to see them more.

Deirdra: Daddy, I want to see you more too.

Liza: (Goes over and sits on her father's lap.)

Therapist: I see Liza went to sit on your lap when you said that you wanted to see them more. (To Mrs. Miller) What is your reaction to what your husband is suggesting?

Mrs. Miller: Mixed. I want to see them more too, but I want help in making the visits better and having a schedule so I know when they're coming.

Therapist: Sounds quite reasonable to me.

Ms. Stein: Charles and I have trouble talking to each other and making plans. I'd like the girls to be with him more too.

Mr. Miller: I agree we do have trouble talking to each other.

Mrs. Miller: I've noticed that and sometimes plans are made at the last minute and we have other plans so the girls are with us and then we have to find a babysitter on Saturday night. That happened last time.

Liza: I didn't like that.

Therapist: (Noticing Liza offered a spontaneous comment) Could you tell us more, Liza?

Liza: I thought I'd be with daddy and Marlene—not a babysitter I didn't even know.

Mr. Miller: It wasn't good.

Therapist: I see. So far we have mentioned these problems in the family: Deirdra and Liza, you are sad about not living with both parents; and you, Ms. Stein and Mr. Miller, have tried to discuss this with the girls, but often these discussions have left you feeling frustrated. One difficulty is arranging visits given the problems you, Ms. Stein, and you, Mr. Miller, have in talking to each other and your (to Mr. Miller) work schedule. Mrs. Miller, you also mentioned that the visits don't go all that well. And, of course, Deirdra, you would like to have a friend in class. Is there anyone or anything we have left out?

Deirdra: Liza doesn't listen to me when I tell her to get dressed.

Therapist: (Notices adults show no verbal or nonverbal response to this.)
    Sounds like you might have to take care of her.
Deirdra: Mommy works and I have to take Liza to school and to the after-
    school program. I have to get her ready to go home from the Cen-
    ter. She is so slow; she never gets dressed herself and then we fight.
Liza: (Unmoved by her sister's comment.)
Mrs. Miller: I've noticed that Deirdra takes on too much responsibility
    for Liza.
Ms. Stein: I don't know about that. After all, I work and I need her help.
Therapist: This leaves us with an important question to consider. To
    what extent might Deirdra be taking on too much of the caretak-
    ing role of Liza and then not being able to have fun enjoying school
    and friendships? (Relates it to problem presented.) Let me give
    you, Mr. and Mrs. Miller, and Ms. Stein, the task to think about
    that. I would like to take some time with you now to draw a geno-
    gram, which is like a family tree. This can help us understand more
    clearly your backgrounds and connections.

    The therapist began working on the genogram with everyone. (See
Figure 6.1.) She moved from the most recent relationship, the Rem cou-

FIGURE 6.1
Stein-Miller Family Genogram at Time of Application

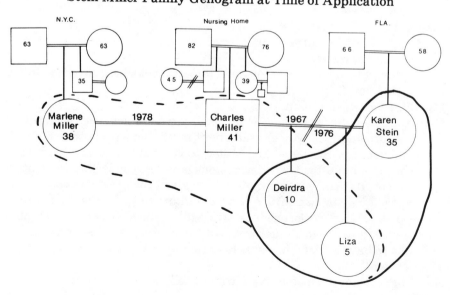

ple, to affirm their presence and reality in the system, and then back in layers through the double single-parent households, to the initial separation of Karen and Charles, then back to the third generation: the family of origin of all of the adults. In this first meeting with the Rem suprasystem the interest was in the bare bones: landmark events and quality of the relationships. There would be opportunity later for more details as evaluation and treatment progressed. Private details of the couple relationship were reserved for the separate meeting with them later in the evaluation. Generally, it is not appropriate to explore these in the presence of the former spouse, and vice versa.

Completing the genogram took most of the remaining time. The therapist made a point of leaving 15 minutes to reach some kind of closure. Experience with Rem families prepares one for increased anxiety and pressure for immediate answers, which once again can surface in the face of the ending of the meeting. Mr. Miller wanted to know: "What should I do with Deirdra?"

The therapist pointed out the complexity of the situation and commented that there would not necessarily be change overnight. She reaffirmed that an important step had already been taken: Those concerned with Deirdra's and Liza's welfare and well-being had been able to sit down together and begin to work towards understanding and resolution. The next steps in the evaluation would be to meet in different subsystems: Ms. Stein and the children, Mr. and Mrs. Miller and the children, the Rem couple, and then Ms. Stein alone. We also planned to confer with the girls' teachers and to request medical reports from their pediatrician.

Separate appointments were set up for these sessions and the fee for the consultation was willingly shared equally by both parents. In this case both parents paid the same fee; the agency's then top fee for a session was split between the two households. Mr. Miller, as mentioned, is an architect. Mrs. Miller is a professor of English, in particular, children's literature, and Ms. Stein is an account executive in a marketing research company.

Discussion

Very early in the session Mrs. Miller comments on the awkwardness of "being all together," i.e., present with her husband's former wife. This reaction is common. Usually the ex-spouse is seen by the new couple as the culprit, a person to be avoided. Meeting this person face to face presents the validation of this perception, as well as the threat of its invalidation. For the former spouse there is the anticipation of two against one, as she sees the Rem couple as adversaries. The children are aware of all the parents' sentiments and are fearful of an explosion and being forced to choose sides.

Because of the explosive potential of these dynamics, most therapists are loathe to see the Rem suprasystem together. However, with experience and determination the therapist can become at ease and learn techniques that maintain order. It is important to recognize that not only are there old injuries but a need to competitively prove oneself is also operative. When the therapist is able to keep individuals focused on the purpose of the meeting, even among the most volatile people, it is possible to achieve a level of collaborative work.

A few minutes into the session, Ms. Stein begins to fight with Mr. Miller. This is common in the Rem suprasystem meetings.The therapist is active and takes control and, as promised, does not let such fighting continue. This couple was able to stop their attack, which is a good diagnostic sign. On a continuum, in the first meeting, a few divorced partners do not fight each other at all, some like Ms. Stein and Mr. Miller do but can be stopped, some need to be stopped several times in a session, and some need to be stopped repeatedly. The therapist has the option to stop the session if it is proving to be too destructive. In a most severe example the bioparents were both remarried and their new spouses joined them in their "hatred" for the former spouse. The four-way meeting took five months of preparation before both Rem couples were willing to listen to each other rather than "spit in their faces."

At the end of this session, the therapist, the parentified child in her own family of origin, is aware of her childhood role as a source of potential countertransference. She is mindful that Deirdra is alert and involved and did in fact get the ball rolling by being the identified patient and responding first in the session. The therapist is aware that she needs to be on guard against having Deirdra be put in the role of her cotherapist.

THE USE OF THE GENOGRAM

Together with the Rem family and the significant suprafamily members, we create a genogram (Guerin and Pendagast, 1976). The genogram is an indispensable treatment tool. It allows us to organize large amounts of data from the complicated histories of the families, and facilitates for the family the process of shifting attention solely from the identified patient to thinking about the Rem suprasystem. The significance of family events over three or more generations comes sharply into focus, as do subsystem interrelationships that often were not previously apparent. Family, marital and individual life cycles are highlighted, including developmental arrests or deficits both horizontally (same generation) and vertically (cross generation). The process of working together on the genogram is itself therapeutic. Affective connections are heightened, and often for the first time each family member feels heard and understood. The complexity and difficulty of each individual's position in the Rem suprasystem are revealed to all. The pseudomutuality and denial of differences so common to Rem subsystems are defused, as each sees how different this Rem family is from the original nuclear system and how diverse have been the histories of the various members. Intergenerational patterns of behavior, as well as timing of deaths, illnesses, divorces, and separations, are clearly depicted. The number of structural shifts, at times involving multiple changes and losses of people, close connections, favorite objects, homes, neighborhoods, and living standards, is dramatically highlighted, facilitating for some a long delayed mourning reaction. If a child's bioparent is not present, we make sure to inquire about him and to include him in order to soften any loyalty conflict the child may be feeling and to support the needed connection to both parents. The therapist's implicit and explicit recognition of significant others in the child's life makes an important statement.

Information specific to the Rem suprasystem is asked for directly, including:

1) *The Present Rem Unit:* Living in, living out and visiting children; when they visit and how often; holiday and vacation schedules; who makes school visits on parents day; and other sensitive living arrangements in the household, like bedrooms, space allocation.
2) *How the Present Rem Unit Was Formed:* The background of the couple's meeting and courtship, and its chronology in relationship to the ending of the previous marriage. How and if the children were prepared for the remarriage; if the former partners knew, were informed, and by whom. Changes in residence, visiting arrangements and other cathected parameters.
3) *The Two Single-Parent Household Structures:* The quality and quantity of time spent with each child by each bioparent; the role of grandparents and significant others during this phase; the quality and quantity of the relationship between the separated spouses.
4) *The Original Nuclear Family System(s):* When, where, why and how this was dissolved; what each adult's and each child's perception was of the dissolution, then and now. Dates of actual physical separation and of the legal divorce. Custody arrangements then and now.

5) *The Families of Origin of All of the Adults:* Assessment of input by each significant person, both historically and in the present. Influence the third generation may be having on the present Rem family and suprasystem.

6) *Mate Choice:* The unconscious as well as conscious factors which may be determining mate choice for this, as well as previous marriages. Are there reasonable expectations and goals for this marriage? Are marriage contracts of the couple concordant, complementary or in conflict (Sager, 1976, pp. 164–180)?

7) *Previous Therapy:* Have there been previous treatment contacts by any family members, either individually or jointly? Why was treatment sought? How long did therapy last, and how was it concluded? What was changed and learned?

8) *Diagnostic:* From the therapist's viewpoint, it is important while completing the genogram to observe overt and covert alliances, power structures, levels of intimacy, bonds between and among members, and patterns of inclusion and exclusion in the Rem suprasystem.

One need not be compulsive about history taking; basic facts will suffice at first, and the rest will unfold as treatment proceeds. We keep the genogram with us in each subsequent meeting with the families and add to it as we move along.

By the end of the first Rem suprasystem meeting, it is usually possible to establish a tentative hypothesis about the purpose the symptom may be serving in the Rem suprasystem. At this point we have the tentative hypothesis that Deirdra's symptom of poor peer relationship is a direct result of her role of parentified child in the Rem suprasystem. Assessment will attempt to answer the question as to what function her parentification serves in the suprasystem, subsystem, and individual. By the end of this session it is also usually possible to have beginning impressions of the individual's intrapsychic world. The therapist notes that all members of the family relate well, are attractive and verbal. Affective range was tense, but when they saw the therapist was in control this tension abated and the work could be done. This is a positive diagnostic sign.

ASSESSMENT PHASE: SEPARATE MEETINGS WITH THE SUBSYSTEMS

The diagnostic task of the separate meetings with the subsystems is to evaluate in greater depth subsystem functioning and the nature of the relationships and to ascertain where each person is in his or her individual, marital, and family life-cycle development and intrapsychic functioning. This knowledge facilitates goal-setting. It is important to set achievable goals with Rem; these should be goals that the family members want for themselves, not necessarily what the therapist thinks they need.

Common treatment goals with Rem families include many that are premised on the acceptance and enhancement of the effectiveness of the Rem suprasystem. the goal-setting process affirms the integrity of the specific Rem unit and that of the other bioparent's household unit. Goals may include any or all of the following:

1) Consolidating the Rem couple as a functioning unit and establishing its position in the Rem family subsystem and suprasystem.
2) Consolidating the parental authority in the Rem suprasystem, optimally forming a collaborative co-parenting team that includes bioparents and stepparents.
3) Helping the children, in turn, to deal with and minimize the continuation and exacerbation of loyalty binds.
4) Facilitating mourning of the old nuclear family, former partners, old neighborhoods, friends and ways of life.
5) Assuring there is a secure place for the child's development in the Rem suprasystem, optimally through the utilization of both family subsystems.
6) Helping family members accept and tolerate their differences from some idealized intact nuclear family model. These may include such differences as lack of complete control over money or children, feelings for individuals in the Rem suprasystem, differences in levels and degrees of bonding in the Rem suprasystem, and differences in rules and expectations of the children in the two households.

Single-Parent Subsystem—Ms. Stein, Deirdra and Liza

Ms. Stein and the girls arrived on time. All three appeared considerably more relaxed than at the first meeting.

Therapist: This is our second meeting together. Tonight I would like to understand more about your life together and how you might want things to be.

Ms. Stein: I'm glad we have this appointment tonight. Deirdra came home from school with the news that the student teacher is leaving next week. There is no reasoning with her.

Deirdra: Why did she start if she knew she would only be with us for three months? She said she would be with us all year.

Ms. Stein: People's schedules change— you can't always plan for everything.

Deirdra: Mommy, you don't understand. She should not have lied to us.

Ms. Stein: Maybe it wasn't a lie. Maybe she didn't know.

Deirdra: But she should have known. She is a teacher!

Ms. Stein: (Exasperated) A student teacher!

Therapist: I see you are both frustrated. This reminds me of your description of your discussion about another loss—Deirdra wanting both parents to be together.

Ms. Stein: Yes. I end up feeling the same way. Rotten.

Therapist: Karen, what happens inside of you when you see Deirdra upset?

Ms. Stein: I don't know—I really don't know.

Therapist: Take a guess.

Ms. Stein: Maybe I get upset too. Listen, I work full-time, take care of the girls, want a life of my own. What do you expect?

Therapist: You are doing so much. I wonder to what extent do you meet your own expectations?

Ms. Stein: When I see the girls upset, I think maybe I'm not a good mother. I run a tight ship and I need to have everything go smoothly.

Therapist: So when you see Deirdra upset that rattles you.

Ms. Stein: Exactly. And when I'm that way nothing works with them.

Therapist: It looks like we need to help you develop more viable ways of relating to them.

Ms. Stein: That's why I'm here.

Therapist: When you sense that Deirdra or Liza is scared or upset could you forget reason for a while and instead reflect to them what you think they are feeling. For example, "Deirdra, you are upset the student teacher left." And then listen to what she has to say.

Ms. Stein: But I want to *do* something.

Therapist: Understandably, since doing something makes you less anxious. In fact, what I am suggesting *is* doing something.

At the therapist's suggestion Ms. Stein and Deirdra replay the beginning of the session. Ms. Stein is able to be more responsive and Deirdra elaborates on how much she liked the student teacher. At this point Liza stops coloring and, half listening, walks to the door.

Deirdra: Where are you going? You can't leave.

Liza: I want a drink of water. I'm thirsty.

Ms. Stein: (Remains silent)

Therapist: (To Liza) Do you think you could wait ten minutes? (She points to clock to show her when ten minutes is up.)

Liza: OK.

Therapist: Let's try to understand what just happened. (To Ms. Stein) What might have been your reaction just now when you heard Deirdra?

Ms. Stein: I guess I thought she is so bossy.

Deirdra: (To Ms. Stein) (Jibingly) Well, if I didn't say anything, you wouldn't.

Ms. Stein: (To Deirdra) (Angrily) That's not true.

Therapist: (To Ms. Stein) What picture might Deirdra have of you that gets you angry?

Ms. Stein: She thinks she is the mother and I just fade out.

Deirdra: I do a lot of things a mother does.

Therapist: (To Ms. Stein) (Mindful of Liza and reaffirming Ms. Stein's role as mother.) What do you think of Liza going out to get a drink of water?

Ms. Stein: It's fine with me. We had pizza for dinner. I know it makes her thirsty.

Liza and Deirdra: (Both go out and get a drink. A playfulness in Deirdra, not evident before, was revealed when she admitted she was thirsty too.)

Ms. Stein: You asked me to think about whether or not Deirdra has too much responsibility. She may, but there is nothing I can do about it. Damn their father—he gets off scot-free and I have to take care of the girls. No wonder he found someone else. If I had his free time, I would too.

Deirdra and Liza: (Return, laughing with wet mouths. Comments from both girls about the new fountain.)

Therapist: Perhaps we could get back to what was mentioned before (a deliberate general statement).

Liza: You mean that Deirdra acts like she is my mother.

Ms. Stein: (Offended) Girls, let's get this clear—I am the mother!

Therapist: Why might there be some confusion about this in the family?

Liza: Because Deirdra's a big boss.

Deirdra: And you are a slowpoke.

Therapist: (Aware that the girls attack each other rather than confront their mother.) Might there be some things the girls do that are beyond their age?

Ms. Stein: (Obviously threatened and criticized by the above comment) Listen, I told you I'm doing my best. I work, take care of the girls, now I go to therapy. What do you want from me?

Therapist: I believe you when you say you are doing your best, but it's not working. Would you be willing to ask the girls what might be too much for them? Remember, listening is doing something.

Ms. Stein: (Half-heartedly) Deirdra, tell me what's too hard.

Deirdra: (Hesitantly) Liza walks so slow in the morning, I'm afraid we will be late.

Therapist: (Aware that Deirdra is again attacking Liza and being protective of her mother. Questions are asked about their morning routine. Ms. Stein walks to the corner with the girls and she leaves them and walks in one direction to the subway and Deirdra and Liza walk two short blocks to school. Deirdra is "in charge" and the girls usually argue all the way to the school.)

Liza: (To Ms. Stein) Mommy, do you think maybe you can walk with us to school?

Ms. Stein: (Angry) This is not going to work. I run a tight ship. I can't do that. Do you have children? Do you know what it is for a working mother to get to work on time? I have a responsible job.

Therapist: You don't *have* to do what they request. Just listen now to what they have to say and we can all evaluate together whether or not this is possible for you never, sometimes, always.

At the therapist's urging Ms. Stein asks the girls to discuss further the morning walk to school. She concludes:

Ms. Stein: (Smiling) I'll tell you what I can do. This Friday I have a 9:30 meeting across town. I'll walk you both to school.

Liza: (Claps her hands.)

Deirdra: (To Liza) Let's not get carried away.

Therapist: (To Deirdra) You may feel two ways about your Mom doing this—glad to have her help but not so glad to give up your role as the important older sister.

Deirdra: I don't know.

Therapist: Time will tell.

The therapist concludes the session by summarizing and suggesting we need to find out if there are other ways to lighten the girls' and Ms. Stein's load. An individual session is scheduled for Ms. Stein.

Discussion

In the single-parent subsystem meeting we find out about the nuts and bolts of daily living in that household. This is important for several reasons. Because the nuclear family structure is no longer operative, we need to know what has taken its place, and how the tasks, roles, and living conditions have evolved since the breakup of the nuclear family. At the time they came to treatment, Ms. Stein had been working full-time for two years. Since she could no longer afford their old apartment, they had moved into their present quarters six months previously. Here, Ms. Stein unilaterally set up the new system and both children complied. Although this left a lot to be desired, Ms. Stein did run her tight ship, go to work, get the children to school, and fed and bathed them each night. The household functioned smoothly, as the family life-cycle tasks were carried on. At the same time Ms. Stein embarked on her first career, continuing her individual life-cycle task. It is Deirdra who is failing to master her individual life-cycle tasks, making friendships, since her role reversal, which is so necessary to the smooth functioning of the household, is impeding her development. Ms. Stein is angry when Deirdra usurps her role in the session. She does not deny it, as some parents do, but instead sees it as a challenge to her authority. In some ways she has created a monster in that her parentified child is now parenting her. She does not like it, but has the need to persist in her behavior rather than change. However, with some therapeutic intervention Ms. Stein is able to consider making a change. Will she?

Rem Family—Mr. and Mrs. Miller and Deirdra and Liza

In the circular seating this time we have the therapist, Liza and Deirdra, then Mr. and Mrs. Miller on the other side of the therapist.

Mr. Miller: I'm glad we're having this meeting. We had a rough weekend —fairly typical for us.
Mrs. Miller, Deirdra, Liza: (Shake heads in agreement)
Therapist: What made it so rough?
Deirdra: Well, Marlene . . .
Therapist: I'm going to interrupt you, Deirdra. I want to hear from your dad. He brought it up. (An intervention aimed at having the adults and not Deirdra be in charge.)
Mr. Miller: (Caught off guard—too ready to give up to Deirdra. Mr. Miller continued in a confused way. With the therapist's questions and direction the following emerged. He picked up the girls after lunch on Saturday and after dinner on Sunday he brought them home. Saturday was fine but Sunday it rained so the family couldn't go to the park. Liza wanted to play dominoes with Mr. Miller. Marlene wanted to do something as a family, like going to

the Museum of Natural History, and Deirdra wanted to play chess with Mr. Miller. Mr. Miller figured everyone would be satisfied by playing Monopoly. The girls would get to play a game and Marlene would get to be together as a family.)

Therapist: What did you want to do?

Mr. Miller: I wanted to make everyone happy.

Therapist: But what would you have liked to do for yourself?

Mr. Miller: I can't answer that.

Therapist: Do you know why not?

Mr. Miller: Because I wanted to watch the football game and how could I want that when I see so little of my children as it is?

Therapist: So, at this point you feel guilty for even wanting that for yourself?

Mr. Miller: Don't you think that's terrible?

Therapist: I'm wondering what is it that does feel so terrible to you about that?

Mr. Miller: As I said, I don't see the girls all that often and when I'm with them I expect to want to spend every moment with them.

Therapist: With that expectation I can understand why you might think you're terrible for wanting to watch the game.

Mr. Miller: (Nods his head in agreement.)

Therapist: So what happened?

Mrs. Miller: Then Deirdra . . .

Therapist: (To Mr. Miller) I see your wife and Deirdra have a tendency to talk for you and you let them.

Mr. Miller: (Confidently) I can talk for myself. Liza was getting bored I suppose and forgot when it was her turn. Then Deirdra got on her case and criticized her. Then Marlene criticized Deirdra in a harsh way so I told her to quit it. She got up and walked out and said, "You are so protective of them—you don't care about me." (To wife) Right?

Mrs. Miller: Close. You do care more about them than me.

Therapist: Wow—it sounds like quite a scene—one pretty common in remarried families.

Mrs. Miller: It was terrible. It was so familiar. You know, I'm the outsider.

Deirdra: I was so angry at Marlene that I wanted to go home.

Lisa: I wanted to go home too.

Mr. Miller: Boy was I frustrated.

Therapist: And you wanted to please everyone and you ended up pleasing no one—including yourself.

Mr. Miller: It always happens that way.

Therapist: That may be part of the problem. When you are all together the only stand you have been able to take so far is one that you think will please everyone. And that is not working. Marlene then feels abandoned by you and the girls want to go home.

Mr. Miller: (Halfheartedly) True. (The hint at a system change makes him withdraw.)

Therapist: (To Mrs. Miller) When you saw Deirdra criticize Liza what was going on inside of you?

Mrs. Miller: I got angry at Deirdra and had to stop her. She takes over so much.

Therapist: Did you think anyone else would stop her if you didn't?

Mrs. Miller: No, I didn't think Charles would. He's so laid back about discipline.

Therapist: So, does it happen that most of the discipline comes from you, the stepmother?

Mrs. Miller: (Sarcastically) The wicked stepmother, because then Charles thinks I'm being too critical.

Therapist: Does everyone see it this way?

Liza: No. Daddy tells us what to do.

Deirdra: He does.

Mr. Miller: But not as often as Marlene would like.

Therapist: So there is some disagreement between the two of you about limits and discipline.

Mr. and Mrs. Miller: Yes.

Therapist: (To Mr. Miller) Your wife said that if she hadn't said something to Deirdra when she was criticizing Liza you would not have. To what extent might that be so or not so from your point of view?

Mr. Miller: I would have said something eventually. What Deirdra was beginning to do was registering with me, but Marlene is so quick to jump in. (At the therapist's urging Mr. Miller says this directly to his wife.)

Mrs. Miller: (To Mr. Miller) I don't really believe you would have said anything.

Mr. Miller: (He begins to back down.) I may have.

Mrs. Miller: Yes, but I can't take being the heavy all the time.

Therapist: Understandably—and they're not even your children.

Mrs. Miller: I know, but why do I keep doing this?

Therapist: It's a good question. Any ideas?

Mrs. Miller: I suppose I don't think Charles will step in even though he just said he would. I still don't believe him.

Therapist: Since you say you don't like being the heavy, and you're not the girls' mother and Charles says he may possibly intervene, I'm wondering if you might want to try something different for yourself.

Mrs. Miller: I'll try anything.

Therapist: (Thinking this is a too pseudomutual response.) Consider this. When the four of you are together and something comes up with the girls and you feel the impulse to step in, might you be willing to hold yourself back for as long as you could and see how Charles responds?

Mrs. Miller: Absolutely.

Therapist: What does everyone think of my suggestion to Marlene?

Deirdra: I like it. After all, she's not my mother and I don't want her to tell me what to do.

Therapist: You mean it might be easier to take it from your dad?

Deirdra: I guess so.

Therapist: (To Mr. Miller) What do you think about this?

Mr. Miller: It makes sense.

Therapist: (To Mr. Miller) I notice that Liza has been playing with the puppets. Do you think she's telling us something?

Mrs. Miller: I notice that she is playing with . . .

Therapist: Let me interrupt you. Could you wait and see what her father will come up with first?

Mrs. Miller: You're right. This may be harder than I thought.

Therapist: It is difficult.

(Mr. Miller does notice that Liza was having the little girl doll and father doll play together. The other female dolls were thrown to the side. The remainder of the session was devoted to a discussion of the girls' first meeting with Marlene—a breakfast at her house which Mr. Miller thought was a "great idea." This first encounter on Marlene's turf set the stage for the shift in control from Mr. Miller to Marlene that the system was reacting to now.)

Discussion

We see the adult who has picked up the parenting task in this household is the stepmother, with the collusion of the biofather. The special appeal of Mrs. Miller to Mr. Miller was her fondness for his children: her willingness to initiate the first contact with them and her specialty in children's literature.

This role is apparently becoming ego alien to Mrs. Miller and she is experiencing frustration with being the "heavy" all the time (a wicked stepmother). At the point that a client expresses discontent or conflict about a role, the therapist moves in to test the client's readiness to change by helping the client develop a goal for himself or herself around this issue. This process enhances autonomy and clarifies the direction of treatment. If at this point the person is able to establish a goal for himself, we suggest a task related to that goal to capitalize on the client's expressed wish to change. The setting of the task is diagnostic, both for the individual and the system. It is important then to follow up in the next meeting to see to what extent the task was carried out and how it was responded to by each person.

By giving Mrs. Miller the task of waiting to see what her husband will do with the girls, rather than jumping in herself, we are aiming for a Rem subsystem change that will have the bioparent parent rather than the stepparent parent.

Individual Session with Ms. Karen Stein

Ms. Stein was seen on her lunch hour and looked attractive in a well-tailored suit. She began by saying that she did manage to walk the girls to school on Friday.

Therapist: How was that for you?
Ms. Stein: No problem. I had some leeway that morning. I felt good about doing that for the girls. (Silence) I love them very much and I know our situation is rough on them. I was glad to give this extra.

The therapist mirrors back to Ms. Stein the smile on her face. Then at the therapist's suggestion Ms. Stein elaborated on her family of origin. She comes from a well-to-do Southern family and is an only child. Her parents were described in an idealized way, although she did admit to a difficult relationship with her mother during adolescence. The divorce was a shock to her parents who still cannot understand "what I'm looking for." She did not find them particularly emotionally supportive during the separation and divorce; however, they did offer financial help. Ms. Stein and the girls visit with her parents at least twice a year. Ms. Stein described her parents in a perfunctory way, and gave the impression of a bright, pseudo-independent girl who at 18 left home to go to college in New York and who since remained both physically and emotionally distant from her parents.

Ms. Stein initiated discussion of her ex-husband.

Ms. Stein: You have to help me with Charles. I can't stand being controlled by him. He sends the check, but when he feels like it and I never know from one weekend to the next where the girls will be. I feel bad for the girls. When they complain about him, would you believe, I make excuses for him!

Therapist: It must be hard for you. What have you tried so far to make the visitation more viable?

Ms. Stein: It is spelled out clearly in the divorce agreement—every other weekend from Friday at 7 P.M. to Sunday 7 P.M. and two weeks in the summer. But he can't keep that. He travels, got married, one thing or another. And I admit some time I change the plan to suit my convenience. I deserve some advantage.

Therapist: Tell me how visitation was arranged last time.

Ms. Stein: The plan now is Charles' plan. He's shortened the time to roughly every other weekend from Saturday afternoon to Sunday evening. But I wanted him to pick the girls up Friday, so I thought about it, and on Wednesday I called him and told him what I wanted. He didn't give me a straight answer, we had some words, and he said he would let me know the next day. I wanted an answer right away because if he can't pick them up I have to arrange a sitter, but he didn't like "being put on the spot." He said he had to discuss it with Marlene. I think he's afraid of her.

Therapist: What finally happened?

Ms. Stein: He picked them up on Saturday morning and I got a sitter for that Friday evening. It is not good for the girls to be so uncertain about where they will be.

Therapist: I agree. When you look back on this incident what could you do differently the next time?

Ms. Stein: I shouldn't wait for the last minute to make plans.

Therapist: You then do place yourself at his mercy.

Ms. Stein: I'd like to plan a schedule at the beginning of the month so I know what's what.

Therapist: That might work, but you'll have to stick to it and just a few minutes ago you mentioned you sometimes bend the plans to suit yourself.

Ms. Stein: I don't like that.

Therapist: But would you be willing at this point to try something else?

Ms. Stein: I think so.

Therapist: I strongly urge you to pick up on your own suggestion and plan visitation at the beginning of the month. In fact I will mention this recommendation to Charles and Marlene if that's OK with you. We could meet together and see what could be worked out, so it's a little easier on all of you.

Discussion

Part of the nuts and bolts of daily living in a Rem suprasystem involves the arrangements and rearrangements of the visitation of the children. It is important in the evaluation phase to find out how the families handle this issue. It is one that may be fraught with confusion, sometimes chaos, and is a potential battleground par excellence for warring ex-spouses. There may be concomitant feelings of helplessness, rage, and despair. In order for the therapist not to get caught up in this, it is advisable to begin with finding out what took place the last time there was a visit. As in taking a sex history in sex therapy, the therapist needs to be as specific as possible in finding out how plans were arrived at and how they were executed. Notice that in this session the therapist does not get caught up in Ms. Stein's sense of helplessness, but moves to focus on the last visitation. What is unearthed is the ongoing battle between the old partners. In asking Ms. Stein how she might do it differently next time, the therapist is exploring Ms. Stein's level of investment in the battle and openness for change.

On a continuum we see some divorced bioparents who can develop a viable visitation structure on their own. Some need conjoint interventions to make this possible. At the extreme end there are some couples who are unable to give up the battle and cannot form a co-parenting coalition even in this one area.

Rem Couple Session—Mr. and Mrs. Miller

Mrs. Miller began the session by saying that the previous weekend visit with the girls was "good." She did hold back "somewhat" in her impulse to discipline the girls and plan the day. It was "hard" but she saw that Mr. Miller became more involved, especially in not letting Deirdra "boss" Liza. Mr. Miller agreed and elaborated on an incident where he, rather than Deirdra, helped Liza find her missing sneaker.

Some time was then devoted to the genogram, the history of their relationship and family of origin. The couple both agreed that they "loved" each other, and that sex was "terrific" when they had it about three times a week. They each reached orgasm and their grins affirmed this. They are both involved and successful in their professions and supportive of each other's career aspirations. The "only" areas of conflict are the girls and Ms. Stein.

Mrs. Miller: What can we do about Karen's control of our lives? She called yesterday to say she wants Charles to start the weekend on Friday evening. What gall. She wants to go away for the weekend. Of course—she gets enough child support—$900 a month.

Therapist: It must be upsetting to think that Karen is controlling your life. But let me understand the communication between the two of you. (to Mrs. Miller) How did you find out what Karen wanted?

Mrs. Miller: The usual way. Charles speaks to her on the phone and then immediately comes in and tells me what she wants.

Therapist: Tell me exactly what happened this time.

Mr. Miller: That's not hard. I told her just what she said, "Karen wants to go away for the weekend and wants us to pick up the girls on Friday."

Therapist: And then what happened?

Mr. Miller: Marlene got upset! I told her she was getting carried away and then she said something about my protecting Karen. A mess— not atypical though.

Therapist: I know—a fairly common interaction in Rem families. (Again reinforcing that this situation is not unique.)

Mrs. Miller: Really?

Therapist: Really.

Mr. Miller: And I thought we were unique.

Therapist: (to Mr. Miller) What was your reaction when Karen said this to you?

Mr. Miller: I'm not sure, but I don't like the way she orders me around. I have plans for the weekend too.

Therapist: But you didn't say this to Marlene. You only gave her Karen's request.

Mr. Miller: Right. What are you driving at?

Therapist: (to Mrs. Miller) Did you ask Charles what he thought about Karen's plans?

Mrs. Miller: (quizzically) No—I just react.

Therapist: Could it be that you express the feelings for your husband?

Mr. Miller: She is certainly more emotional.

Therapist: (to Mr. Miller) In this situation you had an emotional reaction but chose not to express it, and Marlene didn't ask about what you feel and think, but instead reacted.

Mrs. Miller: Are you suggesting that when Charles gives me one of Karen's messages I should first ask what he thinks?

Therapist: Well, I wonder if that would help?

Mrs. Miller: I think it may be worth trying. That way I could get a clearer picture of your (to Charles) reaction first, before jumping in.

Therapist: (encouraging interaction between the two of them to detriangulate from Ms. Stein) Do the two of you sit down together and talk about when it would be best for each of you to have the girls? (encouraging individuation) What you *each* may like?

Mr. Miller: We don't. We talk about doing that but haven't done it yet. I know Marlene prefers it when the girls are not here so I avoid the subject.

Therapist: The work of therapy is checking out the perceptions we have of our mate. Charles, could you check out with Marlene if it is true that she prefers it when the girls are not around? (He does and she responds.)

Mrs. Miller: I do prefer it when it is just the two of us. (Sarcastically) Have you forgotten we are newlyweds?

Mr. Miller: (to Therapist) See, I told you she doesn't want them around.

Therapist: I didn't hear her say that.

Mrs. Miller: I didn't say that. I prefer it when it is just you and me, but I'm not ready to write off the girls. I have a hard time with Deirdra, but I really enjoy Liza.

Therapist: (to Mr. Miller) Could you begin to believe her?

Mr. Miller: Food for thought.

Discussion

At this point the therapist has a better sense of how this couple functions, the projections they resonate from, how conflicts are instigated and dealt with, and the system changes needed for improved functioning. The extent to which the original couple has not succeeded in becoming emotionally divorced is becoming clearer.

Mrs. Miller mentioned that she is in analysis and has been for three years. She and her analyst have discussed her involvement in the Rem therapy and both feel positive about it.

The Rem suprasystem is fertile ground for creating triangles with the former spouse. This is done here by scapegoating Ms. Stein. The Rem couple can then experience closeness and are able to avoid confronting one another and dealing with their own relationship and the possible threat of discontent there. This defense breaks down when one of the partners, usually the remarried spouse, goes over and joins with, or is perceived as joining with, the ex-spouse. At this point the odd person out in the triangle is the new spouse, who then reacts by becoming aggressive or withdrawn, or by triangulating in someone else, often a child. This snowballing interaction needs to be stopped.

In this session the therapist affirms the partners' feeling of being victimized by Ms. Stein, but does not encourage them to maintain this focus. The refocusing takes place when the communication that led to the triangulating is reviewed with them and Mr. Miller is encouraged to speak for himself, rather than for his ex-wife. In this way, Mr. Miller is directed by the therapist to express his own point of view and interact with his present wife, and Mrs. Miller is directed to interact with him in the here and now of the session, rather than focusing on the ex-spouse.

It is important that the therapist not buy into the couple's no-win position and go along with a focus on the complaints about the "other." A balance is to be found between affirming their feelings and remaining mindful of the need to refocus. On a continuum, some couples can be refocused after their feelings are affirmed, while others may need several affirmations before they are ready to move on. Some are unable to be moved from this position, and couples treatment may have to be terminated. Once the triangulating is stopped in a session, then, as we can see in the process with the Millers, the couple issues are available to work on. In this instance, it may well be that their receptivity to the work is heightened by the fact that Mrs. Miller has been in analysis for three years.

Meeting with Teachers

The close proximity of the office to the school made a school visit easily possible. The girls were aware of the therapist's plan to meet with their teachers.

Deirdra's teacher mentioned she called Ms. Stein after Deirdra discussed with her the title for the diary she is compiling in class. She wanted to title it, "The Vampire in Me," but when her teacher recoiled and said that wasn't a good title, she changed it to "Old Before My Time." The teacher was sensitive enough to admit that she was frightened by Deirdra's anger and did not handle the situation well. This title and the teacher's description of Deirdra in school corroborated the therapist's thinking that Deirdra had too much responsibility placed on her. Deirdra's feelings about the loss of the student teacher were also discussed. Deirdra's school work was generally on a superior level.

All the teachers had noticed the girls, especially Deirdra's "overconcern" with Liza, and the squabbling between them. Liza's teacher noticed an improvement in her spirits in the past two weeks. The meeting with the teachers reaffirms the diagnostic thinking that Deirdra is the parentified child and is angry about being in that position.

Reports from their pediatrician were negative for pathology and showed normal developmental milestones.

EVALUATION DISCUSSION

This concludes the evaluation phase of treatment. While evaluation proceeded, treatment had begun. All relevant members of the Rem suprasystem had been seen together and the subsystems had been seen separately. School contact had been made and reports from pediatricians received. At this point we are able to conceptualize the process and dynamics more fully using the system-cycle-psyche frame of reference discussed in the beginning of the chapter. Since we are using an artificial paradigm to explain an integrated, continually changing entity, there will inevitably be some apparent redundancy as we discuss the Rem suprasystem from the perspectives of systems, cycles, and psyche.

System Frame

Rem suprasystem

By having Deirdra parent, the bioparents abdicate the system's need for them to function as a parental pair even though they are no longer a marital pair. In this way they can avoid each other. Mr. Miller can limit his contact with his children and everyone avoids addressing the reality of the breakup of the nuclear family and the mourning experience. Thus, on an affective level the old nuclear family continues to exist and the Rem family is prevented from consolidating. The suprasystem is on the verge of developing severe malfunction because Deirdra, the key to the system's uneasy homeostasis, is beginning to develop symptoms because the system is not fulfilling her life-cycle needs.

Subsystem level

1) Bioparent subsystem. By having Deirdra parent, the bioparents can abdicate their need to function as a parental pair. In this way they avoid each other and the reminder of the reality of the breakup of their marriage and can avoid mourning. Thus affectively the first marriage and nuclear family still exists. Each parent sees the other as impossible to negotiate with. Ms. Stein sees Mr. Miller as the disinterested parent who has all the power. Mr. Miller sees Ms. Stein as the controlling parent who has all the power. By seeing his ex-wife in this way he can rationalize to himself and others his limited involvement with his children. When Ms. Stein and Mr. Miller discuss visitation they are hostile to each other, which serves as a defense against their positive feelings.

The children are angry at both parents. They complain to Ms. Stein about their father. Her response, which is protective of him, fails to affirm their feelings and leaves them no choice but to bicker and fight with each other.

2) Rem couple. Initially, with Deirdra as the parentified child, and Ms. Stein scapegoated as the wicked ex-spouse, romantic short-term bonding could continue relatively unimpeded. Thus the Rem couple did not have to deal with parenting issues and their differences and conflicts about this. By remaining in the short-term bonding stage the couple was protected from the inevitable disillusionment built into the transition to long-term bonding. Mr. Miller was able to be involved with both women and not take a stand with either one. However, at this time the couple is less invested in Deirdra being the parentified child. Mr. Miller feels torn by his need to satisfy his daughters, his wife, and his ex-wife and thus fails to take a stand. His wife does take a stand with the girls. He criticizes her stand rather than give support or take over himself. Thus, Mrs. Miller has taken on the parenting responsibilities and is beginning to feel, act and be seen as the wicked stepmother. By seeing his wife as a wicked stepmother, Mr. Miller can blame his noninvolvement with his children on her. By seeing his children less he attempts to continue his romantic bonding.

3) Rem subsystem. At this point the Rem family has not moved towards consolidation. Mr. Miller's abdication of his parenting responsibility in his household and Mrs. Miller's assumption of parenting functions make her the target of the girls' displaced anger at him. Even if the element of displacement was not operative, we would expect the children to be angry and upset with the new Rem partner.

4) Single-parent subsystem. Ms. Stein does not experience the full impact of the loss of her parental partner because Deirdra becomes her surrogate parental partner.

5) Sibling subsystem. Deirdra parents Liza and Liza's need to be parented feeds Deirdra. Thus both girls, in appearing self-sufficient unto themselves, do not have to experience the loss of their parental unit and the nuclear family. The sibling bickering is a displacement of their anger and aggression towards their parents and preserves the needed connection to both parents. If either parent could have listened to the children's feelings, we can speculate that this would not have happened.

Cycle Frame

Rem suprasystem

From the life-cycle task framework we see that all members of the Rem suprasystem are denying the loss of the old nuclear family and, therefore, are unable to accept the existence of the new configurations (Rem couple, Rem family, and single-parent family) and are thwarted in their ongoing developmental processes and performance of life-cycle tasks. The suprasystem is ready to develop severe malfunction, as it is failing to provide sufficient flexibility to provide an appropriate matrix in which life-cycle "living out" can progress.

Subsystem level

1) Old marital subsystem. Ms. Stein and Mr. Miller, though legally divorced, are not emotionally divorced. They have not been able to function as a parental pair and neither has been able to make mature emotional investments in a new partner. Their anger and fighting are the superficial bond; the children are the vehicle for its expression. They have not been able to see or deal with their continued positive feelings for each other. Mr. Miller can't accept his responsibilities to his ex-wife or children.

2) Rem couple life cycle. Mr. and Mrs. Miller initially were in the romantic bonding phase and now Mrs. Miller has taken on the parenting. This is not good-enough parenting to meet the children's needs. Mr. and Mrs. Miller have not confronted their marital issues, e.g., power struggles, projective identifications, and have not been able to move on to the next phase of their marital cycle—plans to have or not have a mutual child.

3) Rem family life cycle. The Rem family subsystem has not consolidated. Mrs. Miller's premature parenting of the children puts her in the wicked stepmother position and thus the girls' anger at their father is displaced onto her. Roles of adults and children among the four are not clear.

4) Single-parent family life cycle. In the single-parent household, Ms. Stein is allowing and encouraging Deirdra to perform age-inappropriate parenting tasks with Liza. Ms. Stein takes on a pseudo-martyr role when she attempts to have Mr. Miller spend more time with his children. However, her way of doing this is designed more to precipitate a fight between them than to resolve the visitation issue. She keeps an efficient system functioning by parentifying Deirdra. In the process she sacrifices some of her capacity to give warmth to her daughters. The children are reacting to this now and are asking for more of her.

5) Sibling life cycle. Both children are given more responsibility than is age-appropriate and are therefore unable to perform their individual age-appropriate life-cycle tasks of developing peer relationships and having fun (industry vs. inferiority).

6) Individual life cycle. Ms. Stein has developed her own career since the divorce. She maintains friendships and does date occasionally, although she has not formed a new attachment. In her old marital life cycle she is legally but not emotionally divorced. In her family life cycle a co-parenting arrangement has not been made. She avoids contact with Mr. Miller, delegates too much of her parental role to Deirdra.

Mr. Miller in his individual life cycle is doing well professionally. In his old marital life cycle he is legally but not emotionally divorced. In the old family life cycle he is skirting his parental responsibilities. A co-parenting arrangement has not been made and he is remiss in child support payments and has progressively shortened visitation. In his new marital life cycle he remains in the short-term bonding period. In his new family life cycle he is not parenting his girls well enough qualitatively and quantitatively. It seems that the issue of the mutual child has not been addressed.

Mrs. Miller in her individual life cycle is functioning well professionally and is working on her individuation from her family of origin in her own analysis. In her marital life cycle she is enjoying her romantic bonding. In her family life cycle she is prematurely and unfortunately called upon to parent two young girls before having had the experience of developing and mastering parenting skills with her own children. It seems the issue of having her own child is on the back burner—or is it?

Deirdra is functioning well academically but is not developing peer relationships. In her family life cycle her assigned role of older child/older sister has been changed to that of parentified child. She is angry and depressed.

Liza is functioning well academically but is not developing age-appropriate socialization skills because neither parent is available to parent well enough for her to be the baby in the family and her age-ap-

propriate self. In her family life cycle her task to be the younger child/
younger sister is being short-circuited.

Intrapsychic Frame

Our purpose in using an intrapsychic frame is to have enough information about each person's ego structure, anxiety level, defenses, and
adaptations to make constructive system interventions.

Ms. Stein

Ms. Stein was an only child in a stable, well-to-do Jewish family. Her
father is an attorney and mother a homemaker and active participant in
charitable organizations. She describes her mother as the more dominant force in the family and somewhat intrusive in her life during her
adolescence, although not pathologically so. Ms. Stein's good intellect
was encouraged by both parents, particularly her father who hoped she
would consider law as her profession. Parental introjects indicate a com-
petency in work, friendships, and home management and an intellectual
response to emotions. Anxiety is experienced in the face of feeling helpless, out of control and victimized, and is defended against by the reaction of aggressive attempts to restructure the world around her according to her concept of right and wrong. Displacement and denial are also
defenses used. Ego structure is more flexible; despite an initial rigid presentation, resistance can be worked through and new behavior tried.

Ms. Stein's positive feelings for both girls are evident, as well as her
desire to become a better parent for her own ego gratification and their
well-being. Ms. Stein is attractive and takes pride in her appearance.

Mr. Miller

Mr. Miller also comes from a stable, wealthy Jewish family. His
father was also an attorney and his mother was the dominant one in the
family. He has an older brother and younger sister (see genogram in
Figure 6.1). Introjects, particularly paternal introjects, are harsh and
hard driving. Anxiety is experienced when his autonomy is thwarted;
passive-aggressive provocation, rationalization, and withdrawal are the
defenses used. Despite a rigid, pompous/detached presentation, his ego
structure is flexible enough to engage in and risk new behavior. Mr.
Miller's fondness for his present wife and daughters is warmly, albeit
distantly, evident.

Mrs. Miller

Mrs. Miller comes from a stable, working-class Jewish family. She has a younger brother. Her mother suffered from numerous psychosomatic ills and she felt closer to her father. Mrs. Miller comes across as the most emotionally available of the adults. She too, like Ms. Stein, is articulate, competent, and controlling, although not as aggressive. Major defenses are reaction formation used in the same way as Ms. Stein, intellectualization, and withdrawal. It is worth noting that Mrs. Miller, Ms. Stein, and Deirdra all use reaction formation as a defensive response to Mr. Miller's passivity and indecisiveness.

Deirdra

Deirdra is an intelligent, sensitive, compliant child—one well endowed to be the surrogate for the absent parent. Like her mother and stepmother, she uses the defenses of reaction formation and displacement in the face of anxiety. Her harsh maternal and paternal introjects are evidenced in her interactions with her sister. Her anger towards her parents is projected in her class diary entitled, "The Vampire in Me" and "Old Before My Time." Deirdra, like her mother, is extroverted by nature and needs peer contacts.

Liza

Liza, like Deirdra, is an intelligent, compliant child. She has no healthy outlet for her anger and aggression except to bicker with her sister; there is evidence of a reactive depression. She, more like Mr. Miller, is an introverted child. Liza quietly falls into the role of being withdrawn. The system has been teaching her all too effectively that being a withdrawn child is the safest way for her to be rewarded. Direct assertion of her own initiative is generally stymied.

By the end of the assessment phase, the following systemic and individual goals were agreed upon.

TREATMENT GOALS

Rem Suprasystem

To begin the process of having all members accept and integrate the ongoing existence of the Rem couple and the reality that childrearing takes place in two households. Since the grandparents have not been particularly involved in the parenting, this will make the task less complicated.

Bioparent Subsystem

To develop a bioparent coalition.

Rem Family Subsystem

To have Deirdra and Mrs. Miller give up their parenting functions and have Mr. Miller take on parenting responsibilities.

Rem Couple Subsystem

At this point the Rem couple claims the relationship is fine. The only problems are with the girls and Ms. Stein. They are not ready to set a goal for their relationship.

Single-Parent Subsystem

To have Ms. Stein pick up more of the daily parenting responsibilities, which since the divorce have largely been carried by Deirdra.
To have Deirdra and Liza begin to let go of their entrenched surrogate parenting system and be children.

Sibling Subsystem

To have Deirdra and Liza begin to let go of their entrenched surrogate parenting system and be children in both households.

Individual Goals

Mr. Miller

To spend more time with his daughters and take greater parenting responsibility.

Mrs. Miller

To move out of the wicked stepmother role and not to parent in place of her husband.

Ms. Stein

To begin to work out a more viable visitation plan with her ex-husband so she will no longer have to make up for his lack of involvement with the children and will have more free time for herself.

Deirdra

To develop friendships.

Liza

To get more time with both parents.

Anticipation of Other Needs

Although these issues have not been stated as goals, the therapist is aware that the original marital partners have yet to complete their emotional divorce. The therapist anticipates that once the Rem couple no longer triangulates with Ms. Stein, they will need help in learning how to negotiate their differences.

TREATMENT PLAN

In order to achieve these goals, the family therapy modality would be primary. The single-parent subsystem is to meet one week and the Rem family subsystem the following week. Thus the girls were seen every week. On an as-needed basis, individual and couple (Rem couple, bioparents) sessions would be available. Sessions could be split in part so individuals would have some time alone with the therapist if this would appear to be indicated.

At this point a joint session with Ms. Stein and Mr. Miller was not indicated since, as early as the end phase of the evaluation, both bioparents were able to be more responsive to the girls' needs and were able to co-parent in a more workable way so that visits were planned and had more predictability. Both parents attended open school week and individually had contact with the staff at the afterschool center. Mr. Miller's child support checks came more reliably. These changes underscore that assessment *is* treatment. The dialectic process will continue, with treatment necessitating further assessment, which, in turn, will modify treatment.

CHAPTER 7

Middle and Termination Phases of Treatment

The middle phase of treatment addresses itself to the achievement of the goals set at the end of the evaluation phase. This is done on systemic, life-cycle, and individual levels. New information or changed circumstances may necessitate a modification of goals. Any changes are to be agreed upon by all concerned persons.

The therapist as organizer of the treatment process must be particularly attuned to role changes and the heightened tension within the suprasystem when any of the subsystem goals is about to be realized. At these times the system is threatened and an individual's anxiety may need to be contained in order to prevent precipitous acts that would be antithetical to the stated goals. In Rem, the undercurrent of loss, disruption, and failure creates a strong pull. During periods of transition and change, the system needs to be contained and protected as the new structure is forming.

Some families can do well with just a telephone contact. Most families need a session in which their anxieties can begin to be rechanneled or diffused. Some families need several sessions and perhaps extra time to help them move through the transition. In the following excerpted sessions we shall see that the therapist used several techniques to contain and lower the level of anxiety in the Rem suprasystem as the family members moved towards the goals they had set for themselves.

MIDDLE PHASE OF TREATMENT

Single-parent Subsystem

Despite Ms. Stein's initial anxiety, she was able rather quickly and with a minimum of resistance to move to take on more maternal tasks with Liza, so Deirdra could be free to be a 10-year-old. Occasionally she walked the girls to school and picked them up at the afterschool center. She relieved Deirdra of the duties of dressing Liza and helping her with her bath, games, and school projects. She was also able to be more nurturing to Deirdra. She took time and effort to learn how to make French braids, the newest style at the girls' school, and did this for Deirdra frequently. With the therapist's direction, she was able to meet with the group leaders at the afterschool program and elicit their help in seeing to it that they, rather than Deirdra, helped Liza prepare to go home and to move towards taking age-appropriate responsibility for herself. She also encouraged the leaders to have Deirdra stay with her group rather than leave to check on her sister. When the girls visited with their maternal grandparents, Ms. Stein was able to inform her parents about the problems in the family and also urge them not to let Deirdra take control of Liza. A sign of Ms. Stein's strength was her emerging intuitive sense of anticipating potentially difficult situations and her ability to ask the therapist for help.

The following session took place nine weeks after the first suprafamily session. In this session all family members' resistance to the system change of deparentifying Deirdra is evident.

Deirdra: I had a sleepover on Saturday and we stayed up all night.

Ms. Stein: (sarcastically) A regular social butterfly.

Therapist: I detect a note of sarcasm in your voice. (The therapist thinks to herself that Ms. Stein is uneasy with Deirdra's new peer involvement.)

Ms. Stein: She came home exhausted and cranky the next day.

Deirdra: But, Mom, you don't understand. It was so much fun.

Ms. Stein: Deirdra, I had enough with this sleepover already.

Therapist: Karen, I'd like to understand your reaction better.

Ms. Stein: I don't understand it myself. I'm glad Deirdra is having fun and is being invited to other girls' houses, but I'm just in a rotten mood.

Therapist: (to everyone) Sometimes this happens to us. We want something very much, but when we get it we are not as happy as we thought. (to Ms. Stein) What about Deirdra having dates with friends might not be so fine for you? (Note how the therapist avoids having Ms. Stein feel defensive.)

Ms. Stein: (reluctantly) Well, since the divorce she has been a great help to me and I missed her help on Sunday morning. I could not sleep late. Liza wanted me. When Deirdra has a playdate I have to make plans for Liza as well. Before it was so much easier for me because I knew the girls would be together. (angrily) After a day of work and then a few hours with the girls, I hate to have to start arranging babysitting and playdates. It gets me mad.

Therapist: (to Ms. Stein) Understandably. (notices the girls look scared) What might it be like for you, Deirdra and Liza, right now when you see your Mom angry?

Deirdra: I don't like it.

Liza: Are you angry at me?

Ms. Stein: No. I'm angry at the situation. It is hard being a single parent.

Therapist: Yes, it certainly is, and you probably miss Deirdra's help.

Deirdra: Mommy, I don't have to have dates.

Ms. Stein: No, that is not the answer. I'm glad you have friends. Remember that is why we came here.

Therapist: And something has changed for everyone since we have been working together. And as I said before, you might not like everything about the change.

Liza: I miss Deirdra too. (She starts to cry.) I'm afraid you don't love me anymore.

Deirdra: (cries too) I do love you.

Therapist: (To Deirdra) You're crying too.

Deirdra: I get sad when Liza is sad. (to Liza) I don't want to hurt you; I just want to have friends.

Liza: (Looks to her mother. Ms. Stein takes her on her lap.)

Ms. Stein: (to therapist) I didn't know it would be this complicated.

Therapist: How could you have known? You've been taken by surprise by your own reaction, and the girls' too. In some way does this relate to your own experience as a child with your parents?

Ms. Stein: I don't know. (pause) My mother always encouraged me to do things and then would be sarcastic when I reached my goal, much the same way I did with Deirdra.

Therapist: So she wasn't too encouraging of your meeting your needs.

Ms. Stein: (to therapist) I hadn't thought of it in that way, but you're probably right.

Deirdra: I could see Grandma Ruth doing that. She still does it.

Ms. Stein: (laugh—to Deirdra) You're probably right. Like mother—like daughter.

Therapist: I know that is a familiar cliché, but I don't see it that way. You have done something tonight that I don't think your mother has ever done.

Ms. Stein: (smile) What do you mean?

Therapist: You're attempting to understand what makes you anxious and causes you to respond with sarcasm.

Ms. Stein: That's true.

Therapist: And that matters to you. Change is difficult and in this family tonight we identified everyone's growing pains. Liza, your growing pain is that as Deirdra makes friends and spends time with them, you're scared your sister doesn't love you anymore or as much. Deirdra, your growing pain is that you're afraid that by doing what you want for yourself and being with friends you are hurting your mom and sister. And Ms. Stein, your older daughter is moving away from you. That, in and of itself, is usually hard but in your situation as a single parent you are losing someone who helped you out—made things easier for you. At least it appeared so on the surface.

Ms. Stein: So what do we do about this?

Therapist: We do what we have done tonight. Keep talking about it together here and keep working on it with one another. It can take time to get used to changes. As you are all feeling now—it's uncomfortable and upsetting until we have more practice and a better feel for it.

There was a stillness in the room—a mixture of sadness, relief and calm. The three all walked out quietly.

Discussion

As the system change goal of having Deirdra let go of her role as the parentified child is happening, we have the resistance to this change emerge in this session. The therapist explores the resistance and in the process gives credence to Ms. Stein's realistic overload as a full-time working mother of two girls. When working with the single-parent subsystem in a Rem suprasystem, it is crucial to affirm the wear and tear on the single parent. This is imperative in the face of the vacuum created by the systemic change of deparentifying the parentified child. Without such affirmation the vacuum is likely to be refilled by the parentified child, who hates to see her parent unhappy. Notice Deirdra's offer in this session to give up her playdates again for her mother's relief.

This session also illustrates the heightened anxiety experienced by family members who have lived through the separation, divorce, remarriage process. Ms. Stein's final question about what to do with what the therapist labeled as each one's growing pains reflects this intensity of anxiety. The therapist's response to her question serves to create a bridge and a holding environment for the subsystem which will enable them to sustain themselves through this transition as the new structure forms. Our goal is that the new subsystem formed by the bioparent coalition will eventually relieve Ms. Stein so she does not need to call on Deirdra or Deirdra doesn't need to offer her help.

Rem Family Subsystem

The mutually agreed upon goal of having Mr. Miller take a more active parenting role rather than Mrs. Miller had worked to everyone's satisfaction over a two-month period when the following resistance was reported. Mr. and Mrs. Miller came in feeling "disgusted"; the children appeared tense. Liza said she didn't want to come to the session. A similar "disaster" to the one described in the assessment session occurred when Mrs. Miller and the girls all had a different plan for Sunday afternoon, and Mr. Miller again attempted to find a "solution" that would make everyone "happy."

At this point the therapist thought that something more than the verbal dialogue of the previous sessions was needed. She felt that she and the family were ready for the emotional impact that family sculpting often produces.

Therapist: I'd like to suggest something different this evening. It's called family sculpting. Instead of using words, as we have done in the past, to describe situations and feelings, I am asking you to use actions instead. A common occurrence in your family is when Marlene, Deirdra and Liza (speaking directly to them) want Charles' attention and you, Charles, attempt to please them all.

Mrs. Miller: (somewhat anxiously) What do you have in mind?

Therapist: For Charles to stand up in the middle of the room and all three of you to try to get his attention, but remember—no words. Afterwards, we will discuss our reaction.

Mr. Miller: Sounds silly to me.

Therapist: It may be, but might you be willing to do it?

Mr. Miller: OK, but I'm not a very good actor. (He stands up.)

Therapist: (Stands up, chairs are moved back so there is more room. Mrs. Miller and the girls stand up and with the therapist's suggestion place themselves near Mr. Miller.) Again, what I would like to see is the three of you get your father's/husband's attention, and you, Charles, do what you typically do in this situation.

Sculpture: All three began to pull Mr. Miller and he offers little, if any, resistance. Deirdra pulls at one arm, Marlene the other, and Liza his sweater. Liza then assumed a sexy pose and struts in front of him, Deirdra follows suit, and then Marlene begins to massage his neck. Mr. Miller smiles faintly and attempts to move around so he can have his arms around all three. In doing this he pushes Deirdra and Marlene together and then they begin pushing each other. For a few moments Mr. Miller and Liza stand arm in arm and look happy. He then attempts to get between Marlene and Deirdra and again hug all three at the same time. All three move around, elbow the others away, and Mr. Miller contours his body until he trips and falls.

Mr. Miller: (a mixture of anger and embarrassment) I had enough of this.

Therapist: Agreed. (They go back to their seats.)

Mr. Miller: It is a silly game. You're going to tell me it shows something about us. I won't believe it.

Therapist: (Senses that Mr. Miller is angry and in the past has needed time to cool off so she decides to back off now and ask others about their reaction.) Charles, I do hear you, but let's see what each person's reaction is to what just happened.

Liza: The best part was when Deirdra and Marlene were fighting because then I got daddy all to myself.

Therapist: You certainly did for a while. Now I can understand why you might want the two of them to fight.

Liza: (smiling) Yes.

Therapist: (Notices that Mr. Miller seems calmer and is listening.)

Mrs. Miller: I could take this seriously because for me it felt the way I did on Sunday. A lot of competition. (to therapist and Charles) Did you see how seductive these two can be. I don't like competition!

Deirdra: Neither do I. I always want to be the winner and I didn't win anything—no one got anything in that game. Except Liza. (angrily) She got daddy for a while. (to Liza) I'm not fighting with Marlene just so you can have daddy all to yourself. Daddy, you could have hurt yourself.

Mr. Miller: I see that you all think this is important but I don't.

Therapist: (Aware that Mr. Miller's style is to defend his anxiety by getting into a battle.) You're not going to take this seriously at this time.

Mr. Miller: Right.

Therapist: What might stop you?

Mr. Miller: It is a game.

Mrs. Miller: Charles, you are being thick. It does bring out something about the way we relate.

Mr. Miller: I disagree. You're reading too much into it.

Therapist: (Aware of the marital dynamic: Mr. Miller's anxiety can be displaced by an argument with his wife.) Suffice to say at this time that you (to Charles) are not going to take this to heart. (Therapist carefully uses the word heart, because she feels that Mr. Miller is defending against strong feelings.)

Mr. Miller: (Eyes well up with tears.) When I did the sculpture, I realized that I really wanted to be with Liza, just Liza. (He begins to cry. Marlene puts her hand on his back and girls listen attentively.) (To Liza) You were only a baby when I left. It was a few days after your first birthday. The day I left, your mother was holding you and you waved goodbye. It was the first time I saw you wave. I didn't even know you knew how to wave. I walked out and felt sick. This is the first time I'm crying though. Liza, I really don't know you that well and I want to.

Liza: (Walks over and sits on his lap and they hug.)

Marlene & Deirdra: (Watch contentedly; a calm silence in the room.)

Therapist: (Therapist decides not to say anything specifically to Charles because that in fact would break the connection that she feels now exists. She is aware that her thought to say something to him comes from her own countertransferential fear of closeness.)

Mr. Miller: I just took a stand and now I'm afraid Marlene and Deirdra are angry at me. Are you?

Mrs. Miller: No.

Deirdra: No. (Pause, then in a joking and teasing manner.) But maybe I will be later.

Therapist: (To Mr. Miller) You get anxious when you think you have angered someone you love and perhaps this prevents you from taking a stand.

Mr. Miller: I think so.

Therapist: We will continue next time. (When they get their coats both Mrs. Miller then Deirdra spontaneously hug Mr. Miller.)

Discussion

We have found that family sculpting (Duhl, Kantor, and Duhl, 1973) is a valuable tool in working with Rem families. The emotional impact often generated by this nonverbal experience can pave the way for multilevel change. Papp (1976), who emphasizes the movement aspect of sculpting and therefore calls it choreography, makes this point:

> Most family problems become locked into linguistic traps. Families are adept at intellectual exercises that use language to deny, rationalize, accuse, defend, and cover up secret family rules. These exercises, through repetition and predictability, conceal problems into a frozen form. This form is changed by the choreography, which transcends language. It introduces the element of the unexpected, the unknown, the unpredictable. Family members seldom surprise one another by what they say, since they have heard it all before. They are surprised by what they choreograph because they haven't seen it before. Freed from words, the underlying emotional tracts on which the family runs emerge. Once these are made explicit, alternative pathways can be explored (p. 466).

In this session Mr. Miller is quite defensive/anxious about this unknown form of self-expression. However, the therapist persists and Mr. Miller is able to participate with dramatic and unexpected results.

In family choreography it is crucial for the therapist to leave enough time to debrief each of the participants. In this part of the process we see that Mr. Miller is initially very defensive and wants to deny the importance by undoing the experience, "It is a silly game. You're going to tell me it shows something about us. I won't believe it." The therapist respects his resistance and opens up the discussion to the other family members. Later, when the therapist nonjudgmentally affirms his need not to take this "to heart," Mr. Miller, much to everyone's surprise, reveals for the first time his deep feelings of loss. It is the opening up of the mourning issue that paves the way for systemic and individual goals to be attained.

This choreography had other surprises that added to the therapist's and family's understanding of their subsystem and themselves, in particular, the young girls' ability to seductively woo their father away from their stepmother and into contact with them. Mrs. Miller's reactive response in kind to this behavior is striking. This dynamic, so common in Rem, is often reported by stepparents in sessions and discounted by the bioparent and often the therapist. This discounting can invalidate the stepparent's reality. This choreography brought the action into the treatment process in a way that could not be denied.

Another surprise was Liza's powerful capacity to win her father when her stepmother and sister clashed. She saw this clearly and made no bones about thinking this was terrific!

Ms. Stein and Mr. Miller

As was mentioned at the end of Chapter 6, the improved functioning of the bioparent subsystem did not necessitate a joint session with Ms. Stein and Mr. Miller. Three months into treatment the calm was punctuated with a storm. Ms. Stein telephoned, which she had not done before, to report that the day before she did not have heat and hot water. She called Charles to ask him to pick up the girls; he refused; they argued; finally, he said he was no longer sending child support and she hung up. Ms. Stein agreed to come to a session with him the next day. The therapist telephoned Mr. Miller and he, too, was available for the session.

Therapist: (Absolutely taken aback. Ms. Stein and Mr. Miller look gorgeous. She has never seen them look so well. Ms. Stein is stylishly dressed: silk blouse, velvet suit, high sling-back heels, hair and make-up au courant. Mr. Miller, wearing what looks like a new suit and tie, is clean shaven and smells woodsy. The therapist feels embarrassed and identifies her feeling as being the third wheel around two lovers.)

Ms. Stein: You never cease to amaze me, Charlie (unconsciously using the more familiar name). I thought you turned over a new leaf and would show you care about your daughters.

Mr. Miller: I do.

Ms. Stein: I thought you did, but last night was the last straw. When I called to say we had no heat and hot water, you had to think about whether or not it was good for you to take them. What kind of a father are you?

Mr. Miller: (Defensively) Listen, Karen, you forget I work, I teach. I can't be at your beck and call.

Ms. Stein: Beck and call, you have to be kidding—just some fatherly concern when your daughters are freezing.

Mr. Miller: Well, I'm very busy.

Therapist: You really do know each other. You certainly know each other's buttons. You, Karen, criticize Charles as a father; you, Charles, in turn withdraw your support as a parent and, Karen, you criticize more and so on in a vicious cycle.

Ms. Stein: That may be true, but in the dead of winter I can't believe any father would want his children to freeze.

Mr. Miller: I think you're exaggerating. It's April and you have plenty of blankets. You can't just demand I take them on cue.

Therapist: I want to describe again what happens. Karen, you attack Charles as a father and, Charles, you withdraw your support and so on and so on as the anger mounts.

(This goes on for about another ten minutes and the therapist repeats the same intervention twice more. The therapist feels that her interventions are being heard and the cycle might be loosening. The arguing is not getting out of hand.)

Ms. Stein: You give so little it amazes me.

Mr. Miller: What do you mean? I give you so much money that you can go away on weekend trips.

Ms. Stein: Wait a minute! I work and earn a damn good salary.

Mr. Miller: OK. I'm sorry.

Therapist: (Eager to fan the spark of this moment.) You broke the vicious cycle. Karen, when you were attacked when Charles said he gives you money for your weekends away, you didn't say something critical back. And, Charles, you apologized.

Mr. Miller: Please repeat that.

Therapist: (Repeats her last intervention.)

Ms. Stein & Mr. Miller: (Thoughtful silence. For the first time there is a calm in the room.)

Mr. Miller: (To therapist) Are you suggesting we bury the hatchet?

Therapist: Might you?

Mr. Miller: Well this fighting is getting ridiculous already.

Ms. Stein: It is so damn familiar.

Mr. Miller: And we've been divorced five years.

Therapist: There is a difference between a legal divorce and an emotional divorce. The way you know each other's sore spots and use this knowledge to attack each other is evidence that there is not enough of an emotional divorce.

Mr. Miller: Karen, I'll bury my hatchet if you bury yours.

Ms. Stein: Sounds like a good idea. You bury the hatchet first.

Mr. Miller: You should bury yours first; you're the one with the acerbic tongue.

Ms. Stein: But I have custody of the girls.

Therapist: (Somewhat amused by their battle at this point) Folks, it doesn't work that way. It is up to each of you to decide if you are ready to bury your *own* hatchet.

Ms. Stein: (To therapist) You mean I have to decide whether or not I want to respond nastily to Charles for the rest of my life regardless of what he does?

Therapist: Might that be worth considering?

Ms. Stein: Maybe.

Therapist: I suggest that you both might want to think about what your own individual investment is in maintaining the battle and what your life would be like if you gave it up.

Mr. Miller: Are you suggesting that my battle with Karen is preventing me from doing more important things in my other life?

Therapist: Perhaps this is true for both of you.

(Brief silence. During this time the therapist thinks to herself that if this couple had had some good marital counseling, they may have made it together. She wonders and thinks that quite possibly Ms. Stein and Mr. Miller are thinking the same thing. She is not sure how, or at all, to respond to the moment and opts to do nothing at all.)* Let's end with that question.

Within two weeks of this session, Ms. Stein reported in a family session, when 20 minutes were set aside for her to be seen individually, that she was making gains in controlling her sarcasm to Charles. She concluded, "I'm surprised how naturally the barbs at him come to me." In the same time frame Mr. Miller reported in a couple session that, "At long last I have given my secretary the responsibility of sending the child support check out on the first of the month." When Mrs. Miller's response was elicited, she agreed, "The other way was ridiculous and besides I'm not as angry at Karen anymore now that I don't fall into Charles' traps." Charles spontaneously commented, "I haven't been setting them." Mrs. Miller reminded him of a time just yesterday that he did and he responded, "Give me a break, I'm just learning."

Discussion

In the context of the treatment process, this crisis was precipitated by the restructuring of the Rem suprasystem. Ms. Stein and Mr. Miller were beginning to develop a quite viable co-parenting structure, in contrast to their previous cut-off laissez-faire arrangement. This was made possible because the Rem couple subsystem had made gains in detriangulating from Ms. Stein and they were beginning to confront the differences between them that had not been available to them heretofore. The impact of this on Ms. Stein was the actual loss of the old attachment to Mr. Miller. His reaction was to be particularly vulnerable to her need to pull him back, given the emerging closeness with his new wife. When a vacuum such as this is created in the Rem suprasystem by the treat-

---

*It is interesting to note that in a Rem couple's group, this point has been initiated by couples and addressed.

ment interventions, we can anticipate enormous anxiety and a crisis to attempt to restore the old equilibrium in the system. The task of the therapist at this time is to help the family use the crisis as an opportunity for greater differentiation in the system and individuation of the self. In this instance, the therapist felt that in order to facilitate this shift, a session with the original marital partners was needed. By making herself available to them she created a bridge/holding environment so that the transition could be made.

It is interesting that at this juncture the therapist experiences Ms. Stein and Mr. Miller as a marital pair rather than a parental pair, a view substantiated by their seductive appearance and erotic chemistry. The old (still alive) marital bond is addressed by the therapist reflecting (several times) their well tuned interaction and fanning with all her might the first shift in their mutual process. The possibility of differentiation is brought up by Mr. Miller and considered by Ms. Stein, but then is used by each of them to embark on another battle. Their collusion is high. The therapist highlights the old marital life-cycle task to them: "It is up to each of you to decide if you are ready to bury your *own* hatchet." She tests their readiness to change by raising the question: "What is your own individual investment in maintaining the battle and what would your life be like if you gave it up?"

This much progress in one meeting is unusual. On a continuum this couple's availability to begin their emotional divorce is high. At the other extreme we have couples who can never bury the hatchet regardless of therapeutic interventions. In the middle, where most couples are, we have couples who need treatment to get to this point. Unworkable are those remarriages where the new spouse(s) gets in on the act and cannot tolerate the burial of the hatchet.

A follow-up to a meeting of this significance is essential. As mentioned, both Ms. Stein and Mr. Miller are able to begin their emotional divorce by taking very specific actions. Ms. Stein restrains herself from expressing her hostility; Mr. Miller controls his provocativeness and gives his secretary the responsibility of sending the child support check on the first of every month. Mrs. Miller supports this. A new structure in the system has developed. The therapist affirms these new actions that solidified the structure.

The therapist's particular skillfulness in this session needs to be elaborated. She remained neutral and nonjudgmental and allowed herself to be reminded again that there may not be a divorce in the unconscious. Peck (1974) would go so far as to say that there is *no* divorce in the unconscious. He uses the term "divorce ambivalence" (p. 221) to describe the "schizogenic experience of feeling still married to the same person from whom the divorce is obtained." Therapists who take superego positions with divorced partners—that they should not still be attached, especially erotically, that they should not be fighting with one another, etc.—run the risk of not being able to help the partners make the needed transition to an emotional divorce.

Over the course of treatment the therapist had learned that Ms. Stein and Mr. Miller dated each other for two years prior to the marriage. After two years of marriage Deirdra was born and their relationship became problematic. Ms. Stein was home taking care of Deirdra and Mr. Miller was building his career and away from home often. Both felt overburdened and alone. Ms. Stein's harsh criticism of her husband was responded to with increasing withdrawal and despondency. Both felt that the birth of another child, initiated by Ms. Stein, would help the marriage. After the birth of Liza things went from bad to worse. Ms. Stein initiated the divorce and Mr. Miller admitted that, though he himself was not ready to initiate such an action, he was willing to go along with her decision. They separated and a year later were divorced.

Home Visit: Single-parent Subsystem

Two months after the joint session with Ms. Stein and Mr. Miller, Ms. Stein called fifteen minutes before the session to say that she anticipated being at least 20 minutes late. She ordered Chinese food for dinner and the restaurant's prompt delivery still had not arrived. She called the restaurant and the food was on the way. She wondered, since the therapist's office was near her home, if she would be willing to join them for dinner and have the session at their home. The therapist thought for a brief moment and mentioned that she had just had dinner so she would not be able to eat again, but she would be over. Her willingness was based on her positive feelings about Ms. Stein's ability to move from an initial resistant, withholding position to a flexible and more giving response to her daughters. She saw Ms. Stein's request as being in the spirit of her newfound creative parenting. A few weeks prior, the issue of a home visit had been initiated by Liza, who wanted the therapist to see her new doll house. Liza also let it be known that she was tired by 7 P.M. and didn't like leaving the house. Ms. Stein and Deirdra had enthusiastically seconded Liza's idea.

The therapist arrived at the same time as the Chinese food. This gave the girls a chance to show the therapist their room and toys while Ms. Stein set the table. The girls shared a good-sized room, which was relatively neat, but not overly so. Some toys were clearly Deirdra's—board games, a recorder; some were clearly Liza's—doll house, lego sets; other toys were community property—art materials, clay. The girls were not shy and in a warm spirited way competed to get the therapist's attention by showing her their prize possessions.

Liza had recently requested and received a doll house from her mother for her birthday. Her play with it is indicative of her greater relatedness to herself, family, teachers, peers, people in general. In the living room of the doll house she happily pointed out the daddy doll and his younger daughter on his lap. One mother was in the kitchen, the other in the garden, and the sister was with the other children, but in view of the living room window.

Deirdra played the recorder. Her enjoyment and intensity were equally balanced.

Dinner conversation consisted of the girls' reporting the events of the day, first Deirdra, then Liza. Both revealed some minor complaints about school, but in general they had a good day at school and the after-school center. Deirdra's prior criticism of her classmates was noticeably absent. The therapist did not feel excluded, and in response to her question they all agreed that this was a typical dinner talk. When the therapist asked if Ms. Stein also spoke about her day, they all agreed that she usually did not. Ms. Stein asked the girls if they wanted to hear (an example of her greater relatedness), and they did. She spoke about her work on a particular marketing campaign and the girls, especially Deirdra, asked very intelligent questions. Deirdra suggested that from now on, "Mommy should be included in the news of the day." Increased evidence of Deirdra's sense of humor was emerging.

After dinner Ms. Stein wanted to show the therapist around and the girls had a chance to watch their favorite television show. This was a genuine treat since they had missed it since they began therapy.

As expected, the apartment was tastefully decorated. The therapist was surprised, however, to see a third bedroom which was the television room. The therapist wondered to herself why each girl did not have her own room. She opted not to comment about it, but instead stored this information.

Ms. Stein pointed out several photographs.

Ms. Stein: This was taken in Hawaii.
Therapist: What a magnificant sunset.
Ms. Stein: Look at this one. (A primitive South Sea village)
Therapist: I like it.
Ms. Stein: (Warmly) Charles took them.
Therapist: (Struck by the warmth expressed.)
Ms. Stein: (In the same warm tone she proceeds to talk about their trip

to Hawaii and their early romantic bonding. She looks up at the photo.) Gosh, he is a talent. I used to love to watch him take pictures and work at his drawing board. (Defensively) Too bad he's crazy.

Therapist: There are things about him that you miss.

Ms. Stein: Is that normal?

Therapist: Of course.

Ms. Stein: I don't want to be married to him, but I do miss the things I liked about him and the good times. (Silence) (Anxiously) This frightens me. (Silence) I'm afraid I will want him back. But I don't want him back! I just miss his . . . his devotion to his work and sharing that with him.

Therapist: Makes sense to me.

Ms. Stein: (Takes down a photo album that she had hidden in the closet. She shows the therapist the album that contains many pictures of her and Charles and Deirdra and some that include Liza.) I'm probably not so angry if I can look at these. Do you think the girls would like to see them?

Therapist: Are you ready to show them?

Ms. Stein: I think so, but I'm not sure. I would like to. They should get a chance to see their baby pictures. They have seen many, but there are many they haven't seen. (Smiling at a picture of Liza at age four months.) But what will they think? Maybe that I miss their father. I could say I do miss the things I liked about him. I think I can handle it. I want to show them.

The session ends with the therapist saying goodbye to the girls. All three walk her to the door. Ms. Stein asks the girls if they want to see more photos of when they were babies. They happily agree.

The therapist left feeling warm about the session and closer to all three. Ms. Stein was more at ease and the girls were more like children on their own turf. All were gracious and generous to each other and to the therapist. She felt invited into their world.

Discussion

Home visits with Rem have always proven to be significant both for diagnostic and treatment purposes. The home itself is an excellent indicator of where family members are in their mourning of the "old" and their integration of the Rem into their present lives. The therapist sees how much of the "old" has been preserved, how much of the "new" (if any) has been integrated, and if there is a blend of the old and new in the home. Bloch (1973) demonstrated that the home visit can be a tour through time and space; the external space mirrors the internal space. With the therapist as a guide, the tour of the past as evidenced in the home can facilitate the reactivation of memories.

On this home visit, we see that Ms. Stein has kept her former husband's photographs of Hawaii on the wall of her new apartment. The therapist's comments about them reactivated Ms. Stein's positive feelings and memories about her ex-husband. This enabled the therapist to validate them and reinforce that the feelings do not necessarily have to lead to an action. For example, Ms. Stein can miss him and still not want to be married to him. In doing this, the therapist paved the way for Ms. Stein to experience the sadness that is part of any emotional divorce. The therapist felt that if the home visit had not been made, this material probably would not have emerged. Ms. Stein is then able to broach the loss of the nuclear family by "taking out of the closet" the old family album and sharing it with the therapist and then with the children.

Significant also in this home visit is Liza's doll house configuration, where the younger daughter doll and the father doll are together in the living room, and the sister doll is outside, but in view. The therapist interprets this to herself to reflect the continuing strength of Liza's need for and attachment to her sister. Interestingly, from this scene it appears that Liza's affective attachments are to father and sister. Mother and stepmother are on the scene but out of view—mother is in the kitchen and stepmother is in the garden.

The therapist inadvertently had not asked about the sleeping arrangements and living space, and she was surprised to see the third bedroom in the home and that Deirdra and Liza still shared a room. She felt that with Deirdra's increasing individuation, combined with her mother's greater acceptance of it, the third bedroom would become an issue. The therapist decided not to mention it, since she felt it would be premature at this point. Also, it is bad manners to go to visit somebody's house and start re-allocating rooms!

Rem Couple

Four months into treatment, both Mr. and Mrs. Miller had made gains in avoiding setting themselves into triangles with Ms. Stein. Thus their pseudomutuality, supported by scapegoating the "evil" ex-spouse, was weakened. Difficulty in resolving their newly surfacing conflicts was more evident and a couple session was scheduled.

Mr. Miller: (To Mrs. Miller) Karen called me at the office today. We have the girls next weekend. It's a three-day weekend and she wanted to know if I would keep the girls an extra day. I thought about it and I like the idea, especially since they will be in Florida for the following two weeks.

Mrs. Miller: There is no satisfying that woman.

Mr. Miller: Let's not get sidetracked. *I* want the girls for the extra day.

Mrs. Miller: I don't. I have exams to mark. I'm expecting my period. I'm tired.

Mr. Miller: (annoyed) OK. Let's just forget it.

Mrs. Miller: (annoyed too) Fine with me.

Therapist: (to Mr. Miller) I wonder if you are really ready to foget it. (To Mrs. Miller) And if it really is fine with you.

Mr. Miller: (to therapist) Of course I don't want to forget it, but once Marlene makes up her mind, it is set. There is no getting through to her.

Therapist: So your anger might come from your anticipation that you will not be heard.

Mr. Miller: Correct.

Therapist: (to Mrs. Miller) And what picture do you have of your husband that gets you angry.

Mrs. Miller: I see him sulking in front of the TV because he didn't get his way.

Therapist: So as soon as you begin to negotiate together, these pictures come up and you're both stymied.

Mr. and Mrs. Miller: (Shake their heads in agreement.)

Therapist: Granted, sometimes you do sulk, Charles, and sometimes you, Marlene, come across as inflexible, but who from your past may you be reacting to as well?

Mrs. Miller: My dad. To this day, he's the world's worst sulker.

Mr. Miller: (to Mrs. Miller) I've seen him in action; he's worse than I've ever been.

Therapist: (to Mr. Miller) What about you? Who are you bringing with you when you have to negotiate for yourself?

Mr. Miller: (silence) I suppose my dad. He ruled the house with an iron hand. Now he tries to rule the nursing home that way too.

Therapist: Anyone else?

Mr. Miller: (silence) Oh! Karen, of course!

Mrs. Miller: (to therapist) It's one thing to be seen as your spouse's parent, but to be mistaken for his ex-wife is too much! (to Mr. Miller angrily) How many times have I told you that I'm not Karen? Try me!

Mr. Miller: (Moved back in his chair, looks somewhat shaken.)

Therapist: (to Mr. Miller) Might you want to tell Marlene your reaction to what she just said and how she said it?

Mr. Miller: (to Mrs. Miller) Believe it or not, your tone of voice turns me off.

Therapist: How might it make you feel?

Mr. Miller: (hesitant) A little scared. Your words say one thing but your tone is far from inviting.

Mrs. Miller: I can't believe I scare you.

Mr. Miller: It may not be macho but you do.

Therapist: (to Mrs. Miller) Why might it be hard for you to believe that just before you might have scared your husband?

Mrs. Miller: I'm not sure, but I think of myself as a gentle person, sometimes even a pushover, not someone who is agressive.

Therapist: (to Mr. Miller) What is your reaction to what Marlene just said?

Mr. Miller: (to Mrs. Miller) Believe it or not, I see you as all three.

Mrs. Miller: This is certainly new to me.

Therapist: We've gotten to some of what makes it hard for you to negotiate with each other. Charles, you anticipate that Marlene will be as inflexible as your father and Karen and you get frightened by her aggression. Marlene, you anticipate Charles will not be able to negotiate and instead will sulk as your father did. Also, you are unaware that your tone of voice may frighten Charles.

Mrs. Miller: (to therapist) So where do we go from here?

Mr. Miller: Listen, I want the girls to stay over an extra day.

Mrs. Miller: But I have to mark papers.

Mr. Miller: If you can't be with us, then I'll do something with the girls.

Mrs. Miller: How about if we all go out to dinner on Sunday night?

Mr. Miller: Fine. (silence) Are you sure you want to do this?

Mrs. Miller: I wouldn't have come up with the idea, but I can be flexible.

Next Rem couple session

The Tuesday after that weekend. Mr. and Mrs. Miller were seen together; the children had already left for Florida.

Mr. Miller: (to Mrs. Miller) I am so angry at you, I'd like to wring your neck.

Mrs. Miller: I noticed you got a little distant on Monday evening.

Mr. Miller: In my first marriage I would have swallowed my anger and rationalized a way so as not to confront the issue. But I want this marriage to work and you really pissed me off.

Mrs. Miller: (anxiously) What are you talking about?

Mr. Miller: I couldn't believe that you asked me for $7.35 out of my own money to cover the cost of the junk food and nibbles we bought to have in the house for the girls. I say I want to be a family. You say you want to be a family. You say you want to become pregnant. But an incident like this makes me wonder about our marriage!

Mrs. Miller: I think you're making too big a deal of this.

Mr. Miller: This is important to me. I love you.

Mrs. Miller: (flustered—at a loss for words.)

Therapist: (to Mrs. Miller) What's happening to you right now?

Mrs. Miller: I'm surprised. I never saw Charles so angry and so clear about what bothered him. It scares me. (silence) I know he's right and I'm not one to apologize.

Therapist: Really?

Mrs. Miller: It's the closeness. This is something I've been talking about with my analyst. It makes me uncomfortable.

Mr. Miller: But you're the one who is always rapping about getting closer.

Mrs. Miller: Don't take my words so seriously.

Therapist: What might it be about closeness that makes it uncomfortable for you?

Mrs. Miller: I'm afraid I might love Charles more than I do now and then I may lose him.

Therapist: How might you lose him?

Mrs. Miller: I don't know. He'll die, find someone else, be more interested in his career and daughters.

Therapist: And what would you do?

Mrs. Miller: There is nothing I could do.

Therapist: Really?

Mrs. Miller: Really.

Mr. Miller: You mean to say you wouldn't fight for me?

Mrs. Miller: (gulps) I never thought of that. You know I don't like competition.

Mr. Miller: That's right, you never like to keep score when we play cards.

Therapist: To what extent was there competition in your home?

Mrs. Miller: There was no competition. I'm my father's favorite. He preferred my company over my mother's. He still does.

Therapist: No wonder you don't like to compete. You have no experience competing.

Mrs. Miller: Neither does Charles.

Mr. Miller: I was my mother's favorite. I always knew she cared more about me than my dad or brothers.

Therapist: So your experience with competition in your family of origin is the same. It is something that neither one of you has much experience with.

Mr. and Mrs. Miller: (Shake heads in agreement.)

Therapist: Well, there is nothing like your Rem family now to help you learn and master this.

Mrs. Miller: For someone who doesn't like competition I surely jumped in over my head by marrying a man with two adorable daughters and an ex-wife.

Therapist: (Shakes her head.)

Mr. Miller: (Smirking expression on his face.)

Mrs. Miller: (to Mr. Miller) What's so funny?

Mr. Miller: Nothing.

Mrs. Miller: Come on Charles, I know you, come clean.

Mr. Miller: (Hesitantly) I kind of like it having three women competing for me.

Mrs. Miller: I know you do. Sometimes I think too much. If we have a child it has to be a boy.

Mr. Miller: Another girl—the idea doesn't sound so bad after all.

Therapist: (Enjoying the playfulness not evidenced before.)

Mrs. Miller: All kidding aside. When the four of us are together why don't you come over and make me feel special?

Mr. Miller: (Somewhat critically) Do you really mean this?

Mrs. Miller: Well - yes. Kiss me, give me a hug. Refer to me as your "wife" rather than by my name.

Mr. Miller: That would be hard. I'm not one to compete either.

Therapist: As I said before, there is nothing as fine as a Rem family to help you learn this.

Mr. Miller: (Half-joking, half sarcastic) Gosh, thanks a lot.

Mrs. Miller: Ditto for me.

Therapist: (Thinks what a wonderful way to express their ambivalence about the possibility of change/closeness.)

Discussion

Four months into treatment Mr. and Mrs. Miller had made gains in avoiding triangles with Ms. Stein. Ms. Stein had begun to experience her mourning reaction to the loss of Mr. Miller and was thus more separate and even less reactive to him. Given these dynamics, we can anticipate the Rem couple's difficulty with one another beginning to surface. This is a vulnerable time for the Rem couple and their suprasystem. For the Rem couple the short-term bonding begins to pale; individual idealizations begin to crumble. The old pathways for coping with anxiety—

scapegoating of a child, triangulating with an ex-spouse on an unconscious level—may feel like the lesser of two evils. Again, we see that a
vacuum has been created in the Rem suprasystem, and the therapist offers a couple session for the purpose of creating an interim holding
structure that will contain their immediate anxiety and prevent the regression while the structure is being developed.

The process of sorting out the projected identifications (Zinner, 1976)
with parental and ex-spouse figures does much to allay their anxiety
and facilitates the beginning of the negotiation of differences. For Mr.
and Mrs. Miller healthy self-assertion and competition are difficult,
since neither had a good-enough experience in the families of origin of being accepted for himself or herself, including his or her competitive
strivings. The information that they individually shared about being
the favored love object of their parent of the opposite sex leads us to this
hypothesis.

We can see that Mr. Miller's fear of another marital failure, i.e., "In
my first marriage I would have swallowed my answer . . . ," motivates
him to deliberately respond differently, and his wife's individual treatment, i.e., "It's the closeness. This is something I've been talking about
with my analyst," bodes well for the success of these therapeutic interventions.

TERMINATION PHASE

By the end of five months of treatment, improved functioning in all
parts of the Rem family suprasystem was noted. The goals that had
been agreed upon during the assessment phase had been reached in
varying degrees and the new structures had begun to be consolidated.
Contact with the school indicated that Deirdra was getting along with
her peers and occasionally (great success) had to be reprimanded for being "too silly." Liza's mood swings were fewer and not as marked.
Rather than being thought of by her teachers as "unhappy," she was
now seen as a somewhat introverted child who was becoming more responsive.

Termination of treatment coincided with the end of the school year
and summer vacations; the children would be in a sleep-away camp for
three weeks, followed by vacations away with their mother and then
father and stepmother.

The month of June focused on terminating and termination issues.

Follow-up sessions with the Rem family and the single-parent family
were planned for the fall to assess the ongoing consolidation of the sys-

temic, life-cycle, and intrapsychic changes. The prognosis was seen as good.

Single-parent Subsystem

The two sessions prior to this session dealt with Deirdra's resistance to giving up her role as surrogate mother to Liza. This was evidenced by her criticism of her mother's care of Liza and her regression to checking up on Liza at school. Deirdra was able to relate this to missing her role as the caretaker, the "important" person, and "just missing being with my sister." Liza acknowledged this feeling as well and was able to elaborate on it in her own words. Deirdra's ability to work through separation-individuation issues with her sister (family as well) was evidenced in this first termination session.

Deirdra: I've been thinking about this; I want my own room. When my friends come over I want some privacy. All my friends have their own room. Mom, could I move into the television room tonight?

Ms. Stein: (Angrily but with a touch of delight) There is never a dull minute with you. I have to think about this idea.

Liza: (Starts to cry.)

Ms. Stein: What's wrong?

Liza: I don't want Deirdra to be in another room. (To Deirdra) I promise I won't bother you and your friends ever again.

Deirdra: Liza, this doesn't mean I don't love you. I just want my own room.

Liza: Please don't leave me.

Therapist: (to Liza) You're not ready to have her move to another room yet.

Liza: Yes. We're not together so much anymore during the day so at night I like her close by.

Ms. Stein: Well, it certainly will not happen tonight. I have to get used to this idea and my first reaction is no!

Deirdra: Why not?

Ms. Stein: The television room is a family room; we sometimes eat there; guests occasionally stay over.

Deirdra: But Gail has her own room.

Ms. Stein: Don't compare yourself to Gail. You have a big room now with plenty of space.

Deirdra: But I'm getting older and I need privacy.

Ms. Stein: (to therapist) She sounds like a teenager. I can't handle this.

Therapist: What might make you think you can't handle this?

Ms. Stein: She took me by surprise and I don't like surprises and I feel she is pressuring me and I can't think then.

Therapist: Do you think you could tell Deirdra that? (Ms. Stein does.)

Deirdra: But this is important to me.

Therapist: How so?

Deirdra: Like I said, all my friends have their own room. I'm growing up and you get new things when you grow up. Mommy, do you remember after Liza was toilet trained she got a bed. Well this is the same thing.

Ms. Stein: I can't give you an answer tonight.

Deirdra: When could you?

Ms. Stein: I don't know yet.

Deirdra: Darn! (Kicks her feet, folds her arms.)

Ms. Stein: You're angry, but I'm sorry I have to think about this. And your pressuring me won't help. It only gets me angry at you.

Deirdra: (gruffly) OK.

Therapist: (to Deirdra) I hear that this is important to you. You wanted an answer tonight and you didn't get what you hoped for and you are angry. Do you think you can live with this feeling inside of you for a while without trying to convince your mother?

Deirdra: Maybe for two days!

Therapist: : (to Ms. Stein) What do you think of that?

Ms. Stein: (to Deirdra) Please do it. I think you could.

Deirdra: (smiles) OK. But will you think about it?

Ms. Stein: Yes.

Therapist: (to Liza) Liza, you too have a lot of feelings about this.

Liza: Yea, I'm worried it will happen.

Therapist: And your mom is not ready to come up with an answer yet, so it's hard not knowing what will be.

Liza: Well, I'm going to pray to God for Him to keep things the way they are.

Therapist: (Impressed with her solution.)

Ms. Stein: That sounds like a good idea.

Therapist: (Suggests an individual session to Ms. Stein since she experienced her as confused, perhaps blocked on the issue of Deirdra's growing individuation and resignation from the mother-surrogate assignment. Ms. Stein agrees.)

Discussion

On a systemic level this session highlights Deirdra's increasing separation and differentiation from her mother and sister and her old role of the parentified child. Both Ms. Stein and Liza respond with anxiety to her move. Ms. Stein and Deirdra's battle about Deirdra's getting her own room was kept from escalating. The therapist intervened by acknowledging the importance of this to Deirdra, accepting her anger, and suggesting an intermediary step where Deirdra would stop pursuing the issue "a while." A time limit on controlling her frustration was a possibility that was in Deirdra's grasp. Ms. Stein, too, was glad to halt the escalation. She did so by promising to think about the issue rather than keep it a closed case.

Here again we see the therapist creating a holding environment at the turning point of another level of differentiation in the subsystem. Liza's anxiety is expressed directly in the session—a far cry from the withdrawn, inarticulate child who needed others to speak and emote for her in the earliest contacts. She is now able to mourn and have her feelings accepted in the subsystem.

From the individual life-cycle framework we can see that Deirdra has resumed her developmental processes, reflecting that her needs are now being met well enough. Her wish for privacy and a room of her own is age-appropriate.

The therapist, in order to facilitate this further differentiation, offers Ms. Stein an individual session for the purpose of containing her anxiety and exploring its dynamic roots.

Ms. Stein

Ms. Stein began the session right away.

Ms. Stein: Deirdra really threw me when she asked about having her own room. I didn't expect that. At least not so soon. I don't like the idea.

Therapist: Tell me more.

Ms. Stein: What's to say. It's the television area, den, guest room all in one. I grew up in a big house and we had lots of space. I have to settle for this room serving all three purposes. I'm not ready to give it up. Deirdra should not want this so soon.

Therapist: It seems you may have had a different time frame.

Ms. Stein: I think so—maybe two, three years later. She is growing up too fast. And little Liza—would you believe she had her first sleepover last week. It gave Deirdra and me a chance to be together and that was fun.

Therapist: That's good to hear. The girls are growing up.

Ms. Stein: Why don't I want to hear that?

Therapist: Any ideas?

Ms. Stein: As much as I complain about the responsibility, I like being so important to them. I'm not ready to give that up.

Therapist: Deirdra certainly challenges you.

Ms. Stein: She always did. She walked, talked, even was toilet-trained before I expected it. I noticed that she is just starting to develop breasts at ten and a half!

Therapist: (nods)

Ms. Stein: I feel funny saying this, but when she mentioned wanting privacy I thought of her masturbating. Makes me uncomfortable to think of her as sexual.

Therapist: How so?

Ms. Stein: I think of my sex life or lack of it. If one daughter wants privacy and another has a sleepover, it's time for me to have a man. I'm less involved with Charles. He has remarried and I think I would like to also.

Therapist: When you think about wanting to find a partner, might the guest room have special significance as a way to negotiate your sex life with the girls around?

Ms. Stein: It had been in the past, but now it's not that important. I have more time away from the girls. I want a relationship and someone I would care about; he would have to be sensitive to my kids. We would have to work out together the time and place for our sex life. A father without custody sure has it easier!

Therapist: We've been talking about losses: your girls' growing up, Deirdra's loss of innocence, your emotional divorce—and our relationship will end until we meet for the follow-up meeting in the fall.

Ms. Stein: That's a lot of losses, and I'm not ready to lose one more thing. The room stays as is for now. I need the summer to think about it.

Therapist: That sounds true to you.

Ms. Stein: It is. Liza will be glad. Deirdra won't, but I'm the mother and I'm not ready.

Therapist: And I would think that Deirdra and Liza are not so fixed in what they say they want.

Ms. Stein: Ambivalent, right?

Therapist: Probably.

Ms. Stein: (warmly) Whenever I hear that word or am aware that I feel two ways about something I'll think of you.

Therapist: Thank you.

Ms. Stein: (In tears) I'll miss you. I can't believe I'm crying. (Pause) And you're teary too. This whole therapy thing never ceases to amaze me.

Therapist: Amaze you?

Ms. Stein: Yes. I cry, you cry. Deirdra has friends. I get my check on time. The girls see their father more often and I'm talking about wanting another husband.

Therapist: The "I cry, you cry" choked you up.

Ms. Stein: That's the hardest to talk about. Don't make me. (Silence. Ms. Stein notices clock.) Saved by the bell. (Both hug.)

Discussion

In this session we see the parallel process of Ms. Stein expressing her readiness to continue her own life-cycle needs, another reflection of her emotional divorce, and the subsequent resumption of her own developmental processes. She says she is ready to find herself a man.

In this session we also find out that Liza had her first sleepover. This is further indication that she too has resumed her own individual life-cycle tasks and her mother is ready to allow it.

Final Session—Single-parent Subsystem

Ms. Stein and the girls had done some shopping for camp prior to the session and the girls began by expressing their excitement about their new purchases and asking their mother questions they already knew the answer to about camp. Quite atypically no one brought up an issue for discussion. The therapist, aware of their anxiety about termination, began after a short silence.

Therapist: In the past month we've had someone mention the number of sessions left, but tonight so far no one has.

Liza: (to her mother) How many more sessions?

Ms. Stein: Liza, I think you know it's our last meeting.

Liza: (in caricature imitates crying) Boo, booo.

Ms. Stein: You're being silly.

Deirdra: It's not like we'll never see you again. We'll see you in September.

Ms. Stein: That's right.

Therapist: I have a sneaking suspicion that it might be hard for everyone to say goodbye.

Liza: (jokingly) Goodbye.

Deirdra: Goodbye. (Humorously walks to door, waves and returns to her seat.)

Therapist: Why might it be easier to make a joke of this?

Ms. Stein: Well, I don't want to cry again about missing you.

Deirdra: (surprised) You cried in your session!

Ms. Stein: Well, I did. Therapy is very important to me. She (nodding toward therapist) helped me understand you girls better—and myself.

Deirdra: I know and I decided I'm going to be a family therapist when I grow up. I know a lot about it already. Make sure each person talks for himself, have people talk to each other, go to the home. I could go on.

Therapist: (Amused, delighted and thinking she'll probably make a good family therapist at that.) I know you could, but instead, could you tell me how you might want me to feel about you wanting to be a family therapist.

Deirdra: Oh happy.

Therapist: How so?

Deirdra: I'm happier now. I might get my own room and I have friends and I know my mommy and daddy love me and my sister.

Therapist: Sounds good.

Ms. Stein: It is good. What about you, Liza?

Liza: What?

Ms. Stein: Do you want to say how things are better for you now that we have been in therapy.

Liza: Do I have to?

Ms. Stein: Try.

Liza: I like spending more time with you and with daddy, but I don't like it when Deirdra is not home when I want someone to play with.

Therapist: So not all the changes make you feel happy.

Liza: Right.

Deirdra: I thought that after therapy I wouldn't feel sad that my parents are divorced. (starting to cry) But I still do.

Therapist: (Remembers the first session and thinks we've come full circle.)

Ms. Stein: Come here. (Motions for Deirdra to come sit on her lap.)

Deirdra: (Sits on her mother's lap and cries) (To Liza) Why aren't you crying?

Liza: I don't have tears in my eyes.

Deirdra: (to Ms. Stein) Mommy, why isn't she crying?

Ms. Stein: She might not feel the way you do.

Liza: That's it.

Deirdra: (to Ms. Stein) Will I always cry about this?

Ms. Stein: I hope not but I don't know.

Therapist: What do you think?

Deirdra: Will, I don't cry about it every time I think about it but today I did.

Therapist: Any idea why today it made you cry?

Deirdra: Saying goodbye I think.

Therapist: That could do it. This is a pain that you live with all the time, but at certain times you feel the pain a lot, sometimes just a little, sometimes not at all. But the pain will always be there.

Deirdra: Like my warts. The doctor said I have a virus for warts under my skin and sometimes the warts come out but the virus is always there. That sounds the same to me.

Ms. Stein: Good comparison.

Therapist: (Noticing Ms. Stein looks sad) What about you, Karen, might you have a pain inside you that relates to what Deirdra is talking about?

Ms. Stein: I do. When I got married and had children I thought it would last—the family would last. (to Deirdra and Liza) My parents are still together and I feel terrible that I couldn't give this to you.

Deirdra: Mommy, don't feel sad.

Ms. Stein: If there is one thing I learned here, it is that you should be allowed to feel what you feel. So Deirdra don't try to make me feel better. You feel sad about having divorced parents and I feel sad about being a divorced parent. I have warts, too, you know.

Deirdra: (Looks relieved.)

Therapist: I see we only have a few minutes left, and I want to make sure I have my turn to say that I am very happy to have had a chance to get to know all of you better.

Ms. Stein, Deirdra and Liza: (all smiles)

Liza: Will you miss us?

Deirdra: (to Liza) She said she would.

Liza: She did not.

Therapist: (Aware of interaction between the girls, but decides to pick up with Liza) (to Liza) Might you want me to miss you?

Liza: (sheepishly) I think so.

Therapist: Liza, help me understand what missing means to you?

Liza: I don't know. Well, you think about the person—the thought just comes into your mind when you don't even expect it. Like when you're eating lunch or coloring.

Therapist: And what feelings go with the thought?

Liza: Sad. (silence) But maybe a little happy because yesterday I thought of grandma and good times. (to therapist) So could you think about me?

Therapist: I think that will happen to me too. Just when I least expect it, I'll find myself thinking of you, and I'll feel good.

Liza: (Smiles, shyly turns head)

Deirdra: (also sheepishly) Me too?

Therapist: Of course, I'll miss you.

Ms. Stein: I know I had strong feelings about you, but the girls' feelings I didn't know were so strong. But that's the way therapy has been. I found out they have a lot of feelings about a lot of things. Me too.

All: (Spontaneous hugs and "see you.")

Discussion

Termination can be a reminder of previous losses and often sets off a return to the functioning that was evident at the start of therapy. Particularly in Rem we see the resurgence of the sorrow for the loss of the original, nuclear family. It is important that the therapist not minimize this reality. In this session we see that the therapist not only affirms the sorrow of the parent and child, but also acknowledges it as a reality that will be a part of their lives forever.

Rem Family Subsystem

Mr. Miller: Last weekend was not a good weekend. I got into an argument with Marlene. Deirdra and Liza were not getting along. (to Liza and Deirdra) At one point I thought of sending you home. (to therapist) And, I am happy to say, I don't have an ounce of guilt about admitting it.

Therapist: (Thinks to herself—certainly a more human father than the man who played marathon Monopoly.)

Mrs. Miller: Not good—it was terrible. I know it is none of my business —it's between Charles and Liza—but when she is so contrary with him it bothers me and I attacked both of them.

Liza: That's when I thought of calling my mommy and going home.

Therapist: Tonight is our last meeting until we have a follow-up meeting in September to see how things are going. But as we've discussed in the past few weeks, the family all said they were ready to end therapy.

Mr. Miller: Well, now I'm wondering if we should end.

Mrs. Miller: Me too.

Deirdra: We could meet two more times. Then I'm going to camp.

Therapist: We planned for this to be our last session. Now I hear second thoughts. What could this mean?

Mrs. Miller: We're not ready to end yet.

(Prolonged silence.)

Therapist: Let's see if we could understand the silence by finding out what you may have been thinking or feeling at that time.

(All report responses that had them thinking about something outside the session, e.g., Mr. Miller was thinking about work. The therapist reflects this back to them and wonders out loud.)

Therapist: What can we make of this?

Mrs. Miller: Maybe we don't want to talk about ending.

Therapist: Might that be true for you?

Mrs. Miller: Maybe I don't like to say goodbye—who does?

Therapist: Why might this goodbye be especially hard?

Mrs. Miller: I'm worried that things will fall apart again, but not really, because last weekend was the exception when it used to be the rule. Facing doing this on my own is scary. You have listened to me. I really felt understood and it's hard to consider giving that up. (to Charles) I was obnoxious on Sunday. I'm sorry. (to Liza) I'm sorry I lost my temper and yelled.

Mr. Miller: (to Mrs. Miller) I was in a rotten mood and I did make matters worse. I'm ready to try it without therapy. Of course, I was never big on this to begin with, but I'm satisfied with my life. I feel closer to all of you.

Therapist: Might "all of you" include me as well?

Mr. Miller: Well I was referring to my wife and daughters. But I like you.

Therapist: (Smiles.)

Deirdra: Daddy, remember how you didn't want to do the sculpture?

Mr. Miller: Yes, that was a memorable time because it helped me get closer to Liza.

Deirdra: Yes—now I have to share you more.

Mr. Miller: That's true. Before I couldn't shut you up when you insisted on all my attention. Now, let's put Sunday aside, I usually can.

Mrs. Miller: (to Deirdra) But now that your father is with Liza more, you and I have become friends. We spend time together and sometimes we have fun.

Deirdra: Like when you taught me how to do needlepoint?

Mrs. Miller: Yes. And I said I'll teach you to embroider as well.

Deirdra: Do you know how to knit?

Mrs. Miller: Sure. Do you want to learn?

Deirdra: (All smiles—looks to Liza who smiles back.)

Therapist: (Thinks here it comes—the issue of the mutual child).

Mrs. Miller: What's this all about?

Deirdra: Liza, you say.

Liza: No, you're older.

Deirdra: If you have a baby, I'll learn to knit.

Liza: Are you going to have a baby?

Mrs. Miller: I'm not pregnant.

Mr. Miller: We're talking about it.

Girls: (Giggle)

Therapist: It seems that everyone has been thinking about this. What could we make of this?

Deirdra: I want a sister or brother. I could babysit.

Liza: Me too.

Mr. Miller: Let's not get so excited. It takes a long time for a baby to come.

Therapist: I think that talking about the possibility of a baby in the family says something about how you all feel about each other.

Mrs. Miller: Things are not perfect but I feel we'll make it.

Mr. Miller: I want to. We will.

Deirdra: (to Mr. Miller) I don't think about you and mommy getting together any more.

Mr. Miller: You got it. I'm married to Marlene.

Liza: Daddy, I know that.

Discussion

As is often the case in termination, the family regressed to the level of their presenting behavior over the weekend and arrived at the final session ready to battle each other and convince the therapist not to let them go. The therapist assessed that their weekend behavior was reactive to the termination.

From the life-cycle framework we see that the Rem family has begun to consolidate. The wish for a "baby" is evidence of their readiness to resume their family developmental processes; a good-enough mourning has taken place. In some families there can be a pseudo-consolidation and flight into a wish for or actual pregnancy to avoid mourning.

Rem Couple

At what was to be the last session with Mr. and Mrs. Miller, the couple opted for four more joint sessions to look more closely at the mutual child issue that came to life in the final family sessions.

Mrs. Miller used the girls' enthusiasm, her recent 38th birthday, and articles on childbirth later in life to champion her cause. Mr. Miller experienced this "hard sell" as a demand and characteristically withdrew and expressed only the negative side of her ambivalence. In response, Mrs. Miller shared only the positive side of her ambivalence and a power struggle ensued. In the couple sessions the therapist spelled out this dynamic and explored the family of origin projections. Mr. Miller was seeing his wife as his controlling mother and Mrs. Miller was seeing her husband as her withholding father. Once the dynamics were discussed the couple was able to explore both sides of their own ambivalence and resolve the issue of the mutual child. The latter part of the fourth session follows:

Mr. Miller: (To Mrs. Miller) I didn't tell you this but on Sunday when I saw you writing to the girls I was so happy.

Mrs. Miller: Really, it was no big deal.

Mr. Miller: Come on, listen to me. It made me feel I won't have to choose between my daughters and my wife. And believe me for a divorced father that's important.

Mrs. Miller: I'm glad it made you happy. I feel that we are becoming a family. (to therapist) I never told you this but I always felt like I had an ally in you and I needed that. Being the new member is a lonely position.

Therapist: I'm glad I was able to help you feel less alone.

Mr. Miller: Without this therapy, which I might add I was rather dubious about, I don't think I'd be willing to consider a child of our own. But I think this is going to work.

Mrs. Miller: What are you saying?

Mr. Miller: I'm willing to go along with your desire to have a baby. I'm willing to for you.

Mrs. Miller: But I know your feelings about babies—sharing me, 3 A.M. feedings, private school tuition, etc.

Mr. Miller: That has not changed, but what has changed is my feelings for you.

Mrs. Miller: Are you serious?

Therapist: I'm wondering why it's hard for you to accept what he's offering.

Mrs. Miller: So much closeness, it embarrasses me (begins to cry).

Mr. Miller: (Goes over and takes her in his arms.)

Mrs. Miller: (Half crying—half laughing) This means I can throw away my diaphragm.

Mr. Miller: I would say so.

Discussion

In this final session we see that the consolidation of the Rem couple and Rem family has indeed taken place. Mrs. Miller's spontaneous gesture of writing to the girls at camp is welcomed by Mr. Miller. He can enjoy the relief of not anticipating that he will have to choose between his wife and daughters. The feelings of well-being generated by the consolidation provide the impetus for the couple to explore the next marital life cycle task: the resolution of the mutual child issue.

FOLLOW-UP

Three Months After Termination

There was a follow-up meeting after the summer with Ms. Stein, Deirdra and Liza and a meeting with Mr. and Mrs. Miller and Deirdra and Liza.

The gains of treatment had been sustained and additional sessions were not requested by the family, nor did the therapist think they were indicated.

Both girls did well in camp activities, relating well with both peers and counselors. Deirdra happily announced that over the summer her mother moved her things into the den and now it's her room. Liza, with a mixture of stoicism and humorous acceptance, added that she was "expecting this" and thinks, "I'll live."

At the later stage of treatment with Ms. Stein, especially in the individual sessions, the therapist suggested that Ms. Stein might want to consider some more individual work. Ms. Stein was clear that that didn't really interest her, but she would consider it if she felt something was preventing her from becoming remarried. Over the summer Ms. Stein began dating a man she knew casually at work. He was divorced and had a thirteen-year-old son who lived with his ex-wife. By September they had an "exclusive" relationship and Ms. Stein felt hopeful and was "in love." All five had been together a number of times and, despite some rough times where all three children competed for attention and Deirdra began bossing Liza, it was working out well.

Mr. and Mrs. Miller and the girls were satisfied with how things were going. Mrs. Miller was upset that she didn't get pregnant immediately, but was trying to find comfort in her gynecologist's advice "Relax, have a lot of sex, and see me in six months."

Twelve Months After Termination

Mr. and Mrs. Miller reapplied for treatment with infertility the presenting problem. The pressure of the time clock, the ordeal of charts and schedules, and the intimidations and humiliations of modern medical fertility procedures exacerbated marital discord.

The couple were seen for eight sessions and were able to put an outer limit on when they would stop trying to conceive. Mr. Miller suggested that if it was not possible for them to have their own child, he would consider adoption. Four months later Mrs. Miller called to say she was pregnant and happy.

Ms. Stein continued her relationship with the divorced man mentioned in the three-month follow-up. The girls continued to do well. Deirdra excelled academically now more than ever. She was selected to attend a public school for gifted children.

Several months later Ms. Stein contacted the therapist to let her know that she planned to be married in three months and she and her fiance had found a large apartment with a room for each child. She said that she had considered coming to see the therapist a number of times when things got rough, but was able to work things out without her. In her words, "Somehow just the thought that I could call you relaxed me enough to find an answer."

TERMINATION EVALUATION

This section recapitulates the systems-life cycles-psyche themes, summarizing, in an organized way, how each level has been considered and affected by the treatment process.

Systemic Frame

Rem suprasystem

All the members of the suprasystem, including biograndparents and stepgrandparents, show evidence of acceptance and integration of the Rem family. The stepgrandparents remember the girls' birthdays and the couple's anniversary. Mr. Miller's parents want to know if they can expect another grandchild. Mr. Miller's sister, who has a close relationship with Ms. Stein, has also developed a friendship with Mrs. Miller. Some friendships from Mr. Miller's previous marriage have continued; others have elected to be friendly with Ms. Stein, a few with both.

Bioparent subsystem

Ms. Stein and Mr. Miller have developed a bioparent coalition as evidenced by the development of the following new structures: operational visitation plans, predictable child support payments, and school involvement of both parents. There is now, more often than not, open communication between the parents about their children.

Rem subsystem

Mr. Miller has taken on much more of the parenting relationship. This has enabled Mrs. Miller to develop a separate relationship with both girls.

Rem couple subsystem

During the middle stage of treatment the Rem couple moved from experiencing the girls as their only problem to acknowledging difficulties between themselves. This recognition motivated them to work on their relationship and greater well being is evident.

Single-parent subsystem

Ms. Stein is better able to parent both Deirdra and Liza; both girls are now able to be children again, and to individuate at a more appropriate pace. Home life is a generally relaxed, cooperative system with mother in charge. Ms. Stein shares more of her life and experiences with her daughters. Preparation for her remarriage is being pursued.

Sibling subsystem

The girls now have available parental figures in their parents and are freer to be children in both households.

Life-cycle Frame

Rem suprasystem

The Rem suprasystem has been able to mourn the loss of the old nuclear family and has begun to accept and integrate the new configurations: Rem family, single-parent family, and a new set of stepgrandparents.

Old marital life cycle

Ms. Stein and Mr. Miller have made gains in becoming emotionally divorced. Both have been able to move on to form gratifying new attachments.

Old nuclear family life cycle

As a result of the emotional divorce, Ms. Stein and Mr. Miller are better able to function as a parental pair. A channel has been opened for all members to give affective expression to their feelings about the loss of the nuclear family.

Rem couple life cycle

Mr. and Mrs. Miller have confronted their marital difficulties and have begun to work through a resolution of them. The issue of the mutual child has been resolved insofar as conscious desire to have a child is concerned.

Rem family life cycle

The Rem family consolidation is progressing well. Mr. Miller has begun to take on the primary parenting responsibilities; this has enabled Mrs. Miller to develop separate relationships with each child. The girls' loyalty conflicts have diminished greatly.

Single-parent family life cycle

Ms. Stein has taken on some of the parenting tasks that were inappropriately assigned to the two girls. This freed them to be children again. Ms. Stein went on to develop a new attachment and the single-parent family is on its way to become a Rem family.

Individual life cycle

Ms. Stein has progressed in her career too. She has formed a new attachment and is planning to remarry. In her old marital life cycle she has made gains in becoming emotionally divorced. In the old family life cycle a viable co-parenting arrangement has been made with her ex-husband. She is now better able to parent the girls. She is planning to remarry shortly.

Mr. Miller began to do even better professionally. In his old marital life cycle he has made gains in becoming emotionally divorced and in accepting an appropriate relationship with his former wife. In the old family life cycle he was able to form a co-parenting coalition with his first wife. In his new marital life cycle he deepened his relationship with his wife which led to the decision to have a mutual child. He is pleased by the pregnancy. In his Rem family life cycle he is parenting his daughters and looking forward to his child with Mrs. Miller.

Mrs. Miller continues to function well professionally and has begun to terminate her analysis. In her marital life cycle she has deepened her commitment to her husband. In her family life cycle she has done much to move out of the position of the wicked stepmother, and has developed good relationships with each of the girls. She has resolved the issue of a mutual child and was pregnant at time of last contact.

Deirdra is functioning better in school in both academic and socialization skills. In both families she is now being a child. Sibling relations are more fun. At her own pace (and somewhat faster at first than her mother could accept) she is moving towards further age-appropriate individuation.

Liza is also doing much better in school in both academic and socialization skills. In both families she is now being an age-appropriate child. Sibling relations have been painful at the points of Deirdra's greater separation, but all parental figures have stepped in to fill the vacuum. A more appropriate sibling relationship has emerged.

Psyche Frame

Our psyche frame helped us to make appropriate system interventions. Clearly the systemic interventions led to needs being met well enough so that the developmental processes were resumed and behavioral changes were made. To what extent this led to intrapsychic change is not known, except by deduction from observable changes in behavior.

Ms. Stein had the resources to fight and struggle, largely in a positive way, to make her divorce and mothering a viable situation. Therapy helped her to change her intrapsychic dynamics enough so that she could accept divorce, share parenting with her ex-spouse, and free herself to embark on a new love relationship. She has less of a need to repress and isolate her affect and to strike out aggressively and control others. In its place there is a better sense of well-being. With her defenses softened she has been able to be vulnerable enough to form another love relationship and to consider remarriage.

Mr. Miller is less fearful to ask for what he wants or to fail to take a position out of fear he will not be loved. These changes are indicative of significant intrapsychic changes. His defenses of withdrawal and projection are less utilized. Mr. Miller married two intelligent, mildly compulsive women who are too ready to take over control when he fails to assert his position. He is beginning to take a stand and Marlene is more ready to accept and value his assertiveness.

Mrs. Miller has grown in her recognition of her own value as a person and a woman. This has helped her to be at ease with the children too. Her husband's desire to have a child with her has given her the assurance of Charles's love. Her need to fill the vacuum made by her husband's passivity is less operative.

Deirdra's changes are dramatic. Her school work is excellent. She is no longer the parentified child. Without rebelling she has requested and insisted on room to grow (if you will forgive the pun). She is now moving on a healthy emotional growth line. Oedipal resolution seems to have worked out well. She is able to accept and utilize well what she gets from both households, as does Liza.

Liza's reactive depression is gone. Her school work is going well. She now expresses her feelings more openly as well as in her play (placing the sister doll where she is outside but visible). She no longer uses childish ploys to get her emotional necessities. Rage towards mother and father, with fear of desertion, are no longer present. She has sufficient security and self-respect to have ongoing peer relationships—and need no longer cling to Deirdra. She did well at camp in a new peer environment. Her oedipal issues are out in the open without a need for subterfuge.

Mother's remarriage may stir up some insecurities but both girls are better prepared to deal with this situation than they were with their parent's separation, divorce and father's remarriage.

Any of these five persons, given sufficient stress may fall back on outmoded adaptations. But the threshold for doing so is likely to be much higher. The bed of the stream has been changed; the river is likely to flow in a different direction henceforth.

SUMMARY

The Stein-Miller case, presented extensively in these two chapters, illustrates our model utilizing direct treatment with subsystems as well as the suprasystem. It illustrates our conceptualization of the need to understand families on family systems, life-cycle, and intrapsychic levels: the system-cycle-psyche frame.

On a continuum the Stein-Miller case is a highly successful treatment example as far as the attainment of the original goals for all three levels. On the other end of the continuum are Rem families who are never able to consolidate because the Rem suprasystem denies the existence of the Rem family and the loss of the nuclear family. In these cases growth is arrested on all three levels. In the middle—and most of the families we have treated would be placed here—are Rem suprasystems and subsystems that are in more conflict about Rem family consolidation and the acceptance of the loss of the nuclear family than is evidenced in the Stein-Miller case. For some families, treatment would need to span a longer time to achieve the goals of this case. Other families can achieve a decreased intensity and frequency of dysfunctional behavior but cannot reach the degree of resolution we see in the Stein-Miller outcome.

The successful outcome of this case can be attributed to: the available ego strengths of all family members, the seeking of treatment before entropy set in, the excellent resources of school and afterschool center, the skill of the therapist and the supervisory and team support available to her, and an agency hospitable to Rem treatment. We chose this case since it illustrates a wide variety of Rem issues and the treatment of them. Throughout the remaining chapters, specific modalities and techniques will be used as we discuss particular subsystems and special problems that surface in Rem.

CHAPTER 8

Marital Therapy with the Remarried Couple

In Chapter 4, using the marital contract and marital typologies as a frame of reference, we outlined an approach to understand the myriad complaints that couples present. In this section we begin to look at the actual therapeutic work with couples in light of the special issues of Rem.

Many Rem couples seek treatment because of marital dysfunction, but more often these couples seek treatment because of the children. Our approach to assessment is to initially include as many members as possible of the Rem family suprasystem who impinge on the couple and the Rem family subsystems. We then work down from the family suprasystem to the subsystems. As assessment proceeds, we determine the most likely combinations of people to work with to effect the agreed upon goals (see Chapter 6). Eventually, we may or may not work with the Rem couple alone. Usually, when the child is descapegoated, or the most pressing needs of the child are being met, we do find it is important for the Rem couple to focus on their own relationship.

COMMON COMPLAINTS PRESENTED BY REM COUPLES

Those Rem couples who are aware that they are a dysfunctional pair are likely to have complaints caused by a lack of intimacy (often expressed as poor communication), power or control problems, and inclusion-exclusion conflicts. These are not dissimilar to problems experienced by any marital pair. We shall focus here on those areas we have found to be the most commonly associated with Rem.

Children and Stepchildren

Just as in first marriages, couples may focus their attention on the behavioral problems of a child and deny the marital conflict. At the same time, the child's behavior can unify spouses around an issue and help them keep their family functioning at the price of having a symptomatic child. Wynne et al. (1958) have pointedly described how married couples often display this type of scapegoating and pseudomutuality. In Rem, pseudomutuality and scapegoating of children can be impelled by an intense fear of another marital failure on everyone's part. The following case example illustrates this with particular poignancy:

> The remarried couple, the Shynes, brought Mr. Shyne's son Peter, age 10, to the clinic because of numerous complaints about the boy's slowness, laziness, selfishness, lying, disrespectfulness, etc. Peter was an average student. He was not a behavior problem in school, but was pseudomature and related more successfully to his parent's friends than his own. Peter's father was the custodial parent because his mother wanted to pursue her career. On weekends he saw his biomother and had a peer-like relationship with her and her sophisticated friends.
>
> At home, Peter was extremely slow and resistant to doing household chores and his homework. This precipitated both his father's and stepmother's criticism and lectures about his future if he didn't shape up. Peter would become angry to the point of tears; then there would be a huge outpouring of emotion from all parties, apologies, and a temporary smoothing over of the situation.
>
> Assessment suggested to us that the problem lay within the marital Rem subsystem but the couple would have none of it. They felt very threatened and redoubled their scapegoating of Peter. The family was seen conjointly for a period of a year, and while the child's peer relations improved, as did his behavior at home, Mr. and Mrs. S, as a united front, continued to pressure, criticize, and discount any gains Peter made. Peter accepted the role of scapegoat and the identified patient and collaborated in hiding the poor relationship his stepmother and father shared. The therapist was unable to break down the pseudomutuality of the couple since the family colluded as a strong force to maintain it. All three family members avoided discussing verboten topics and secrets, such as the fact that Mr. S had another marriage prior to that with Peter's mother and that he had a grown son by this marriage. Therapy ended through mutual agreement with minimal gains.

The couple reapplied about six months later around a "crisis" when Peter's biomother verbally attacked him for not visiting her more frequently now that he was more involved with his peer group. Peter complained, "She never asks me what I want to do; I just have to go along with her and her friends."

Perhaps because they were not the focus this time around, the Shynes had their guards down and were much more open with the therapist about the disastrous turn their marriage had been taking. Concurrently they were much more tolerant of Peter's foibles, which had decreased in frequency. However open they were, they refused the offer of marital work, so help was given to Peter and his biomother around their issues.

Mr. S called again about one year later when Mrs. S was about to leave him. At this point he requested couple help in the hope that she would reconsider. However, she refused since she had "made up my mind." Mr. S then projected all his depression onto Peter and became excessively concerned about how the boy would react to the loss. Peter and his father were seen around the restructuring of their household. In the course of this work Mr. S revealed the intense marital discord that he had covered over for years. He related this partly to his need to make this marriage work "no matter what" after two other failures."

Due to the rigidity of this family and its ability to close the therapist out during the first course of family treatment, it was not possible to penetrate the pseudomutuality and address the couple issues. It is appropriate to question our judgment about having continued treatment on the Rem couple's terms with Peter colluding. In retrospect we felt we had little choice in this instance, although some staff members felt that in this case more dramatic techniques may have been effective. Initially, treatment ended with a slight reduction of tension, with the therapist being seen as a resource to whom the family returned several times. When the couple reapplied and revealed their marital difficulties, they still refused couple work, probably because of fear of what would happen if they were to really confront one another and a defensively determined shared fantasy that "time would heal." The therapist at this time verbally acknowledged the partners' problems but made a conscious decision not to push them too hard for marital work but to "leave the door open" should they wish to return. This was because of the therapist's sense that they needed to control therapy and that too much pushing would force the couple to retreat and to intensify scapegoating the child. Although the couple never did avail themselves of the offer of marital work, they did continue to call upon the therapist from time to time as Peter grew into adolescence.

Complaints About Spouse's Parenting

Couples will often seek help with complaints about the parenting style of one another. By the time treatment is sought, the couple (and children) usually have experienced hard times that have left them feeling unloved, frustrated or worse. Stereotypically, the bioparent is "too soft" and the stepparent "too hard." The stepparent complains that the child is ruining the marriage and the bioparent comes to the child's defense and criticizes the stepparent's parenting.

The dynamics in these situations are complex and are often motivated by conscious and contradictory unconscious forces. In a remarriage, the bioparent consciously usually wants a helpmate in parenting tasks and a parent surrogate for the child; less available to consciousness are the bioparent's negative feelings about the stepparent's "intruding" on his or her relationship with the child. Depending on the degree to which the stepparent is viewed as an intruder, this dynamic may lead the bioparent to undermine the stepparent's effectiveness with the child. In the most severe cases, the bioparent attempts to divide and conquer the stepparent and child and therefore remain in a position of power in the triangle. To complicate this even further, bioparents, stepparents, and stepchildren share the myth of the "wicked stepparent" and its counter myth of "instant love" that is expected of stepparent and stepchild. In some instances the stepparent, especially if he or she does not have children, may have unrealistic expectations of children in general and the stepchild specifically.

We frequently find that the Rem family system and members of the suprasystem as well are intent on imagining an idealized relationship between bioparent and child by scapegoating the stepparent. Schulman (1972) describes passive parents who keep out of significant transactions with their child, which then allows them to criticize the spouse for whatever transactions he or she has with the child. The stepparent (more often stepmother) who rushes in to fill the parenting vacuum falls into the trap of becoming the disciplinarian, whereas the bioparent, by default, emerges as the softer, kinder, more giving parent. The predicament of the stepparent's role adds to her feelings of helplessness and engenders anger that is usually turned against the child, and the tragic spiral continues as the marital pair is at war with each other and "the child is the cause of it all." A child of the same sex as the stepparent often presents a more difficult situation, since there is greater oedipal competition for the bioparent.

In the following example some of the dynamics described are evident:

Mr. and Mrs. Pinella applied for treatment seven months after their marriage, the second for both. Mrs. P initiated the request for treatment with a complaint about her husband's "inability" to get along with her seven-year-old son Warren. Mrs. P was divorced when Warren was two and his father died a year later. Mr. P had been divorced three years when he remarried and he had two daughters, ages eight and 10, who lived with their mother and her new husband near the Pinellas' home.

Mrs. P had developed a close relationship with her bright but somewhat socially immature son. She had not dated until Warren was five. Mr. P was the first man she dated seriously and she was particularly attracted to his "take charge" manner with her and her boy. After six weeks of seeing one another, Mr. P suggested that he meet her son. Mrs. P thought she had found the "perfect father" for Warren. Friends and relatives agreed. When Mr. and Mrs. P first spoke of marriage, Mr. P even spoke of adopting Warren.

At the time of application to the clinic, their honeymoon period had come to a quick halt. Mrs. P had become progressively inattentive to setting expectations for Warren or disciplining him and Mr. P in inverse proportion to her passivity increasingly filled the void. Giving no positive direction to Warren herself, Mrs. P criticized her husband for how he dealt with the child and acted as Warren's advocate at court. Mr. P became increasingly resentful; his approach to Warren becoming more authoritarian and rigid. In response, Mrs. P and Warren joined forces against this "wicked stepfather." Mr. P described himself as the "outsider and

FIGURE 8.1
Pinella Family Genogram

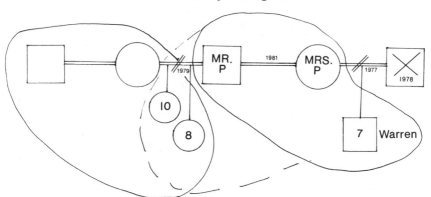

outcast," and was bitter towards his wife's behavior. He received
no support from his wife, and no discussions were held to try to
agree upon a philosophy of childrearing.

Treatment in couple and family sessions shed light on Mrs. P's
ambivalence about accepting Mr. P into her family. She said she
"went along" with Mr. P's original plans to meet her son and told
Warren at that time, "There is someone who wants to meet you."
Warren asked, "Is he an ogre?" Warren recalls that Mrs. P did not
answer his question.

Goals were agreed upon to include Mr. P in the family, for Mrs.
P to take a more active part in the rule setting and adherence and
for Mr. P not to feel he should have major parenting responsibility
for Warren. Treatment focused on having Mrs. P take a more active role in the parenting of her son. This involved enabling her to
assert to her husband her own thoughts and wishes about parenting, rather than confronting, provoking and triangulating as she
had heretofore. In this way Mrs. P did not have to take a "too leni-
ent" position in response to Mr. P's hard line.

When Mrs. P discussed with her husband problems of Warren's
discipline, it brought forth a more moderate response from Mr. P.
Mr. P, like Mrs. Miller in Chapter 6, was motivated to move away
from his controlling behavior because of his anxiety about feeling
forced to behave in a way that made him act like a "wicked stepparent." Eventually, a parental coalition developed where Mr. P
was able to help his wife both nurture and set limits with her son.
This was hard for Mrs. P, who unconsciously saw in Mr. P the person who was to rescue her from the frustrating task of relating to
Warren and who also would be her hatchet man to carry out her aggressive feelings for her son. In order for this parental coalition to
develop, Mr. P had to deal with her anxiety about running the risk
of getting her husband angry, since she did not always agree with
his ideas about parenting. Mr. P was confronted with his ego-alien
dependency yearnings, which were stirred by his contact with
Warren, as well as the fact that, contrary to his image of himself,
he often came across as terrifying and unpleasant when he was
angry.

The Rem family system was further complicated by the fact that
Mr. P had two "perfectly behaved, well mannered and helpful
daughters," who "never created problems" during their bimonthly
weekend visits. Mr. P would compare his "wonderful" daughters to
Mrs. P's "difficult son." In defense, Mrs. P answered with, "Well,
girls are easier."

A session with all five revealed that the girls sensed the tension
in the home, were fearful of their father's temper, and were deliberate in their behavior not to upset him and to protect Warren, of
whom they were fond. They openly admitted that they showed on-

ly "company manners" when they visited and the "real me" was
not such a "goody-goody." The girls were given permission by the
therapist to be themselves and run the risk of causing a little trouble. They did, learning they did not have to be perfect in order to
support their father's competitiveness.

Mr. P at this point understood his contribution to the problem.
The competition between the parents abated and the tension in the
home decreased. Structurally, Mr. P became more involved in being a parent to his daughters; Mrs. P became more involved in being a parent to her son and the couple began to function as a co-parenting team rather than adversaries. The three children continued
to get along well.

Conflicts About Having a Mutual Child

This conflict usually occurs when one spouse has children from a previous marriage and the other does not. However, we now see an increasing number of men and a smaller number of women who have no children
and do not want any. Most often it is the woman who feels the "time
clock" ticking away the years and feels she has to make some decision
before her age excludes her from having children. Often this conflict can
be understood in terms of the life cycle of each member of the couple,
where one feels he or she is beyond the "baby stage" and the other feels
ready and wanting. Sometimes the couple has made a genuine or "understood" agreement before the marriage, but then one or the other
wants to alter the contract as changes occur in feelings, circumstances,
finances, and in the Rem family suprasystem. Changes in contractual
terms, often made unilaterally, evolve unnoticed for a time and are not
discussed by the couple. The first step is to bring them to light and foster discussion to work towards resolution. (See Chapter 12 for a more detailed discussion of the mutual child.)

Conflicts About Money

Older couples may seek help around the question of wills and distribution of property among "his, hers and theirs." When the couple remarries later in life, it is common to have emotion-laden differences
about whether "his" or "her" children or the "new" spouse should be
favored in the inheritance. This brings up issues of competition, favorit-
ism, and how much one is valued by one's mate and one's grown children. It is not unusual that the bioparent may be caught between loyalty and affection for the new spouse and grown children, and feel forced
to choose who comes first. Adult children may feel that all money and

goods that belonged to their parent are rightfully theirs. Prenuptial agreements that may have appeared reasonable and were not resented when signed before marriage can be inappropriate after the couple has been married a number of years. For example, an agreement to leave the major part of an estate to one's children may need to be changed some years later. The spouse is now likely to require greater protection and security, as well as being accepted as a family member. Becoming informed of their parent's intent to change the prenuptial agreement, adult children may bring pressure to bear on their bioparent to continue to designate them as prime or even sole heir. Such intrafamilial strife can be very nasty and hurtful.

With younger Rem couples, conflicts about money often relate to the amount of child support and alimony paid out or received and how that deprives the Rem family. Divorce means, for the vast majority of families, that both households will have to lower their living standards. Sometimes the former wife suffers unjustly; sometimes the husband. Courts are filled with cases of inequities. Children, former wife, and Rem couple feel the financial strain. Two households just cannot have as high a standard of living on the same income as does one household.

Money struggles bring out the worst in everyone concerned: husbands, wives, and attorneys. These battles are motivated by reality and emotional factors—fear, humiliation, anger, revenge, avarice, territoriality, guilt, and chauvanism. Some of the problems over money that existed early on in the divorce between partners may have been resolved by the time remarriage takes place. All too often, however, some problems still remain or are exacerbated at the time of the remarriage. A former wife may feel that now she and her children will be really deserted by her ex-spouse. A new husband may find that the expense of another marriage strains his budget too greatly and that he cannot fulfill the promises regarding living standards made to his new spouse during their courtship. Or he may resent what he feels to be an unfair amount of child support or alimony he is committed to pay. The new spouse may feel *her* income goes to pay *his* alimony and child support obligations, or that they are restricted as a family because of his "unfair" obligation to his other family.

Money must be dealt with as a reality. When working with couples it is important to try to lessen the impact of the symbolic meanings of money. For example, a woman constantly complained of the money her husband sent monthly to his former wife; it appeared to be obsessing her and poisoning their relationship. Apparently, she and her husband had ample funds for their current and retirement needs. However, her husband had never completed an appropriate emotional divorce from his former wife and often compared the two women to the disadvantage of the second wife. When his provocative behavior was dealt with in treatment, his wife's obsession about money withered.

The money a spouse (usually the husband) earns may not be sufficient; he cannot afford to remarry and be the prime wage earner for two households. Often funds would be adequate if he had not been married before. This reality factor hopefully should be laid out before marriage, so that the pair can decide whether or not they can afford or wish to get married, what potential they have together for improving their financial position, and whether or not the standard of living that will be available to them is acceptable to both. To first begin to face this problem after marriage is more difficult because feelings of having been deceived incite the potential for marital dysfunction.

The Wright family illustrates a common issue. The original contract concerning monetary matters was accepted readily by both partners. Then factors outside the Rem family, but in the suprasystem, suddenly changed the situation and the new de facto contract was not acceptable to one of the Rem spouses.

> The Wrights were a Rem couple with three of Mrs. Wright's children living in the household. Mr. Wright's children resided with his ex-wife in another state so that their visits were limited to once or twice a year. Mr. W had chronic underemployment and achievement problems, but Mrs. W had forged a successful career after her divorce, and consequently she carried the family. This arrangement worked well, with Mr. W carrying more household responsibilities during his periods of unemployment. The sand in the machine occurred when his first wife was hospitalized with a terminal illness and his two children had to move in with the couple. Mrs. W was tremendously resentful of the added financial and emotional burden, focused on Mr. W becoming a "real man," pushed him to "succeed," and threatened to leave him if he did not.

Mrs. Wright was unwilling for "my hard-earned salary" to go to others who had not been included in her original "contract" with her husband. Baer (1972) expounds on this point when she makes clear how money that goes to a former spouse may be a realistic deprivation for the Rem family, but that emotional and symbolic meanings of the money can also be an overdetermining factor to produce disruptive behavior in Rem spouses. When money that goes to a former wife or children is seen by the second spouse as depriving her of love and consideration, no logic or reason can ease the tension and conflict.

Negative Use of Ex-spouse

Former spouses of their own volition may be an irritant to the Rem couple. Some may be litigious, continuing a struggle that should have ended a long time ago, or be determined to keep their former spouse from enjoying life in view of the injury done to them. Others may suffer mental illness. In Chapter 15 we discuss the mentally disturbed former spouse; here we will focus on the Rem couple's interactions.

Manifestations of destructive behavior between Rem spouses can run the spectrum from mild irritation that increases in severity through jealousy and irrational hatred towards a partner's former spouse. There are usually three main characters in the drama: current husband, wife, and the ex-spouse of either one. Sometimes other characters are involved: children, the other partner's former mate, parents of the adults, and friends. But the central figures usually remain the three adults, with children seen as representing the other spouse.

Let us consider the ex-spouse a constant for a moment and focus on the interplay of the Rem couple. If the two new spouses are emotionally divorced enough from their past loves, and are mature people who can be open with each other, and neither has a characterological disorder, nor is the least bit neurotic, psychotic, borderline or senile, they can usually deal with and weather the provocations of the most difficult ex-spouse. However, since few among us can claim this state of perfection, an ex-spouse can be the object that the Rem couple uses to provoke all degrees of negative processes between them, from mild irritation to insane jealousy and the contemplation of murder.

Competitiveness and various degrees of jealousy are the most common reactions. All too often these are stimulated by one spouse who still has an incomplete emotional divorce or even a sadistic desire to stimulate a competition of the former and present partner for him. In fantasy, and occasionally in fact, one spouse will harbor a Captain's Paradise model and occasionally even fantasy a ménage à trois. Some enjoy trying to arrange social events (aside from the "milestone" events discussed in Chapter 11) that will include current and ex-spouse. There are some former spouses who meet to share time and sex together, often enjoying an intimacy they never had or had only fleetingly when married. Bergman's film, "Scenes from a Marriage," expressed the poignancy of this type of incomplete divorce most perceptively. In these instances, and in a thousand less explicit ways, one can fire the insecurity, anger, and jealousy of one's present spouse.

On the other side of the coin is the new spouse who has a need to be involved in triangles and is overly curious about his/her mate's previous and ongoing relationship with his/her former spouse. Also, some new spouses have such underlying insecurity that there is no combination of expressions of love, attentiveness, and continued support that can assure him/her that the mate is no longer affectively and/or sexually involved with a former mate. For the extreme of this type of person the mere existence of someone whom the mate once loved, cared for, and had sex with is sufficient to poison the relationship.

Spouses' children from a previous marriage can be seen as instruments and projections of the former spouse and may not be accepted for themselves; hence they often are seen as the enemy. On the other hand, the guilty or not emotionally divorced new spouse can use his children against his current spouse or feel torn apart by his poorly conceived divided loyalties, as was Mr. Miller (see Chapters 6 and 7).

Lingering affection for the former spouse and incomplete emotional divorce, guilt about leaving, need to triangulate the former spouse into the present marriage, need to maintain an entourage of former mates—all contribute on a conscious and unconscious level to how that person relates to former and present spouses. Sometimes the partner fears that angering the ex-spouse will have retaliatory effect on the children and/or affect visitation and finances.

If the former spouse is not married or involved in a new relationship, this can increase the psychic threat to the new partner. Clinically, we look at how the previously married spouse may play into this potential to arouse jealousy, anger, and hostility, perhaps by not taking a firm stand if the previous partner is intrusive or by being subtly seductive and provocative. How often, why, and where a person talks on the telephone with the former spouse or the frequency of references to her in social situations can exacerbate jealousy and rivalry and lead to the present mate's accusation: "You're nicer to her than to me! I'm just your *second* wife!" The mate with a former spouse is often unaware of how provocative he or she can be or of his/her underlying motivations.

In the case that follows, Mrs. Wilder was unaware of how her fear of intimacy following her divorce affected her second husband. He, on the other hand, thought her to be in love still with her first husband and projected his negative feelings onto her son as the ever-present symbol of her first husband.

Mr. Wilder married a woman with a nine-year-old son, Henry, four years after her divorce. Her former husband had left on short notice without Mrs. Wilder's being aware of any evidence of the customary prodromal signs. He announced he no longer loved her and now loved someone else. Henry was said to look like his father and to have a similar outgoing personality. Mrs. W had never affected a complete emotional divorce from her husband. When discussing her divorce with friends, she discussed her husband's action without recrimination and with an edge of compassion for him, still professing not to understand what had happened.

The presenting problem of the Rem family was the poor relationship Mr. W had with Henry. Mr. W, shortly after marriage, seemed to develop a strong distaste for his stepson, was curt with him, found fault, lectured him on being thoughtful of others, and, Henry and his mother felt, was too punitive. There was no physical violence. Early on in the evaluation it was clear that Mrs. W and her son had an age-appropriate parent-child relationship. When the couple was seen alone, Mr. W felt his wife to be cool and distant. She was attentive, apparently loving, but he felt she was not passionate or fully with him. Mrs. W said she was what she was, that she did love her husband and enjoyed sex with him, but did at times feel guilty, like she had no right to be with him, almost (said with an easy laugh) as if she were having an affair with him and couldn't let herself go because she was guilty.

Treatment proceeded with the couple based on discovering that Mr. W felt his wife never fully gave herself to him and that she still appeared to love her first husband. Mr. W had taken an antipathy to the child, perceiving him as an extension of his father who was standing between him and his wife, as he slowly came to feel she was always vaguely inaccessible to him.

In talking through their marriage contracts, it was apparent that Mr. W wanted a more passionate and romantic bonding; Mrs. W had no desire or need to merge. She believed she loved Mr. W in her way, but she had great need to avoid emotional intimacy and to have lots of space and time to herself. Her emotions ran deep but she believed they should be muted, soft, and measured.

Mr. W was a romantic partner, Mrs. W a parallel partner. In individual sessions Mrs. W revealed she had been a romantic partner with her first husband (from her description of him, he took shape as a rational partner who enjoyed her as the affective expresser while he was "cool"): "I did not wish it, but one day I just realized I could never let myself go again and love as I had with Calvin. It just hurt too much."

In a conjoint session, Mrs. W explained her feelings to her husband. They were both moved to tears. He felt remorse because of his behavior to the boy. He recognized his wife's need to limit her demonstration of love and intimacy. Mrs. W entered individual treatment. Having emerged in her mid-thirties as the classical picture of a beautiful, cool, unattainable woman, she recognized that her romantic and her parallel behavior with her two husbands were opposite sides of the same coin. Superficially, the limited adaptations available to her could be seen as having their roots in her own nuclear family, where two narcissistic parents gave her little love.

The description of this family indicates how Mr. W's hostility to Henry was a displacement of his jealousy of his wife's first husband because he believed she still loved him. Actually, the fact of his wife's distance was not based on love for another man *but on her fear of loving.* Inadequacy on his part played no role in Mrs. W's behavior towards him. Reassured of this, he became an effective stepfather and was able to give his wife time and opportunity to work through her underlying problems, a mature manifestation of love on his part.

The Wilder situation also illustrates the use of a variety of modalities: Rem family therapy (ex-husband was not included because Mrs. Wilder's problem was accepted by her not to be based on unfinished business with her former husband, but on her own self-image as determined by her parental introjects), couple treatment, and psychoanalytic psychotherapy.

Jealousy within the Rem couple subsystem can be based on a partner's fear of sexual inadequacy. Some partners want to know details about their mate's prior sex life or constantly wonder how they compare as lovers. Some Rem partners do compare the current mate to former lovers in their own minds or in conversations with the new spouses. To do the latter is likely to be detrimental to the current relationship and mutual sexual enjoyment. In the following example the situation got out of hand and touched off a paranoid reaction in an at-risk husband.

Mr. and Mrs. Gulden requested treatment because their marriage, the second for Mrs. G and first for Mr. G, was endangered by Mr. G's jealousy. Mr. G had become increasingly jealous when his wife would not join him in repeating to friends uncomplimentary anecdotes about her former husband. He regarded her not cooperating in the denigration of her former husband to be evidence of her continued affection. He persisted despite her repeatedly requesting him not to, since it embarrased her and she felt it was not appropriate because he revealed confidential information.

She then told him she would never tell him anything again about her past life. Mr. G tested her on her resolution and she held fast. He then began to accuse her of protecting her former husband because she still loved him and preferred her ex-spouse to him. She protested, reminded him of why she had left her first husband and of her many demonstrations of love to Mr. G. Born of his own insecurity, he then stated that her former spouse must have been a better lover than he. Sensing danger in this tack, she had said she did not wish to discuss the matter further. Mr. G persisted. She remained silent. Her silence was taken by the now somewhat irrational Mr. G to mean that her first husband *was* a better lover and she must still be seeing him. He became suspicious, questioned her constantly about her whereabouts, checked her purse, closet, and chest of drawers, telephone bills, called her where she had said she would be later in the day to check on her, checked the mileage on her car, came back to the apartment several times after she had left to see if her diaphragm was in its place, began to question friends and portrayed other paranoid behavior.

Home life had become a series of inquisitions, denials and arguments. She sensed something irrational and became frightened; she told him that he was sexually superior. Mr. G refused to believe her and demanded details: how large was his penis compared to the other man, who gave her better orgasms, had she learned this nuance or that nuance of sex play from her former husband, etc. He finally agreed to come for therapy with his wife because of his love for her and to "arrive at the truth."

After evaluation it was apparent that couple therapy could be used only in a limited way to assemble historical data, e.g., his mother had "betrayed" his father by having several affairs in which he had been used as an accomplice by his mother. Mr. G regarded his father as a weak fool whom he was determined not to emulate. The couple therapy served to lessen any subtle provocation on his wife's part, but more importantly allowed for the eliciting of data that finally convinced him to accept individual therapy after two months.

EVALUATING THE MARITAL SYSTEM

Regardless of the original reason for requesting help, it is almost always essential in Rem situations for the therapist to be able to evaluate the marital relationship. History-taking and exploration of relationships in the Rem family suprasystem often reveal areas which relate to stress between the spouses which were not mentioned as the presenting complaint. This material needs to be handled by the therapist with sensitivity to the spouses' need to preserve the integrity of their relationship, concomitant with their fear of another failure where they will repeat the same destructive patterns as in the previous relationship. One finds that these fears may lead couples to conceal information about previous relationships from the therapist and/or from other family members. Developing a genogram will often bring secret prior relationships into the open.

When the couple presents itself with a marital difficulty, the clinician can be more direct. However, even then, it behooves the therapist to have at least one family session to assess the total family picture. It is usually contraindicated to involve former spouses in the program at this point if complaints focus on the couple's interaction. A former spouse may need to be brought in later as assessment progresses, if the emotional divorce is not complete and/or parent-child relationships are problematic.

We use the individual marital contract concepts and the typologies (see Chapter 4) to provide a perspective from which to understand the problems the couple experience. While the reminder list of contractual terms itself may not be used or appropriate in the evaluation stages of every couple, the parameters of the contract and the typologies can be kept in mind by the clinician to develop a set of hypotheses about the couple's interaction, their complementarity, and the areas of conflict.

The reminder list designed for the couple is included in Appendix A. It can be given to a couple to talk through together, writing down the significant items and detailing differences. For others, particularly those who cannot discuss without ending up in pitched battles, it is wiser to ask them to write out their responses separately and discuss them in the session.

In understanding the Rem couple, the parameters which are particularly pertinent are:

1) Expectations regarding the spouse's relation to the stepchildren.
2) Expectations about who will take care of the family and/or who will be in charge of the couple relationship.
3) Expectations regarding money and responsibilities for financial support.
4) Expectations regarding the inclusion or exclusion of members of the Rem family suprasystem and the inclusion or exclusion of the noncustodial children.
5) Expectations regarding closeness/distance, autonomy/dependence.
6) Differences in where each spouse is in his or her individual life cycle and their willingness and ability to fulfill an appropriate role in the marital and family life cycles.
7) Anxieties about another marital failure and how these are handled or denied. How the partner reacts to these fears.
8) Fears of loneliness or abandonment.
9) How the former relationship impedes on the present; transferential-like reactions from the former spouse to the present one.
10) Differences and similarities in the individual contracts and interactional contract in the present and past relationship.

In the process of evaluating the Rem couple, we clarify the expectations of each member on conscious, preconscious, and unconscious levels. In doing this, the clinician orders the material for the spouses, who usually are confused, angry, accusatory, and unable to "get a handle" on what went amiss. In the initial stages of evaluation, we use joint interviews, as well as at least one individual interview with each person. The individual interviews are important to elicit negative feelings about one's spouse, illegal activities, conduct in the past one is ashamed of, and extramarital relations. If there is a current, meaningful extramarital relationship which is secret, we would not be able to do couple therapy unless this relationship were to be terminated. We find that to proceed otherwise creates a false basis for couple therapy; sexual and caring potential is drained away and the therapist becomes a partner to a charade. If the person does not wish to terminate the second relationship, other modes of therapy besides conjoint may be offered. Sometimes we may not be able to arrive at a basis for a therapeutic contract.

THERAPEUTIC APPROACHES, PRINCIPLES AND TECHNIQUES

In working therapeutically with the Rem couple, the clinician makes use of his general marital, family, and individual therapy skills, as well as his awareness of the special issues that distinguish a Rem marriage from a first marriage. With some couples, an educational or group guidance approach may supply the needed support and open enough vistas to make marital therapy per se unnecessary. In this section, we address ourselves to those Rem couples where fundamental differences and difficulties between partners indicate the need for more than an educational approach.

Modalities: Group and Conjoint

Our approach to the Rem couple is a flexibe one. The interventions we use range from insight-oriented methods, to systems interactional interventions, to behavioral techniques. The theoretical basis for these techniques also varies from psychoanalytic to general systems theory to formulations based on learning theory. Most work with the Rem couple is conjoint, but this does not exclude the possibility of seeing the couple with their children, individually, with an ex-spouse, or in groups.

Rem couple groups have proven to be especially effective because the group allows the spouses time to focus on themselves and their relationship; most likely, they have not had the chance to consolidate in this way since they had to become an "instant family." In the group, couples are free for the moment from the interruption and focus on children. This can be an anxiety-producing but rewarding experience. Since there are several (usually four) couples in the group, there is enough pressure and a common desire to "leave the children out of it," "not blame the children," "not use the children as the issue and bond between us." Couples see in the group that they are not so unique, that other people share their problems. The group process can take some of the heat out of issues, as well as lead to productive problem-solving and the modeling of solutions.

The option also exists of including the children for a few sessions *if* problems and ages are similar. The children, particularly adolescents, sometimes meet in their own group. We have tried multiple family group therapy with families which had a wide diversity of problems and children of differing ages. This did not work out because there were too many people whose needs were too great and too varied. We do believe that multiple family therapy might be effective if less chaotic cases are selected.

In an "alumni" meeting of a Rem couples group treated at our agency, several of the couples agreed to talk about their group therapeutic experience before a professional audience for training purposes. Most meaningful was the couples' sensitivity to one another's feelings and situations, and the caution with which they approached the most difficult topics: sex, money, and their feelings (both positive and negative) about their living or deceased, former and current spouses. The Rem couples group experience was part of a total treatment plan for each of these families, which had included some individual marital work prior to the group. As shown in the following, the group might be used to move the couple out of a deadlock or off a plateau which had developed during couple therapy.

Mr. and Mrs. Collins were a couple who had lived together for five years. Mrs. C complained, "Saul is too harsh with his daughters; they're 11 and 14. He's too arbitrary and ready to be angry with them. I'm glad they only visit one day a weekend. It upsets me so to see what he does to them." Mr. C thought that his wife exaggerated and added, "How would she know? She doesn't have children and doesn't want any." He then became silent.

Mr. C was extremely guarded in sessions. He denied being aware of any feelings and answered tersely. Mrs. C too was guarded but somewhat less so. Communication between them and with the therapist was sparse and nonrevealing, except for the high level of defensiveness it portrayed.

The therapist was unable to help them get through their communication impasse. At a team conference the suggestion was made, and accepted by the therapist, that Mr. and Mrs. C join an open-ended Rem couples group. It was felt that the group would be an excellent alternate treatment modality for a number of reasons: The pressure would not be on them to "produce"; they might find it easier to speak up for other persons in the group than for themselves; they might see that their problems were shared by others; and the group process would add an important ingredient beyond that of the authority of the therapist.

Mr. and Mrs. C had their own cautious momentum about getting involved in the group. After about six weeks Mr. C found himself getting angry at a woman in the group because he felt she was being very insensitive to her husband's feelings. This led to other members' being able to penetrate the couple's lowered defenses and information began to emerge: that Mrs. C came from a home in which she had been mentally and physically abused. She identified with a man in the group who had abused his children. (The therapist now hypothesized some of Mrs. C's reaction to her husband's criticism of his daughters was a positive identification with his girls and a reaction formation to her own aggressive impulses.)

Mr. C heard the experiences of other women in the group who had raised their children alone. Eventually this opened the way for him to better understand his former wife and subsequently his daughters. Over nine months these two closed-off partners became group members who gave to and received from the group, one another, and others in their lives.

Use of the Marital Contract

The marital contract provides a conceptual framework to understand and make order out of the morass of material a couple brings in. It makes understandable what the marital conflict is about on superficial as well as deeper intrapsychic and couple system levels. When couples present the clinician with typical complaints over money, sex, time, discipline, friends, etc., the use of the contract concept makes it possible to go beyond these complaints to the more basic issues which underlie them. These include power, inclusion/exclusion, closeness/distance, and passive/assertive parameters, as well as others (see Chapter 4 and Appendix A for detailed information about the marriage contracts, behavioral profiles, and the interactional "contracts" or scripts). Contracts help the therapist assess the marriage at the present moment. One must be cognizant, however, that one or both partners may change the contract without informing the other. Sometimes couples are not conscious themselves of the changes they have instituted. Unilateral changes in ground rules can provoke hostility.

Contracts are useful not only for purposes of diagnosis but also to help guide the ongoing treatment program and cue the therapist to productive areas for intervention. By observing the interaction of the couple and their history, the clinician can construct the interactional contracts which are the preconscious ground rules of the game for the couples' interaction. Sager states that:

> Early in treatment I usually start to orient spouses to work toward a single contract as a means to achieve a better relationship. Often this is at first done implicitly, as the three of us compare the terms of the two separate contracts that have been verbalized or written out by the couple. In its broadest sense the road we travel along toward the goal of a single contract is the work of therapy. The terms of the contract must be the choice of the two spouses, not mine. I try to be a guide, a facilitator, a remover of road blocks. I draw their attention to the problem areas as well as those that are congruent and complementary. I devise tasks to change their behavior towards each other, and I interpret their intrapsychic and system dynamics to them when I think that will help. I relate the present to the past; to their parents' marriage and their relationships with their parents, to their role assignment in their family of origin, to their relationship with siblings and how this may affect their current marital behavior; and to other life experiences when any of this is indicated. I manipulate their system on their behalf, with their consent and cooperation (1976, p. 196).

Using the two individual contracts and the interactional one, the therapist helps the couple work towards a single contract. Although all the elements in the new single contract may not please each spouse, the single contract is based on many quid pro quos which the spouses agree upon and find acceptable without one feeling defeated or overwhelmed by the other. The agreements they develop are ones they both must have the capacity to fulfill, and are also dynamic agreements, which must be renegotiated periodically. There must be differences between them; they do not have to act, feel or look alike; but they must respect the differences and still accept each other despite them, if not for them. How love and affection are expressed is often an area that requires attention. Spouses are prone to fail to see an expression of love when it is not done in a style they know well.

The following case example is a session that relates to a change in a significant quid pro quo agreement that was not clearly expressed in the Johnsons' marriage contract.

> Mr. and Mrs. Johnson have been married for five years. Mr. Johnson has a 13-year-old daughter, Eunice, from this first marriage who visits with them. Mrs. Johnson, also previously married, had no children. The couple now have a mutual son, Justin, age three. Treatment was sought because of marital conflicts.

Mr. Johnson: What do you mean, $75 is too much for a Christmas gift for Eunice? We always spend more than that.

Mrs. Johnson: But we can't afford that now.

Mr. J.: You think you're such a hot-shot stepmother, but you care much more about Justin. I could not believe that last week, for no occasion at all, you bought him those expensive blocks. You do care more about him than you do about Eunice!

Mrs. J.: I do. He's my child—our child—lest you forget.

Mr. J.: I thought you would love Eunice as much as if she were your child. You did say that.

Mrs. J.: I did, but what did I know? I didn't have my own child then. I had no basis for comparing experiences I had not yet experienced.

Therapist: So the original contract you made five years ago was that you, Mrs. Johnson, would love and treat Eunice as if she were your child which, I gather, meant you would go along with your husband's ideas about presents to Eunice.

Mrs. J.: Right, and dancing lessons, camp—you name it. I went along with it.

Th.: (to Mr. Johnson) And what were you going to give in return?

Mr. J.: Well, we didn't talk about it but it was one of those things you would call kind of understood and agreed upon. In return, I guess, I would go along with her wanting to have a baby.

Th.: I see, but now that you have a son you feel that Mrs. Johnson is less caring about your daughter and not living up to her part of the contract.

Mr. J.: True.

Mrs. J.: We can't afford it.

Mr. J.: But you just got Justin those expensive blocks; 36 bucks.

Mrs. J.: And besides, we don't spend $60 a week child support for him. I won't even mention the alimony.

Th.: The situation has changed for both of you over the past five years. You, Mrs. Johnson, are no longer willing to go along with your husband when it relates to giving things to Eunice. Let's consider what you might be willing to give now. To

start, what amount of money would you be willing to appropriate from the family budget for a Christmas gift for Eunice?

Mrs. J.: This is hard, because I'm not used to saying no to Fred
when it comes to Eunice.

Th.: I see that.

Mrs. J.: Fifty dollars seem generous to me.

Mr. J.: For Christmas; I wouldn't call it generous. I think it's
cheap.

Mrs. J.: I don't. We have a lot of expenses now. When you wrote
the bills last week you said that and we agreed we want to live
within our means.

Mr. J.: (begrudgingly) Well, I'll just take out the rest from my own
money.

Mrs. J.: That sounds OK with me.

Th.: And what might the two of you want to do about your son?

Mr. J.: Good idea. Let's decide about how much we are going to
spend on him for Christmas. A $36 set of blocks just because
it's Tuesday doesn't make sense to me.

Mrs. J.: You tell me.

Mr. J.: Forty dollars.

Mrs. J.: That's fine; we'll decide on a limit for each child for Christmas, birthdays, and so on. And if I want to buy him blocks or
something on a whim I'll take it out of my own money and
you do the same for Eunice. And I can do that for her too if I
want and you can for Justin. (Mr. Johnson nods agreement.)
What hurts me, however, is that you don't think I'm a good
stepmother.

Mr. J.: That's true. I would like you to love Eunice as much as you
do Justin.

Mrs. J.: But I don't. There is a difference. I love her and most of the
time in the last two years I like being with her, but I feel closer to Justin. I saw and felt him being born; I nursed him.

Th.: To what extent do you think you're a good stepmother?

Mrs. J.: I must be getting there because before, when Fred would
criticize me, I would get hysterical. Now it's a mixture of anger and more sadness. This is my reality. He doesn't feel I
quite measure up to being a good stepmother.

Th.: So this is a source of tension and disappointment you both live
with now?

Mr. J.: Yes, hopefully this new plan won't rub our faces in it the
way it has.

Th.: I hope so.

The Johnsons illustrate the importance of reviewing "contractual"
agreements. Mr. Johnson extracted a promise from his fiancée five

years ago that she responded to in good faith, not having any knowlege-
able basis for knowing how she might feel in the future. Mr. Johnson's
request was motivated by the best of intentions plus anxiety about losing the love of his daughter, guilt about the divorce and the wish to supply a new "nuclear" family for Eunice when she visited his home. Mr.
Johnson felt he had kept his part of the contract, an unspoken pact, by
having Justin with his wife.

Treatment in this session dealt directly with clarifying the old contractual term, getting open agreement on the new one, and working out
an interesting quid pro quo. More work, of course, had to be done, but
this was sufficient for that day. Part of the remaining work had to do
with Mr. Johnson's not realizing he did not fully accept his own son but
thought of him as Mrs. Johnson's. Thus, it was as if each had his/her own
biochild and the other was a stepchild. After more feelings and problems
emerged in the quid pro quo situation, the husband was better able to
understand Mrs. Johnson's feelings of differentiation between biochild
and stepchild. Mrs. Johnson apparently sensed the future movement
when she wisely pointed out that they each might be moved to spend
some of their own money for either of the two children.

Mr. Johnson would also have to appreciate better his attachment to
his former wife and his guilt towards her and Eunice; apparently he did
not appreciate all that his first wife gave to his daughter. The therapist
made no attempt to deal with these other issues in this session; to have
done so would have been an intrusion. These issues surfaced later.

SPECIAL ISSUES OF REM COUPLES

The Former Spouse

In addition to the clinician's sensitivity to how Rem spouses are influenced by their families of origin, there needs to be sensitivity to how
the current marriage is influenced by the past relationship and by the
present relationship to the former spouse. We ask Rem couples to include in their individual marital contracts information about their previous marriages. We are particularly interested in whether or not the
relationship to the new spouse is different from or similar to that with the
former spouse and whether or not there has been growth in terms of a
more mature choice of object, affect and behavior. A discussion of the
former marriage or relationship is necessarily a charged one for both
people, and therefore the clinician needs to be sensitive to this and, at
the same time, comfortable himself with the emotions this material may

elicit. All too often clinicians avoid talking about former marriages and collude with clients in denying their importance or even that they ever existed.

The feelings about the former spouse, both expressed and unexpressed, may span the spectrum from very active hostility, anger and denigration, to passivity, "no feelings," and neutrality, to guilt, self-blame, continued mild affection, love and a desire or fantasy of reuniting "some day" and of having regular or sporadic sex together. These feelings, attitudes, and behaviors probably overlay a lack of mourning for the former spouse and appropriate closure of the former relationship. Talking through and recognizing both the positive and negative aspects of that former life and "laying to rest" the past, insofar as possible, can deflect or neutralize the intrusion of the past relationship.

Steve and Hilda Gould presented themselves as a remarried couple with problems in the relationship. Mr. Gould's first wife had died of cancer, leaving two daughters 10 and 13. Mr. G remarried Hilda Crocese two years later and this relationship was stormy. Mrs. G was extremely narcissistic and could not comprehend why the children did not like her. They persisted in seeing her as the wicked witch and their dead mother as the good angel. The biomother had been a teacher in a local school and was loved and respected in the community. Mr. G was a guarded, defensive man who had never mourned his first wife; five months into the therapy he began to let go. He had cast Mrs. G as the witch-whore-seductress, with his dead wife as the saint. He could not connect with his second wife until mourning took place so that he finally could lay his dead wife "to rest" and feel free to love and have for himself.

It is often helpful for the couple to look at: 1) how the past relationship is being projected into the present; 2) the way their own behavior duplicates the past and stimulates a similar response from their present mate; and 3) the way one can overreact when there is something (positive or negative) in the present relationship that conjures up the past spouse. One has to look at whether either spouse tries to "force" the mate into behaving as the ex-spouse had. A period of testing often takes place in courtship, but, as time goes on, some mates push harder to bring forth negative reactions. Sensing this and unconsciously wanting to comply, partners will often fall into behaving as their partners "demand"—even to their own disadvantage. A subtle struggle often goes on as to which mate will press the other into his/her procrustean bed; sometimes one "wins out" for certain situations, the second for the others.

A peculiar variation of the first wife who has not been put to rest is seen when a spouse marries "for the children," but marries a person he cannot love, as if to prove his continued love for the deceased spouse. These marriages do not stand much of a chance to be gratifying for the children or either Rem spouse.

In dealing with the issue of the former spouse, the clinician should be aware of how much the ex-spouse intrudes into the new marriage, both physically by being close by or making frequent phone calls and symbolically in the form of furniture, dishes, even the conjugal bed that may have seen service in a previous marriage. Sometimes friends are tolerated who are loyal to the ex-spouse and do not accept the new marriage. All this contributes to the new spouse's sense of being on the "outside" rather than truly paired with the new mate. The current spouse may unwittingly encourage this reaction, as Joe Davidson did in Chapter 1, by staying on the telephone too long, talking too nicely, being avidly solicitous of his ex-wife—all ostensibly to stay on her "good" side so she would not interfere in his relationship with the children.

These common Rem couple complaints about inclusion/exclusion do not occur in first marriages in the same way; "mother-in-law" or "father-in-law" intrusion is just not the same as "ex-spouse" intrusion. These surface complaints usually relate to the Rem spouses' deeper mutual expectations of each other; what each one wants to give and receive in return. For example, one mate's involvement with the ex-spouse may be an expression of his expectation in the current relationship in terms of independence and/or distance from the current spouse. The current spouse may have expected her new husband/wife to "drop" the former spouse so they could become a closeknit couple devoting much time and energy to each other. They can renegotiate their expressed and unexpressed expectations of each other in this area, but in Rem there is still the reality of having to deal with the ex-spouse in *some way* acceptable to all adults involved.

What the new spouse does vis-à-vis the former spouse affects the current pairing. It is important when one or both adults of a new marriage have been married previously that they do not deny their history. One's children and former spouses can't be wished away. The remarried are not "innocents." When faced, the historical reality need not negatively affect the new relationship; its denial, however, can be a most serious negative prognostic sign.

When an ex-spouse is damaged in some way, physically or emotionally, or perhaps has not set himself or herself up in a satisfactory life situation, the potential for serious problems exists. Often, the spouse, out of guilt, feels he/she has to rescue or accommodate the former mate, for fear of damaging him/her or the children further. To go overboard in this direction is not unusual:

Mr. Turner's former wife, who had been hospitalized several times since their divorce ten years earlier, came twice a week to the Ts' apartment to visit with their son. This was to spare the son having to see the poor living conditions of his mother, who still resided in a furnished room, although she could afford an apartment. Mr. T didn't feel his ex-wife could "handle" any other visiting arrangement and was hesitant to confront her for fear she would "fly off the handle." The present Mrs. Turner felt these visits were an unnecessary intrusion into their home and resented the former Mrs. T's helping herself to food and then leaving the dirty dishes.

In the couple sessions, it became clear that both Mr. and Mrs. T felt invaded by his former wife. They had polarized around the issue, with the present Mrs. T being the vocal, complaining bad one and Mr. T being the good, calm, soothing, moderating one. In addition to the concrete issue of how to deal with the intrusion, the visits had become the focus for a negative marital interactional script for the Turners.

After some discussion, which at one point included Mr. T's adolescent son, a more rational way of handling the visits from the ex-spouse was considered. Mr. T was able to relate his unwillingness to confront his ex-wife with his own anger at her illness and ineffectiveness as a mother and also his extreme guilt for having divorced her. His guilt also invaded the relationship with his son, whom he was unable to confront when the boy truanted from school, stayed in his room, and refused to accept help. For the present Mrs. T, her husband's inability to take charge as a parent and mate felt as if he had broken an agreement he had made with her—to be an all around benevolent authority.

Mr. T's guilt and dependency had to be relieved if he were to give himself peace and be an effective father, husband, *and* ex-spouse. This required a deeper appreciation of his long-standing need not to be able to allow himself to have for himself. He finally was able to determine a limited and appropriate sense of obligations to others instead of his guilt-ridden stance that dated to his "obligation" to become the man of the house after his father's death when he was 11. The present Mrs. T recognized her "fill the vacuum role." She accepted a goal to allow Mr. T to take charge, rather than denigrating his efforts in that direction as she had been.

An ex-spouse and a "former life" can also intrude in the current marriage in the form of lifestyle differences, tastes, ideals, values, political viewpoints which may have been acquired through experience with and influence of the former spouse. To the extent a new spouse identifies these as representing a predecessor's imprimatur on the spouse, they can invoke jealousy, competition and resentment in the current relationship.

Mr. and Mrs. Lewis were married for 10 years. Although she was involved in her own career as a psychologist, Mrs. L's relationship with her husband during the late sixties and early seventies was very much influenced by his liberal political points of view and his ideas about social change. Since she wasn't really committed to politics, she adopted his viewpoint without much thought.

Her current husband, Mr. James, resented the influence Mr. L still seemed to have over Mrs. James in absentia. They had many arguments over her "liberalism" until she finally adopted a more conservative stance to appease him, rationalizing that the political scene was of no essential importance.

However, she had a growing awareness of her capitulation to her husband in many areas because of her fear of provoking arguments and his temper, which occasionally was violent. The couple came for treatment as Mr. J became dissatisfied sexually and emotionally with his wife when she distanced herself more and more from him in order to avoid confrontation. The issue of giving in to him as appeasement was seen to be a pattern for her, held over from her first marriage and even from needing to be the lovable nondisruptive child, who therefore would be rewarded for being "a good girl."

Mr. J, who had also been married before, needed to look at his violent outbursts as they related to his partner's showing any thoughts or positions that differed from his. He perceived these differences to be "disrespectful" of him as a man, and a reminder of the humiliation caused him by his first wife's numerous, poorly disguised extramarital affairs.

Sexuality and Rem

Just as clinicians may avoid dealing with the ex-spouse, so, too, they may avoid inquiring and dealing with the area of sexuality. Frequently, we have found that sex is better for both Rem partners than it had been in the previous relationships. This can be related to greater maturity, more experience, clarity as to sexual needs, and a better marital situation. Still, the clinician should be able to inquire into sexuality in such a way as to be able to place sexual difficulties into perspective and to be able to determine whether sexual problems are secondary to marital difficulty, whether marital difficulty is secondary to sexual problems or whether there is a sexual problem that predates the current relationship and ripples out to affect other areas of the couple's well-being. The current relationship may be too poor to tackle sexual problems until other areas are dealt with. These issues are discussed more completely elsewhere (Sager, 1974, 1976).

Premarital sex is usually good for Rem couples because many partners do not want to enter into a marriage where sex is not up to their expectations. At the start of a new relationship one or both partners may have a situational dysfunction based on guilt towards a former partner, apprehension at the thought of achieving the sought-after gratifying relationship, or uneasiness with a relative stranger. One person may experience insecurity about one's ability to perform sexually with a new partner. The dysfunction is likely to pass shortly when it is situational and the new partner is not setting off associations on some level that remind one of unhappy experiences in the past. A single gesture, personality trait, or physical characteristic may become a symbol for the totality of the negatively viewed person or experience. Reassurance or relaxation techniques to decrease the focus in performance are often all that is therapeutically necessary.

After marriage, sex usually remains satisfactory, although frequency may decrease as the partners continue on in a familiar conjugal bed and are joined by the reality problems of daily living. However, we have been impressed with the number of Rem couples who continue an active and pleasurable sexual relationship. As in any committed relationship, it is necessary to give thought, attention, and discussion to keeping sex creative.

Sexual ennui, inhibition, and lack of sexual desire are all terms that refer to a lack of wanting to initiate or to respond to the initiation of sexual activity. It can be sporadic, cyclical, or continuous. It may apply for both partners, for one, or for each at different times. Kaplan (1979) has elaborated on the many psychological, interactional, and somatic etiological possibilities. When both partners have no desire, it is not as likely to emerge as a complaint as when one feels deprived by the other's lack of sexual interest. We have no hard data, but sexual ennui is possibly less common in Rem couples than in first married couples of similar age. This observation may, however, be due to the fact that the Rem couple's marriage has been of shorter duration. More study is required before conclusions can be drawn.

Sexual ennui in spouses who are not dysfunctional and who enjoy sex when they are sufficiently aroused to follow through is not necessarily a manifestation of pathology. Yet, it can be a most difficult problem to overcome because of the many subtle unconscious forces that can be contributory. Taking a careful sexual, marital, and medical history is necessary. This should be followed by referral for medical and laboratory examination to rule out somatic and endocrinological factors as well as the many prescription and common street drugs that may inhibit sexual desire. When either or both partners find the lack of desire to be ego-alien, and this state has not responded to the therapist's efforts, the couple should be referred for consultation to a qualified sexologist whose training and experience are broadly based, encompassing knowledge of the various relevant medical and psychological disciplines.

Of particular relevance for Rem couples is the degree to which the past relationship plays into sexual difficulties and may produce or exacerbate them. This can be by one partner's verbally comparing his current partner's performance to that of the former partner, or through unexpressed comparison which may block sexual pleasure in the present. Sometimes, one partner will be inordinately curious about his partner's past sexual life. He or she may find this inquiry stimulating, or he/she can use it as a barometer of the current relationship or as a way for projecting blame on the dysfunctional partner ("You could have orgasms with him. Why not with me?"). Another way the past may play into the present is where there is a widowed spouse who through guilt over pleasure with the new partner or through unresolved mourning develops a sexual dysfunction. In men, this is often manifested as secondary erectile dysfunction; in women as an orgastic problem.

Fear of Another Failure

While often first-time married couples openly admit that they don't know whether to stay together or separate, with Rem couples we more often see two ends of the continuum on the staying together-separating issue. Some couples present a united front (often against the scapegoated child) to conceal marital difficulties because of fear of another failure; other couples present with such brittleness that to get them to explore the possibility of improving what they have is extremely difficult. These couples often act as if they would rather be right than happy.

There also may be a tendency to solve Rem issues by dropping the partner at the first sign of trouble. The "dropper" may rush headlong into another relationship with no hiatus or pause to look at and modify himself. The tendency to drop and rush into relationships with a melange of children trailing behind has lately been aptly referred to as a "chronically reconstituting family," for we don't see that in this situation any degree of stabilization has taken place.

This discussion is not exhaustive. Some of the common presenting complaints of Rem couples have been elaborated and some general approaches to evaluating the marital system and effective modalities of therapy have been indicated. The former spouse, sex, and the possibility of another failure are important issues that clinicians must help the Rem couple confront. The key for the clinician is to have an armamentarium of skills, knowledge of Rem issues, comfort with being involved with families, and the personal ability to detach himself or herself sufficiently from the marital dyad, so that he/she does not become lost, over-identified with the spouses' problems, and confused by the complexity of the couple's interaction and conflicts.

CHAPTER 9

The Child and the Children's Subsystem

A child whose parent remarries is a child who has experienced the separation and divorce of his parents or the death of one parent. Such events are important and meaningful at any developmental level. The process of working through such changes and accepting the remarriage has a spectrum of responses. For some children the remarriage may be welcomed; at the other extreme, some children never accept the remarriage. In the middle are most children who, with time and appreciation of their feelings by the parenting adults, can find a place for themselves in the Rem family and the Rem suprasystem. This chapter focuses on these issues for the child under the age of 12.

A young man, at 22, wrote the following to his father 12 years after a bitterly fought separation and divorce. Both his bioparents are now friendly and have been constructive co-parents for several years. Even the most acrimonious divorces can heal for adults and their children when fears, jealousies, and old injuries can finally be put aside:

There was much error, wrong and hurt done in the way the break-up and settlement was handled. Leaving Mom was not wrong, but many of the means chosen, often out of uncontrolled anger and hatred, to handle the situation were not right. But as you know, and as I have told you and written it before, what became most important for me a while back was to forgive the past so that we could set ourselves to live for what we have now. I don't condone the past but I can't hold onto it and let it be wall and barrier to what the present and future holds for you and me, for two people whose lives

222

mean a great deal to one another. I came to realize that that's what I had to do because I love you. And I was able to do it also because the turmoil had subsided. But it has not been this way only with you. With Mom too I have had to overcome much anger and bitterness which was a harsh barrier between us.

My feelings about your remarriage* are only good ones. I have certainly never felt any negative feelings towards Lily because you married her in place of Mom. I have only felt glad and happy for both of you to have found someone again to share your lives with in happiness. And I have never had any conflict between loving a stepmother and a mother. It is easy to accept Lily as your new wife but also very importantly as someone who has also entered my life in a meaningful way. She is your wife and my stepmother, and each of those actualities has an important meaning to me.

Take care and send my love to Lily.

> I love you,
> Walt

Major shifts in families can have both positive and negative effects on individual members. On the positive side, for children in a Rem situation, are the possibilities of increased affection, additional opportunities to identify with and introject other male and female parental figures, great individual enrichment through exposure to a variety of persons and lifestyles, and a better feel for and confidence in marriage because of seeing the bioparent in a new, successful relationship.

On the negative side, the child whose parent remarries has already experienced a series of stresses and major changes; the new complexities, rejections, hurts, loyalty conflicts, and other pressures which come as baggage with remarriage often contribute to symptomatic behavior that appears or becomes more pronounced after the remarriage.

INCIDENCE OF PROBLEMS AMONG REM CHILDREN

In our assessment and treatment of 213 Rem families during an 18-month period from September 1977 to March 1979, a total of 367 children were included. Table 9.1 shows the percent of the total number of manifesting behavioral disturbances; any child might have revealed one or more of these forms of behavior.

Only 9% of the 367 children assessed were considered to be free of in-

---

*Six years after the divorce—*eds.*

TABLE 9.1

Therapist's Assessment of Problems in Rem Children Under 18

1. Dysfunctional relationship with parent(s), total		83%
a. with custodial parent	37%	
b. with noncustodial parent	30%	
c. with stepparent	34%	
2. Impulse control problems (including substance abuse)		38%
3. School problems		36%
4. Depressed state		29%
5. Pseudo-independence/maturity		23%
6. Extruded child (psychologically and/or physically, including battered child)		23%
7. Disturbance in peer relationships		21%
8. Psychosomatic complaints		12%

ternalized or behavioral problems. The 91% who were assessed as having problems did not necessarily have difficulties of a severity or etiological nature to indicate a need for therapeutic intervention. Many of these children could be dealt with through an educational or guidance program for parents or in a peer group. We did not compare this group, who were seen in a clinical setting, to Rem families who were not seekers of help or to the children of intact, nuclear families.

This chapter is drawn from our work with these 213 Rem families with 367 children, plus an additional number seen from mid 1979 to mid 1981, to bring the total to over 350 Rem families and more than 700 children. These families were seen in consultation and treatment at the Remarried Consultation Service (RCS). Only about 10 children were in our residential programs; the others were seen in our clinic with their families. In addition, an even greater number of Rem situations were seen in the Agency's other outpatient, residential, day school programs, and mental health consultation assignments.

In some instances when children had clinically significant problems, marital complaints were the presenting problem. More frequently, the child's behavior would be seen by the adults as the reason for seeking assistance. We conceptualize the child's problem in terms of how it arises and is maintained by the Rem family suprasystem and its subsystems; we also consider the child's functioning prior to Rem.

The focus in this chapter will be on the child under 12 who has at least one bioparent who has remarried and whose bioparents' marriage ended by divorce or death. The relevant literature will be briefly reviewed. The major stress points for the child will be outlined. The effect of this stress on development and coping patterns will also be considered. Variables we have found to be significant for the child to flourish in Rem and what the child may experience emotionally and interactionally will be discussed. The final part of the chapter deals with the kind of problems children in Rem often manifest and some of the special issues in dealing with these problems.

RESEARCH ON THE CHILDREN OF DIVORCE

The most extensive work has been done by Wallerstein and Kelly (1974, a, b; 1976, 1980, a, b; Kelly and Wallerstein, 1976, 1977; Kelly, 1981), who use the developmental stages of children to explore the different effects of divorce on children at varying ages. A constant finding that held for all age groups is that the *quality and consistency* of the custodial parental relationship is crucial to the successful adjustment of the child to the separation. Their findings are summarized in Table 9.2.

The conclusions that may cautiously be drawn from their study are that follow-up one year after separation reveals that girls between the ages of 3¾ and 4¾ were the most vulnerable; that the 9–10-year-old group were equally distressed, but of the 7–8-year-old group only half as many were in worse condition than earlier. Those who fared best were the adolescents; most proceeded normally or were at even an enhanced level, as a result of their mastery of separation.

Wallerstein and Kelly provide the most complete developmental description of children of divorce to date, but isolate the child from the familial system, i.e., they investigated the intrapsychic and life-cycle behavioral issues, but eschewed the interactional and systemic processes. Their population is skewed toward an upper-middle-class white group and hence generalizations may not be valid.

Tessman (1978) uses extensive case material and substantiates Wallerstein and Kelly's finding of the importance of the child's relationship with the remaining parent in helping the child weather the loss:

Age in itself appeared to be less prognostic of the degree to which the child worked through the loss than were several other factors, such as the home-parent's eventual well-being; the child's relationship to the parents before the loss and their manner of coping with stress; and the availability of appropriately supportive relationships during the period of stress (p. 492).

TABLE 9.2
Children's Reactions to Parental Parting

Age Group	Reactions to Separation	Follow-up one year later
Preschool 2½–3¼	Regression, forgetfulness, bewilderment, aggression and neediness.	50% of children had problems.
3¾–4¾	Guilt, depression, diminished self-esteem and self-image.	Most vulnerable were girls 3¾–4¾ years.
5–6	Anxiety and regression, whininess, mood changes, tantrums, separation problems.	
Latency 7–8	Loss of age-appropriate defenses, intense sadness and longing, loyalty conflicts.	23% were in worse condition.
9–10	Conscious and intense anger toward parents, struggle to master through denial, courage, bravado, support-seeking, movement, fears, identify problems, somatic, school problems.	50% were in worse condition.
Adolescence	Extremely painful feelings, concern about financial needs and their future as marital partners; precipitous deidealization of parents; precipitous independence.	Most proceeded normally at level equivalent to previous level or enhanced by mastery of separation.

Adapted from Wallerstein and Kelly, 1980a, b; and Crohn et al., 1981.

However, the assumption here is that the noncustodial parent does not continue to play a role with the child. The variable of the parent who leaves the home but continues a responsible, loving, and visible role with the child is not considered. The "child of divorce" is considered largely in the literature in isolation and not within the context of his suprafamily system.* We find that in many cases *both* bioparents wish to continue a consistent and responsible involvement with their child.

Lamb (1977) reviewed the relevant research conducted by developmental psychologists and from that data evaluated the effects of divorce on children's personality development. He concludes that:

---

*An extensive study of childhood bereavement is reported by Furman (1974). The author also notes that the child's relationship with the surviving parent is essential to the grieving process.

As we survey and evaluate the evidence concerning the effects of divorce on personality development, there appear to be only two conclusions that we can state with relative certainty and assurance. The first is that the children of divorced parents, compared with the children of intact families, are "at risk" for psychological damage. The second conclusion, however, comprises an important qualification: It is not possible to specify flatly "the effects of divorce," because there are no sequelae that can be identified as the inevitable consequences of divorce and family dissolution. Divorce can be beneficial to children, inasmuch as it signals the termination of hostilities, uncertainties, and harmful hatefulness. On the other hand, family dissolution and the associated severance of important formative relationships can be damaging to the psychosocial adjustment of young children (p. 171).

RESEARCH ON THE ADJUSTMENT OF CHILDREN TO STEPFAMILIES

The professional literature concerning stepchildren and stepparents is minimal. Generally, the research data are not generalizable. In research about stepchildren, the primary issue addressed is whether children in Rem fare better, as well, or worse in terms of their "mental health" as children living in nuclear families. The results are not conclusive.

Bernard (1971) investigated the mental health of stepchildren using university students and found no significant difference in terms of stability, self-sufficiency, or dominance compared to non-stepchildren. The ability to develop and maintain an intimate love relationship with an appropriate mate was not examined in this study or in any other.

Bohannan (1975) focused on stepfathers and stepchildren, finding that stepchildren rated themselves as happy, successful, and achieving as often as did non-stepchildren with their biofathers. Interestingly, Bohannan found that stepfathers may be promulgating negative images of themselves, since natural fathers rated their children as significantly happier than the stepfathers rated their stepchildren, although neither the mothers nor the stepchildren perceived themselves as less happy. Bohannan further suggested that the *outcome* for children with stepfathers is the same as with natural fathers and that what may ultimately be more important to understand is the process: both the specific kinds of adjustment such children must make, and the long-term effect on the character structure that relationships with two or more father figures might create.

Other researchers have found that the mental health consequences for children living in Rem are worse than living in a divorced family, and both are worse than living in an intact family. Langner and Michael (1963) and Rosenberg (1965) each used large-scale random samples of stepchildren and found that the mental health of the stepchildren compared adversely with non-stepchildren. Similarly, Bowerman and Irish (1962) found that the relationships of stepchildren to their stepparent, as well as to their remarried bioparent, were marked by greater levels of uncertainty of feelings, insecurity of position and strain, than were those to be found in non-step homes. The authors also found that stepfathers appear to fare better than do stepmothers with stepchildren. They also found a higher average adjustment towards the stepparent when the previous marriage was ended by divorce rather than death.

CLINICAL STUDIES

The clinical studies concentrate particularly on adaptation to remarriage, on the myths that surround the stepfamily and interfere with adaptation, and on the lack of clear role definitions available to stepparents and stepchildren. Evidence exists that such myths and role difficulties also exist in the nonclinical population.

Bitterman (1968) examined 145 active family service cases of remarriage and found most clients denied the full implication of remarriage and stepparenting. The children's normal development of loving and being loved was disrupted, they experienced problems in dealing with their parents' sexuality, and there were loyalty conflicts between the bioparent and the stepparent.

Research concerning the children and Rem is scant and not generalizable to a nonclinical population. No research on children and Rem has been done which is longitudinal, using a nonclinical sample. Findings are not consistent, and so clinicians who generally see children in "trouble" form their own subjective opinions based on their own criteria, experiences, values, and prejudices.

MAJOR STRESS POINTS FOR THE CHILD

The individual life cycle of the child is disrupted initially with the separation of the bioparents. In the family life cycle he or she becomes a member of two single-parent families. This cycle is disrupted again with the remarriage of one or both bioparents, which adds one or two new family life-cycle tracks. What follows is a description of the child's experience in the process of becoming a Rem family. The response of the child is contingent on genetic, developmental, systemic, intrapsychic, and environmental influences.

Disruption in the Nuclear Household

Prior to separation, the child is a witness to covert or open conflict between the parents. He may be excluded from their difficulties or drawn in as one who is blamed or used in the struggle of one against the other. He may have failed at being expected to "cure" a failing marriage, or his normal developmental needs may have "caused" the pressure between the parents. One or both parents may have inappropriately used him as a confidant and adviser, or the parents' difficulty may have been kept a "secret." The child feels a pull to each parent: He may blame himself as the cause of their problems and experience the impending threat to his security. He fears abandonment, which then seems a reality when one parent leaves. The reality of his parents' actions and decisions may play into his fantasized wishes and/or fears.

One eight-year-old boy, whose parents had recently separated and were arguing, vividly expressed his emotions in the following dream:

I am on a swinging bridge made of sticks—it's a hanging bridge. On each shore there's a monster trying to get the other monster. I don't know what to do; I'm afraid. I jump off the bridge into the water and swim away. The monsters eat each other up.

When a parent is ill, particularly from a protracted illness, the child's other parent may also be unavailable emotionally or physically; the child may witness frightening or overwhelming medical conditions and procedures. He may watch helplessly as the formerly well parent deteriorates; moreover, his own needs no longer can be properly tended to. If the death of his parent is accidental and sudden, there is no preparatory time; the child precipitously experiences a major loss. With a parent's death, the child may be part of funeral rituals that may help him with the loss or traumatize him further, or he may be lied to and excluded. There may be feelings of guilt, self-blame, anger, sadness, fear, or relief.

In both separation and death, the child loses his "holding environment" (Winnicott, 1965). The two-parent home in which he was nurtured is no more, and, depending on circumstances, he may become pseudo-independent or regress to an earlier developmental level. How he will adjust also depends on the circumstances and his level of development. With the youngest children (under 18 months), if the supportive environment continues, there is likely to be less reaction in the child than between 18 months and 39 months, where regression would be common and expected, as well as bewilderment, aggression, and increased demandingness. With children between four and six years of age, guilt, depression, diminished self-esteem, anxiety, tantrums, and separation problems may occur. With younger latency-aged children, there may be a loss of age-appropriate defenses, and with older children, intense anger at parents and problems in school. Wallerstein and Kelly summarize their findings in their book (1980b). Our work indicates that those children who have had uninterrupted support of both bioparents after divorce, and where the parents do not foster loyalty conflicts, suffer the least damage.

Double Single-parent Household

With separation, both parents have their own household, the double single-parent stage. If a spouse has died, the surviving parent is the truly "single" parent. Both parents may desire to be part of the child's care system and to provide emotional, physical, and financial support. These parents seek to cooperate around their children and form a co-parenting team.

With separation, the child is most typically (nine times out of ten) in his mother's custody with visits to his father. His immediate reaction may be one of relief that the hostility of the marriage has ended. With death, the surviving parent may be depressed and consequently unavailable to the child. In such instances the child is at high risk. Typically, the mother may return to work and there may be a radical shift downward in the family's standard of living. Mother and child may return to live with the maternal grandparents who may then become surrogate parents. This attachment may be life-saving for some children. However, if the mother is once again a child in her parents' household and then a peer to her own child, the child runs the risk of another loss. There can be a marital-like bonding between the custodial parent and the child and intensification of Oedipal wishes and fears, particularly from age four to six. In response to this, the child may become extremely enmeshed or defend against the inappropriate close bonding by opposition and hostility. He may parent the parent and be overly concerned with the parent's well-being, or may parent a sibling, as Deirdra did for her sister, Liza, in the case presented in Chapters 6 and 7.

When the custodial or surviving parent begins to date and becomes increasingly involved with a new partner, the child is in danger of being extruded and there is the threat of another loss. He may become symptomatic, withdraw, compete with his parent for or against the new mate, display hostility, align with the grandparents against the parent, or leave the home in favor of the other parent's household. If there is loyalty to the dead or absent parent, or unresolved mourning, the resistance to the new parenting figure may be extremely intense.

It is important in the "single" stage for both parents to demonstrate love to their children and to be available to them, but it is also important to help them maintain their age-appropriate roles and to know that their parents have adult friends, including those of the opposite sex, who are important to them. Thus, when mother or father remarries, the children have known their stepparent and have gradually redefined their relationship with the person who first was the parent's friend, then the parent's lover, and then either live-in mate or spouse.

As increasing numbers of former spouses who share visiting or custody arrangements are on good co-parenting terms, the ex-spouse should be told of an impending marriage or committed relationship (move in) before it happens and preferably by the former spouse directly. This helps to defuse reactions that could be hurtful to the children.

Occurrence of Remarriage

The child's fantasy of uniting his bioparents is challenged when one parent remarries. Younger children who may have imagined or wished that a dead parent would return can be struck with the finality of the death at the time of remarriage. While to the parent the remarriage is a joyful occasion, to many children the wedding is a time of mourning, with a renewed sense of loss.

The child may experience the remarriage as a "second divorce," particularly if he played the role of surrogate mate or there was a quasi-symbiotic relationship during the double single-parent stage. At remarriage his role is usurped by the new spouse; if there are stepsiblings his ordinal position as youngest or oldest or as the only boy or only girl may also be changed. Extreme denial of the remarriage may take place, as in the following example.

Katherine's father and his woman friend of two years decided to live together. Both gave up their small apartments and together they rented a larger one that included a room for Katherine when she stayed over. Katherine, age seven, was told beforehand (no reaction) and then visited with them twice at the new apartment (no reaction). One month after the couple had their new apartment together, Katherine and her father walked by the woman friend's former residence. Katherine asked her father if they would be visiting her there that day.

Although to the parent remarriage means the anticipation of greater stability, to the child it may mean changes in role, living arrangement, standard of living, school, and peers. Once more he has to deal with two "parents" in a household, as well as siblings who may be strangers. The relationships with the noncustodial parent and with grandparents, who may not have yet relinquished their interim role of surrogate parents, may be affected. His live-in household may also change as children from the "other family" visit with their noncustodial parent on weekends.

The child has involuntarily become a part of an extremely complicated family suprasystem. He has incomplete knowledge of its structure and function. His expectations are based on the experience in his nuclear family, popular screen and television ideas about families ("The Brady Bunch"), his fantasies of a "new life," and prejudiced folklore about the stepfamily. The Rem family's goal of consolidating into a viable unit must consider the child's previous life and the issues that remain unresolved for him.

VARIABLES AFFECTING THE CHILD'S SUCCESSFUL ADAPTATION TO REM

There are several variables that facilitate or impede the child's adaptation to Rem. These include constitutional, intrapsychic, historical, interactional, and environmental factors. Our findings relevant to these parameters concur with those of several other authors (Bernard, 1971; Duberman, 1973; Gardner, 1976; Messinger, 1976; Ransom et al., 1979; Tessman, 1978).

Constitutional and Intrapsychic

Constitutional and intrapsychic variables are strong determinants of the way the child meets life situations and of his "fit" in the family system. His intrapsychic dynamics, his personality strengths and deficits, shape the options available to him for coping with change and stress, as well as the way he deals with the conflicts within himself, his family system, and subsystems. All of these influence how he manages his Rem situation and how his Rem situation manages him.

The child's age at the time of remarriage is influential also: The very young child (under five years) and the older adolescent (above 18) tend to assimilate into Rem most easily; the middle age groups present the most problems.

Mourning the Loss of the Nuclear Family

The way in which the bioparents responded to the loss involved in the marital breakup is meaningful for the child and affects his ability to use Rem as a positive force. If the parents are unable to mourn the loss of the spouse and nuclear family, they will be unable to provide good-enough pathways for the child to mourn. The degree of emotional attachment then remaining will hamper the child's acceptance of the Rem family.

Where there has been intense bonding between the child and his custodial parent during the double single-parent stage, both parent and child may find it difficult to relinquish this exclusivity and allow room for the stepparent. The time span between marriages is an important variable here. If double single parenthood lasts a long time, the parent-child roles may be rigidified and resistant to change; if the period of single parenthood is short, it is likely that the mourning processes have not been completed for the child and parent. Based on our clinical observations, but without adequate research of nonclinical families, we suggest not less than one year and up to three years to be the optimum period of time for single parenthood after divorce.

Which Parent in Which Household Remarries

Currently women at the ratio of nine to one retain custody of their children. This means that in the vast majority of Rem families the custodial children have a stepfather. Stepmothers predominate in the non-custodial households. Yet it is the stepmother who is most often cast in the role of the wicked stepparent. The wicked stepmother myth may in part be based on a prior historical time when only men had legal status. Custody of a child, with rare exception, was lodged with the father. It was not until the middle of the nineteenth century that the "tender years" presumption evolved and custody of a child moved in the direction of the mother because she was seen as more nurturing and more crucial to the developing child during the first seven years (tender years) of life (Wald, 1981).

Each type of household, with visiting children or custodial children, presents its own challenges. The most complex situation is where both Rem adults are custodial parents. Perhaps equally complex is where one Rem adult is a custodial parent and the other a visited parent: Children leave and visiting children appear. This is what we have defined as the "revolving door" syndrome in Rem.

It has been our observation that it is more difficult for the child when it is the custodial parent who remarries rather than the visited parent. This follows from the fact that there is less disruption in the primary household of the child. However, it is not uncommon that the remarriage of a noncustodial parent will reverberate in the single-parent subsystem to the extent that the custodial parent may be motivated to make a major shift—begin to date, move in with someone, want to move to another city or state, etc.

The Relationship Between the Bioparents

If there is ongoing hostility between the bioparents, the child's adaptation to Rem is more difficult. The hostility is often played out by using the child as a messenger between households or negatively identifying him with the ex-spouse ("You're just like your father—no good").

The child needs permission (emotionally) from both bioparents to become a real member of Rem. If he perceives that his unmarried bioparent is unhappy, he may feel too guilty to begin to attach to the stepparent. When a parent has died, the child needs a sense that the deceased parent would have approved of the remarriage and the child's new parental bond. Sometimes this is achieved by the approval of the surviving grandparents, sometimes through discussion with the surviving parent or approval of other members of the Rem family suprasystem.

When a custodial parent has remarried, that parent may be freed from the burdens of single parenthood and may become more accessible to the child. However, there can be withdrawal from the child because of the new marital and familial pulls. In these instances the remarriage is another loss for the child and may affect his development adversely. It is up to the remarrying parent to maintain the connection with his child, despite any possible rejections, withdrawal, and hostility from the child. In the long run, such persistence pays off.

Contractual Expectations

Children and adults enter Rem with a variety of expectations, both conscious and unconscious, stated and unstated. These expectations relate to what the child expects to receive from his parent, stepparent, and stepsibs, and what he expects to give in return; they also relate to what he expects the family as a whole to be, who will have authority over whom, how responsibilities will be divided, what the behavioral and cultural ground rules might be. The child has a set of expectations of what he wishes to receive and to give, similar to the "contracts" of two marital partners.

What is crucial is to what extent the child's contract melds or conflicts with those of the other Rem family subsystem members. For example, the child may want to depend on his stepparent as a parent, while the stepparent may expect more of a pal or peer-like relationship with the child. Often the custodial parent expects his new spouse to take over rearing and/or discipline of the child, while the child expects that the bioparent will continue to be the primary caretaker. It is common that a childless stepparent will see in the child the opportunity to have reciprocal parent-child love fulfilled, while the child sees this demand as disloyal to his other bioparent. Or, the child may see the remarriage as a chance to reexperience a more complete parental home with structure and stability, while the parent's and stepparent's contracts are to be primarily mates and secondarily parents. All the possible contractual conflicts between the child and family, their intensity, and how they are resolved contribute to the child's adjustment in Rem.

Stepsibling Subsystem

The children's subsystem of the original nuclear family experiences changes prior to the remarriage. With the separation of their parents, the children may remain physically in one household or be split between the two households. Emotionally they may join together in a compensatory dependent relationship or they may remain isolated from one another. Their reaction is very much determined by their parents' needs and availability to them.

The subsystem of children from the nuclear family probably has been stabilized by the time of the remarriage. Remarriage causes another disruption in the sibling subsystem. Ordinal positions may change, competition may be heightened (stepsibs are often the same age and sex, in the same grade), roles change, e.g., the responsible oldest may suddenly be the youngest or an infantalized youngest may lose his special position.

The stepsibling subsystem can facilitate the adjustment of children to Rem ("We're all in this together") or can be maladaptive, especially when there is a great deal of competition for the adults and when there are striking differences in school achievement and financial resources.

Sometimes stepsiblings know each other from school or the community and have established a friendship before their respective parents remarried. They then find themselves together in a household as "siblings." This is a radical shift in roles, degree of intimacy, and level of relating.

Life-cycle Conflict

The degree to which the child's life-cycle stage or developmental needs blend or conflict with the phases of Rem influences positively or negatively the child's prognosis for a successful adjustment and ability to develop in a growth-nurturing ambience. For instance, a built-in conflict exists between the child's needs for parenting and the Rem couple's need for a period of romantic bonding.

Frequently, problems arise in a new Rem family when there is a prepubescent child who is rapidly becoming aware of his sexuality. With parental remarriage still in the short-term bonding stage, sexuality and romance may pervade the household and be overstimulating to the youngster. The youngster can react in a number of ways:

1) with anger at and resentment of parental sexuality;
2) by acting out sexually himself;
3) by dealing with the intensity of his own conflicting feelings by withdrawing or pushing away the adults;
4) by developing values and morals that differ greatly from the parents' wishes and teachings.

The new couple may be so preoccupied with their own love needs that they overlook important age-appropriate needs of the children. The child who becomes the squeaky wheel and protests this relative neglect may get his needs met or may become symptomatic or the scapegoat for the adults' dyadic problems.

Cultural, Religious, Socioeconomic Factors

Divergent cultural, religious, and socioeconomic backgrounds are frequent in Rem households. Often the home household and the visited household are divergent too. How these differences are dealt with is an important consideration. If differences are respected both between households and within each household, a more favorable situation for the child will be established.

Differences in households may be disproportionately overemphasized when one or both bioparents are not adequately emotionally divorced and use the child to strike out at one another. It is often difficult for a divorced parent to accept that his child will not be raised as he would have raised the child himself.

Financial Gulfs

The degree to which stepsiblings experience financial inequality due to differences in resources of families of origin may adversely affect the child's adaptation to Rem, particularly if the gulfs are large. This can exacerbate the sense of competition, deprivation and isolation. For some children it produces a defensiveness about their less financially achieving bioparent, for others a negative sense of worth of themselves and their bioparent. Values are sometimes quite warped.

The Rem Family Suprasystem

Grandparents and extended family such as aunts and uncles can play a highly significant part in the adaptation of the child to Rem, particularly if they were deeply involved with the child during the double single-parent stage. Their approval may be needed for the child to feel free to form new attachments. Unfortunately, parts of the suprasystem may hang on to the child and/or interpret the remarriage as a disloyalty to the "old" family or to a deceased parent. The community is also influential, to the extent that Rem is or is not commonplace and blends in with the environment. With other children available who have stepparents, the child can find peer support and learn ways of coping with his situation. Many school programs now include discussions in class of divorce and remarriage with an exchange of feelings and experiences by the students (see Chapter 16).

Change of Residence, School, Peer Group

The integration of the child into Rem is more difficult if he is uprooted and moved to a new community and new school, and therefore needs to make new friends. It is preferable, although not always possible, if something in the child's outside life can remain continuous rather than subjecting him to total upheaval.

THE EXPERIENCE OF REM FROM A CHILD'S PERSPECTIVE

Positive Potential

There are many positive aspects of the multiplicity of Rem for the child. After seeing a destructive marital relationship between his bioparents, he may gain positive models and a feeling of stability from the loving interaction of the Rem couple. He may get care and attention from his stepparents, sibs, and grandparents that add to the bounty from bioparents. The multiplicity of personalities, styles of living, and values may give the child the rich mosaic of life in an extended family without its structural certitude and monolithicity. A stepparent offers the child opportunities for selective identification and may compensate for limitations in the bioparents. A child whose mother is a stern, distant person may look to the warmth and gentleness of his stepmother as a way of getting some other needs gratified. His father may love him but have a limited education; the child may find intellectual stimulation in a brighter or more educated stepfather. His breadth of choice of a future mate is broadened insofar as he is influenced by parental introjects and projections (Dicks, 1967).

Multiplicity of Relationships

In order to understand how the child experiences Rem, one needs to be aware of the multidimensional system of interaction. The young child, perhaps depleted by the events leading to Rem, has to rally his forces and begin to understand and relate to the Rem family suprasystem where the number of members has increased and the rules have become increasingly unclear. There is a likelihood that any move he makes will reverberate in at least two households. When a child asks for help with his homework from his stepfather, there are implications for his biofather living on the other side of town and for his stepsiblings who see their stepbrother take their father's time. A holiday or a birthday is not just a day to be enjoyed anymore, but a time of tension to make sure everyone in the family is satisfied and no parent or stepparent feels slighted by where and how the child chooses to spend his time.

If the Rem household is a destructive one, the child may be able to leave the noxious environment by spending weekends in the household of the other bioparent:

> John, age eight, lives with his mother and stepfather in a tense home where he is not allowed to assert himself or be angry, but he is constantly castigated for being passive and stupid. When he spends weekends with his father and stepmother, he is able to speak up and get positive encouragement for his point of view. Although this is confusing to John, without his weekends he may grow up believing that being himself is a dangerous and impossible idea.

For the child, shifting back and forth between households may not have a positive effect; rather, it may make him experience himself emotionally as an orphan. One must keep in mind that vertically the child has already had several household changes and now horizontally he has to relate to at least two households, both of which may also not be constant. For instance:

> A 10-year-old girl residing with her mother and stepfather is an only child during the week, and the oldest child on the weekends when her stepfather's toddler children come to visit. When she visits her biofather, who has a young teenage stepdaughter, she then becomes the younger child in that household.

The systems and roles in each household may be quite different, and the reentry from one to another is typically difficult for the child in that a sense of loss may occur each time. However, as the child becomes older and/or becomes familiar with the to and fro pattern, reentry and separation usually become easier. The entire process becomes much easier when the adults do not stimulate the child's loyalty conflicts and do not use him/her in their own conflicts.

Divided Loyalties

If the households of the ex-spouses are hostile, the child may be used as a mediator between them. Divided loyalties between his feelings for the two bioparents and between the bioparents and the stepparents are common. The child can feel he has to choose between parents; the anxiety engendered by this may cause him to withdraw to a pseudo-independent regressed stance. He may experience divided loyalties between his natural siblings and stepsiblings, particularly where a stepsibling is close in age and becomes a buddy to the child, thereby usurping the exclusive role his biosibling may formerly have had.

Divided loyalties can extend to grandparents and other parts of the suprasystem. A child may like his new, acquired stepgrandparents, but may feel the resentment of this by the biograndparents.

Pseudo-independence

The pseudo-independent stance of a child will often have originated during the double single-parent stage, when the child was left to his own devices in the midst of post-divorce chaos. This stance is the direct result of the loss of the child's "holding environment." This pseudo-independence may become reinforced or heightened by the remarriage. For example:

Annie, in the custody of her mother, was 11 when her father remarried a woman with two children. Prior to this, Annie had been
responsible for herself while her busy professional mother worked.
Her visits to her father, who was very attentive, had been times
when she could be a "child" again. After the remarriage and with
her father's increasing involvement with his new wife, stepchildren, and then a new baby, Annie became engrossed in her peer
group and then exclusively with one boy to the extent that she
formed a premature couple bond with him. With this pseudo-independent stance, she opposed all parental dictates, became sexually
involved, and made the demands of an older adolescent. When
these were denied, she and her boyfriend would disappear for days
and engage in minor delinquent activities. The extrusion of Annie
was reversed when her mother, in therapy, learned to be more attentive to her needs. Her father and stepmother, also with the help
of therapy, included her more in their family, allowing her to be the
older child. She became very attached to their baby. As her needs
were met, she dropped her boyfriend and developed ties with a
group of peers.

Often the child will repress hostility he feels toward his bioparent for
fear of another abandonment and will project his hostility onto the stepparent. If even this expression of conflict is too dangerous, the child
may withdraw into a depression that is synergized by unresolved
mourning. A parent who has also repressed mourning may feel threatened by the child's grief and attempt to cut it off. The child may withdraw further into depressive mourning or act it out in rebelliousness
and antisocial behavior.

Incest Fears

The incidence of household incest between stepparent and child and
among stepsiblings is higher than among their biological counterparts.
The tragedy of Phaedra is not unique. The weakened incest taboos in
the Rem family may prevent the child from reaching out to the stepparent for normal parenting. The Rem couple is at the start of a new
marriage and sexuality pervades the household. A child's Oedipal-like
attachment to a stepparent is not as safe as that to a bioparent. For a
mother to watch her five-year-old daughter flirt with her daddy can be a
threatening experience. But if "daddy" is a stepfather, all three family
members may experience anxiety, which may be defended against by
withdrawal and distancing that is maintained by a constant series of
hostile acts (see Chapter 13).

CLINICAL ASPECTS

Initial Stages

An understanding of the suprasystem and its subsystems, the matrix for the child's existence, is essential in working with children of Rem. Although the treatment process may involve one or more subsystems of the Rem family suprasystem, it is important to keep in mind how the treated part fits into the entirety of interrelated persons. For the child, the ex-spouse bioparent must often be our concern on equal terms with the new adult couple and all the children.

The general approach we utilize in initiating assessment and treatment in Rem families with children was discussed in the first part of Chapter 6. We underscore, however, the importance of trying to have all the members of the child's two households and other significant members of the Rem family suprasystem attend the first session. By significant, we mean those who have input, at least currently, that affects the child's well-being. Most commonly, this includes all bio- and stepparents, bio- and stepsiblings, and grandparents.

It is most important to emphasize that it is the parenting and stepparenting issues, not the ex-marital issues (such as alimony) which are the adults' and our common agenda. It is then up to the therapist to be directive and maintain the limits of the agenda during the sessions. Whom to include, when to include them, and how to set up a session are matters of diagnostic acumen, artful timing, and sensitivity on the part of the therapist. Conceptualizing the suprafamily system and the dynamics of its parts makes it much easier to make these determinations. Our objective is to produce change as effectively and rapidly as possible. Understanding the suprafamily system and including appropriate subsystems in the treatment program minimize the sources of resistance to change and maximize the potential for change.

It is paramount that the therapist be flexible. For example, it is often necessary to see each bioparent separately to facilitate trust in the therapist or to promote comfort in the joint sessions. The clinician may have to enlist a co-therapist for another part of the system, which may be in an isolated role position and in need of support. A noncustodial parent, after a bitter divorce and custodial fight, may feel that the Rem family's therapist must be allied with his former spouse and antagonist. To be included in the treatment program, he may need his own therapist to meet with individually for one session and then act as a support/interpreter for him in conjoint sessions. We utilize a model for this that is adopted from MacGregor et al.'s (1964) multiple impact family therapy.

Often, for a brief period different therapists may be assigned for the child or children, the Rem couple, and the former spouse. They may meet separately with the assigned subsystem, as well as in the entire group meeting. When a co-therapist is not available, one therapist can meet separately with different subsystems for a brief time.

Goal Setting

"Treatment" actually begins with the first phone call. The therapist's acceptance that "you can't go home again" and that the Rem family will never be the same as the "original" family (nor should it be) promotes realistic goals of individuation and differentiation of system members. Goals are set both for the family as a whole and for the individual members. It is necessary to consider the noncustodial bioparent as well as the Rem family and the child. The therapist's knowledge of family and child development, as well as his special knowledge of Rem, comes into play in setting goals and throughout the entire treatment process.

TREATMENT TECHNIQUES

Clinicians working with remarried families must keep in mind the special Rem issues, as well as emotional and interactional issues which are universal rather than unique to Rem. They should involve the family in clear contracting and goal setting and be able to assign tasks as indicated to facilitate goal attainment. In addition, they should be able to intervene at different levels of understanding: systemic, life-cycle, and intrapsychic.

We employ a multimodal technique in the sense that we include individual, couple, and conjoint family therapy as well as groups, multiple family therapy and network therapy, in various combinations when and as needed. Decisions regarding the timing of the various modalities and who shall be included or what subsystems worked with at any time are essential to developing a workable approach to a particular family.

Different issues and techniques may necessarily be involved for the variations of Rem that are seen by the clinician. There are some common Rem family issues which are often addressed that have direct bearing on the child's functioning: unresolved mourning, the special use of history, clarification of expectations of roles and relationships for the child and all adults, and exploration of myths.

Unresolved mourning can be a major block to the consolidation of the

Rem family. Here mourning is referred to in the larger sense of the failure to grieve for the absent or dead parent, for the loss of the "old family" and way of life. The therapist may find the expression of this in the child's inability to adjust to a new school or neighborhood, in longing for the former place of residence, or through more indirect expression such as complaints about food. The therapist may then involve the family in a mourning process. This can be done with the original nuclear family as a whole, or it may be more relevant to break the family into bio-units, so the child is seen separately with each of the biological parents and sibs, as was done in the Stein-Miller case in Chapters 6 and 7.

A primary difference in Rem family therapy as compared to treatment of the intact family is the *special use and meaning of history.* Many family therapists approach work with the nuclear family with a deemphasis on history and concentration on the here-and-now interaction; however, with Rem families history is vital. History determines cross-generational alliances which are reinforced by blood ties.

History-taking can also be used to create a bond for the two newly joined families. It is a way for family members to become acquainted and introduced to each other. This often has not occurred as a pre-Rem process but is vital for the family to be able to appreciate and respect one another. The therapist may then use this material to make connections for the family in terms of similarities and differences.

Peck (1974) points out that it is the Rem family's press for members to be the same and intolerance of variation which promotes pseudomutuality in the family and precipitates further disruption and crises. The therapist can highlight the variety of feelings, attitudes, values, and behavior to illustrate that differences are not only there, but are to be expected and accepted. Paradoxically, stressing difference rather than pushing for harmony can facilitate the growth of Rem in a more genuine way.

Instruments for a Diagnostic Assessment

When indicated, the therapist may get a clearer picture of the child's development and current functioning through obtaining and interpreting a developmental history and through judiciously using psychological testing and school reports. Although our approach is to work "down" from the Rem suprasystem to the subsystems to the individuals, this does not preclude using these assessment instruments in selected cases. For example, there may be a question about a child's school failure relating to learning difficulties, or symptoms such as impulsivity or depression relating to an undiagnosed medical condition. Sometimes, problems in a child predate the remarriage or predate the death of a bioparent or the divorce. Family functioning and Rem issues may exacerbate or exaggerate a problem which is medical or learning-related. We prefer to see the individual and systemic issues as interconnected factors with interconnected levels of understanding rather than be caught in an either/or conflict.

Individual Sessions with a Child

It is not antithetical to our approach to provide individual sessions for the child; we do not religiously adhere to only seeing the Rem family subsystem or other parts of the suprasystem conjointly. There should be a rationale for seeing the child alone: for instance, if there are severe loyalty conflicts for the child between two sets of parents, or if the child has been abused or molested. Choosing to see the child alone will also depend on the therapist's bias, comfort, and orientation, as well as the child's motivation and the parent's ability to descapegoat. Seeing a child alone too early in the course of treatment may preclude meaningful involvement of the adults in therapy. Child treatment later on is usually more acceptable to the child and less likely to be unconsciously sabotaged by the adults, who no longer need the scapegoat and are prepared to offer the child a healthier and more nurturing environment.

Play Therapy

Play materials in the office facilitate contact with young children. While this is obvious, it is not common for therapists who see many couples and families to think of having play materials available. These may include at least two sets of family figures, with a few additional figures to represent significant others in the child's life. In some situations two simple doll houses could be most helpful. Cars, trucks, pistols, checkers, crayons, paper and clay are also suggested. The therapist's comfort and familiarity with the use of play as well as other techniques are illustrated in the following vignette:

> During the first of three planned sessions, Richard, age nine, was reluctant to talk, but the medium of play allowed him to become occupied and somewhat freer to verbalize. He responded positively when his clay productions were praised. He talked about his school experience and said that he understood that he had so much difficulty because he was a dumb boy and could not do better. There was a sense of helplessness and hopelessness in this child.

During the second session Richard was more withdrawn and it was difficult to elicit much from him. However, in preparing for the third and final sessions, the therapist anticipated this recurrence and set up a tape recorder and planned to use Gardner's mutual story-telling technique (Gardner, 1976) as a means of involving Richard during the session. He responded positively to this invitation and initially told a story of his time with his mother and his weekends with his father.

Richard told a story of a dragon who lived in a cave and went out into the forest every night and found people, dragged them back to his cave, killed them and ate them. A boy became lost in the forest and found his way to the cave. The dragon was very angry and asked what the boy was doing there. When the boy said that he was lost, the dragon said that if he was not out of the cave in five seconds he would be killed and eaten. The boy ran out of the cave and ran and ran into the forest until he came into another cave. In this cave there was another dragon and the exact same thing happened. The boy ran back to the first cave and told the dragon to come into the middle of the forest and he would have a surprise for him. The boy then ran to the second cave, which was five miles away, and told the same thing to the second dragon. The boy then went to the village and told all the people that they did not have to worry about the dragons any more. He was certain that, since he had learned that the two dragons used to be married to each other but were divorced, and since they hated one another so much, the two dragons would meet in the middle of the forest and would kill each other. The boy then returned to the middle of the forest and to his surprise the two dragons were talking and laughing together. They told him that they had decided that they wanted to live together again and they lived happily ever after. The boy told them that they didn't have to worry because he would bring them food every day so that they no longer had to kill the people or animals for food.

This was the end of Richard's story. Without the therapist having to mirror Richard's feelings by telling another story, he was able to discuss his great sadness about his parents' divorce, the loyalty bind he experienced, and his wish that they would reunite.

The Children's "Contract"

Just as the marital contract is used with adults to clarify couple issues, the children's contract (see Appendix B) can be used with children age 10 and older to help elucidate what the child expects to receive and give in relating to the adults and other children in his family and subsystems. Not a contract in the legal sense, the children's "contract" can tap into expectations and attitudes which the child was not aware of or could not verbalize. It is an instrument that outlines several parameters of frequent concern for Rem children and is meant as a reminder list. The child can discuss his ideas, hopes and fears, hopefully to reach some agreement on the terms. It can be written by the child or, for some, it would be better to just be talked through at home or with the family in session and then with the therapist. Parts of the reminder list can be used by the therapist to discuss selected parameters with the child and his concerned adults during sessions.

Other Techniques

In families with young children, it can be useful to employ in family and individual sessions the natural media of the child: play, fantasy, acting, drawing, movement, role playing, and an endless host of others. We have found sculpting to be particularly useful in helping define emotional boundaries and issues such as inclusion and exclusion in the family (see sculpting session in Chapter 7). In addition, we often role play with a family member or have children take parental roles and vice versa to help develop empathy and also to diffuse some of the circular and nonproductive repetitive interaction. We may request the parent or stepparent to play with the child in the session; in response we may observe and perhaps interpret and redirect. The entire repertoire of techniques with children should be available, keeping in mind the objective of achieving the established goals by the most parsimonious means.

PROBLEMS OF THE THERAPIST

Therapists' reactions to working with Rem have been discussed fully in Chapter 5. We will emphasize here a few points relevant to work with Rem children. Where there has been desertion or death by a bioparent, hostility on the part of a stepparent, neglect, overprotectiveness or indulgence on the part of a bioparent, it is common for the therapist to want to rescue the child from the situation. Hostility towards the "offending" adult has to be guarded against.

It is important for the therapist to be alert to the need for children in Rem families to preserve the positive parts of their images of both bioparents. Children are defensive of their parental images; an attack on a parent is an attack on them. The therapist has to counter the parental tendency to polarize the child's feelings so that one parent is all good, the other parent and/or stepparent all bad. This type of splitting often produces devastating results in the child's sense of self and of his parents. The therapist may unwittingly play out his nontherapeutic reaction in sessions by allying with the child against the "bad" parent or by competing with the parent for the child's affection. If the family denies their conflicts and focuses their trouble on the child, the therapist may sense that certain material is forbidden, join the denial, focus on the child and/or encourage pseudo-mutuality.

Therapists who are stepparents themselves may over-identify with stepparents, especially when a child is particularly hostile and rejecting of the stepparents' efforts to reach him/her.

SUMMARY

It is important that we learn how to make the Rem suprasystem work best for children and adults. For the children in Rem, the multiplicity of relationships, personalities, values and lifestyles can be extremely enriching, devastating or a combination of both. The child experiences a combination of home lives that he would not have been exposed to in an intact nuclear family. Under the best circumstances and with non-hostile co-parental planning, Rem can provide an alternative family lifestyle that is different from that of a few generations ago but need be no worse or better than others.

Increasing public awareness of the incidence of remarriage, and knowledge that the adjustment to Rem is difficult for all concerned, even under the best psychological and material circumstances, is reflected in the fact that parents now focus on problems sooner, with some parents seeking preventative help before remarriage in the form of educational groups at community resources, health-oriented rap groups at clinics and from self-help sources. Schools have begun to have class discussions about separation, divorce and remarriage. Teachers are alert to look for effects of family disruption in their charges and to seek help when necessary (see Chapter 16).

In our clinical work with children of remarriage we are increasingly seeing referrals of a child and his family before problems are at crisis proportions, although crisis situations are still in the majority. We emphasize the importance of including in assessment, and as indicated, in treatment too, all the involved members of the child's suprasystem. To exclude noncustodial parents or ex-spouses and stepparents will usually mean that the therapeutic effort will be short-circuited in some way, the child leaving each session to return to an unchanged noxious system environment.

CHAPTER 10

The Adolescent
in the Rem Family

Let us remind ourselves who the adolescent is before considering the adolescent in the Rem family. It is probably easier to understand who the adolescent is not. He is not a child, and he is not an adult. In primitive cultures the period of adolescence may be quite short and include just an initiation or rite of passage ceremony. In contemporary highly technical societies the adolescent years are being extended because the complicated roles and perplexing tasks adults must assume require more time and energy to learn. In this context, we can say that our adolescent is one who is expected to be giving up the role of the child but who is not yet expected to have integrated the tasks required to assume the role of the adult. Biologically he is adult; sociologically and psychologically he is maintained in a dependent condition.

However, even with this sketch the normal adolescent is not a person who is easily described. Through history the typical adolescent's behavior, at best, has been depicted as rebellious and, at worst, has been diagnosed as pathological. Consider the remarks Anthony (1969, p. 77) selected to quote:

Socrates:
    Our adolescents now seem to love luxury. They have bad manners and contempt for authority. They show disrespect for adults and spend their time hanging around places gossiping with one another. . . . They are ready to contradict their parents, monopolize the conversation in company, eat gluttonously, and tyrannize their teachers.

248

We will not be discussing the "disturbed" adolescent in this chapter. We will be describing the "normal" adolescent and the more complex family suprasystem the Rem constellation presents to the youth as he struggles to become an adult. In this way the strengths of the adolescent, as well as his limitations, will be seen. After all, while displaying rebellious, obnoxious and hostile behavior, the adolescent does love intensely, has lofty ideals and values and can be very generous, at least to people outside his family. In no other population is it more important to keep in mind that there is a reverse side of equal intensity to the manifest behavior. This knowledge can be utilized by the therapist to help the Rem family and adolescent survive, laugh, and grow with the reassurance that adolescents really do mature into adults.

When we add to the many forces at play in the adolescent's growth towards individuation the series of upheavals of parental dissonance, separation, divorce, and then one or both parents remarrying, it is a wonder that so many do as well as they do in Rem situations. Our findings confirm those of Wallerstein and Kelly (1980b) that adolescents recover from the emotional fallout of separation and divorce better than do younger children. However, in Rem homes we often find they have more difficulties than do prepubescent youngsters unless they are accepted in the household by the adults with understanding and flexibility. They require the freedom to move in and out of many aspects of family life, and to give and to take from two households as they move towards greater individuation and peer culture involvement.

The experience of being an adolescent in a Rem family is different from the experience of being an adolescent in a nuclear family. It is different for the adults as well. In the first part of this chapter we will address these issues by:

1) defining the preadolescent and adolescent life tasks;
2) comparing and contrasting how each task is played out in the nuclear and Rem family;
3) defining the parental task in the nuclear and Rem family that relates to the particular adolescent task;
4) describing the therapeutic interventions necessary to help the adolescent and Rem family deal with their particular tasks.

The format of a chart that compares and contrasts the ideally functioning nuclear family and the Rem family is used. While this tends to exaggerate both situations, we use it since it organizes a vast amount of information that highlights the complexity of the Rem experience.

To develop a sense of identity is an ongoing life process, but it is during adolescence that this challenge is predominant. The adolescent's life tasks discussed are by no means conclusive but are salient to forming enough of an identity to move along the continuum to adult functioning.

The second part of the chapter focuses on the treatment of the adolescent in the Rem system, with discussion of:

1) progressive forms of the extruded adolescent syndrome;
2) treatment modalities;
3) case examples:
   a) growth-producing extrusion;
   b) destructive extrusion;
   c) extrusion from and return to Rem family.

A COMPARISON OF THE ADOLESCENT IN THE NUCLEAR AND REM FAMILY

Preadolescent Life-cycle Task

The preadolescent family experience is one where the previous epigenetic crisis—trust vs. mistrust, autonomy vs. shame, initiative vs. guilt, industry vs. inferiority—is resolved so that the next crisis—e.g., identity vs. identity confusion—can be met. "Crisis is used in a developmental sense to connote not a threat of catastrophe, but a turning point, a crucial period of increased vulnerability and heightened potential, and therefore, the ontogenetic source of generational strength and maladjustment" (Erikson, 1968, p. 96).

Preadolescent Task—Nuclear

Since the marital and parental tasks have been shared by the same two adults, there is more likely to have been created a stable enough environment for the adolescent to master the previous stages so that he can meet the next age-appropriate challenge with a shift in instinctual energy for and vulnerability to the crisis (Erikson, 1968).

Preadolescent Task—Rem

It is harder to master preadolescent life tasks since the stability of the home environment has gone through a period of enough discord to disrupt the nuclear family. The double single-parent phase and then the remarriage of one or both parents may have caused the child/adolescent to to take on inappropriate roles and responsibilities: parent's confidant, pseudo-spouse, parentified child. Loyalty bonds, chronic sorrow for the loss of

Parental Task—Nuclear
To create a stable enough home environment with the optimal amount of frustration to encourage the preadolescent to move to the next challenge. Environment must begin to encourage risk-taking and provide for rapprochement opportunities.

Parents begin to reinvest in their marital relationship.

nuclear family, and abandonment fears are often issues.

Parental Task—Rem
Same. Also included is the parental task to help the preadolescent express his reaction to the loss of the nuclear family, in particular abandonment fears, since in the nuclear family differences were responded to by divorce.

Bonding of the Rem couple but the Rem parent needs to function as a parental partner with the new spouse and the new former spouse.

Therapeutic tasks

1) To help Rem families with the above tasks. Particular attention needs to be given to assess the extent to which the family has dealt with the loss of the nuclear family. Unresolved mourning may be sapping vital energy from all family members which is needed to master their individual, family and Rem life-cycle tasks.
2) To help the family learn to negotiate differences which might not have been done in the nuclear family or family of origin. With the preadolescent there is a need to begin to shift from arbitrary authority to the negotiation of differences (Rhodes, 1977).

Adolescent Life-cycle Task

To begin to terminate the role of the child in the family and move to begin the role of an adult in the family.

Adolescent Task—Nuclear
It is difficult at best, but it is a single termination process and a single beginning with the same constant parental and sibling figures.

Adolescent Task—Rem
There is a double termination process—the loss of the role as the child and the loss of the nuclear family. There is also a double beginning process—the beginning of the adult role in the family and the beginning as a new member in the Rem family.* The

---

*We are grateful to Joseph G. Moore for his formulation of this double process concept.

closer the divorce and remarriage is to the adolescent phase, the more simultaneous and therefore the more intense the double aspect of the terminations' and beginnings' processes is likely to be felt.

Parental Task—Nuclear
To facilitate more independent functioning with a bifocaled vision of the adolescent's often denied dependency yearnings. To allow for regression and rapprochement refueling.

To encourage sibling support for the adolescent's more adult functioning.

Parental Task—Rem
Same, but more difficult since the task of the Rem family to consolidate is antithetical to the adolescent's task to move away from the family. The challenge is for the Rem family to integrate the adolescent as an adolescent and not as a child or adult.

Therapeutic tasks

1) To help the Rem family, which may be in its unstable and anxious beginnings, integrate an adolescent as an adolescent who by his very nature is protean in physical and psychological development and needs to begin to leave the family.
2) To confront the Rem suprasystem with its responsibility to the adolescent who is withdrawn, grandiose, unsure, self-centered, generous, pseudomutual, pseudo-independent, tenaciously hostile, self-destructive, romantically merged, or extruded.

Adolescent Life-cycle Task

To discern critically and integrate successfully those aspects of his parents' personality/identity that will be helpful to the youth as an adult.

Adolescent Task—Nuclear
The environment usually lends itself to have the adolescent express various aspects of the parents' personalities. There is some criticism often ambivalently expressed, "Oh you are just like your father/mother," but a

Adolescent Task—Rem
More difficult in Rem because the expression of, "Oh you are just like your father/mother," often has a negative connotation because the bioparent may not be able to recognize or acknowledge any positive aspect of the other

general feeling of acceptance of the adolescent prevails.

parent. This tends to place the adolescent in a loyalty bind. In extreme situations, when the adolescent expresses a positive connection to one parent, the other parent feels betrayed. In order to survive with this parent (usually the custodial parent), the adolescent may need to reject/split off all aspects of the other parent. Indirect, unconscious, often negative aspects of the rejected parent may find expression. In the positive sense, the addition of a stepparent may provide the adolescent with a person with whom to form a positive identification. Multiple identifications can offer the adolescent a variety of extended options. The Rem couple can provide a more viable marital role model. In the negative sense, multiple identification can lead to identity confusion, especially if parental figures operate counter to each other and thrust different values and points of view on the adolescent.

Parental Task—Nuclear

To create a family atmosphere wherein the adolescent can test out aspects of both parents' personalities. This requires an "accepting enough" atmosphere where he can evaluate and make choices about role identification, rather than become involved in power struggles and dyadic alliances against the other parent.

The adolescent is not an adult and limit-setting is still needed. Limit-setting should consider age-appropriate behavior and needs for greater independence.

Parental Task—Rem

Same, but may be more difficult because of a parent's unresolved feelings, e.g., consciously angry but often unconsciously positive sentiments for the divorced/deceased spouse. Bioparents' ongoing functioning as a parental pair affects this task as well. Consider how regular child support payments can influence a parent. It may be harder for the bioparent to encourage identification with a stepparent of the same sex, since he may feel as if his marital and parental role has been usurped;

competitive, jealous, and angry
reactions may be common.

Therapeutic task

1) To help the adolescent and parental figures integrate a realistic picture of both parents, a picture that considers each parent's strengths and weaknesses.
2) To help parental figures understand that the adolescent needs to identify with both parents and other significant adults, including stepparents. To help them create an atmosphere where this is possible.

   Wallerstein and Kelly's (1980, b, p. 76) research findings state: "The most tragic situations for the child were those in which mother and stepfather demanded that the child renounce his or her love for the father as the price for acceptance and affection within the remarried family. Such children were severely troubled and depressed, too preoccupied with the chronic unresolvable conflict to learn to develop at a normal pace."
3) To attempt assiduously to include both biological parents in treatment since without both parental contacts it becomes hard not to assume one parent's view of the other. If personal contact is not possible, telephone and/or written communication is the next best alternative. A prime example is an incident where a biomother complained that her ex-husband did not care about their pill-popping teenage son. She complained that when she attempted to discuss the problem with him he "tuned out." When he was seen (quite willingly contrary to his wife's caveat regarding his attitude about "shrinks"), he complained that his ex-wife was emotional when she spoke about their son and spoke in her mother tongue, Portugese, a language he did not understand.
4) To see that positive and not destructive identification with parental figures is encouraged.

Adolescent Life-cycle Task

To integrate affect and develop self-control by mastering the expression of heavily charged feelings and impulses. To learn how to negotiate with adults since the parental decision-making that was prevalent during latency is no longer appropriate.

Adolescent Task—Nuclear	*Adolescent Task—Rem*
The adolescent experiences frequent mood swings. It is common for the adolescent to move	Same mood swings prevail but anger toward parents may be more intense since they "failed"

quickly from intense feelings of love to bitter feelings of hate; noble idealism to narrow prejudice; sublime elation to acute depression. In expressing these affects the adolescent can seem like a young child (angry outbursts, verbal tirades, temper tantrums) or an adult (thoughtful debates, philosophic discussions). The adolescent is more likely to be able to risk expressing a wide range of feelings—more predictably anger, criticism, and doubt, but occasionally softer emotions—since the family history is more likely to have provided a stable enough home environment where abandonment fears usually have not and will not become an issue. Family history is one where there is a greater likelihood for differences to have been negotiated successfully.

to provide the stable nuclear family—"a holding environment." The inhibition of the expression of feelings towards parents may be common because of loyalty conflicts and abandonment fears. The family history is one where differences have led to separation. Ambivalence and anger about the situation are often displaced onto the stepparent. In her study of more than 2,000 marriages, Bernard (1971) found that very young children and older adolescents tend to accept a stepparent more easily than those in between.

Parental Task—Nuclear

To lovingly survive what is apparently the normal process of adolescent passage by containing and establishing parameters for the expression of anger, criticism, and normal (from the parental viewpoint) adolescent unpleasantness. Humor, objectivity, knowledge of normal adolescent behavior, and mutual parental support are necessary to weather attacks that threaten self-esteem. Without these defenses parents are more apt to become intimidated, feel weary, and then respond with arbitrary control, withdrawal, or expulsion.

A "loving fight" (Stierlin, 1979, p. 93) must develop between the parents and adoles-

Parental Task—Rem

Same, but often harder to accept the adolescent's anger and criticism since parents, in various degrees, may feel guilty for not providing their child with a stable nuclear family. Even a parent who is a widow may feel this way. There is less likelihood of a bioparent support system. Spouse (stepparent) support may not be forthcoming, especially when the stepparent has no prior positive history with the adolescent. The stepparent may feel more threatened by the adolescent's expression of anger because their relationship has only just begun. Expectations, rules, and roles should be clearly defined. In particular, the biopar-

cent where differences are negotiated with the goal of mutual accommodation and limit-setting based on the adolescent's need for growing independence.

ent must clearly define his dual role as spouse to his mate and parent to his adolescent. In the Rem system nothing can be taken for granted. The lack of models, the open system, and the newness of relationships obfuscate the standards of acceptable behavior. Family discussions that answer questions and define rules and responsibilities are helpful.

Therapeutic tasks

1) To help parents and adolescents continue to work through the anger and sorrow of the real (as opposed to the adolescent's symbolic) loss of the nuclear family. To help parents forgive themselves for "failing" to provide a stable nuclear family.
2) To help the Rem family subsystem appropriately express and hear family members' thoughts and feelings with the goal of mitigating the tendency to scapegoat (usually the adolescent or stepparent) or extrude the adolescent.
3) To clarify the range of normal adolescent behavior in nuclear and Rem families so that parents and adolescents can gain some objectivity about their situation.
4) To help Rem family members clearly define their expectations, rules, roles. In particular to help the bioparent, the power base of the triangle, define his roles of spouse and parent within the Rem subsystem and clearly state these roles to the Rem family.
5) To encourage mutual parental support systems (bioparent/stepparent, bioparent/bioparent) and parental coalition (bioparent/stepparent) so that they can all ride the wave of adolescence together and the adolescent can feel as much security as possible in this new Rem suprasystem.

Adolescent Life-cycle Task

Puberty brings hormonal, physical, and psychosexual growth. The adolescent becomes a more sexually directed being whose task is to rechannel Oedipal feelings and begin to form psychosexual relationships with peers.

Adolescent Task—Nuclear
There is a constant marital/pa-

Adolescent Task—Rem
What might have been an in-

rental pair who have developed a stable sexual relationship. The sexual atmosphere in the home has been woven into the fabric of family life. Parents have been together for several years and secure sexual expressions have replaced heightened sexuality of earlier times.

Incest taboo usually prevails vis-à-vis parents to children and between siblings.

tense, somewhat sexualized bond with parent of the opposite sex is "usurped" by the new spouse. While in the long run it is in the adolescent's best interest to be released from such a bond, initially it may be difficult and some adolescents have referred to this as a "second divorce."

The sexual atmosphere in the Rem household is heightened. The closer the remarriage is to the onset of adolescence, the greater the likelihood for 1) sexual attraction, often mutual, between stepparent and stepadolescent; 2) sexual attraction between stepsibs.

There is some loosening of the incest taboo. Members have not grown up together and a blood bond does not exist. Therefore, there may be a greater potential for household sexual activity or a more stressful reaction formation to the impulse.

Parental Task—Nuclear
To reinvest in the marital relationship. The adolescent needs to know again that he lost the Oedipal struggle, but is attractive enough physically and emotionally to have age-appropriate psychosexual relationships with peers.

To help the adolescent master the vicissitudes of closeness without using sexuality impulsively. To help the adolescent distinguish between intimacy and pseudo-intimacy. To continue to encourage sibling support for the adolescent's greater peer involvement. This may require exploring fears about the loss of the adolescent sibling.

Parental Task—Rem
Same, but more difficult to be available to the adolescent when energy is devoted to Rem consolidation, especially during the romantic short-term bonding stage and/or birth of a mutual child.

If the adolescent has "won" the Oedipal battle in the double single-parent stage, he may experience his parent's remarriage as his now having lost out. The parent's remarriage becomes a divorce for him; the stepparent is seen as his enemy.

Rem can provide the adolescent with a positive marital pair role model to neutralize the prior experience so that age-appropri-

ate psychosexual relationships
with peers can be pursued with
enthusiasm.

Due to heightened intrafamilial sexual feelings among stepparent, stepadolescent, and stepsiblings, the parents need to convey the limits of sexual expression so that the adolescent feels
safe.

Therapeutic tasks

1) To address and distinguish between physical attractions, enjoyable flirtations, normal arousal, and destructive sexual expressions. Sexual experiences between stepsibs needs to be evaluated
and is not necessarily cause for alarm.
2) To clarify that sexual thoughts and fantasies about family members are natural and not the same as actions. An open discussion
about this can dilute the intensity of these feelings.
3) To assess sexual behavior, overt and covert, of Rem family members to make sure that generational boundaries are maintained in
an atmosphere that also permits the expression of healthy sexuality. (For more complete discussion see Chapter 13.)
4) To work towards the consolidation of the Rem couple but, at the
same time, address the adolescent's need to venture out and come
home again. Bioparents, stepparents, and adolescents need to be
helped to work out mutually acceptable age-appropriate ways to
continue to experience themselves as significant to each other.

THE TREATMENT OF THE ADOLESCENT IN THE REM FAMILY

Wald's study on the number of years couples have been remarried at
the time of the first application and then of reapplication for help reveals that, although the highest number of applications comes during
the first year of the remarriage, many reapplications are made when
children reach adolescence (Wald, 1981). Our experience with Rem families supports this finding. Just as in nuclear families, the turmoil of adolescence in Rem families can stir issues that heretofore had been quelled.
In its positive aspect, the resurfacing of these issues provides the family
with an opportunity for greater mastery.

The dysfunctional Rem couple can interact with a disturbed or even
"normal" adolescent to produce the extruded adolescent syndrome.

The syndrome is progressive and begins with forms of subtle disengagement of Rem family members and concludes with forms of banishment of the adolescent. The syndrome is a system problem where the Rem couple's excluding behavior provokes the adolescent to react in a manner that elicits a still more negative and distancing response from the Rem couple. A reciprocating negative interaction between youth and adults builds up to an ultimate crescendo that eventuates a self-imposed or commanded banishment. While all degrees of extrusion can and do occur in most families, we have found that in Rem families with an adolescent all too often the extrusion is skewed toward more severe consequences. The degree of extrusion is inversely proportionate to the degree of Rem family consolidation, i.e., the more severe the extrusion the less evidence of Rem family consolidation.

In Rem families where the extruded adolescent syndrome occurs, the factors impeding consolidation have included:

1) The Rem couple's limited ability to resolve conflicts without using rigid rule setting and/or threats of, or actual, abandonment.
2) Characterological deficits in the adults in the system.
3) The Rem couple's fear of another failure—hence a denial of marital problems in the new family.
4) Adults' reaction formation to their anxiety about not being a consolidated family often leads the adults to insist that the adolescent spend more time with them than is appropriate to the adolescent's need to have peer involvement or to be by himself.
5) The projection of marital difficulties onto the adolescent, who becomes the scapegoat or the adolescent may be seen as the reminder or ghost of the previous marriage and the incarnation of the ex-spouse.
6) Immediate gratification needs replace problem-solving. These Rem families have few support systems and opportunities for refueling.
7) An acrimonious rather than cooperative relationship between the bioparental pair.
8) The adolescent's intense loyalty conflicts leave him feeling helpless, frustrated, and overwhelmed.
9) The unresolved mourning of the original nuclear family.
10) Neither bioparent's household really welcomes and wants the adolescent as he is.

Extrusion is a form of scapegoating. However, there are some characteristic differences. When an identified patient is scapegoated, he is usually pulled in and enmeshed within the family system. The family needs him to stay within the home where he performs a central function in maintaining the system's homeostasis. In extrusion there is an intense magical fantasy. The Rem family believes that if the adolescent physically leaves, the problems of the system will vanish. He is highly cathected to do so as the physical embodiment of the system's pain (history, ghosts, projections, etc.) and hence he must be banished from the household.

There is a danger in extrusion. If the adolescent leaves, there is a lessened chance of working out a resolution. If a child is scapegoated and remains within the household, there is a greater possibility that problems may eventually be resolved. However, extrusion is not necessarily a negative resolution to the Rem suprasystem's conflicts. An adolescent may be better off in boarding school, college, or his own apartment where he can grow and individuate. Remaining within the Rem household may overwhelm the adolescent with conflicts that hinder separation.

Forms of Extrusion

Table 10.1 shows the progressive forms of extrusion. To reiterate, this is a system problem. It is not important whether the adult's behavior initially provokes the adolescent to respond in an alienating way or vice versa. A reciprocating negative interaction is set up that tends to escalate if not interrupted; if interrupted, it is likely to return with the next minor incident unless different coping behavior can then take place within the system.

Of interest is our finding that stepsiblings often act as allies to the adolescent who is the identified patient and fight the extrusion. Perhaps defensively they sense the system's need for a scapegoat. In nuclear families siblings are usually in collusion with the myth that the identified patient is the problem and are fearful of what would occur if the family's problems were exposed. In the Rem subsystem, siblings and stepsiblings are less likely to be invested in the family myth and this leaves an opening for family members and the therapist to challenge it.

Birth of a mutual child can have an effect on the range of extrusion responses. During the pregnancy the adolescent may become anxious about his value and position in the family and sexually stimulated by fantasies of the adult's physical closeness and respond with a reaction formation form of self-extrusion. The Rem parents may become absorbed in the birth of their own child and extrude the adolescent. However, the birth of the infant often will provide a cohesive line/blood tie and common goal for all Rem family members, so that the extrusion behavior is not as necessary. The adolescent may become restituted by attaching to the baby and investing it with the nurturance he wants for himself. The attachment to the half-sibling may bring a better acceptance of the stepparent, who may then respond in kind.

TABLE 10.1
Extrusion of an Adolescent

Form of Extrusion	Parent's Response	Adolescent's Response
Subtle disengagement	Honeymoon period; preoccupation with new mate in short-term bonding phase; preoccupation with mutual child	Isolation; compulsive peer involvement to the exclusion of parents; pseudo-independent posture; compliant child/ pseudomutual child
Open hostility	Victim: "What is he doing to us?" Verbal abuse; physical attack	Victim: "What are they doing to me?" Hostile retorts; violent responses
Threats of extrusion	"I'll send you away to" . . . mother/father, suprafamily member, boarding school, court, childcare facility, hospital, etc.	"I want out from you too" . . . mother/father, suprafamily member, significant other, boarding school, etc. Suicidal threat and gestures; substance abuse; eating disorders; first flight—"I'll reject you before you reject me."
Temporary extrusions —spontaneous outbursts of rage.	Adolescent is temporarily sent away to mother/father, suprafamily member, childcare agency, etc.	Chronic periodic runaway and return; periodic merger with other systems: intense romantic involvement, friend's family, significant adults, substance abuse
Planned permanent extrusions	Change in custody arrangement to other parent or suprafamily member; boarding school. Geographic cure: kibbutz, study abroad, adolescent helped to relocate in distant state	Adapts well to new plan and grows to independent living; runaway; drug and alcohol addiction Hospitalization; delinquent behavior
Banishment	Throwaway—no contact with child: "You are not my child; you can never come back."	Suicide; runaway—missing person; cults; criminal behavior; jail; determination to make it on his own; attaches himself to parental surrogate

Evaluation and Treatment

Evaluation and treatment, in general, need not vary greatly from those outlined in Chapters 6 and 7. However, for adolescents we are very sensitive to an openly or subtly expressed desire to be seen alone. We then will use our judgment as to when and how to include significant Rem suprasystem members. It is important to take a careful developmental, school, medical, and social history. Determination of age-appropriate functioning prior to separation, after divorce, and at remarriage are important. Obviously, a youngster who always has functioned poorly is quite different from one who has done well until two months ago when his mother remarried.

Treatment Modalities

In the treatment of Rem families with an adolescent we use a multimodal approach that combines individual, family, and couple sessions. It is more common for us to use individual sessions for adolescents in Rem families than in nuclear families since adolescents in Rem families often have a greater need to test reality, ventilate anger, explore their ambivalence about autonomy, and mourn their losses. Individual sessions with the adolescent are most often utilized during the beginning phase of treatment. In the later phases, when libidinal energy begins to be rechanneled into the adolescent life tasks previously described, the adolescent often opts to terminate the individual sessions but continue in family sessions.

The mutual aid that group members can offer one another as they work on common tasks make Rem adolescent groups a productive and freeing treatment experience. In the case of Rem adolescents, these tasks include mourning the loss of the nuclear family and integration into the Rem family, as well as the normal tasks of adolescence. Often the adolescent's feelings of isolation are compounded by the misapprehension that he is the only one going through this particular dilemma. The group gives the adolescent the chance to test this reality.

Within our Rem multifamily therapy (MFT) group, teenagers receive support from each other and welcome the opportunity to talk about their concerns, particularly their ambivalent feelings toward their noncustodial parent or the Rem adults. When a custodial parent berated an absent, noncustodial parent to the adolescent, the other parents in the group were able to witness the devastating effects on the child's ego. This then led them to be supportive to both the adolescent and the parent and then to be more respectful with their own child or stepchild.

A very poignant exchange occurred when a mother (abandoned by her first husband years previously when she was pregnant with her third child) was denigrating her former husband to her teenage daughter—"He's no good, he's trash, he doesn't love you, he never did." In a breathtaking response, this very tough street kid wailed out, "But he's part of me. . . . When you destroy him you tear me apart." The silence within the group underlined the difficult situation of separating the issues: that adults are ex-marital partners but not ex-parents, and anger and resentment toward a former spouse are often justified, but need to be separated from their parental roles.

MFT is often a treatment of choice for Rem families with an adolescent. The group usually has a maximum of four families and two co-therapists working in a 90-minute session. It is not uncommon to have 20 or more members in an MFT group.

Case Examples

The following are three case examples of the extruded adolescent syndrome. One describes an extrusion that proved growth producing; the second unfortunately was not; and in the third the adolescent is extruded from the Rem household for two years and then returns (see Genogram).

When Maggie Jones, age 16, rejected a group home placement at another agency on the grounds that she could not identify with the girls from a lower socioeconomic class and found the rules too restrictive, she and her family were referred to the Remarried Consultation Service for outpatient counseling. Quite atypically, Maggie made the initial telephone call and repeated the same complaint she had when she went to the other agency: She and her mother were not getting along and she wondered if they should live together.

Since Mr. and Mrs. Jones' divorce when Maggie was five she lived with her mother. When Maggie was 14, her mother and male friend,

FIGURE 10.1
Jones Family Genogram

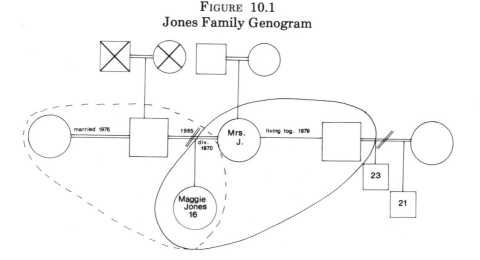

a divorced man with two young adult sons, moved into their apartment. Her father remarried a single woman when Maggie was 11. The family's original application for a residential placement was prompted by extrusion threats from Maggie's mother. These threats and mutually virulent outbursts exacerbated when Maggie entered her senior year at high school and began to apply to out-of-town colleges. The anticipated extended physical separation of the mother from her daughter made Maggie anxious and put her rather limited borderline mother in a panic state. As in the past, but now more intensely, Maggie's pseudo-independent behavior, i.e., "Don't tell me what to do," alternated with regressive behavior, i.e., "I can't do anything." Her mother's responses were equally extreme. They were punitive, i.e., "You'll do as I say" or permissive, i.e., "Whatever you do is fine." Both mother and daughter were depressed, threatened extrusion, and Maggie was temporarily extruded. In the past five years Maggie "shuttled" between her maternal and paternal households numerous times; grandparents and suprasystem members were not available. At the age of 14 she spent a week alone in a hotel. Maggie describes herself as "the first shopping bag child."

Mr. Jones and his new wife didn't have sufficient room for Maggie to live in their one-bedroom apartment. They made no genuine effort to get a two-bedroom apartment. Her presence interfered with the couple's extended romantic bonding and caused them to end up at loggerheads. Father and stepmother saw Maggie as the ghost of the previous "disastrous marriage," and this was further complicated by the second Mrs. Jones' mother and Maggie's mother having the same severe psychosomatic preoccupations and ailments.

Shortly after Maggie's initial application, all Rem family members were contacted, with an assiduous outreach to Maggie's mother who reluctantly conceded to come in for "one" individual session. Maggie was locked out of her mother's apartment. Although this had been threatened for years, her mother had finally changed the locks. As in the past, Maggie sought refuge in her father's home.

Mr. Jones and his wife agreed to have Maggie stay with them until an alternate living plan could be worked out. All agreed, and we supported their conclusion, that Maggie's prior living arrangement was not a viable plan for Maggie or other family members. At this phase of treatment Maggie was seen with her father and stepmother in family sessions and individually.

Within one week after Maggie was with them, Mr. and Mrs. Jones were in a battle and felt unable to resolve their conflicts short of physically separating from each other. Sorting out their projections revealed that Mr. Jones anticipated that his wife wanted Maggie out "yesterday," and Mrs. Jones anticipated that her husband wanted Maggie to remain permanently. Each read the other's unconscious somewhat correctly. In fact, when they were able to separate themselves from their projections, both had set a limit of three weeks longer. Maggie herself "yearned" for there to be room for her in their home. The direct expression of this to them, followed by their refusal to let her stay past three weeks, helped her to accept the reality that this would not be. Her own limit to stay with them then became not more than a month.

The couple was then helped to move from their permissive response of leaving Maggie on her own to find a new place to live without being given limits and guidelines, to the direction of making it a family effort. Financial limits, location options, possible alternative living arrangements and priorities were voiced by all family members. A week later, when Maggie did not follow through on some of the telephoning she previously took on as "easy" to do, Mr. and Mrs. Jones were furious. Mrs. Jones initially expressed this anger for the couple in the family session. This attack was stopped and rechanneled by the therapist into the possibility that Maggie may have bitten off more than she could chew and her father, stepmother, and therapist each had had a part in allowing her to do so. This enabled Maggie to ask for help with a task that proved to be "beyond" her. Mr. Jones' anger at his ex-wife and resistance to parenting his daughter were expressed in his angry retort, "Why do I have to do everything; she has a mother!" At that point the therapist firmly but warmly reminded him, "That is true, but you are the healthier parent." Mr. Jones was then able to offer Maggie his assistance and the search for the best place for her to live became a father/daughter project. This alliance did much to improve their relationship and mitigate against the Rem subsystem's need for a wicked stepmother. A women's residential hotel that had a limited in loco parentis structure and was near Mr. and Mrs. Jones' apartment house was chosen and worked out well.

Family sessions continued for two months after Maggie moved into the hotel with more work on the Rem family consolidation that had begun at the point of crisis. Maggie's stepmother became increasingly able to be a positive role model. After the family sessions the couple contracted for four months of couple sessions to work out better ways to resolve their marital dissonance. In Rem couples we have found that after problems with the adolescent have been resolved, the couple is then often more willing to look at their difficulties, but not before, as is sometimes possible in nuclear families.

Once Maggie was living on her own she initiated contact with her mother and their relationship was less volatile. Despite Maggie's and the therapist's urging, her mother refused individual or joint sessions.

Maggie's individual sessions, which began during the early stage of treatment in conjunction with the family sessions, continued for six months after the family sessions terminated. During the first phase the individual sessions were used to support Maggie's available ego strength, encourage her good functioning in school, test reality, and discharge feelings. A poignant dream illustrates this. At the third session Maggie, at the therapist's inquiry, told of a dream where she buys the Rolling Stones album she always wanted. When she hurriedly opens it up she sees that the record inside is not by the Rolling Stones but by a group, Blood, Sweat and Tears. She wonders, is this a Rolling Stones album with the wrong record or a Blood, Sweat and Tears album with the wrong cover? She feels frustrated and wakes up. Maggie was able to associate the feeling of frustration in the dream to the frustration she feels about accepting that her extrusion from both parents' homes is "for real." Associations to blood, sweat and tears led her to express anger, fear and grief about her predicament.

With the help of a stable living situation, better relationships with her father, mother and stepmother, and ongoing treatment, Maggie began to reach her high academic potential and enjoyed and maintained appropriate peer relationships. She was accepted to an out-of-town college and a local college. Her father and stepmother urged her to attend the out-of-town college and consider their apartment to be "home base" on school breaks. After careful consideration in individual sessions, Maggie chose the local college with dormitory accommodations since she felt more "secure" with her own room. This choice also left open the possibility of more individual and family sessions with the family.

The following example of extrusion became known to us through the Cult Clinic at the Jewish Board of Family and Children's Services.* This clinic services families whose teenagers, young adults, and sometimes senior citizens have become members of a cult.

Mrs. Langer, a divorced woman of 57, applied to the Cult Clinic. Her son Ezra, age 18, had been a member of a cult for 13 months at the time of application. Ezra maintained sporadic collect telephone contact with both his parents. While he usually sounded "brainwashed," his mother felt that recently he was more lucid. He began to express some dissatisfaction with the cult's leader and the hard work he was required to do.

Ezra's bioparents were seen for the first session. Subsequent

---

*Arnold Markowitz, Director of the Cult Clinic and a former staff member of the Remarried Consultation Service, supplied this case.

FIGURE 10.2
Langer Family Genogram

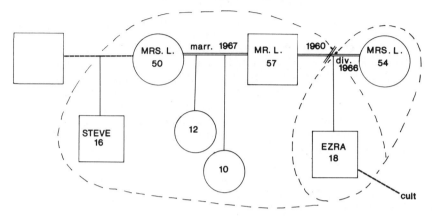

sessions included Mr. Langer and his Rem family and individual
sessions for all family members. The following case history was
pieced together.

Ezra's parents divorced when he was four years old. Mrs. Langer
had custody of Ezra and Mr. Langer moved to another state and
shortly thereafter remarried a woman with an out-of-wedlock son
who was two and a half years younger than Ezra. Mr. Langer and
his second wife then had two daughters. A successful business-
man, Mr. Langer always contributed child support, albeit unpre-
dictably paid, but he became less and less involved in Ezra's emotional life as his Rem family grew. Ezra's mother felt that total
responsibility for their son was "dumped" onto her lap. In junior
high school Ezra's grades went from bad to worse. There were
three aborted attempts at therapy. By his sophomore year of high
school Ezra was truanting often and was frequently high on marijuana. A year later when his mother found out he was dealing in
drugs, she panicked, became enraged, and felt she could not handle
him. She extruded him to live with his father. Mr. Langer thought
his ex-wife was always too permissive with Ezra and that his "firm
hand," a home in the suburbs, and stable Rem family would be the
answer.

In the Rem household the second Mrs. Langer was wary of this
abrupt change; she was especially wary of Ezra's influence on her
children. She had never developed a more than polite and distant
relationship with Ezra, but felt that she owed it to her husband to
go along with the plan since he had been so good to her and her son.
The typology of this remarriage was Mr. Langer/parental (rescuer)

partner and Mrs. Langer/childlike partner. Ezra and his step- and half-siblings expressed positive feelings about the arrangement and the family's spacious house was a plus.

The four-month honeymoon period ended when Mrs. Langer, Ezra's stepmother, found Ezra and her son smoking marijuana. Despite her son's acknowledgment that he was the one who initiated the incident, Mrs. Langer saw Ezra as the culprit. Mr. Langer admitted, with minimal regret, that he was unwilling to give his son the benefit of the doubt and risk the possibility of causing a rift with his wife. In the two months that followed, the father-son relationship became increasingly more disaffected. The children's relationships remained good but had to be surreptitious. Ezra was an outcast in the home.

Over a long holiday weekend, Ezra was urged by his father and stepmother to stay home and study (ostensibly for his own good) rather than join the family on a camping trip. At this point Ezra no longer offered even minimal resistance to being extruded from the family.

When Mr. and Mrs. Langer returned they found a note from Ezra stating that he was with friends and would not be coming home until the weekend. The adults admitted feeling disgusted with Ezra but relieved. A week later he came home during the day and took all his valuable possessions. Despite Mrs. Langer's admonishment he did not wait for his father. Mrs. Langer described him as "not in this world." When she questioned if he was high, he replied that he was "high on love" and had found "a real family" and his "spiritual mother and father." Mr. and Mrs. Langer admitted that they were worried but decided to give it some time before contacting Ezra's mother since, in the past, Ezra, despite his initial enthusiasm, was unable to follow through on his commitments. Ezra himself called his mother three weeks later. She then contacted her former husband and their well oiled mutual blame system was immediately set in motion.

By the time the family was seen in treatment, the parents and stepmother were ambivalent about Ezra's involvement in the cult. They were fearful of his safety, both physical and emotional, but did not want Ezra to return to live with them. His bioparents and stepparent expressed that parenting Ezra was a frustrating and unrewarding experience that was beyond them. In this way, the parents were in collusion to extrude Ezra. Ezra's half- and stepsiblings were more able than the adults to express their guilt, anger and grief, and the sessions with them had therapeutic value. Although there was evidence of marital discord seething just below the surface, the Rem couple denied this and preferred to scapegoat Ezra and the "nightmare" he had caused the family. Mr. Langer and his family terminated at this point.

Mrs. Langer, Ezra's mother, continued for three months longer in a group for parents whose children are in cults. She made some gains in resolving her ambivalence about Ezra's membership in the cult and was able to let him know, via his collect telephone contact, that she did not approve of what he was doing and wanted him home.

At a four-month follow-up contact, Mrs. Langer had repeated her feelings to her son on two occasions but Ezra remained obdurate.

In the example that follows, an adolescent boy was extruded from the Rem home for almost two years and then returned after the newly married couple had consolidated their relationship.

Mr. and Mrs. Amato were both remarried. Mr. Amato, age 42, had no children from his previous marriage which ended five years prior to his remarriage. Mrs. Amato, age 37, had a son, Bruce, age 12. Bruce's biofather had left the household and moved to Arizona when Bruce was a year old. Child support payments were sporadic and birthday gifts, which had been sent each year, were usually appropriate for a younger child. Bruce's father never availed himself of his full visitation rights, and when Bruce did visit with him during summer vacations, he left him alone for much of the time with his current live-in woman friend.

During a lengthy single-parent household stage, Mrs. Amato and Bruce had developed a close relationship; they felt they had only one another. Mrs. Amato worked hard so her son could go to a private school. Bruce was a B student, excelled in athletics, and was a "good son," i.e., did not cause his mother any trouble. Mr. Amato was the first man Mrs. Amato had been serious about; they

FIGURE 10.3
Amato Family Genogram

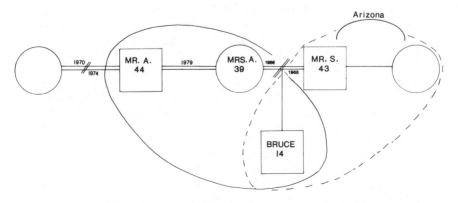

had worked together for a year before they had their first date. Bruce was 11 at that time.

During their ten-month romantic courtship the couple spent many weekends away and had a "joyous" two-week vacation. During this time Bruce was "cooperative." He stayed with relatives and friends.

Mr. Amato and his stepson were standoffish from the beginning. Despite efforts on Mr. Amato's part to try to fill in as father, his sense of order and rigid intergenerational boundaries were antithetical to Bruce's upbringing. In addition, Mr. Amato had an underlying competitiveness with Bruce for Mrs. Amato's attention and affection.

When the honeymoon was over and the conflicts were out in the open, Mrs. Amato was overprotective of her son. Despite her deep love for her husband, she found herself supporting Bruce in most situations, which invariably undermined Mr. Amato's authority and relationship with Bruce. This enraged Mr. Amato. Bruce started to do poorly at school, was noted to be inattentive in class, and began to associate with older boys who smoked marijuana.

Two years after the remarriage, the Rem family came for help. Mr. Amato immediately stated that Bruce's behavior at home and at school "is impossible." Bruce was 14, a tall, good-looking boy who initially seemed a bit spaced out. He had recently been found smoking marijuana in the boy's lavatory, and the school made involvement in treatment a condition for his continued attendance. His previous good record kept him from being expelled. Mrs. Amato admitted there was a problem but that her son wasn't as bad as described. Her saying this started her husband off on a heated accounting of Bruce's transgressions of commission and omission.

After three months of therapy, Rem family consolidation did not improve, since Mr. Amato's agenda was to get Bruce out of the house. Bruce made little effort to stop his self-extruding behavior, e.g., cutting school, defying curfews. The major change that took place during the therapy was that Mrs. Amato was willing to accede to her husband's request. Since all three agreed that the biofather could not and would not provide a home for Bruce, a preparatory boarding school was selected. Bruce openly voiced his discontent over the plan and stated he felt powerless against three adults: his mother, stepfather, and therapist. Bruce attempted to make his mother feel guilty enough to change her mind, but she did not alter her position. Begrudgingly, he left for the school with a meager willingness to consider that this might in fact be better for him (this he had confided in an individual session).

Over the ensuing 18 months the marital relationship solidified. The original couple typology of Mr. Amato/rational partner and Mrs. Amato/childlike partner moved in the direction of an equal-equal partnership. Bruce, however, continued to do poorly in school and occasionally defied school rules. After the first year he was not "invited" back to the school because they felt he needed a less competitive setting with academic supports readily available. Testing had revealed high average intelligence and no evidence of a learning disability. On home visits he insisted he did not want to be away at school, and that he would continue to do poorly unless allowed to come home. His mother felt guilty and torn but opted to side with her husband, especially since she was happy in her marriage.

Mr. Amato, now more secure in his marriage, verbalized that their approach to Bruce must be wrong and he was willing to have Bruce home, attend a highly individualized tutorial school (which he had already inquired about), and return to family therapy to see if they can now all learn to get along.

The dynamics of the son's rejection by his biofather, his 12-year exclusive interdependence with his mother, the intensity of Mr. and Mrs. Amato's short-term bonding, and Mr. Amato's own history of rejection by two emotionally unavailable parents and a former wife made the extrusion inevitable under the given set of conditions. Mr. Amato felt that he had finally found his ideal lover-partner and he would not let anyone interfere with his long awaited happiness. With the marital relationship consolidated, he now was able to identify with Bruce in a positive way that allowed him to deal with the mother-son subsystem from a position of security and self-assurance. He became a mature, effective, and caring stepfather.

Extrusion of the adolescent is not the only evidence of disturbed behavior in a Rem family adolescent; the adolescents may become depressed, scapegoated, bound in or act out, involved in substance abuse or criminal activity. We have focused on the extrusion because it represents an extreme solution that usually is the result of unsuccessful attempts to arrive at another resolution. Understanding extrusion and the interplay of the myriad forces that lead to it calls upon all the skills of the therapist. As we begin to understand the Rem suprasystem and adolescence better, our abilities to be able to help families avoid extrusion will increase. Yet, there will continue to be a need for many youths to seek another place, another home.

CONCLUSION

In 1981 the MacNeil/Lehrer report (1981) aired a documentary "Gang Violence" that raised the point that although runaway shelters are increasing, America does not like to face up to the problems caused by profound social change. Remarriage is a profound social change and the interfacing of normal adolescent development with a dysfunctional Rem system is more likely to result in the more extreme forms of extrusion. Our hope is that short-term crisis residences would be set up to provide a temporary living arrangement for the system-extruded adolescent. An adjunct to this would be family, individual, adolescent, and group sessions in which to explore problems and find short- and long-term solutions. The goal would be to return the adolescent to the home or alternative living arrangement with all family members having a deeper insight into their problem and a better sense of the services available to help towards a resolution.

Our long-range goal with all adolescents is for them to develop enough of an identity so that the process of separation and individuation that culminates with having established the basis for achieving good object relations is achieved. Anthony (1969, p. 71) describes how "a new relationship then becomes possible in which two adults, linked by mutual happy memories, find to their surprise (not knowing the strength of the identification processes) that they have many interests in common and discover a new mature pleasure in each other as people."

SECTION III

Special Issues of Remarriage

CHAPTER 11

Family Milestones: Weddings, Funerals, Holidays and Rites of Passage

Divorced parents do not stand in the receiving line together. If the bride's mother and stepfather are giving the wedding, she alone or both are in the line—but not the bride's father. If her father and stepmother are giving the wedding, they, as host and hostess, stand in line, and the bride's mother is merely an honored guest. If neither has remarried, only the bride's mother should be in the line unless he is giving the reception. In that case the estranged wife would not act as hostess, but the godmother of the bride, or an aunt, or even a very close family friend would receive in her place. When the groom's parents are divorced, his mother joins him in the line, and neither his father nor his stepfather need be there, which eliminates all complications.

> *The New Emily Post's Etiquette,*
> Elizabeth L. Post

Judy (parents divorced: mother single, father newly-rewed) arranged the seating plan of the star-crossed people and then proceeded to solve the other hierarchical and diplomatic problems— the wedding procession and the receiving line—by abolishing them. She and her father would be the only ones to walk down the aisle; congratulations would be received informally.

> "A Wedding With Some Relative Problems,"
> Nancy Love

These contemporary quotes highlight that special occasions in Rem families are complicated, as well as stressful, events. The normal separation anxiety associated with the milestone usually finds expression in the surfacing of heretofore unresolved issues for the original family members: old hurts, anger, guilt, reunion fantasies of children and adults, parental competition, and chronic sorrow for the loss of the nuclear family. This emotional stirring has a ripple effect on the Rem family and Rem suprasystem. These are the times when family members extend their circle of significant others, including future in-laws or a favorite teacher. Statements from adults and children referring to "being on show", "feeling exposed," "wanting to disappear," or "needing to divide in half," "grin and bear it," and "get it over with" speak to this additional strain.

Those Rem families who have not functioned as or acknowledged the existence of their suprafamily are forced to do so when tickets for a graduation are distributed or guest lists and seating arrangements are drawn up. Milestone events for a child of divorced and remarried parents elicit more polarized feelings among suprafamily members than are likely to occur when that child had a parent who died and the widowed parent remarried.

It is not surprising that issues related to and aroused by Rem family celebrations are often the precipitant to treatment or the initial problem presented. Of 18 consecutive Rem families who applied to one of our agency offices, four presented with problems related to milestone situations. In two families the precipitant to their application was when the stepmother was not invited to a child's graduation. In another example a recently remarried widow and widower applied when the new wife was "snubbed in front of everyone" by her husband's daughters at the bris (religious circumcision) of the first grandson. Another application was a direct plea for help from a shocked man whose soon-to-be bride "refused" to have his five-year-old daughter at their forthcoming wedding.

During the same time period we saw a Rem family in treatment where some intense emotional reactions needed to be worked through around everyone's involvement in a bar mitzvah. In another ongoing case a suicidal 15-year-old boy and his twice remarried father broached their feelings about this young man's not having had a bar mitzvah. The precipitant to these discussions was the upcoming bar mitzvah preparations of another son from the second terminated marriage where a much more viable parental relationship existed. There was also an emergency recontacting of the therapist for a one-session meeting to help a remarried woman with custody of her two adolescents decide whether or not she would attend the funeral of her former father-in-law.

In helping Rem families deal with these issues we have used the following points of reference.

UNDERSTANDING FAMILY BOUNDARIES

How a family, nuclear or Rem, responds to a special occasion provides a unique opportunity to study the family's boundaries. The term boundary refers to those factors that contribute to the sense of identity, differentiating the members of one group from another. These include shared experience, space, property, ritual activities, and beliefs. Walker and Messinger (1979) remind us that boundaries can be physical, such as the walls of a house and the fences or hedges separating it from its neighbors, or psychological, such as the implicit boundaries defining the degree of intimacy and physical closeness members share with each other and nonmembers.

In Rem, in particular, at the boundaries we have the chance to assess to what extent the loss of the nuclear family and the new Rem family have been integrated. At one end of the continuum we have the family with oceanic-permissive boundaries. In a working-class Protestant family the oldest brother, age 63—the patriarchcal head—stated, "Once a member of the clan, always a member of the clan." His younger brother's present and former wives both attended almost all "clan" functions—weddings, baptisms, or Thanksgiving dinners. When the next generation had its first divorce and remarriage, the former wife and child were "of course" invited to Christmas dinner without any prior discussion with the Rem couple.

At the other end of the continuum we have families with very rigid boundaries. The divorced partner is "out," "as good as dead." He or she is included in plans only begrudgingly, if at all. In another working-class Protestant family the parents divorced when all the children were grown and living on their own. The father then remarried. Prior to his son's wedding he received a letter from his adult daughters urging him to "come alone or don't come at all."

Between these two extremes there is a range of more flexible behavior that takes into account blood ties, preferences, loyalties, sensibilities, the reality of the loss of the nuclear family, remarriage(s), and sensitivity to the impact of exclusion or inclusion on others. It is the therapeutic task to help families see if they can arrive at an acceptable middle ground.

EMPATHIC CONNECTION TO ALL POINTS OF VIEW

There is no right or wrong way to deal with family milestones in Rem families. Unlike Emily Post, we do not have handy rules of thumb. Instead we help people express their different points of view, including views that do not mesh with the consensus or are the mixed feelings of loyalty conflicts. Often this process and the statement, "Everyone's point of view is well taken and understandable," provide an empathic connection to the individuals and the Rem situation. Consider the following example. A teenage girl wants "just my parents" and not her well-liked stepmother to attend her high school graduation. She doesn't want to have to make "awkward introductions," worry about her mother sitting alone, and wonder how tense they all will be. She says with feeling. "When I march in I don't want to have to search out *two* sets of people!" Her mother agrees with her daughter but for different reasons. She would like to share this happy event just with her daughter and her former husband (and continued co-parent). Historically they both delighted in and mobilized around their daughter's academic promise and worked hard to split the cost for her private school tuition. The father cautiously admitted that he felt some of this himself, but he also wanted his present wife to be there. He was grateful that she had supported him in taking on the additional expense of private school education. The stepmother did want to attend the graduation. She wanted to share it with her husband and stepdaughter. She too had made some financial sacrifices so that her stepdaughter could graduate from this school.

UNCOVERING PRECONSCIOUS AND UNCONSCIOUS MOTIVATION AND FAMILY OF ORIGIN REPLAY

After we elicit ambivalent and contrary points of view and make an empathic connection, we further the alliance, both therapeutic and familial, by sorting out preconscious and unconscious motivation and family of origin issues. For example, for this intellectually gifted high school graduate, her father's four years of remarriage did nothing to neutralize her fantasy of parental reunion. The graduation resurfaced chronic sorrowful issues.

FACTORS IN DECISION-MAKING

We emphasize that coming to a decision in matters like this is difficult because "you cannot please everyone" and more often than not there will be those who are dissatisfied. We tell the family that the Rem situation is different from nuclear families in that the pervasive feeling tone of the occasion is accompanied by the resurgence of feelings of loss and the awkwardness of mixing new matches. Some people experience shame and embarrassment because they feel that "step" is a stigma. We remind families that most often the occasion is a happy one where the joy of the event could prevail over old hurts. At the point that individuals and families have worked this through, we have been delightfully surprised at some of the innovative ways potentially disquieting situations have been resolved. People can have two festive meals in one day; a divorced woman can participate in the church choir on the day of her daughter's confirmation rather than "share the same pew" as her ex-husband, his wife and their sons; a wedding given by two remarried parents of the bride can have invitations with just the name of the bride and groom.

Mr. and Mrs. Nathan applied for treatment shortly after their remarriage because of Mr. Nathan's problematic relationship with Saul, his 10-year-old stepson. Mrs. Nathan had been divorced for three years and Mr. Nathan had divorced just prior to his courtship with Mrs. Nathan. Mr. Nathan's two daughters, Carol, age 16, and Roberta, age 11, lived with their mother in another state and visited every third weekend. Mr. Nathan came from an intact nuclear family where boundaries tended to be "good natured" and "very flexible." He was three years older than his younger sister. Mrs. Nathan was a latency-age child when her divorced mother remarried and produced another child, which caused Mrs. Nathan to feel displaced and extruded from the Rem family. Primary marital topology—Mr. Nathan/parental rescuer; Mrs. Nathan/childlike rescuee.

After six family sessions, Mr. and Mrs. Nathan joined a Rem couples group. Ten months later family sessions with another Rem therapist were added to the treatment plan. At the first family session, which included Mr. and Mrs. Nathan and Saul, a genogram was done as a way for the family to introduce themselves to the new therapist. In discussing his family, Mr. Nathan mentioned that in six months his sister's oldest son would be celebrating his bar mitzvah. The therapist made a mental note of this and four months later when the event was mentioned in passing by Saul, the therapist picked up on it. The spouses responded in their typical polarized view and the following transpired:

Therapist: I'd like to hear more about the upcoming bar mitzvah.
Mrs. Nathan: (Angrily) I don't want Ethel (Mr. Nathan's ex-wife)

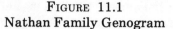

FIGURE 11.1
Nathan Family Genogram

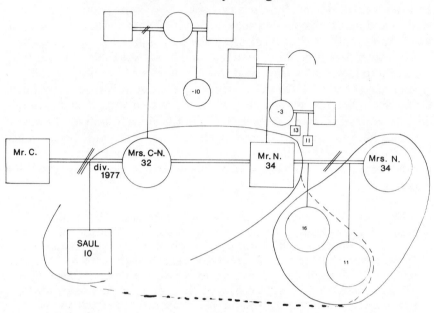

to attend. After all, there has been a divorce—what's done is
over! (Statement of her own family of origin experience.)

Mr. Nathan: That's impossible—Ethel and my sister have been
friends for 15 years. They sat together when Carol had her
bas mitzvah.

Mrs. Nathan: (Barely letting her husband finish his sentence) But
you were married to Ethel then!

Therapist: (Aware of the mounting tension and proclivity of the
couple to escalate into a verbal free-for-all) Let's stop right
here. (Forcefully setting limits) I can tell this is a charged
subject for both of you because, as in the past, you are both
taking an extreme and opposite point of view.

Mr. Nathan: You mean she says black and I say white as if it's a re-
flex action?

Therapist: Exactly. (Pleased that Mr. Nathan now was able to understand and use an appropriate metaphor to describe their
interaction) (Talking to both) Let's try to understand your
position and see if it is possible to find a middle ground.

Mr. Nathan: I cannot imagine Ethel not being there.

Mrs. Nathan: (Starting to attack) Oh Al. You are such a . . .

Therapist: (Interrupting) I remind you both that we cannot get any work done if either one attacks when you hear a different point of view.

Mr. Nathan: In my family everyone is included at a simcha (celebration). They would go into hock and have gone into hock rather than invite fewer people. My sister and mother talk to Ethel often. I'm sure the girls think she will be invited.

Therapist: It would be very difficult to confront the family with a different way of doing things. (Boundary issue address)

Mr. Nathan: Maybe impossible.

Therapist: Maybe.

Mrs. Nathan: (Ready to attack what she calls Mr. Nathan's negativism) Oh you are so n . . . (She catches herself and covers her mouth).

Therapist: (Smile to Mrs. Nathan; to Mr. Nathan) How might you like things to be for you at this bar mitzvah?

Mr. Nathan: I don't know—I never thought about it before. (Moving chair back and showing other fidgeting signs of anxiety.)

Therapist: Try to think.

Mr. Nathan: (After some thought where everyone was now able to sit with the silence) Perhaps Ethel can come to the synagogue and Kiddush (wine and ritual breaking of bread) right after the service but just Cynthia (Mrs. Nathan) and I could be invited to the affair in the evening. (Smile on his face)

Mrs. Nathan: (A hint of a smile on her face)

Therapist: Tell me more.

Mr. Nathan: That way everyone will be satisfied.

Therapist: I don't know about that, but let's consider it.

Mrs. Nathan: I could live with that. But what about the girls? They are very protective of their mother, but on the other hand if she is not there they would not have to be jumping back and forth between two parents all evening.

Saul: (Talking to his mother) I think it is a good idea because you would not have to be tense the whole time—just half the time.

All: (Laughing)

Therapist: You see that it could be better for your Mom, but I wonder how it might be better for you.

Saul: You know, I think I have to comfort my mother when she's upset. This way I could be with the kids at the kids' table.

Therapist: That does sound better for you.

Mr. Nathan: I wonder how the girls would feel about this?

Therapist: To what extent might you be willing to ask them and then let us know what they say?

(The girls were included in family sessions when they visited during school vacations. Since it would be impossible for them to come to the following session, Mr. Nathan's discussion with them was an alternate plan. Strengthening Mr. Nathan's ties to his daughters and moving away from his overinvolvement with his stepson were goals of treatment. The therapist proceeds to elicit from Mr. and Mrs. Nathan and Saul how Ethel, Mr. Nathan's parents, sister, brother-in-law, nephew, etc. may view their plan. To Mr. Nathan, thinking that his ambivalence was not addressed enough.) Perhaps there is a part of you that might want Ethel there?

Mr. Nathan: (Looking at Mrs. Nathan—responding hesitantly) I suppose so. I would like it if she did not *want* to come. I don't want to hurt Ethel any more; I left her. Also she is not a bad person.

Therapist: I'm sure she is not. (Supporting positive feelings for former wife)

Mrs. Nathan: (Becoming anxious and then typically aggressive) Would you believe he feels protective of her!

Therapist: (To Mrs. Nathan and in a lighthearted tone) It happens in the best of Rem families. I've noticed my husband is sometimes protective of his former wife. I don't like it when it happens, but it does sometimes.

Mrs. Nathan: (Looking calmer—a hint of a smile possibly due to the alliance with therapist and therapist's modeling.)

Therapist: (To Mr. Nathan) The way you suggested to chance things. (Therapist notices the slip—chance for change and uses it). It is a chance—a risk that you might want to take. To confront the way your family does things and let go of some of the protective and guilt feelings you have towards Ethel.

In the next family session Mr. Nathan reported that he had discussed the matter with his daughters when they visited and his older daughter urged him, "Don't hurt Mommy again." His younger daughter did not express strong feelings either way. Mr. Nathan "got scared" when he heard his older daughter's admonishment, but he reconsidered and wanted to continue discussing putting his plan into action. The focus of the session was developing the strategy to follow through with his plan. Mr. Nathan would speak to his sister first, and then, if she agreed, he would speak to his brother-in-law. Perhaps both Mr. and Mrs. Nathan would visit them. Mr. Nathan and his sister would decide who would tell their parents. His sister and/or her husband would tell Mr. Nathan's ex-wife. Saul did not have much to contribute to the session verbally but seeing his mother and stepfather work on issues and resolve matters together was important for him. In this session his usual restlessness was minimal. A week later Mr. Nathan reported that there had been some heated discussion, but his sister and brother-in-law had telephoned the previous evening to say they would go along with his request.

Three days before the bar mitzvah both the couples' group therapist and family therapist got a frantic call from Mr. Nathan. His sister could not carry out the agreed upon plan and his ex-wife was invited to the evening affair as well. The "change of heart" had come about after a telephone call between Mr. Nathan's sister and their mother. An emergency session with either, "preferably both," therapists was requested since his wife was refusing to attend.

The therapists met and after careful consideration decided not to give an "emergency session." Their decision was based on the fact that the couple had done a lot of work in resolving the issue and a feeling that they could resolve the new dilemma. The family therapist, because she had done most of the work with the couple around this particular issue, got back to them and shared both therapists' thinking and decision. The therapist empathized that it was indeed an unfortunate turn of events, but whatever they decided would be awkward and someone would be displeased. We would deal with this and the aftermath of the event at the next session. The couple offered only minimal resistance to this. Mrs. Nathan decided to go to the bar mitzvah when her husband said, "I want you by my side." This was happily shared at the next session; all agreed they were able "to get into the joyful spirit of the celebration" and wanted to move to another subject now.

Milestone events are integral to the growing individual and family. At best life is not static and, while these special occasions in Rem can and usually do cause emotional stirring, more often and more importantly they are a time to rejoice and an opportunity to further master the tasks of the individual and Rem family life cycle.

CHAPTER 12

Progeny Perhaps:
Deciding About a
Mutual Child

In Chapter 3 we discussed in detail how differences in individual and marital life-cycle needs can present problems for the Rem couple. Nowhere is this issue more pronounced than in the decision to have or not to have a mutual child.

A Rem couple may request counseling with this as the problem presented or the problem may surface when the couple is already in treatment. In both instances couples reveal similar dynamics in their unwritten and unspoken marital contract (see Chapter 4). In the courtship and honeymoon period, often both partners were ambivalent about a mutual child, aptly described by one husband as "a definite maybe possibility." There was mutual agreement, sometimes but not always verbalized, to "put this issue on the back burner," with concerns about career goals, financial solvency, and Rem family consolidation taking priority. However, preconscious and unconscious contracts are such that each spouse believes the other will "want what I want" or that the partner can be changed, convinced, or manipulated to his/her point of view. Concurrent with this, more on a conscious and preconscious level, the clock counts down the childbearing years for women and childrearing years for men.

At the time the couple seeks treatment for this issue or brings it up in ongoing treatment, the homeostasis that enabled the issue to be dormant is no longer working for one or both partners. As one previously married but childless man retorted to his wife, who had a preadolescent daughter from her former marriage, "Five thousand dollars in savings is enough of a cushion for me. I don't need any more before I have kids." Always, the reality of the time limitations and sometimes family, peer, and medical profession pressure sway the balance. Precipitants to treatment have included the birth of a baby to a relative or friend or to one's former spouse, pressure from parents who want a grandchild, an increased level of intimacy or distancing for the couple, as well as an intense desire to have one's own child.

Treatment with these couples has the following phases:

1) Exploration of the homeostatic balance and the factors involved in the shift.

2) Exploration of the nature and degree of each partner's ambivalence. The ambivalence often has a "political," "environmental," "societal" component expressed as questions about zero population growth, importance of the survival of a race and/or religion, and security of the world in general. The ambivalence always has an interpersonal component resonating from attitudes and feelings about the commitment to and stability of the present marriage. There is also an intrapsychic component that touches issues of dependency, possessiveness, sexuality, and generativity. For those who have had children, the pleasures, pain, and "routine inconveniences" of childrearing are reviewed. These components all have conscious, preconscious, and unconscious levels of awareness.

3) An assessment of the extent to which each partner has worked out his/her ambivalence enough to act in an autonomous way.

4) In cases where both are "clear" but have different resolutions the couple can consider these options:
   a) One partner is willing to "go along with"—"give in"—to the other spouse's wishes.
   b) Separation/divorce.
   c) Wait and see, with or without a specific time limit, which is different from option d.
   d) Continue to try to convince one another, either by both actively pleading their case, or by one actively pleading and the other passively but resolutely "treading water" in his/her position.

If individuals have really resolved their ambivalence, this last way of relating is not an option and couples who choose it may not be certain enough about their desire and/or fearful of separation. Depending on the degree of sophistication, intelligence, and maturity of the couple, these choices may or may not have to be clearly spelled out by the therapist. Reaching a decision, however, involves hard work.

CASE ILLUSTRATIONS

Case 1

Mr. Rogers is a boyish-looking 47-year-old executive in the publishing business who was divorced nine years ago, with two sons now 25 and 21. At the time of application he and the second Mrs.

FIGURE 12.1
Rogers Family Genogram

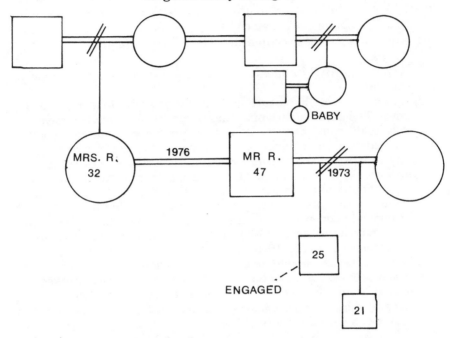

Rogers, a 32-year-old magazine editor, who had not been previously married, had just celebrated their sixth anniversary. Their primary marital relationship was Mr. Rogers/parental, Mrs. Rogers/
childlike. Mutual career aspirations provided the homeostasis for
this hardworking couple in a hard-driving profession. The couple's
anniversary coincided with Mr. Rogers' promotion to a long
sought position and Mrs. Rogers' gynecologist urging "a rest
from the pill." If that was not enough, Mrs. Rogers' younger stepsister had a baby and Mr. Rogers' older son announced his engagement. (If a wedding is planned, can becoming a grandparent be far
behind?)

The couple had discussed the issue of having a mutual child prior
to marriage and Mr. Rogers was ambivalent, but stated he "could
consider one." Mrs. Rogers initiated the treatment contact. Mr.
Rogers had spent "sleepless nights of soul searching," during
which time he reviewed the pleasures and pains of raising his sons
and was now "clear" that he did not want another child and
"would not change my mind." An exploration of Mrs. Rogers' ambivalence revealed that she, too, had resolved this issue but in

favor of having a child. Interventions that aimed at urging each partner to convince the other of his/her point of view validated their steadfastness of position for the couple and therapist. With both partners "loyal" to what would be psychologically true to them, and not being of a masochistic character structure or defense, this couple chose divorce.

To reach this decision, treatment focused on first helping the couple "make sense" of their oxymoronic dilemma—"the divorce of a good marriage." Explaining it in the context of their "needs no longer being met *enough* to continue their relationship" helped provide the middle ground between the extremes of a good and bad marriage and also demonstrated empathy for the importance of their individual needs to have and not have a child. The couple was then urged to move from the intellectual to the emotional response to their situation. The pain associated with the loss of the relationship and "a wake for the child we didn't have" was felt by both partners in varying degrees. Also judiciously balanced and explored was the "joy" and "excitement" of being true to oneself and the fear of the future. Mrs. Rogers wondered if she would again meet a man she wanted to marry, and what would happen if she found out she could not conceive. Mr. Rogers considered the positive and negatives of setting up his own home again.

Just prior to coming to their decision to separate, the couple spent time with Mrs. Rogers' stepsister and her new baby. In the session that followed, Mrs. Rogers "checked again" to see if Mr. Rogers had changed his mind. He replied, "The thought had not occurred to me." Treatment with this couple spanned three months. By termination they had begun to live apart.

Although the possibility of individual treatment was discussed, both agreed that they did not feel a need for this. A six-month follow-up contact revealed that both were starting lives independent of each other. Contact with each other was less and less frequent and both were beginning to go to parties. Divorce proceedings with one lawyer had begun.

Case 2

Mr. and Mrs. Miller, the couple discussed in Chapters 6 and 7, were content to put the issue of a mutual child aside for almost a year, during which time they enjoyed an active and erotic sexual relationship. Mrs. Miller did want a child of her own and tended to deny Mr. Miller's comments that his first marriage began to fall apart after the birth of Deirdra and finally ended two years later, after Liza was born. Each was hopeful that the partner would "come around" to his/her point of view. For Mr. Miller this meant his wife would find enough maternal gratification in being the stepmother of his two growing daughters. For Mrs. Miller this meant that her husband would change his mind and want a child with her once he saw that they had a stable marriage.

At the end of the honeymoon stage which was followed by five months of treatment where Rem family consolidation was the goal, Mrs. Miller began to "panic" about her age and childbearing possibilities. She wanted to "conceive right away." Mr. Miller saw her panic as a "demand" on him and in his characteristic way began to withdraw and express only the negative side of his ambivalence. Mrs. Miller made this the arena for a full-blown power struggle when she shared only the positive side of her ambivalence. In unlocking this impasse the couple's fear of closeness was explored and their characteristic response, where Mrs. Miller becomes actively controlling and Mr. Miller passive-aggressively withholding, was reflected to them. Mr. and Mrs. Miller were then able to discuss both sides of their ambivalence about a mutual child and Mr. Miller, despite strong feelings about 2:00 A.M. feedings "again" and sharing his wife, was willing to go along with her wishes. His own words to her: "I want to do this for you." Treatment ended at this point.

One year later the couple reapplied with infertility the presenting problem. The pressure of the time clock, ordeal of charts and schedules, late but ever present menstruation, and intimidations and humiliations of modern medical procedures exacerbated the destructive marital interaction previously described. Mr. Miller's sperm count was "low normal" and Mrs. Miller's fallopian tubes were blocked. Mrs. Miller blamed her husband for the infertility and he agreed. Interventions that highlighted his anger and frustration helped Mr. Miller say, "I'm doing all that I can including my first thing in the morning jerk-off session at the doctor's office and I'm sorry that is not enough for you. Get off my back and I'll raise my sperm count." Indeed, within one month he did; the marital interaction improved but the infertility persisted. At termination the spouses were able to mutually agree on an outside date to let go of efforts to conceive and Mr. Miller initiated the idea of adopting a child. At a 12-month follow-up Mrs. Miller had not been able to conceive and the couple had begun to pursue the adoption of an infant.

LONGING TO HAVE CHILDREN

In working with couples with this issue, both men and women speak of a "longing," "destiny," "lifelong fantasy" to have a child. In many instances otherwise articulate people are at a loss for words to describe this primal feeling. Those with words hear the echo of the Biblical commandment, "Be fruitful and multiply." Harding (1975, p. 159), a Jungian analyst, in her discussion of maternity concurs with this when she states, " . . . the true fulfillment of each individual is not to be found through the satisfaction of his/her personal desires alone, but also through an allegiance to the aims of another part of his psyche which is in harmony with the movement of life through the generations." At the writing of the first draft of this chapter, one of the authors considered stating that women feel this commandment more strongly since, in our practice, women and not men were willing to divorce because of this. Within a matter of weeks that therapist's stereotype was shattered. A 39-year-old college professor, whose 10-year-old daughter had lived with her biomother since the divorce six years ago, "surprised" his 32-year-old ambitious public relations executive wife of four years with his "strong desire to be a family." After three months of treatment, when his wife chose to "peak" in her career for the next two years and "then see what happens," he was not willing to wait any longer and chose to separate.

For Rem couples who choose not to have a mutual child and remain together, the decision is fraught with emotion. When the relationship is not working out, there is relief, "At least this time I was smart enough not to have a child." When the relationship is working out, this decision is experienced as a "loss," a "void," and an absence of an outward symbol of credibility and status of their present relationship to themselves, their family, and the world.

> Mrs. Allen, a divorced, childless nurse, age 41, had been married for four years to a 46-year-old dentist who had two children from his previous marriage. Prior to treatment, which had been initiated because of problems with Dr. Allen's daughter, the couple decided not to have a mutual child. At a point in treatment when the two were becoming more intimate, Mrs. Allen shared a dream where she was standing alone at her husband's funeral and his children were being comforted by their mother. This dream helped both partners to get in touch with their feeling a lack of credibility and completeness as a result of their decision not to have a mutual child.

Countertransference reactions to such a primal issue can be intense. This, compounded by the timeliness of this issue in the marital lives of some of our Rem team members, produced energetic discussions where personal biases and values needed to be aired. Our team meeting discussion paralleled the clinician's tendency to be critical of the couple and look for "the real issue," i.e., pathology, and then to go to the other extreme and see just health. To avoid this countertransferential flipflop, a purview is needed of: interpersonal and intrapsychic dynamics, individual and marital life-cycle tasks, and the importance for some of the primordial "destiny" or "instinct" to procreate. Time with the couple, a comfortableness with uncertainty where clinical and personal judgments are delayed, and a careful ongoing review of one's work are essential.

THE MUTUAL CHILD

The birth of a mutual child can have dramatic effects in the Rem family. In its negative aspect it is an added stress emotionally, physically, and financially that can threaten the stability of the Rem family and exacerbate abandonment fears, especially in stepsiblings who do not live in the Rem household. In its positive aspect it helps towards Rem family consolidation by providing a "blood tie" for all involved and possibly realigning parental responsibilities in a more adaptive way. The most common example of this is the overinvolved, childless stepparent, usually stepmother, who can now turn over some of her control to her husband, the father of his children, so she can ready herself to become and be the parent to "my child." Often the experience of being a parent from day one, as opposed to becoming a stepparent in medias res, humbles the stepparent to the vicissitudes of parenting. This can lead to a greater acceptance rather than harsh criticism of one's spouse's vulnerabilities vis-à-vis his children and to a more realistic and sensitive acceptance of the stepchild. For the marital couple this affirms their relationship and deepens their commitment as they are now *both* a marital and parental pair.

In the following case example the admonishment from his two-year-old son helped a man control his verbal and physical attacks on his stepson.

Mr. Levinson, age 39, and his wife, age 40, applied for counseling ten months after their marriage because of Mr. Levinson's volatile relationship with his stepson, Robert, age nine. Mr. Levinson had been married before; his wife had died in an auto accident. Mrs. Levinson's first husband had sporadic contact with Robert. At the time of application Mrs. Levinson was five months pregnant. The pregnancy was not planned but very much "wanted" by the Rem couple. The limited impulse control of all family members demonstrated by Mr. Levinson's aggressive criticism, Mrs. Levinson's passive-aggressive efforts to pit son and stepfather against each other, and Robert's immature behavior made change difficult.

Throughout treatment, spanning three years, the therapist had some family sessions with the new baby and the then toddler to capitalize on the family's positive feelings for the baby as leverage for greater self-control. Progress was slow but steady. At age two, baby Bill approached his father and yelled, "No, no, no," when Mr. Levinson was berating his stepson. Mr. Levinson was both "shocked" and "scared" by his son's response. He was fearful of having his own child suffer from the "fallout" of his battles with Robert. His son's frightened expression and well spoken warning became the beacon that enabled Mr. Levinson to exercise a degree of self-control not heretofore thought possible by him, his family, and the therapist.

What is it like to be the mutual child in a Rem family? Our practice so far has not given us many opportunities to explore this. But the first reported dream of a three-year-old whose half-sister visits every other weekend from across the river in New Jersey points to both the pleasure and pain of this experience. The little girl's bedroom overlooks the river and in the dream—"My sister is swimming to see me." When she woke up she immediately looked out the window and cried because "Melissa is not there." In another example, a preschooler finally surmises that her half-brother's mother and her mother are not the same, "There are two mommies, but we share our Daddy."

Katherine Baker, a social worker and mother of two teenage mutual children, is particularly interested in the maturation of mutual children. In a personal correspondence to our team she writes:

> Mutual children seem so especially selected to receive a tremendous amount of family intensity and bonding with the parent who has not previously had children. As such, they might easily become "at risk" when they are beginning to negotiate separation in early adolescence. Following the development of mutual children would necessitate a family long-term study, but perhaps an awareness of the burdens of such intense bonding and of their fulfilling such a symbolically unifying role in their families would be useful to clinicians working with the Rem couple at the time of their decision to conceive.

In summary, the issue of a mutual child is complicated for Rem families in both the decision-making and adjustment stages. The birth of a mutual child, agreement not to have a mutual child, and agreement to divorce because this difference cannot be resolved any other way are all outcomes of this dilemma. In working with these families, no matter what the decision may be, we see people struggling within themselves and with the partner and in that process there is always birth. To quote e.e. cummings (1954, p. 331):

> We can never be born enough. We are human beings; for whom birth is a supremely welcome mystery, the mystery of growing: that mystery which happens only and whenever we are faithful to ourselves.

CHAPTER 13

Loosened Sexual Boundaries

In Rem families there is a loosening of sexual boundaries, related to the structural nature of the step position, which is nonbiological, non-legal, and typically has not involved proximity or developmental ties between step-related persons over the years of growth and development of family relationships. Indeed, the only tie that step-related persons share is the close social and spatial tie with its potential for emotional attachments to grow over time (Wald, 1981).

This loosening is also related to the heightened affectionate and sexual atmosphere in the home during the new couple's early romantic bonding period. A pubescent teenager, especially with pubescent step-siblings of the opposite sex, can further intensify the sexual climate in the Rem household. In our work with Rem families we have seen that responses to the loosening of sexual boundaries have run the gamut from pleasurable fantasies, increased anxiety, repressed thoughts and distancing behavior, angry and violent fighting as a defense against sexual stirrings, to the most extreme and unfortunate circumstance of a sexual relationship between stepparent and stepchild. Our term for this is not incest, since there is no blood tie, but instead *household sexual abuse*. We use the term stepparent to include both the married and committed relationship partner of the biological parent. Geiser (1979) uses the term "psychological incest"—a violation not of a biological barrier but of a psychological bond that exists between people who call themselves "family."

The loosening of sexual boundaries in remarried families certainly

293

does not lead automatically and inexorably to sexual abuse. Remarried families are usually capable of coping with this added stress as they are with other stresses in their lives. Among remarried families who seek treatment we have seen how the new sexual tensions can be dealt with effectively.

Robert, a 15-year-old, made sexual overtures toward his 11½-year-old stepsister, Marge. Marge complained about this to her mother. Mother determined that Robert had kissed Marge on the lips and tried to feel her breasts. Marge had told him to leave her alone and he walked away "mumbling." Marge's mother told her she did the right thing to tell her about this, that such things happen in homes but that it shouldn't, and that she would talk to Robert's father. Mrs. Simmons informed her husband of his son's actions, and he discussed the issue fully with Robert. No further sexual advances were made. Marge felt secure with her mother's support. The matter was not a troublesome issue between the two parents. Actually, Robert and Marge developed a good brother-sister type of relationship and both were comfortable in their home.

In an individual session a 38-year-old stepmother of a shapely 15-year-old spoke of feeling anxious when her Rem family visited with her brother's Rem family for the weekend. On further exploration, she revealed that her stepdaughter and her brother's handsome stepson, age 17, got along "famously." She wondered then, and more freely now, what would happen should these stepcousins marry. Her brother's stepson might be her stepson-in-law and "sharing a son with my brother is too close to home." This woman was now more able to discuss heretofore repressed sexual feelings towards her brother.

In the middle stage of treatment with a Rem family with a 16-year-old boy from the maternal side and a 15-year-old boy and a 17-year-old girl from the paternal side, the therapist wondered out loud why in four years they had not been able to *all* be together at the summer house. Rem family consolidation was difficult for this family and this intervention was directed at that issue. All agreed it was the "one bathroom problem." The therapist's response, "unisex toilet," elicited chuckles. Further probing revealed that the toilet seat either up or down meant that, "The men have a penis and women a vagina. There is a difference!" The bathroom opened the door for all Rem family members to openly express for the first time sexual feelings for each other. A month later, despite the renamed "sexy bathroom," all were able to spend the weekend together.

Treatment considerations include the therapist's comfort in relating to sexual material and the importance of clarifying that sexual thoughts and fantasies about family members are natural and not the same as actions. An open discussion about this can dilute the intensity of these feelings so that channels can be opened for the expression of healthy sexuality.

In the following example there is greater loosening of sexual boundaries when the mother of two children divorced their father and then lived with a man 28 years her senior. Two years after separating from this older man, she married his son. The treatment considerations mentioned above were helpful in bringing about improved family functioning.

Mrs. Prince applied for treatment for her daughter, Juanita, age 15, who was frequently truant from school, defiant of curfews, and generally "fresh and disrespectful." Mrs. P made her application when Juanita had just returned home after a five-week aborted stay in Florida with her biological father, his new wife and her twin daughters, age 13. After strategic telephone work, Mrs. P was able to bring to the first session her husband, their two-year-old daughter, and her two children from her previous marriage, Juanita and George, age 12.

In the first session, Mrs. P was quite vituperative toward Juanita, whose defiance of limits and uncooperativeness with household chores were "the problem." All others were steadfastly silent. Family sessions were judged not a viable enough modality for Juanita to be heard and she was given the opportunity to meet with another therapist—a young social work student who had a facility for establishing good rapport with adolescents.

FIGURE 13.1
Prince Family Genogram

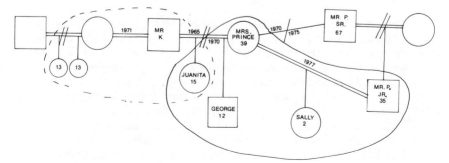

At the seventh session, after Juanita had relentlessly tested the therapist and Mrs. P had made several attempts to sabotage treatment, Juanita nervously revealed that she had left out an important person in the genogram that she had previously done with the therapist. A year after her parents divorced, her mother had a "live-in" relationship with the father of Mr. P. This lasted two years and two years later Mrs. P married Mr. Prince, Jr., whom she had met when he visited with his father. Juanita was relieved to expose this "family secret." The dynamic implications of this loosening of the intrafamilial sexual boundaries were explored. Juanita was aware that she was voluptuous, despite her silent prayers not to grow anymore, and that she was more attractive than her dowdy, flat-chested mother. She did not like it when her mother worked the night shift and she was alone with her stepfather, her brother, and the baby. Usually at these times Juanita missed curfew and was severely criticized by her mother and stepfather. Once the secret was revealed, the family dynamics of Juanita's rebelliousness, Mrs. P's aggressive efforts to divide and conquer her husband and daughter, and Juanita's and Mr. P's isolation in the house were viewed as maneuvers to defend against sexual fears/wishes.

After careful exploration and preparation Juanita agreed to let her therapist bring up the secret at a family session. Once it was mentioned, fears were diffused and Juanita's attractiveness was acknowledged by Mr. and Mrs. P and her pubescent brother. Mrs. P made a genuine connection to her daughter when she said, "I would not allow any hanky-panky incest to happen." Mr. P agreed. Some of the wife/mother duties heretofore assigned to Juanita were now shared by Mr. and Mrs. P. The Rem family household became "home" for Juanita and a more nurturing environment for everyone.

In the next case example, sexual boundaries loosened sufficiently to allow a single incident of household sexual abuse:

Mrs. Rosenwald had stated on the phone that she was very upset. Her daughter Jan, age 15, had told her that the night before, her stepfather, Mr. Rosenwald, had come to her room when she was almost asleep, had felt her breasts, and had just begun to touch her vaginal area when she pretended to moan in her sleep and began to turn over. She was afraid to let him know she was awake. When confronted by his wife, Mr. Rosenwald first denied this and said Jan probably dreamed it, but he then acknowledged his actions and agreed to come to the agency. Mr. and Mrs. Rosenwald had utilized the agency's remarried family life education services when they were considering marriage.

In the conjoint session with her husband, Mrs. Rosenwald opened up the issue immediately, Mr. Rosenwald said he did not really know why he had the urge to "play with" Jan. When he returned from urinating during the night, he noticed her door was open. She was asleep, and he wanted to touch her "very gently while she slept." He had an erection very quickly but lost it just as fast when he thought she was awakening. He felt guilty and ashamed of his behavior. His sexual relationship with his wife was gratifying and exciting to both of them.

On further exploration Mr. Rosenwald said that he had a good relationship with his stepson, Barry, and that they enjoyed lots of things together (confirmed by Mrs. Rosenwald), but that Jan was always an enigma to him. He felt she wouldn't let him get close to her, no matter how he had tried. This was confirmed again by Mrs. Rosenwald, who said she and her husband had discussed this many times.

Mr. Rosenwald was an attractive man, one who gave off a sense of sexual vitality. We suggested to him that perhaps his stepdaughter felt sexual stirrings in his presence without quite knowing what they were and, as a result, unconsciously held him at a distance and was unable to allow herself warm friendly feelings. He thought this might be so. We also suggested she might eschew being very friendly with Mr. Rosenwald because it might make her feel disloyal to her father.

We urged the couple to talk together to Jan about our meeting and praise her for asking her mother for help. Mr. Rosenwald was helped to tell Jan how he felt about his behavior and to reassure her it wouldn't happen again.

Mr. Rosenwald said he preferred that we not inform Jan's father about the incident because he felt ashamed and because he knew that his wife's first husband was always trying to find an excuse to harass them. We saw nothing to be gained at this time by involving Jan's father; we believed the behavior would not be repeated and there was no need to consider an alternative placement for Jan. However, we did recommend a Rem family meeting with Jan and Barry along with Mr. and Mrs. Rosenwald. We did so because we wanted to better understand the dynamic of Jan's and Mr. Rosenwald's distancing in the context of the Rem family system. We also wanted Barry to be there because to establish a family secret that excluded him was not constructive for Rem family consolidation. Furthermore, such a session possibly could provide an opportunity for Barry and Jan to decathect any sexual stirrings or fantasies they might have about one another.

Two sessions were held. After 18 months, a follow-up revealed that there was no recurrence of sexual molestation. Jan and Mr.

Rosenwald developed an appropriately friendly and affectionate relationship. Jan was emerging as a well individuated youngster and was preparing to leave for college.

In this instance Jan's telling her mother of the molestation brought prompt and effective remedial and preventive attention. She felt supported by her mother, by the agency staff, and, after some time, by her stepfather.

In this case and the case of Mrs. Prince and Juanita, a biological parent was able to protect her child. In other families, the biological parent(s) have made no move or ineffectual moves to protect their child and overt sexual behavior and repetitive incidents of household sexual abuse have occurred.

INCIDENCE OF SEXUAL ABUSE

Statistical data gathered by DeFrancis, former Executive Director of the Children's Division of the American Humane Association, in his 1969 study of 250 families with sexually abused children, showed that 27% of the offenders in these cases lived in the child's home; 97% of the offenders in his study were male; the ratio among victims was 10 females to 1 male. Burgess, Holstrom, and McCausland found over half the cases in their 1977 study involved the father or stepfather. All offenders were male; of the 44 child victims two were male. Berliner's (1977) data on sexual abuse of children revealed 75% of assailants were the father or stepfather of the child, and 7% were the mother's live-in male friend; 99% of the offenders were male; 95% of the child victims were female.

Several factors have combined to bring about the reporting of higher levels of child abuse—an increase of 47% from 1975 to 1978 according to the 1978 Annual Report of National Analysis of Official Child Neglect and Abuse Reporting. Foremost is the passage of The Child Abuse and Treatment Act of 1974, which reflects the evolution toward improved expanded child protective law. This comprehensive act also established the National Council of Child Abuse and Neglect. Presently all 50 states have enacted legislation mandating the reporting of child maltreatment. These reporting laws continue to be refined and modified to broaden the range of reportable conditions and to increase the group of mandated reporters. In fact, many states now require anyone who suspects that a child has been abused or neglected to report it. Further, most states now accept reports from anyone, mandated or not, including anonymous sources (National Analysis of Official Child Neglect and Abuse Report, 1979).

Other factors contributing to the higher reports of incidence of child abuse, in particular sexual abuse, include the public's greater willingness to talk about sex in general and specifically with a therapist, and the greater awareness of the problem through the media (Geiser, 1979). Of specific interest in Rem situations is the weakening of the taboo against incest due to the presence of stepparents in so many more homes. De-Francis (1969) has noted that both bioparents were present in only 40% of the cases studied. For obvious reasons, we do not have accurate data on household sexual abuse in Rem families or in intact ones. Although more study is needed of these situations, it appears that the Rem family is less likely to reinforce incestuous relationships through the conspiracy of silence and unconscious collusion that is found in the nuclear family (Wald, 1981).

Particularly, we are concerned here with household sexual abuse on the part of stepfathers towards their stepdaughters. The common dynamics, treatment conceptualizations, and a lengthy case example of this form of household sexual abuse will be discussed.

COMMON DYNAMICS

In both professional and nonprofessional literature, child victims of sexual abuse, like rape victims, have too often been blamed for the attack. Lolita, the child in Nabokov's novel, has become a household word that encapsulates this insinuation. We believe a child is not a partner, nor an accomplice, nor an accessory to the act. Rather, the child is a captive who is usually too frightened, threatened, or overwhelmed to flee the assailant. Whether coaxed, cajoled, or willingly drawn into the act, the child has no experience to guess what it is he or she is being asked to participate in. How can there be consent when one does not know what one is consenting to, what will happen next, nor what the short or long-range consequences of the act might be? Even a "seductive" child with clear intentions of seeking affection and approval through physical contact cannot understand what is involved in the expressions of sexual need. In no way can the child be considered the perpetrator of the deed.

Burgess and Holstrom (1975) have written, regarding inability to consent:

The victims' collaboration comes about because of their inability to consent or not consent due to their stage of personality or cognitive development. It should be noted that we do not define ability to consent arbitrarily by age. In all these cases, the primary person involved, the assailant, stands in a relationship of power over the secondary person, the victim, because of being older, being an authority figure, or for some other reason (p. 11).

They elaborate on the "other reasons":

The assailant gains access to this victim by three methods: a) pressures the victim to take material goods; b) pressures the victim to accept human contact; and c) pressures the victim to believe the sexual activity is appropriate and enjoyable. In each of these approaches, the assailant makes sure the victim gets something out of the sexual encounter; thus at the time the encounter is not a totally negative experience for the victim (p. 11).

The authority figure sometimes explains his sexual behavior for the victim's benefit:

. . . . the activity is often presented as being instructional. The offender appears to take a teacher-role. He first shows by demonstration on the child what to do sexually and then asks for a return demonstration on himself. . . . The motivational intent in sex-pressure assaults is to gain sexual control of the child by developing a willing or consenting sexual relationship. Sexuality appears to be in the service of the offender's need to dominate in order to receive affection and physical contact (p. 240).

The need to dominate is the most pervasive element in the dynamics of the offender and is evident in the centripetal rather than centrifugal pulls in these family systems. The assailant and the consenting parent fear the loss of the child to others outside of the system. There is the denial of the importance and often existence of the noncustodial parent and fiats against allowing the child to develop normal social relationships, particularly with those of the opposite sex. Going outside the household for normal age-appropriate sexual experience is strongly discouraged and is seen as a sign of disloyalty to the family.

We can postulate further as to the intrapsychic dynamics of the assailant. In cases where the early history of the assailant is available to us there is evidence of suppressed anger toward the maternal figure for perceived deprivation and for failure to promote a strong parental bond:

John left home at age 11, when he chose to live in a boarding school in another part of the country. He claims he identified with his father, entered his father's vocational field, but admits he remembers being unfairly punished and put down by his father. He remembers his mother failed to defend him against his father and states she was ungiving, uncaring, and self-involved.

Murray at age nine had been forced by his father to hide in the attic and keep watch through a slit in the floor over his mother's bedroom. When she had a lover, he was to report it to his father.

The child's rage toward the mother is projected toward other females, and, as is the case with rape, the sexual behaviors which are subsequently acted out are not a function of sexual desire but of aggression. Assailants who have defended their actions as educational admit they did not tolerate their victim's refusals.

The common dynamics of the consenting mother reveal a dependent personality who is fearful of losing the interest and protection of the powerful authority figure in the household, and thus she is ready to see the assailant's demands as acceptable and appropriate. There are indications as well of the consenting mother's abstinence or avoidance of sexual pleasures because of physical illness or emotional problems and a subsequent offering of the child to the stepfather. Our findings in this area with Rem families are similar to those found in nuclear families and confirm those reported by Lustig, Dresser, Spellman, and Murray (1966), who state:

In these families both the mother and father seemed to define and experience the daughter as a maternal object, projecting onto the daughter their own maternal introjects and sexual fantasies. . . . Central findings included generalized role reversal and ego fusion between mother and daughter, fear of abandonment through family disintegration among all protagonists, the sexual expression of pregenital anger and/or dependency wishes, and the need of both parents to maintain a public façade of role competence (pp. 38–39).

The noncustodial biological father has proven not to be a force to contend with either because of death, desertion, absence, inconsistent involvement, or the limitations of his own dependent personality. This perpetuates the family system where the authoritarian stepfather can be in charge because the mother is isolated from her original parental partner and the child feels abandoned by her father.

Jill, age 13: Tell my dad? You have to be joking. He wouldn't believe me and if he did, he wouldn't do anything to help me.

In cases of household sexual abuse we have seen, the child has always been the identified patient and complaints presented have included: depression, suicidal gestures, persistent abusiveness and/or withdrawal between child and stepparent, adolescent rebelliousness, or poor school achievement. Only after a relationship had been established with the therapist did the child, in an individual session, hesitantly introduce the abuse problem.

In incest cases there is usually a remainder of affection towards the father. Although there is confusion and guilt present, the child does not wish to abandon or be abandoned by the biological father. She continues to long for his acceptance and love or for his other involvements in her and the family's life. In household sexual abuse where the stepfather was the abuser, the child has wished to leave the home to escape the assailant and her mother who is seen by the child as colluding in the abuse. In these latter cases, the absence of the blood and historical ties has left the child without anything with which to counter the post abuse feelings of anger, resentment, helplessness, powerlessness, and hopelessness. The fear of the stepfather's authority over her and over the household leaves the child with flight fantasies, which she may be able to present to the therapist with the hope that these will be fulfilled.

The depression in the abused child is linked to self-reproaches, the turning of the origianlly object-directed aggression against the self (Bibring, 1953). Depression can also be based on recognition of being in a hopeless situation with no exit apparent. Abused children have expressed self-hatred for not being strong enough to get away and guilt for being "so weak." The following description of extreme sexual abuse is not unique, unfortunately.

Ann, age 42, recounted the sexual abuse of her own early childhood. Her father had been killed, and her mother, pregnant with Ann, turned to prostitution. After some years of being shuttled back and forth between her mother and maternal grandmother, Ann lived from ages four to five with her mother and the mother's live-in boyfriend. She remembered two things about that time: The boyfriend sexually and physically abused her, and parties would take place at their home where she was passed around from one man to another and her mother laughed and participated in threats made against her when she struggled to break away. She remembered a man who put his penis in her mouth and told her "little worms would go down her throat into her stomach and swim around." She remembers anal and vaginal assaults, with bodies all around her. Ann states: "I should have run away. Even though I was only four or five, I could have taken care of myself. I was already making my own meals."

Anger at the parent is often too frightening to be consciously acknowledged and is masked by the child's anger at the offender. When even that outlet for anger is blocked, severe depression and/or suicidal ideation and acts may follow.

In his report on the child sex victim, Schultz (1973) states that, "It is not the sexual assault that usually creates trauma, but the child's parents' behavior upon its discovery, and the effect of this on the child." This may or may not be true for victims of one-time stranger attacks, but some children who are terrified into submission by a household member on a repeated basis have been able to voice extreme disappointment and utter abandonment in the parent's failure to respond. This is particularly so in Rem situations when the biological parent dismisses the child's complaint.

> Heidi, age 15, the object of her stepbrother's sexual advances, states with great feeling: Why do they leave me alone in the house with him after I've told them how he bothers me?

TREATMENT APPROACHES

In the play *Hippolytus* by Euripides, Phaedra speaks to her nurse about her sexual encounter with her stepson:

Phaedra: Ah! Would thou couldst say for me what I have to tell.
Nurse: I am no prophetess to unriddle secrets.

In cases of household sexual abuse (and incest cases as well) the task of the therapist is, indeed, to unriddle secrets, since the problem presented is not the abuse. Rather, the problem presented is most often, but not always, depression or acting-out behavior in the child who is being sexually abused. We need to learn what it is the child means to say by such actions. Sexual abuse has heretofore been too difficult an issue to verbalize directly, and smoke screens have been erected in a defensive posture.

The genogram and the clues that emerge during this process with the family help in the unriddling of secrets. In each case of abused children, what is clear and immediately verified by a glance at the genogram is the unavailability of the noncustodial parent and the family myth that the stepfather has taken his place. One stepfather expressed disquiet when the biofather was given a place on the genogram. The importance of including the noncustodial parent in sessions needs to be established from the beginning of treatment, and the genogram serves as the starting-off point from which to assert the bioparent's place in the child's life.

Those treatment modalities utilized and recommended include individual, couple, sibling, Rem family, noncustodial parent and child(ren), and suprafamily sessions. Telephone availability has also proven essential since disparate parts of the family and suprasystem reach out to the therapist at periods of crisis for each person.

An opportunity for all family members to have an individual session is significant since it has been in the individual sessions that young and adolescent girls have broached the subject of the sexual abuse. Female therapists who show that they can handle anger, are in control without being punitive, and are comfortable discussing sexual matters have been more likely to elicit information about sexual abuse. Sgroi (1975, p. 20) states, "Recognition of sexual molestation in a child is entirely dependent on the individual's inherent willingness to entertain the possibility that the condition may exist." With the strength of the therapist to lean on, the child can stand with the new authority figure to face the authority figures in the home who have misused or neglected their power or responsibility to the child. It is essential that the child not find replicated in the therapist the powerlessness the child feels and sees in the parents.

Treatment of the child thus includes the formation of a trusting relationship with the therapist where anger and guilt can be verbalized and the youth's burgeoning assertiveness can be supported. With the establishment of the therapeutic alliance, the client can then see power used to gain safety rather than to endanger safety. Therapists are frank with the children and tell them that they may have to be removed from the home. We are prepared, if it should be necessary, to protect the child by not having her return home that day. We have not had to utilize this recourse to date. However, in some cases, the child's admission of the sexual abuse has meant the breakup of the family. DeFrancis (1969) reports, "A total of 18% of the children were placed away from home, many with friends or relatives." Although children have expressed guilt regarding leaving their mothers, they also feel anger toward them for their collusion in the abuse and this enables them to effect the separation:

> Cathy, age 15: I feel bad about leaving my mother because she needs me, but I know we have to split eventually anyway. When I have my own children I'll never allow her and John to visit me because I'd be afraid of having him near my children.

Thus, the resolution of the problem of the sexual abuse of the child may involve adding new problems to the child's life: the loss of the family and home, loss of friends, neighborhood and school, and the concomitant adjustment to the new family, home, neighborhood, friends and school. What is then lost is not only sexual innocence, but much of what the child knew and had.

Another aspect of the treatment of this problem also entails finding out about the sex life of the adult couple. Often therapists lose sight of the dyad in the attempt to respond to the child's needs. The total treatment plan involves moving the couple from involvement with the child to getting something substantial for themselves.

> Louise, whose husband had sexually abused her 13-year-old daughter, admitted that sex with her husband was a source of constant bickering. She lacked desire and was content with only minimal physical contact. She particularly could not tolerate her husband's advances when she did not want to be touched. Suggestion was made for her to let him know when and where she could be touched. Louise subsequently reported that she felt better about initiating sexual contact and no longer felt "invaded." She had enjoyed intercourse and, for the first time, became aroused and was hopeful that soon she would reach orgasm.

Cases of household sexual abuse are emotionally taxing for the family and the therapist. The support, engagement, and expertise of a team effort are vital to the refueling needs of the therapist. The pooled experience of a team can be most helpful in the planning of strategic intervention and decision-making. Our entire staff or just the team leader and therapist may meet with families and thus help to neutralize the family's idealized expectations and rescue fantasies projected on their therapist. The impact of the family's personal contact and thoughtful engagement with the team underscores for them the seriousness of their problem and enables multiple identifications with men and women. Given this experience, families have been more willing to consider team recommendations.

Case Example

In the following case, household sexual abuse took place between the common-law stepfather and his two stepdaughters with the tacit consent of their mother. This case was followed closely in the Remarried Consultation Service conferences and in supervision. Because of Cindy's two suicidal gestures, immediate psychiatric consultation was arranged for with the director of the service.

Cindy, 16, came for treatment with her mother, Mrs. Adams, 38, her sister Judy, 14, and the mother's live-in male companion, Mr. Smith, 57. Cindy was occasionally rebellious but more often depressed and had recently made two suicidal gestures. All were present for family sessions.

During the first two family sessions Cindy was withdrawn and remained silent except for monosyllabic replies to questions the therapist put directly to her. She sat nearly immobile; her affect was depressed. Mrs. Adams expressed anger at Cindy's refusal to do household chores, and her ineptness when forced to help with the family business. Mr. Smith, too, was angry at this, especially since he saw himself as a loving and caring father to her. There was a strong belief in the myth that this was a normal, legal family. A great deal of denial was in operation: the importance of the biological father to the system, Mrs. Adams' deteriorating condition due to the complications of diabetes and the seriousness of Cindy's suicidal ideation and two suicidal gestures.

With the family present, Cindy was unable to respond openly to the therapist's efforts to reach out to her. A suggestion was made and accepted that she see the therapist for an individual session. Fifteen minutes before the appointed time, Mrs. Adams came to the office to say she had brought Cindy but needed some time to talk alone. It was agreed to see her for 15 minutes and then see Cindy for the scheduled appointment. Mrs. Adams stated she was unhappy with the way Judy was behaving toward Mr. Smith. She reported there was a sexual overtone to the way Judy would snuggle up to Mr. Smith while he lay in bed, and that Judy frequently sat on his lap, which Mrs. Adams felt she should have outgrown. When asked if this disturbed only her or Mr. Smith as well, she said Mr. Smith had asked her to talk about it since it was disturbing to him. Mrs. Adams granted permission for the therapist to bring this up in future family meetings.

Most of the ensuing session with Cindy was spent talking of her suicidal thoughts and actions, and the rage she felt prior to each incident, primarily toward Mr. Smith. She then revealed that he touched her in ways "he should not have" and that he touched Judy as well. When asked to describe what he did, she did in detail and reported he laid on her bed with her, touched her breasts, buttocks and vagina and had her hold his penis. Although there had been no vaginal penetration, he had manually brought her and himself to orgasm. After each incident, Cindy went to the bathroom and vomited. Mr. Smith had initiated this sexual activity when Cindy was about 14, and then involved Judy when she turned 12, two years ago. Judy had confided this to Cindy only recently, and Cindy had then told her about his activities with her as well. Cindy was most upset about two things: her mother's non-intervention and insistence that the door to her bedroom always be left open; and her fear that if she openly complained, Mr. Smith would abandon the family and leave her mother in severe distress because of her emotional dependence on him and her increasingly debilitating physical condition. Clearly not knowing what to do, she hoped the therapist would find a solution. Although concerned about what would happen to Mr. Smith, and how he would react, Cindy agreed to the suggestion that the abuse issue be introduced and discussed at a meeting of the family.

An individual session was arranged for Judy, who revealed Mr. Smith's sexual advances toward her and the same fear of her mother's being abandoned if she resisted. Judy also agreed to a family meeting to open up the issue of the sexual abuse.

The family had met with the psychiatrist during the early phase of treatment and he was included again in the family sessions when the abuse was to be discussed. His presence was essential for several reasons: Two therapists' authority would underscore the cause for alarm about Mr. Smith's behavior; two therapists would also serve to dilute the intensity of each family member's rescue fantasy directed toward the primary therapist; the primary therapist would not have to go it alone when taking on this precarious but crucial therapeutic charge; and the psychiatrist would provide male support. The strategy, discussed by the staff in conference, was to introduce the "family secret" by questioning Mrs. Adams about her previously mentioned concerns regarding Judy's sexual closeness to Mr. Smith, rather than to confront the issue with information provided by the children. It was agreed that the director of the service, in his capacity as consultant, would take therapeutic leadership in the session, while also being sensitive to the family's therapist, who was in closer contact with the family system and its members.

The objectives of this consultation had been decided upon in the staff meeting. These were: a) to open the abuse issue for discussion in the family and to determine its extent; b) to stop the abuse; c) to make clear the legal implications of the abuse; d) to be prepared to immediately remove the girls from the home if it were deemed necessary; and e) to try to avoid endangering the mother's relationship with her common-law husband.

After opening greetings the consultant then brought up the major reasons for the therapist's having requested this second consultation:

Psychiatrist: It seems that there are things going on in the family that do not get discussed openly, for example, I was told by Ms. P (therapist) that you (to Mrs. Adams) mentioned to her that you are concerned about Judy's snuggling up to Mr. Smith in bed.

Mrs. Adams: Yes, I don't think it's healthy.

Mr. Smith: Let me explain. I had two wives who were frigid. I don't want Cindy and Judy to be afraid of sex, so I instructed them just like I did with my own daughter. But I read an article in the local paper a while ago that said this might be bad for them.* (Sounded defensive at first and then more at ease and straightforward)

Psychiatrist: (to Cindy) What was involved?

Cindy: I'm embarrassed to say.

Psychiatrist: Would it be better if I ask you direct questions and you answer?

Cindy: Yes.

Psychiatrist: Did Mr. Smith ever touch your breasts?

Cindy: Yes.

Cindy answered yes to questions about touching her vagina, clitoris and squeezing her buttocks. There was never any vaginal, oral, or rectal penetration.

Judy: (Reported the same information and added) He would call me into his bedroom and was mad at me when I said no. My mother would walk by and not say a thing.

Therapist: How did that make you feel?

Cindy: Very disappointed; she walked by with me too.

Mr. Smith: (Open and volunteering) I showed them my sperm. I thought they should know what it looks like.

Psychiatrist: What was the sexual play that caused you to ejaculate?

Mrs. Adams: He masturbated in the bathroom.

Cindy: Not true. He masturbated in front of me.

Mr. Smith: I object to your term sexual play. This was for education, their own good, and I never forced them to do it.

Cindy: I would say "please no more" and then it would happen again.

Mrs. Adams: But girls, you never told me this.

Judy: I felt guilty. I thought I was taking something away from you.

Mrs. Adams: To me it was only loving; they take it as something illicit.

Cindy: I'm afraid that because of this I will never have an orgasm.

Judy: Will I be able to have babies?

---

*Mr. Smith used the "educational" rationalization referred to earlier.

After giving accurate and reassuring information to the girls, the therapists informed the family that the sexual abuse would have to stop immediately. Mr. Smith claimed, and the girls confirmed, that the abuse had ceased since he read the article three weeks ago. He insisted, however, that he had done nothing wrong and Mrs. Adams vehemently agreed. The psychiatrist was able to support Mr. Smith's awareness of the danger to the girls, his realization that Cindy's presenting symptoms, depression, and suicidal acts had all been cited in the article, and his decision to voluntarily cease his actions. The psychiatrist impressed on Mr. Smith that his actions, regardless of how he perceived them, were illegal.

At staff meeting after this session, there was agreement that it was necessary to find an alternative home for the girls. But as the molestation had ceased and we would continue to follow the family and see the girls separately it was felt that removal need not be done as an emergency. The abuse was reported to the Child Abuse and Maltreatment Register.

Fortuitously an alternative home rapidly became available in a few days, when a maternal relative who was mindful of stress in his sister's home reiterated a previous offer to have the girls live with him and his family. This offer was presented to the family, the therapist spoke with the aunt and uncle and within a few weeks all family members were able to accept the change of residence. The girls' removal from the home was effected with the ready consent of the couple, who came to see it as helpful for the girls as well as for themselves. The girls were followed in a clinic in their new locale. The therapist communicated directly with the new therapist after having received the appropriate releases.

Treatment then focused on improving the couple's relationship. Their sexual needs and the issues between them which had kept them from marrying were addressed. Mr. Smith's three previous failed marriages loomed large in his mind as proof that something goes wrong once a couple is married. Mrs. Adams took this as a sign that she was no different in his eyes from the other women and was hurt by this lack of trust in her. After a few sessions where the issues were explored, the couple made a decision to marry.

Shortly after Cindy and Judy had gone to live with their aunt and uncle, their father, who had been ill, died suddenly. No legal action or change in legal custody was undertaken in relation to the change in residence. In view of the girls' voluntary removal from their mother's home and the cessation of the abuse, no further action was recommended.

Abuse can have profound implications for the future of mental health of the child. Rosenfeld (1977) has traced the evolution of psychiatric ideas about incest from an early conceptualization as etiologic of certain disorders of the child to its later being seen as a symptom of family dysfunction. This latter viewpoint is what we have begun to explore: household sexual abuse as a dysfunction in some remarried families, as incest is a dysfunction in some nuclear families. The Rem situation lowers the threshold at which the incidence of abuse can occur.

The clinician must be alert to the continuum of the loosening of sexual boundaries in remarried families. From the most benign to pernicious situations, the issue needs to be explored so that all family members can feel safe.

CHAPTER 14

Adoption in Remarried Families

The adoption of a stepchild has not been a prominent issue in our practice with Rem families over the past five years. There are a number of reasons for this:

1) Most families we treat have two living bioparents.
2) Our commitment to include the bioparent whom the system might be trying to exclude counteracts the development of the uninvolved-absent parent. In most families both bioparents have been willing to become involved in treatment.
3) Where there is a deceased parent or one who has abandoned the family, the single-parent phase frequently caused a symbiotic-like bond to develop between parent and child, so that Rem family consolidation is, and continues to be, too problematic and tenuous to consider adoption.
4) We treat a clinic population, and historically adoption is "dealing with the strength of society," i.e., people who have problems with reproduction but not with ego deterioration and family system dysfunction (Braden, 1970).

Our knowledge of adoption in Rem families comes largely from a small number of treatment cases, the nonclinic population applying for legal service at the Jewish Board of Family and Children's Services, and the nonclinic population in general. On a conscious level, the following common themes emerge as motivation for adoption:

311

1) Family unity and consolidation.
2) Protection of the child and protection of the child/stepparent dyad in case of the death of the bioparent. Protection of property is mentioned in wealthy families.
3) Acceptance by the Rem family suprasystem and religious affiliates.
4) The natural outgrowth of what already is the voluntary assumption of parental care by a stepparent over another's child, i.e., doctrine of in loco parentis (in place of a parent). Thus, the facts establish the law as opposed to the law establishing the facts in a nonrelated adoption.

On a preconscious and unconscious level there are issues of identity, inclusion/exclusion, acceptance/rejection, possessiveness, abandonment, control, mortality, propinquity, and legacy. In families where the biological parent is deceased, the issue of adoption may arouse fears about the surviving parent's death. Appelberg (1977, p. 33) reminds us that, "Thinking about the possibility of one's death need not be morbid or damaging to one's children, since death is part of life and making provisions for such an eventuality is a duty one owes to the living."

There is no overriding body of federal family law; each state specifies the reciprocal rights and duties of family members. But notably absent from all state statutes is the specification of rights and duties of stepparents toward stepchildren (Wald, 1981). Thus, the doctrine of strangers is operative for steprelated persons. Legally, a stranger is defined as anyone who is in no event resulting from the present state of affairs liable for the other (Black, 1968).

In the adoption of a stepchild, the law operates under two doctrines:

1) *Doctrine of Parental Preference,* which argues that the bioparent is the preferred parent in disputes with a third party, whether a relative, foster parent, adoptive parent, or stepparent. This emphasis is related to the ideology that the parent-child tie is "so rooted in the traditions and conscience of our people as to be ranked as fundamental . . . " (Katz, 1971, p. 6). An increasing number of case decisions demonstrates an expanded application of the doctrine of paternal preference to unwed mothers, so that biofathers have been able to prevent adoptions when the unwed mother of their child has later married and unilaterally agreed to the adoption of the child by the stepfather (Wald, 1981).
2) *Doctrine of the Best Interest of the Child,* which considers two criteria in making this determination: the psychological parent and the child's preference. The "psychological parent," as defined by Goldstein, Freud, and Solnit (1973) is one who, on a continuing,

day-to-day basis, through interaction, companionship, interplay, and mutuality, fulfills the child's psychological needs for a parent, as well as the child's physical needs. The child's preference is considered by the court when the child is of "sufficient age and capacity to reason so as to form an intelligent preference (Mnookin, 1975). This concept is relevant to that of the psychological parent because it may be presumed that the child's preference reflects the child's view of the parent who is the psychological parent for him (Wald, 1981). Others have argued that such a position is untenable because of the difficulties of assessing the more psychological parent when both parents meet the psychological needs of their children in the same or complementary ways (Okpaku, 1976; Stack, 1976). This concept of child's preference also runs the risk of putting the child in a loyalty bind and giving the courts the added tasks of developing methods by which to help children know their feelings and speak openly about them (Wald, 1981).

Among the procedures that have been suggested to deal with the risks and complex questions that are inherent in the principle of children's preference is guardian ad litem (guardian for the suit), representation of the child in the court through advocate lawyers, and the use of neutral mental health professionals to develop factual and objective social studies for the courts to use as a basis for their decisions. Another alternative suggested has been a team approach, in which educators, mental health professionals, and legal representatives explore the issues and make joint recommendations to the court (Wald, 1981).

Current adoption law and practice continue to favor the doctrine of bioparental preference over psychological parental preference and the rights of the absent biofather over the rights of the remarried family unit. Children with living parents can become available for stepparent adoption only through voluntary consent of both parents or through judicial termination of parental rights on the basis of unfitness or abandonment. Therefore, in Rem families where the bioparent has abandoned the child, the court requires that a bona fide "diligent search" for this parent must be done before the court can terminate the bioparent's parental rights. A "diligent search" involves contacting relatives and friends, placing a classified advertisement in the personal column of a newspaper and, most threatening of all, the possibility of finding the person and literally facing the let-well-enough-alone past.

In Rem families where the bioparent is deceased, the adoption procedure is much less complicated. When the parent, stepparent, and stepchild (if old enough) agree to an adoption, they petition the court for a change in legal status. The final stage in both instances involves a court-approved home study, similar to those done in a nonrelated adoption, where the biological parent, stepparent, and child might feel under scrutiny. The above-mentioned gains of adoption override the obstacles for those who choose to pursue this goal.

CASE ILLUSTRATIONS

Mr. Helders, an electrician, and Mrs. Helders, an English teacher, both age 27, lived together for two years prior to their marriage. Four months after the wedding they applied for treatment for Mrs. Helders' son, Steven, age eight, who was not working up to his potential in school and had recently taken money from his mother's pocketbook. A six-session contract that emphasized the systemic change of having Mrs. Helders rather than the stepfather do the major part of the disciplining and limit-setting eased the tension in the family, abated Steven's fear that he was losing his mother, and enabled Mr. Helders and Steven to enjoy mutual interests in athletics. The fact that Mrs. Helders allowed the stepfather-stepson relationship to flourish made the prognosis favorable.

Mrs. Helders' first husband had been out of the picture for five years. With the therapist's lead, Steven was able to ask questions about his father which heretofore had been forbidden. His questions were perfunctorily answered by his mother, who briskly admitted her wish to "forget that relationship." The follow-up telephone contact with Mrs. Helders six months after treatment verified the anticipated good prognosis. Steven had begun to do better in school and there was no repeat incident of stealing.

A year later a letter from Mr. Helders proudly "announced" the upcoming adoption. The therapist responded and invited the family to a follow-up session. In response to the therapist's comment, "I want to hear about the adoption," Steven replied, "Mommy and I have adopted Joe." In response to our laughter, he added, "He's legally ours now." In discussing the procedure Mrs. Helders highlighted her ambivalence. More than anything else she wanted them to be "a family," and was worried about Steven's guardianship if she should die. Mrs. Helders' parents were both dead and an older sibling lived in Europe. However, the diligent search and possibility of finding her former husband were an anathema to her. Mr. Helders was not threatened by the search and encouraged his wife to pursue what was necessary for the completion of the adoption. Steven had known about the plan and was also encouraging.

Steven was told about the possibility of finding his biofather, but this was not opened for discussion by Mrs. Helders. Mr. Helders mentioned that he had asked Steven about this in private, but

Steven was non-committal. In session, Steven reluctantly expressed his ambivalence. He, like his mother, wanted to "put to rest" the issue of his father, but he was curious about his father and his father's interest in horse racing. His drawings of horses had greater significance when this information about his biofather was revealed.

The entire family was positive about the adoption itself but critical about the invasion of privacy they experienced by the court-appointed home study. Steven had not expected the judge to ask him if he wanted to be adopted, and he felt "shy" but "glad" to say "sure." There had been a large extended family party to celebrate the adoption. Steven's friends were present, which eased the name change in school. He continued to call his adoptive father by his first name which seemed comfortable for all. Mr. Helders' siblings, a brother and sister and their spouses, however, were careful to refer to themselves as aunt and uncle rather than the prior first-name basis. Mr. Helders' parents began a savings account for Steven's education as they had done for their other grandchildren. Mr. and Mrs. Helders felt a stronger bond and were in the "talking stage" of considering a mutual child.

In this case example adoption was used to facilitate family consolidation, so aptly described by Steven's perception that he and his mother did the adopting. However, adoption in another family had the opposite effect.

Mrs. Joseph applied for counseling for her son Stuart, age 23, who was showing increasing signs of agoraphobia. There was a history of several aborted therapy experiences where Stuart was diagnosed as schizophrenic. Past therapy consisted of individual sessions for Mr. Joseph, Mrs. Joseph, and Stuart. This time the Josephs were seen as a family for six months and the intense mother/son symbiotic-like relationship and Mr. Joseph's passive, albeit hostile, response to it were challenged.

History-taking, via the genogram, revealed the family secret that Mr. Joseph was not Stuart's biofather but had adopted Stuart when he was four years old. At that time Stuart's biofather had initiated the adoption in exchange for $2,000 needed to cover a debt. Although appalled by the idea of selling the child as chattel, Mr. Joseph went along with his wife's request to "start over and wipe the slate clean."

Further discussion revealed that Mr. Joseph was aware of his wife's sexual attraction to her ex-husband and he felt threatened by this. Thus the $2,000 seemed like a small price to protect family unity. In fact, it had the opposite effect. Mr. Joseph felt resentful of being pushed into a commitment he wasn't ready for and guilty for "buying his son." Mrs. Joseph was aware of her husband's resentment and felt her son needed protection from him. Stuart knew, but could not recall how he knew, about "the price for his head," and this reinforced his negative feelings that he was "no bargain." In this pathological family system, the issue of paradox, where the adoption hindered family consolidation rather than promoted it, became a dynamic theme that did bring about some structural changes, loosening the suction of the mother/son dyad and enabling the adoptive father to be more involved with his wife and son.

In the following case adoption helped a subsystem of the Rem family to consolidate, but left members of the original nuclear family feeling that they were "disposable."

Mrs. Wallace, a 50-year-old divorced woman with two sons, Bruce, age 19, and Andrew, age 17, applied for counseling for both boys because they slept all day and hung out with friends all night. The application was precipitated when Andrew, an unlicensed driver, took his mother's car and got into a minor accident. The boy's father, Mr. Wallace, had left the home seven years before and had been remarried for five years to a divorced woman with a son who was now 10 years old. Mr. Wallace paid child support for Bruce and Andrew during periods of his intermittent employment as an actor and had sporadic contact with both sons.

Despite his former wife's accusation that "Mr. Wallace has another family and has lost interest in us," he readily attended the first assessment session, which consisted of the original nuclear family. When the genogram was done, Mrs. Wallace sarcastically mentioned that her ex-husband had adopted his stepson three years ago. Mr. Wallace agreed that he had mentioned this "in passing" to his boys shortly after the event occurred. Bruce recalled flippantly responding, "Oh that's nice." Andrew was vague about his reaction then and now. The therapist sensed that this was a charged issue and said so to the family. Mr. Wallace, somewhat defensively, spoke of his stepson having been deserted by his father and his not wanting him to be a "fatherless boy." Mrs. Wallace vituperatively added, "But what about your own sons?" Her attack on her ex-husband was stopped by the therapist and the boys were invited to speak for themselves. Bruce expressed, "But your *own* sons are fatherless boys." Andrew, with help from the therapist, was able to say this in his own words. Mrs. Wallace quite sensibly raised for the first time questions about what the adoption meant in terms of her sons' inheritance. Did insurance policies now include another beneficiary?

In this first session the opening up of the issue of the adoption and the way it was handled led to the quick acceptance by all of the treatment goals of strengthening the father-son relationships, developing a working co-parenting alliance of the bioparents of the boys, and consolidating further the Rem family by including Mr. Wallace's sons from his first marriage. Andrew and Bruce had rarely been invited to the Rem household and had felt themselves to be strangers there. Mr. Wallace's first family and progeny had remained a semi-mystery to his second family. This was now about to change. A second assessment session included Mr. Wallace, his second wife, his adopted son, and his two biosons.

THE CHILD'S VIEW OF ADOPTION

So far not enough has been said about the importance of adoption from the child's point of view. The legal tie may strengthen the emotional bonding and give roots to the emerging sense of identity. It is not uncommon in the legal department of the Jewish Board of Family and Children's Services for teenagers and young adults to actively participate in the adoption procedure.

Susan's mother died when she was two years old. By the time she was four her father had remarried and both she and her stepmother enjoyed a mutually gratifying relationship. At 15 her father died and she continued to live with her stepmother. By the time she was 19 her stepmother had remarried and one year later she was adopted by her stepmother and her stepmother's new husband. During the courtship period her stepmother had made known to her future husband her plan to adopt Susan, since this was important to her and to Susan. The Agency attorney speaks of this family's day in court as a joyful event for all three. Susan mentioned that her "parents" would walk her down the aisle at her forthcoming marriage.

According to Goldstein, Freud and Solnit (1973), Susan's relationship with her stepmother is a "common-law parent/child relationship" and the court is favorable to adoptions of this nature. In some instances, court precedent has stipulated continued contact with the bioparent after adoption. This has been done when the adoption of the child is seen as instrumental in facilitating a more stabilized family identity and functioning, and when input from the biological parent is seen as beneficial to the growing child. For example, if the child had lived with the bioparent for a number of years before the divorce and remarriage, it is not thought psychologically sound or even realistic to have the parent disappear. England's Children's Bill of 1975 confers guardianship and limited legal rights to stepparents without diminishing the legal rights of the noncustodial bioparent (Maddox, 1975). We hope the effects of this law will be researched, as it suggests interesting possibilities as well as problems. Contact with the biological parent can prevent the "hidden parent syndrome" (Jolowicz, 1969). In this syndrome the child's ambivalent feelings and questions about the absent, secret, or not discussed bioparent have no outlet and therefore remain submerged and presumably have a deleterious effect on personality development. The most flagrant example is when the child embraces the hidden parent's alleged destructive behavior (negative identification).

According to Wald (1981), the two parallel tracks that are apparent in legal thinking overlook the need for a third track that considers the value and function of the family:

> Two parallel tracks are apparent in legal doctrines and principles that have relevance to the rights and duties among remarried family members and between remarried family members and the noncustodial parents: One balances the rights and obligations of biological and legal parents toward their children after divorce and remarriage; the other protects the rights of children in these circumstances. Both of these tracks reflect positive directions in the evolution of individual human values, but neither includes a focus on the family as a significant societal institution and milieu essential to the emotional health of its members. There is increasing recognition that a third track that seeks to establish criteria and principles to balance the values and functions of the family and the values and rights of individuals is needed (p. 119).

In conclusion, we see that adoption in Rem families, as in nuclear families, is more common in the nonclinical population. It is a step that can encourage or jeopardize family consolidation. We urge a careful exploration with families considering adoption as to their motivation and method. Wald (1981) presents a fascinating case where in one Rem family it is in the stepdaughter's best interest to be adopted but not in the stepson's best interest. In cases that involve a diligent search for the absent parent, much support needs to be given to the family, especially to the parent embarking on this task.

The positive aspects of adoption encourage biological parents and stepparents to take the risks involved. Robert Frost (1962) could have been referring to the family unity adoption may ideally achieve when he said, "Home is the place where, when you have to go there, they have to take you in."

CHAPTER 15

Mentally Ill
Family Members

We operate on the premise that mental illness is a multidetermined state. This is supported by research in the genetics of mental illness, on the families of schizophrenics, and biochemical and neurophysiological investigation into the etiology of mental illness.

Other research indicates that some people will be so mentally ill, possibly for genetic or organic reasons, that no form of treatment now available can help them function within normal limits, and cope with the ordinary stresses of life over a period of time. Others can function if their important social systems (family, work, school) are not stressful. The work of Laqueur (1972) in multiple family therapy with hospitalized schizophrenics and their families supported the importance of changing the identified patient's family system. Using control groups, he found that those families who had multiple family therapy prior to discharge of a schizophrenic young adult were able to appreciably cut down hospital recidivism. These studies were done over a 25-year period at Creedmoor State Hospital in New York and Vermont State Hospital. A smaller but carefully controlled study at Hillside Hospital in New York replicated Laqueur's findings (Lurie and Harold, 1968). The latest research in schizophrenics and their families is summarized by M. J. Goldstein (1981) and brings a new emphasis on the importance of particular family interventions.

Greene (1970) wrote that the marital relationship prognosis was very poor in cases where one partner had a major affective disorder, which has a definite genetic component but also may be exacerbated by major or minor life crisis and hormonal disturbances. Greene and colleagues later reported (1976) that now that drugs are effective in treating the two polarized affective states of this disorder, the prognosis has improved markedly. It is inspiring to witness scientific advances that are so immediately rewarding.

Another difficult marital relationship is likely to occur with a partner whose rigid and authoritarian defenses remain ego-syntonic but where there is no psychosis. These persons need not bear an ominous diagnosis, but their behavior is often intractable and exasperating to those who are dependent on them. Often, the interaction between two partners may readily cause symptomatology to emerge in an at-risk partner. However, it is possible in another marriage for a less vulnerable partner not to develop major symptomatology and to be an effective mate. The mix of the partners in the second marriage may produce an interaction that is not noxious for either spouse.

Research, as well as clinical experience, also supports the idea that severe mental disturbance per se need not be reason for terminating a marriage or writing off a child. Much can be done to restore or develop a person to good functioning when early diagnosis and treatment are instituted. Where indicated, appropriate medication, family therapy, individual therapy, or other modalities should be employed. Multiple modalities are often necessary. Hospitalization or a protective and therapeutic milieu should be considered when there is danger to oneself or others or where the home environment continues to be noxious.

We are long past the day when divorce was automatically viewed by many as evidence of severe pathology in one or both of the mates. However, even with the best therapy currently available, some marriages do founder because of gross or subtle evidence of severely pathological behavior in either or both partners. In some instances mental illnesses may be a significant factor in divorce, while in other situations good dyadic and family system interaction may minimize the devastating effects of individual mental illness.

The Rem situation is further complicated when there is a mentally ill ex-spouse, present spouse, or child. Under mental illness we include: schizophrenic reactions, manic-depressive disease, organic brain syndrome, sociopathic behavior, severe obsessive-compulsive functioning, and other extreme pathologic symptomatology. In this chapter the following will be considered:

1) The mentally ill former spouse who has custody of the child.
2) The mentally ill former spouse whose child lives with the Rem couple.

3) The mentally ill child from a former marriage.
4) The mentally ill spouse in the Rem couple.

MENTALLY ILL FORMER SPOUSE

In the case of a mentally ill former spouse, an emotional divorce is harder to achieve because the disturbed partner, almost always a dependent person, denies the reality of the divorce and continues to act as if the legal agreement, breakup of nuclear family household, and remarriage had not occurred. Frequently, the better functioning spouse may experience a form of survivor's guilt and hostile-protective, as well as genuinely protective, feelings that further hinder the emotional divorce. Legal financial obligations may reinforce this bond.

The effect of this on Rem couple consolidation is at best an impediment and at worst an obstacle that may lead to another divorce. A primary treatment consideration is the need to assess to what extent the healthier partner is letting himself be unduly victimized by the former spouse, and to what extent the new spouse and Rem family system are involved in this dynamic.

> Mr. R "finally" put his foot down and refused to give his ambulatory schizophrenic former wife the recurrent anti-eviction money. His present wife, who had been urging him to "take a stand" for three years, then stymied him by advocating he give the extra money. Exploration revealed that the current Mrs. R had a seriously disturbed mother and needed to replay her role as dutiful caretaker.

In situations where the pathologic former spouse lives with the child it is usually harder for the Rem partner to set limits. On the conscious and reality level, the safety, comfort, and healthy development of the child may be at risk. (We are not referring to life-threatening conditions where the child must not remain with the disturbed parent.) Preconscious forces are operative as well. The noncustodial parent often feels guilty for "abandoning" the child, who has to endure the person he himself could not. There is awareness that if he had remained in the home he could have been a "buffer" or "run interference" between the child and mentally ill parent. This parent is usually genuinely worried about the child in this situation, and feels powerless to have an impact. These feelings of powerlessness may cause a parent to withdraw from the child, deny this feeling and instead project anger and blame onto the child, or be overly protective towards the child and too permissive with setting limits. An appropriately nurturing cooperative effort of the original parental pair is very hard, if not impossible, to achieve.

Mr. R, mentioned above, was not able to take his stand with his schizophrenic former wife until all his children were out of her house. Despite alimony and child support that would allow his former wife an excellent standard of living, he often gave additional money to prevent eviction and "the children being put out into the street." Money and gifts were also used by Mr. R to "soothe" the children's physical and emotional ills. An attempt, albeit an ambivalent one, had been made for the children to live with Mr. R when he remarried, but the children and adults as well opted for the original post-divorce living arrangement. Unfortunately, it was not until two children were out of the house and another was about to leave that Mr. R applied for clinical assistance.

The following case example shows the effect on a child of living with a thrice hospitalized manic-depressive mother.

A pseudo-independent, intelligent teenager, Emily Mazer, age 16, whose family had been known to the agency, requested individual treatment to deal with her "procrastination problem." Emily lived with her mother. Her father, who lived in the same city, had been in a committed relationship for three years and the couple had a mutual child. For the past 10 months his other daughter from his first marriage, Joni, age 11, had lived with the Rem unit.

In uncovering what might be the secondary gains of her "procrastination problem," we found that Emily knew that if she did not get her senior project completed she would not graduate from high school and then would not be able to attend an out-of-town college and instead would be homebound. What became conscious was her ambivalence about her role as her mother's protector and caretaker and her father's monitor of his ex-wife's functioning. At this point family sessions with the Rem suprasystem revealed that all family members were invested in Emily's being the protector of her mother and unconsciously no one wanted her to go *away* to college.

Therapist: (to Emily, Mrs. Mazer, her mother, Mr. Mazer, her father, Ms. Zuckerman, his partner, and Joni) As you all know, Emily and I have been meeting for two months because of her "procrastination problem." When she started she insisted on individual sessions, but now, with my urging, she has agreed to meet with you in order to tell you about her understanding of that problem.

Mr. Mazer: I'm glad we are having this meeting because I want to do everything possible to make sure Emily catches up on her school work, graduates, and gets to go away to college.

Mrs. Mazer: I agree and I know that is what Emily wants too.

Therapist: (Smiling directly at Emily.)

Emily: Well . . . that's not the whole truth. In therapy I found out that I want to go to an out-of-town college, which I knew, but there is a part of me that doesn't want that.

Mr. Mazer: (somewhat anxious) What will you do?

Emily: I don't know yet.

Therapist: Perhaps everyone would like to hear the part of Emily they haven't heard about before.

Mr. Mazer: I would. (All agree.)

Therapist: Emily, are you ready to do this?

Emily: I am, but remember you said you would help me out if I need it. (Welling with tears) I want to go away to college but, Mommy, I'm afraid to leave you alone. The last time you got sick I was the one who realized it and called Dad and got you to the hospital. And Dad, how are you going to know if Mom is OK if I don't tell you?

Mrs. Mazer: Don't be ridiculous. I'll be fine.

Therapist: (to Mrs. Mazer) You get upset when you see Emily scared. I know she is not used to showing that side of her. But perhaps you might have a similar fear?

Mrs. Mazer: I know I feel safer when she is in the house.

Mr. Mazer: I think I do too when I know Emily is with you.

Ms. Zuckerman: I know I do.

Joni: Mommy, do you want me to move back with you when Emily leaves?

Mrs. Mazer: I don't think so. I can see you're doing better now that you are with your father.

Therapist: (to Mrs. Mazer) It seems that everyone is worried about you.

Mrs. Mazer: I'll be fine.

Therapist: Tell us more.

Mrs. Mazer: I'm in therapy. I'm working on my problems. I take my medication. (Emphatically) I want to be fine; I don't want to be hospitalized again!

Therapist: (to everyone) Everyone wants that to be true, but we don't know for sure what will happen. This is the tension everyone in this family lives with, and you may feel this tension more if Emily is away at school.

Everyone: (Heads nod yes.)

As a result of family sessions Emily's mother, who was indeed
anxious about this upcoming empty nest crisis and the possibility
of another breakdown, was able to join a day hospital program. Father and stepmother no longer withdrew their support and were
now able to give the vote of confidence Emily needed to follow
through with school assignments, college applications, and interviews.

At Emily's last individual session before she left for college, she
came in humming this line from a Beatle song, "When I'm away,
I'll write home every day." Emily was able to complete her school
work and graduate, but surely leaving home was a risk for her.
With a little help from the Beatles and a little help in individual
and family therapy, she was able to admit that she was "scared"
and "eager" and worried about her mother. Her prior pseudo-independent posture would not have let her express these sentiments.

When there is a mentally ill former spouse but the child lives with the
Rem couple, the emotional and physical protection of the child is important, especially the emotional protection. The erratic, irascible, and un-
reliable behavior of the pathologic parent can leave the child flooded
with emotion, and the adults often too angry and hard pressed to respond to the child's needs.

Mr. King and Ms. Wilson, his live-in partner of two years, applied for treatment at the suggestion of Ms. W, who was appalled
by nine-year-old Robert's fresh and physically aggressive behavior towards his teacher and peers which she observed when she accompanied him on a class trip. Mr. K had had custody of Robert
since he was three, when his mother had her first psychiatric hospitalization. She had three hospitalizations after that and was now
living in a single room occupancy hotel across town. She did not
contribute to Robert's financial support and telephone contacts,
birthday presents and visits were sporadic and unpredictable.

Just prior to the application for treatment, Robert's mother had
"promised" to make his birthday special by taking him to a movie
and dinner. Mr. K and Ms. W's doubts were assuaged when Robert's mother had regular telephone contact with him for two weeks
prior to the scheduled event. They "even allowed ourselves" to
make their own special plans for that day. On the birthday Robert's
mother never showed up, didn't call, and could not be reached. Mr.
K, Ms. W and Robert got into an altercation and shouting match,
ending with Mr. K's cursing out his former wife in front of Robert.
Robert ran to his room and could not be convinced to come out for
the remainder of his birthday, despite his father's and Ms. W's efforts. His disappointment in his biomother and his anger were po-
tentiated by his stepmother's affection and dependability.

Treatment gave this Rem family unit a chance to ventilate their frustration and sense of helplessness, and helped the adults be there for each other and then act as a parental pair to help Robert deal with his disappointment. When the option was discussed, Robert chose to make plans with his mother and risk disappointment rather than not make plans with her at all. This was a difficult Rem situation that was complicated by the limited income of the two adults, who were just beginning in a new business. However, treatment did help the Rem family consolidate and feel better about the way they got along. Robert's impulse control improved. Support systems from maternal, paternal, and Ms. W's family were recruited to provide respite time for the couple. At the point of termination, the couple found a new apartment together; prior to this Ms. W had moved into Mr. K's and Robert's apartment. This step was seen by them as "being engaged." Several attempts were made to meet Robert's mother, but the therapist and the Rem team, like the family, had to settle for less than what had been hoped for.

In similar situations, the Rem couple often is expected to make "sacrifices" for the sake of the child. The word sacrifice is chosen carefully since it acknowledges the foregoing of something dear to the Rem couple. Some examples of this are when the mentally ill parent is provided with funds for the visit with the child and/or is encouraged to visit the child in the Rem household. In the latter, time and space limits need to be clearly set. When this is not possible, the court can be helpful in mandating supervised visits. Often a relative or friend can be called upon for this function.

MENTALLY ILL CHILD

Except for the pain and despair of having one's child die, the anguish that parents feel when something is seriously wrong, either mentally or physically, with their youngster is probably the most devastating emotion anyone can suffer. The parent's identification with the child as an extension of themselves, together with the old shibboleth about the sins of the parents being visited upon the children, is bound to evoke extreme reactions and feelings (Singer, 1980, p. 242).

In Rem families where a child from the former marriage is mentally ill, it is common for this intense crisis to leave the bioparents locked into a blame system which, in fact, may be an added determinant of the child's symptomatology. In a uni-blame system, the parent who left the home or initiated the divorce may feel more guilty about and responsible for the child's mental illness and his former spouse may be set on convincing the parent that this is so. Both parents agree on who is the one and only culpable party. If the divorce was more or less mutual, a mutual-blame system may result where harsher and harsher aspersions and blame are hurled by both parents. In the most entrenched families, the Rem spouse champions his partner's position and this often leads to the exacerbation of symptoms in the child and diminution of Rem consolidation. In families like this the goal is to develop a parental coalition where placing blame is replaced by a working alliance.

     Mr. and Mrs. Egan, remarried for one year, applied for treatment when Harris, age nine, Mrs. E's son from a former marriage, made a suicidal gesture by swallowing shoe polish. More frequent and increasingly more severe pleas for help, such as psychosomatic complaints, truancy, enuresis, and encopresis, went unheeded by the Rem couple and Mr. and Mrs. Zindel, Harris' father and stepmother. Mr. Z thought that his former wife (now Mrs. Egan), a pediatric nurse, was aware of Harris' difficulties, and since she was the custodial parent it was her responsibility to "right the wrong." Mrs. E thought her former husband, a martinet, had once again taken matters into his own hands. Through the course of treatment the absence of a parental coalition was striking. How both bioparents responded to Harris' escalating pleas for help paralleled an incident where, at three years old, Harris nearly drowned because each parent thought the other was watching him. Treatment helped develop a parental coalition where all four bio- and stepparents (sometimes grandparents included as well) began to talk and listen to Harris. Due to the severity of Harris' depression, a residential treatment program was our recommendation. It was accepted rather than sabotaged.

    In situations where there is a mentally ill child from the former union, the Rem spouses may need to be helped to make a realistic adaptation which includes enabling them to have a life of their own and to make realistic plans for themselves and the child for the future. In another Rem situation a father who left his second wife with their young adult manic-depressive daughter was perpetuating the pathologic family dynamic by giving special consideration and favors to that dyad. His ex-wife deserved something extra, usually money and frequent telephone contact, for "putting up with" their daughter. His daughter's favor was curried in a similar way with the hope that she would "calm down." The Rem couple sought treatment with the new wife's complaint that "we are four people in my bedroom."

MENTALLY ILL REM SPOUSE

A mentally ill spouse in a Rem experience may find the caring and emotional involvement with a former spouse and children fuel for paranoia. Financial responsibilities to them may be incendiary for feelings of deprivation and object loss and concomitant rage. In the following case we have a woman who was indeed "insanely jealous" of her husband's relationship, which appeared to be within an appropriate range, with his ex-wife and young children.

Dr. Leiter, a physician, divorced his wife because of her erratic behavior, irresponsibility in caring for their young children and her persistent and flagrant sexual relationships with several men. Dr. L maintained custody of the children. Three years later he impulsively married the second Mrs. L, a beautiful divorcee who he later discovered had been divorced by her husband because of her uncaring behavior for him and her jealousy of her husband's family. Mrs. L. appealed to him because the two could relax and "be children together." On the air flight that took them away on their honeymoon, Mrs. L asked her husband if he had rewritten his will to include her. His reply that his estate would be divided into thirds, one-third for her and each of his two children, threw her into a rage. She accused him of loving the children more than he loved her and demanded that she should get half with the other half to be divided between the children.

It soon became apparent that any attention he gave his children she regarded as being taken away from her. The marriage survived for five years, with Dr. L trying to appease his wife but stubbornly refusing to change custody of the children to their mother. When upset, Mrs. L would withdraw, drop her cultured veneer and attack her husband with vile language, screaming that she was not only the second wife but second fiddle to the children as well.

Dr. L persisted; at his urging Mrs. L went for psychoanalysis for two and a half years and then joined her husband in marital therapy. Periods of peace and good feelings existed when the spouses were alone together and were able to act like two idyllic adolescent lovers. As soon as the children or anyone else slightly close to Dr. L appeared, Mrs. L's jealousy and rage flared again. Despite protestations of her love for her husband, she found another man "who is unattached and can love me first and only."

Dr. L, an overachiever, perhaps chose these two unattainable women because they ultimately were as rejecting as his mother had been to him. The adolescent love he enjoyed with Mrs. L was a fulfillment of his dream of childhood merger with his mother.

This example of grossly disturbed behavior in a spouse in a

Rem family was a most poignant and painful situation because one partner was trapped by his neurosis and remained in a perpetual blind state of short-term bonding and the other was immersed in her more severe psychopathology. Only in their infantile love periods when they could exclude the rest of the world could they truly enjoy one another.

The last phase of this couple's conjoint treatment was to work out a fair financial settlement and a reasonably amicable divorce. Mrs. L went off with her new lover. Dr. L continued in treatment, applied himself to overcoming his neurosis, and became ready for a more mature and equal love relationship. The children, with minimal treatment but with their father's continued love, support and understanding, are now doing well.

In conclusion, we see that a mentally ill family member in a Rem system has a greater susceptibility to abnormal behavior because of the immediacy of other relationships in the suprasystem. With a former spouse or child it is harder to let go of the emotional bond, which may in turn prevent the Rem couple from mastering its marital and new family life-cycle tasks. The extent to which this can be modified is the therapeutic task, along with finding creative and realistic adaptations to deal with this misfortune. It is important that appropriate diagnostic and treatment consultation be utilized in these situations, so that full advantage is taken of psychotropic drugs, partial hospitalization programs, support groups, and individual therapy, as well as family systems treatment.

SECTION IV

Prevention

CHAPTER 16

Preventive Measures

Optimally Rem members are helped by preventive intervention prior to living together or remarriage. Although often resistant to anticipating trouble until they are in a state of crisis (because of reasons discussed in earlier chapters) there are some approaches which are less threatening.

DIFFERENTIATION OF PREVENTION FROM TREATMENT

It is important to differentiate prevention from treatment. Primary prevention is the prevention of the incidence of specific dysfunction and the promotion of general mental health, with the reduction of the incidences of new cases. Secondary prevention is early case-finding and interruption of the course of a dysfunction and is distinguished from tertiary prevention, which is the rehabilitation and prevention of long-term complications of the dysfunction (Spiro, 1980, pp. 2858–9). Some educational programs and counseling can have tertiary preventive effects on families that have become dysfunctional. Primary and secondary prevention are distinct from treatment in several ways:

1) *Population.* The target group is not identified as "pathological," since the Rem families and pre-Rem families we seek to attract have not identified themselves as having problems. Sometimes the population is heterogeneous with various family configurations

331

wishing to be enlightened about lifestyles which may not directly affect them. The other target population is people who have contact and influence on others, i.e., therapists, physicians, clergy, lawyers, teachers.

2) *Locale.* Preventive programs are more often held in settings which are identified as "normative" rather than "mental health" related facilities: schools, recreation centers, Y's, adult education or extension programs of colleges, workplaces, houses of worship.

3) *Timing.* Prevention with Rem couples and families takes place ideally before the remarriage occurs or prior to the emergence of problems. In contrast, Rem families who apply to clinics for help usually are in the throes of serious dysfunction.

4) *Size of Group.* Generally prevention is done with meetings of larger groups which tend to protect anonymity and allow participants to be as active and self-regulatory as they wish. When a couple contemplating remarriage calls our service for advice in easing the transition, they are seen alone in premarital evaluation. They may then be referred to an educational group of Rem couples, or advised to enter treatment.

5) *Approach.* In prevention, the primary approach is educational: to provide information, answer questions, share experiences with others, make suggestions and help participants use their own resources. There are clear boundaries about what is being discussed, and the leader will be sensitive and capable of setting limits on inappropriate self-exposure. Prevention looks at conscious and pre-conscious issues and system issues, but does not offer interpretations or deal with unconscious data. Prevention aims to create "signal anxiety" by discussing and elaborating on potential danger points in the Rem process and what to do about them. Sometimes, preconscious wishes, conflicts and fantasies are made explicit in preventive discussions in order to define their potential destructiveness— most commonly the wish that the new marriage and family will be perfect. We can explore preconscious issues as they relate to the present Rem situation, but we do not push further into intrapsychic material or intervene directly to change the system. Likewise, a "lid" is put on confrontive or other emotionally charged interaction among group participants. When growth is not possible because of system or individual blocks, educational programs may not be sufficient and treatment may then be indicated.

6) *Purpose.* Preventive methods are instituted to avoid the development of a negative or malfunctional state or to avoid further deterioration. *Treatment* is to rectify what already has become a negative malfunctional state.

In the first part of this chapter we explore primary preventive approaches we have found useful and the institutions and professions that can play significant roles in this work. The second part focuses on secondary prevention—pre-remarriage counseling. Although we will not deal here with preventive measures that can be taken at the time of separation or divorce because they are beyond the scope of this book, actually such measures are of prime importance in minimizing damage at these times as well as setting in motion those factors that can enhance the likelihood of a positive outcome for remarriage. Tertiary prevention (treatment) has been amply covered in the main body of the book. In a sense, all the prior chapters on structure, theory, treatment, and special Rem situations provide a body of information that can be drawn upon as a basis for preventive work, as well as for treatment.

PRIMARY PREVENTION

Primary prevention introduces new educational experiences that will give people added knowledge and understanding, cause them to question their habitual way of thinking, feeling, and acting, and help them develop new methods (where new methods are indicated) of dealing with their family, themselves, and their social environment (Auerbach, 1968).

Educational Programs

The first type of educational program is information-giving through dissemination of printed material and films, television, and radio shows, discussion of what the *New York Times Magazine* featured as "The New Extended Family" (November 23, 1980). This is a one-dimensional broadside approach that hopes to meet the needs of those who hear or read about it but who will not provide feedback.

Various types of group experiences offer more possibilities. In a lecture-discussion group, the leader's brief lecture or film (e.g., "Stepparenting: New Families, Old Ties," Polymorph Films, 1977) is followed by an extensive discussion period in which the presenter or chairperson engages the audience regarding common situations occurring in Rem families in order to raise familiar, minimally threatening issues and to normalize them. Audience members experience relief when they can identify with common situations and hear how others have handled them. It is useful to begin with issues of stepparenting and children and then move to marital issues since it is easier for the adults to start talking about problems "created by the children" than to talk about more anxiety-provoking issues about their marriage. Children's reactions to divorce and remarriage can be normalized; this frees the parents to react more appropriately and/or with less guilt.

The lecture-discussion programs require less of a commitment than do discussion groups. The audience can be large, which appeals to couples who might be frightened by an interactional experience. Several single-evening programs can be set up on an alternate week schedule, creating the opportunity to focus on a specified subject: planning a mutual child, summer plans for children, the grandparents' role in Rem (grandparents to be invited too), monetary problems, graduation, weddings, holidays and other nodal family events. For larger groups, panel discussants also function as small group leaders.

At a PTA-sponsored evening program in a local school, the Rem Consultation Service members gave short presentations of a specific area of Rem and, when appropriate, shared some personal information about themselves, i.e., their own experiences in Rem families. We used a large genogram to explain the complexity of the Rem suprasystem and then referred to it to illustrate a few common characteristics and situations. After a brief question and answer period, each staff member met with a group of the participants to continue the discussion in small groups of approximately 12 people. The leaders took an active role in tuning in to the members' interests and directing the group. In order to protect anonymity, the only source of identification was a sign-up sheet where participants could then request further information—either written material about the service, or a consultation with a staff member. A book display and pertinent articles and bibliographies were available for participants to take home.

Lecture-discussion programs can also be initiated by the professional person as when a staff member, who was consultant to a large "Y" which sponsored day camps for children each summer, was aware that a number of registered families had children who lived out of state and would be visiting them for the summer and attending the day camp. An evening workshop was set up to help parents and stepparents deal with this forthcoming visit. Divorced noncustodial parents, remarried parents, and stepparents attended. The focus was on expectations of themselves and their children prior to, at the beginning, in the middle, and at the close of the visit. In order to stimulate discussion, parents were given a summary chart dealing with the potential emotional reactions of each phase and practical suggestions for each period (see Appendix E). This enhanced the parent's awareness of signal anxiety so that they would be more aware of trouble spots and learn suggested ways to cope with them. For example, several parents said that the initial part of the visit last year had been a flurry of intense activity that left everyone exhausted and depleted. Parents recognized the necessity to slow down and pace themselves and their children more realistically. To maximize the impact of the one session, the leader was prepared to speak about some of the primary issues, such as the child's separation from the custodial parent, the fantasies of the "perfect visit," and the sadness and anger at the termination of the visit. Ongoing consultation was available throughout the summer.

In Rem discussion groups, also known as family life education discussion groups, the content of sessions is initiated by the members. The goal is to help participants become more familiar with the dynamics of the Rem family life cycle, to recognize some of the crisis points in the normal development of the Rem family, to clarify roles, and to enlarge understanding of the complexities of the everyday Rem situation so that they will have a wider background from which to make choices (adapted from Auerbach, 1968, definition of parent group education, pp. 4-5). Leadership in Rem discussion groups calls for skill in group dynamics and expertise in Rem issues.

Groups are often developed specifically for Rem couples since conceptually the marital dyad is the main foundation for the family, and the family system will be more likely to function well if the spouses have a strong coalition. However, recruiting these couples has been difficult. Shortly after our service was organized in 1976, we received several inquiries from other family service agencies and clinics who were offering widely publicized Rem discussion groups but were attracting few people. This paralleled our previous experience when we had advertised a four-session couple workshop on remarriage, at a very nominal fee, for which only four couples registered. The program was offered at a well-known Young Men and Women's Association in New York City with a mailing list of many thousands of which at least 30% were in Rem situations.

Investigation revealed that our publicity design emphasized the negative aspects of Rem situations. People were reluctant to publicly label themselves as stepparents. The style of the various advertising brochures stressed "problems" and the need for help. Nonpathologically oriented advance publicity, which emphasizes coping with situations rather than suffering from problems, is preferable. The use of effective catch phrases that offer identification also helps, e.g.: "Four out of every 10 marriages involves an adult who has been married before." "One out of every four families includes stepchildren." "Eighteen million children under the age of 18 have become part of stepfamilies." "Each year, half a million adults become stepparents." "There is a new type of American family—the stepfamily."

In Rem discussion groups a wide range of Rem issues is covered, enhanced by the openness of individuals in sharing experiences, and the apparent changes in feelings, attitudes, and coping behavior that occur in a comparatively short time (four to eight sessions). For example, in a six-week Rem discussion group consisting of five couples married less than three years, the most recently wed couples initially complained of the burdens of an instant family and resentment of their abbreviated period of romantic bonding. The more experienced Rem couples, by their own example, gave permission to the newlyweds to "indulge" themselves. This led to a general discussion on the need for time alone for the Rem couple and the building up of support systems to make this possible. At the final session all five couples reported having taken specific actions to spend more time together. One couple who worked near each other reported taking a long lunch hour together for the first time. Another couple mobilized stepgrandparents to babysit for the weekend.

Locales for Preventive Services

Family therapists as mental health consultants can expand their impact by educating important social systems which interact with the members of the Rem suprasystem.

School systems

Administrators and teachers can be pivotal in preventive work with children of divorce and remarriage. Understanding Rem dynamics and developing nonjudgmental attitudes are the essential first step in using the school as a focal point for prevention. Here, the school consultant educates staff about children's reactions to divorce, to Rem family suprasystem dynamics, and to the teacher's most helpful role during these times.

Drake (1981) summarizes utilization of school systems in helping children cope with divorce. If we expand this to include both divorce and remarriage, it provides a useful conceptualization of intervention points for teachers and others. Drake argues that helping children through a family crisis or family transition is not outside of the school's domain, although many people would contend that divorce and remarriage are personal and not related to the cognitive functions of the school. Drake (p. 148), however, states that it is unrealistic to expect maximum academic functioning from a child when a family upheaval is taking place without resolution. When families are in transition, the children frequently view teachers as significant, stable adult figures who are in a position to perceive problems in the school setting which may not come out at home or which parents may overlook due to situational preoccupation. The child benefits when the teacher knows about significant events in the child's present or past life.

Drake suggests that teachers or guidance personnel use a checklist of information which is pertinent to the school, but which does not unnecessarily intrude into personal material. We have expanded her checklist to include information on children in Rem (see Appendix D). Drake further suggests that in order to intervene effectively school personnel should be knowledgeable about the effects of divorce on a child at different ages, able to recognize a dysfunctional problem, aware of their own values and biases, and comfortable when speaking with parents about the perceived problem. Moreover, they must be in a position to influence school policy in order to effect change at an administrative level. Rem children feel understood when school personnel are familiar with the Rem family suprasystem and subsystems, children's and adolescent's reactions to remarriage at various ages, the effect on the child of changes in ordinal position, residence, visitation variation, holidays and vacations, graduation, Mother's Day, Father's Day, etc.

The school provides unique intervention opportunities, since children are already grouped by age and academic level. Interventions can be direct one-to-one discussions between child and teacher or group discussion. They can also be indirect parents' meetings on the subject of divorce and/or remarriage, adult education classes about stepparenting, for example: Parent/Stepparents Association. These would not be aimed at treatment for the parents but toward providing information, education, guidelines, and referrals if needed. Such topics may encompass: mentioning the school in child custody and separation agreements, defining the noncustodial parents' accessibility to the child at school and his/her involvement in parent-teacher conferences, notification of illness, invitation to the child's performance in school plays, graduations and the host of other matters that go with parent interest and concern in supporting a child at school. Providing the opportunity for classroom discussion among the children the day after the adult meeting maximizes the potential for child-parent interaction.

School teachers are beginning to report that the once familiar excuse, "My dog chewed up my homework," has been replaced with, "I left it at my father's/mother's house" (Moskowitz, 1981). For preventive work, the whole-class method can be used: All children are included. Guided by the artistry and interests of the teachers, administrators, and PTA, they may include discussions of feelings about divorce/remarriage and types of family configurations, essays about personal experience with loss or change, and/or whatever else surfaces as pertinent for a particular group. The routine class assignment to "draw your family" can be enriched to "Let's see how many different kinds of families and households each of you can draw." The rollicking song "I'm My Own Grandpa" (Lathans-Jaffe) intrigues children to memorization and can be a lighthearted preface to the drawing assignment and subsequent discussions.

Children often describe embarrassment and feeling out of place when "the family" is expected to be of the traditional intact nuclear composition. An assignment such as those mentioned above, within the first few days of school, encourages openness, since the expectation is one of polymorphous family configurations. Children have described elaborately deceptive tales, rather than revealing what they felt to be their own peculiar family situations. Once an ideal fantasy construction has been presented, it is difficult for the child to backtrack, possibly causing further alienation from the teacher and peers. Related children's literature such as *The Boy's and Girl's Book About Divorce* (Gardner, 1971), *A Second Mother for Martha* (Green, 1978), and *All About Families* (Lewis, 1980) should be available in the classroom.

A recent newspaper article documented an elementary school children's project in writing a manual about divorce for other children (Rofes, 1981). In this class 12 out of 16 children came from divorced and/ or remarried households. Such creative projects are engaging ways to approach a complicated subject.

Medical settings

Medicine has responded to the continual pressure of parents' groups and patients by doing an extraordinary job in preparing a couple for the birth and inclusion of children into the family. The husband is taught with his wife to participate as a partner in childbirth and childcare. Literature abounds to help the couple change from a dyad to a triad. However, these practices have not been extended to preparation for the "instant" family of remarriage, territorial problems that emerge, and other related matters of children and parents vis-à-vis step situations. The *Stepfamily Bulletin* (Einstein, 1980–82) in the waiting room magazine collection alerts the patients to the physician's sensitivity and openness to discuss issues relevant to remarriage. Family physicians, as well as medical specialists, are often in an excellent position to advise and help if they are relatively free of judgmental attitudes, e.g., the gynecologist who advises a woman about contraception as she resumes sexual activity or discusses plans to have a mutual child. Other areas include when and how the physician should involve all necessary parental persons in medical disclosure.

An obese 12-year-old boy and his custodial parent (mother) responsibly cooperated in adhering to his weight reduction regime when he was with her. The pediatrician who had prescribed the diet was aware of the divorce and the father's remarriage, but did not think to inform the boy's father or to ask the boy's mother to do so. When the boy visited his father and stepmother, he refused to eat most food offered to him and was thought to be negativistic. Actually, he was ashamed to acknowledge his need to diet; he felt he was not lovable and had no right to impose on his father and stepmother by requiring different food.

If the physician had been alert to the potential problem, he could have discussed it with the mother and son and they could have mapped out appropriate action together.

Physicians often are the first professionals seen during family stress and are sought as sources of information and counseling. Hence, they are in need of training in Rem family dynamics and should reveiw their values regarding this new type of American family; otherwise they, too, may inadvertently promote destructive behavior by commission or omission.

Religious institutions

Religious institutions which recognize and respond to Rem families give a powerful sanction and validation of Rem as an accepted, moral way of life and provide a positive setting for family activities, discussion, and youth groups. In their counseling roles and in their messages to congregations, clergy can be nonjudgmental towards adults in Rem and accept the Rem family with others as a family entity. To do this need not interfere with or contradict the clergy's responsibility to strengthen the intact family and to advise against ill-conceived separations and divorces. Couples clubs, couple enhancement groups, weekend activities, family programs, and other church/synagogue-sponsored activities can provide outreach programs to Rem families. In counseling curricula for the clergy, education about Rem family suprasystems and subsystems should be included to enhance counseling relevance and effectiveness.

Community centers

Community centers are natural settings for Rem families to gather and benefit from programming, such as stepparent and stepchild outings, youth groups, workshops and courses. Berman (1980) describes an unfortunate incident—a Girl Scout leader's insensitivity when a nine-year-old in a Rem family reports, "I have a sister; she was born yesterday." The scout leader responds, "She is not really your sister," and follows with critical, semantic questions that clarify the differences among sister, stepsister, and half-sister. Some consciousness-raising about Rem by the professional staff or the mental health consultant at the community center where this troop met might have brought forth a more compassionate response from the scout leader.

Employee assistance programs

Industrial mental health programs are being developed throughout the country to respond to the individual, family, and work-related problems that affect on-the-job efficiency and morale. The findings demonstrate that these programs can increase productivity, decrease absenteeism, limit staff turnover, and improve the quality of working life. Because separation, divorce, and remarriage affect about 40% of workers, company or union sponsored workshops, discussion groups and lectures/films on remarriage can help increase employees' efficiency and attendance, as well as positively affecting their life in other areas.

Self-help

Several self-help organizations for Rem families are developing. The most comprehensive and effective is The Stepfamily Association of America, Inc., originally conceived by John and Emily Visher (1979). This Association provides educational services for stepfamilies, and the larger community that interacts with them. The local chapters of this nonprofit educational organization are able to supply a support network and advocacy group for stepfamilies. Its national and state divisions have assisted in starting a wide variety of services, including self-help groups, lectures, meetings, community education programs and workshops for Rem members and professionals. Their newsletter includes a regular column addressed to stepchildren issues, written by the children themselves.

Benefits of self-help organizations are rooted in their health rather than pathologic orientation, and in the mutual support system formed by the families themselves. A distinguishing feature of The Stepfamily Association of America is that it has solid professional clinical backing available when requested. Educational programs can be enhanced when lay people share their common problems with occasional professional input. We regard the self-help organization to be a powerful tool for consciousness-raising, support, and development of new models for successful Rem family suprasystem interaction.

Dilemmas of Rem Discussion Group Leaders

Family life educators and other primary prevention specialists are subject to the same personal reactions as are Rem therapists (see Chapter 5). They need supervision, peer support, and special training to help them acknowledge and work with their responses in order to prevent distortions in their work due to unproductive personal or judgmental responses. Flexibility, variety of assignments, peer support, and supervision can help prevent leaders from being overwhelmed. Rem discussion group leaders may need to take strong control of sessions so that painful material does not frighten participants or turn the program into quasi-therapy for one or two of the couples or individuals.

The discussion group leader may refer out to a mental health facility. The leader's familiarity and comfort with Rem facilitate the suggestion as an empathic gesture and not a threatening event that arouses fears and causes the participant to drop out of the program. However, if the leader sees signs of child scapegoating, child abuse, household sexual abuse, dramatic regression, severe depression, or significant self-destructive behavior, he or she may elect to shift to a format of crisis intervention, particularly with impulsive adolescents. If the adolescent runs away, threatens suicide, or engages in significant antisocial activities in response to Rem, the leader must impress upon the family the seriousness of the situation and make an immediate referral.

SECONDARY PREVENTION—PRE-REMARRIAGE COUNSELING

Although there are increasing requests for pre-remarriage counseling, they are disproportionately few compared to the Rem families who call for help in crisis. These not-yet-remarried partners may have experienced some minor difficulties that they wish to "nip in the bud," or they may have unearthed more serious conflicts between themselves or with the children. Other couples call with no specific request, but ask our help in "averting potential problems," in "helping the children adjust," and "what to look for." It is our impression that a higher proportion of Rem couples go for premarital education or counseling than do those entering a first marriage. People in love feel they need no guidance and certainly they do not want to question any misgivings or doubts about their betrothed or themselves. Except for those who wish to be married by particular members of the clergy whose church requires premarital instruction, there appears to be no current way of overcoming mass resistance to premarital education.

Initially, the pre-Rem couples are seen in an exploratory conjoint session. Recommendations for educational or treatment experiences are made depending on the desires of the couple and on our assessment. Our assessment emphasis, in addition to customary factors for any couple, is on the prerequisite attitudes and behavior to help determine their commitment to marriage and to the particulars of their Rem situation. In order to deal with the present and future, we need to understand the past as well, that is: knowledge about each person's family of origin, models for marriage and parenting, previous marriage(s), and models for the future marriage with the spouse-to-be. We would want to ascertain the congruence and conflict of each person's individual, marital, and family life-cycle tracks and explore the Rem family suprasystem and its potential for positive, negative, or neutral influence on the new coupling.

During this process of information-gathering, the pre-Rem couple may begin to understand themselves more profoundly and learn about the complexities of their situation. The Reminder List for Marriage Contract—Rem is given to aid them in this task (see Appendix A). Issues not previously considered by the couple may be disclosed, and other areas of complementarity and strength may be revealed or highlighted in this process. It is very unusual, except in Rem, to have to be concerned about one's own children and/or spouse's children's presence at, and their reaction to, the wedding!

The goal of pre-Rem counseling is to aid the couple in accomplishing the tasks necessary for readying themselves for remarriage or living together. If there are children, the dyad-focused counseling helps make up for the loss of the courtship developmental stage due to the instant family phenomenon. It also brings to the surface child issues which may have been glossed over in the excitement of the impending marriage. If there are no children from previous marriage(s), it is easier to consolidate and become a marital pair with congruent marital cycle needs. The premarital counseling would then focus on any residual feelings (positive or negative) which may impede the new marriage or any repetition of patterns which are of concern to either spouse. How does each partner interact with the other? Are their behavioral profiles reasonably compatible or do they indicate the possibility of the development of debilitating stress? Has the divorced or widowed person learned from past experience? Is he or she now showing a behavioral profile that promises more mature and productive outcomes in the present couple interaction? What are the anxieties, concerns or complaints about themselves or their partners? ("What don't you like about your prospective partner?") Are the individual and couple dynamics different from the prior marriage so that a previous untenable marital situation will not be repeated?

The following are prerequisite attitudes and behavior we look for and encourage with each individual who comes for pre-Rem marital counseling. This is adapted and modified from Carter and McGoldrick's chart (1980, p. 272).

Remarrying Adult

1) Sufficient emotional divorce so that there are no significant secret remnants of wishes to revive the old relationship. Conversely, intense feelings of hatred and desire to injure the former mate suggest continued involvement. Ideally, a range of friendship, without feeling primary responsibility for the other, works well for many former mates. It is possible for many divorced bioparents to discuss and act in concert on major decisions relative to their children, to continue coparenting, and to avoid using the children against the former spouse.

2) Ability to meet affective and financial responsibilities in a new relationship.

3) Clarity and agreement with future partner regarding emotional and practical aspects of their marital contract. Awareness and respectful sensitivity for the new spouse living in the home of, and perhaps sleeping in the same bed as, the former spouse and living in a milieu created by someone else. The new spouse needs to have responsibility and authority in jointly helping to make the "old home" into "their new home." Finances are often difficult for pre-Rem couples to discuss. Davidyne Mayleas (1977) has two excellent chapters (Rewedded Bliss, pp. 39–111) which help to flush out unrealistic financial expectations.

4) Clarity with future partner regarding his or her relationship with the ex-spouse and children and vice versa. Any expectations that the new stepparent will be an instant mother or father or immediately love the children and be loved by them needs to be dispelled. Instead, stepparents and stepchildren are expected to be friends and to allow the relationship and roles to evolve. A negative emotional reaction from children and former spouse to Rem is to be expected sooner or later. The remarrying spouse should understand its source and not overreact. He/she should not expect former and new spouse to like or respect one another, and should be able to examine his/her own role as provocateur in relation to the

attitudes of former and present spouses. Clarity is needed regarding marriage contract and what is wanted and expected.

5) If the future partner has not had children of his/her own, more attention needs to be given to understanding the impact of children who are capable of speaking, acting, etc., and who have a host of feelings towards parents and the "newcomer," who may be seen as "taking my mother's (father's) place in the family."

6) Provision of opportunity for children to get to know their future stepparent several months prior to the marriage; ability to keep the definition of the new relationship open and allow new family member and children to find their own roles. Children must not be asked or allowed to decide whether a potential mate is or is not acceptable. The bioparent should explain in realistic and honest terms what remarriage will mean to them as the parent envisages it: Their family life with the parent will continue; the stepparent can add to their experience by being a friend to them rather than replacing their mother or father. "Step" should be defined in positive terms. It is important for the parent to ask children about their expectations and desires and *listen*. Use of stepparent nomenclature should not be pressed, although future spouse and children may choose to use it.

7) The bioparent should transmit the idea that all the adults are sensitive to the significance of the Rem household vis-à-vis the other parent's home. It is important that all Rem members accept that their family now is a more open system, with more permeable boundaries than those of the intact nuclear family. It is important to continue the same visiting, emotional, and financial commitments to a child that existed prior to Rem. It is necessary for the new couple to consolidate their relationship as much as possible before being overwhelmed by "instant" children and to structure regular time off together without the children. It is also important to structure individual time for each child. Masterminding these schedules is indeed the challenge of Rem!

The following case* is an example of a "family" who had come into treatment prior to any discussion of remarriage. After several months of multimodal therapy, the therapist was able to shift to some preventive work as the adults and children anticipated the forthcoming wedding and subsequent move from the East to West coast.

Steve is an eight-and-a-half-year-old boy referred to the agency

---

*We are grateful to Arlene Lieberman, C.S.W., for this case. Ms. Lieberman is a Fellow in the Advanced Child Therapy Training Program of J.B.F.C.S.

by his father, Mr. Ryan, who had been divorced from Mrs. Ryan when Steve was two-and-a-half years old. After an altercation with his mother, Steve had voluntarily moved from Boston to his father's home in New York, separating him from both his mother and his six-year-old sister. This was the first time he had lived with his father since the divorce. The current household also consisted of the father's committed partner of one year's duration, Mrs. Donohue, and her three-and-a-half-year-old son, John.

Mr. Ryan had contacted the agency because of concern about his son's unhappy, sensitive manner—subject to mood changes, alternately outgoing or reticent and detached, crying easily when frustrated, thumb-sucking and clinging to his teddy bear, and making few friends in his new school. Father reported Steve to be in excellent health with normal developmental history and milestones. In the therapist's effort to engage the biological mother through several long distance phone calls, Mrs. Ryan described Steve as "a little babyish and insecure, a child who overreacted easily" since the divorce.

During the course of therapy, Steve and his father were able to be more openly expressive towards each other. Steve would frequently talk through a hand-crafted cardboard "CBS microphone" he had made as he sat in a special spot which he designated as his "talking chair." When the living together couple decided to wed, and as the therapist explored with the two adults and two children their anticipated reactions and expectations, Steve spontaneously came up with the idea of a checklist, which he painstakingly wrote and then "broadcast" over WKTV TV in a family session. Steve's list read as follows:

1) The Wedding/when and where/everybody's feelings about it ☐

2) Getting a house/how big/where it's going to be ☐

3) John School in California ☐

4 Steve School in California/wondering what it is going to be like/if it's Public or Catholic or Private ☐

5) Family Agency in California. How to find a therapist in California ☐

6) Family members left behind and family visits ☐

7) Making Friends and Neighbor left behind ☐

8) Leaving Lonin (a family friend) in another house in California ☐

9) Transportation in California ☐

This time the child had highlighted his areas of anxiety well in advance of the event, in contrast to his past separations.

Former Spouse

The former spouse should be told of the approaching marriage by the ex-spouse—not by the children. Ex-spouses often anticipate/project a reaction that makes them reluctant to follow through with this. Children are likely to report the forthcoming marriage anyway, but their motives must be examined to see if triangulation factors are involved rather than reality fears. Anxiety may be assuaged in a former spouse by appropriate reassurances backed by concrete demonstration regarding continued financial and co-parenting responsibilities. These efforts are not the same as reporting to or asking approval from one's ex-spouse and should come from strength, not fear. The remarriage of a former spouse often will bring an unexpected exacerbation of earlier feelings of loss, even if the former spouse has been happily remarried him/herself.

The premarriage counseling issues become complicated when they involve people with characterological problems or significant intrapsychic conflict. At these times, more intensive or individual therapy may be required. However, preventive counseling may be beneficial if it is implemented by a therapist who maintains a firm grasp of the dynamics involved and an understanding of human development.

Marriage as Acting Out

The following is an example of a couple on the verge of either breaking off or going full steam ahead with marital plans in an acting-out gesture. Pre-Rem counseling provided a constructive intervention that interrupted the course of a dysfunction.

Sara Martin, 40 years old, called requesting premarital counseling. Both she and her 50-year-old fiancé, Dave Wessler, had been previously married and were anxious about possible difficulties between their two sets of children. Further exploration revealed that, after dating Mrs. M exclusively for a year, Mr. W had suddenly bolted, returning a month later and demanding that they get married, as this would solve all their problems. He felt uncomfortable living with Mrs. M and felt he had no authority with her two teenage children. Traumatized by Mr. W's temporary abandonment, Mrs. M refused to marry without some counseling in order to understand what it was that had made him bolt.

FIGURE 16.1
Martin-Wessler Family Genogram

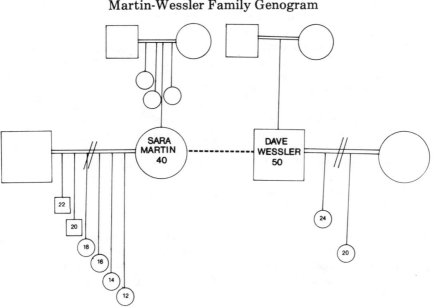

Anamnesis revealed that Mrs. M was the youngest child in a Southern family. She described a painful childhood where she was dominated by a selfish, authoritarian mother who allowed her no self within the relationship, with no possibility of having her needs met or even known.

Mrs. M married at 17 in order to exit from home. Extreme passivity and lack of autonomy regarding birth control resulted in six children. An unavailable husband necessitated her involvement in all household matters: She became more competent and independent and eventually gained the courage to leave.

During her single-parent stage, Mrs. M entered therapy, which she described as having been helpful. She began to grow, found a job as a secretary (which increased her self-confidence), and became president of her church singles group. During the two years of her single life she felt independent and strong.

Mrs. M was presently terrified by her neediness of Mr. W and was worried about being overwhelmed by her dependency yearnings. She polarized her fears as: 1) extreme pseudo-independence and self-righteousness that come from her being unconnected to other human beings; 2) extreme passivity and helplessness which she experienced on one level with her first husband and on a primary level with her mother. Mrs. M was able to express fears that Mr. W would take over, would make all the rules and that she would become a "blob" again. Unconsciously, she had been resisting any authority he might have in the Rem household by sabotaging his effectiveness with the children, thereby keeping him out of the system. Mr. W had been unaware of this and only experienced it as a problem between him and the children.

Mr. Wessler was an only child of Portugese immigrants. He grew up in a sea town in Massachusetts where his father was a fisherman. Father was away at sea for long stretches of time and mother was sickly and often unavailable. Prematurely autonomous and independent, he was withdrawn and expected none of his needs to be met by others. His father was emotionally distant and a martinet when he was home. While in college he met Maureen, an extremely passive, helpless young woman. They married and had two daughters. Mr. W worked hard and became a successful mechanical engineer. Over the years the marriage slowly deteriorated. Maureen continued to withdraw more and more into passivity and would not stay alone in the house when he went on business trips. She refused to work but was also unable to adequately care for the house and children. Mr. W took charge and became the father of a childlike wife. He resented this and initiated a divorce when his daughters became self-sufficient teenagers.

When he met Mrs. M at a church social, he was impressed by her strength and independence. He voiced how glad he was to finally have an equal relationship with a woman. However, he was not accustomed to dealing with a woman who could be assertive and he found her disagreements annoying and confusing. He tended to withdraw when Mrs. M expressed her needs.

Initially, during pre-remarital counseling, the couple was rigidly focused on the role of the two sets of children. Mr. W was dissatisfied with Mrs. M's children's behavior. His own young adult daughters were raised in a stricter, more formal environment. He felt insecure about parenting Mrs. M's children and was unconsciously responding to Mrs. M's sabotage of his entering her system. Mrs. M, on the other hand, was focused on the time when Mr. W's children visited. She found them sullen and withdrawn and believed that they saw her as an evil stepmother. They did actually identify with their helpless biomother.

The therapist joined the couple's resistance about marital issues and had several sessions with the whole "family" around parenting issues. The teenagers seemed to be relatively healthy and were able to ventilate the usual concerns about Rem. However, the sessions were used by the counselor to highlight an approach to the parenting issues which led back to discordance within the marital pair.

Mr. W and Mrs. M began to understand that they had marital problems and agreed to 10 couple counseling sessions. In these, Mr. W became aware that he was unsure of his role as a stepfather or as a member of the household. This caused him to be fearful of expressing any needs or demands. Instead, he complained about minor irritations or occasionally blew up inappropriately. If Mr. W did break out of his characterological pattern of withdrawal and make a demand, Mrs. M would experience him as trying to take over. She would overreact, feel overwhelmed, and lose emotional control. When Mr. W was faced with her crying and attacking, he would further withdraw without expressing his needs. Mrs. M would feel abandoned and react with even more uncontrolled behavior.

Therapy clarified this pattern and the distortions involved; in reality, Mrs. M wanted Mr. W's involvement in many issues but had not been able to see this or ask for it. He was also hesitant to be the caretaker again. Mrs. M began to realize that Mr. W did not have to like everything she did. She was not going to be emotionally abandoned if she acted autonomously. She began to see how her interpretation of Mr. W's expressed opinion as an order was a distortion based on the model of the absolute authority of her dominating mother. Yet, his brusque style at these times did reflect some negative identification with his martinet father, of which he had been unaware. Mr. W was able to clarify his inability to make demands during his childhood because of his mother's frailty and father's rigidity, later reinforced by his ex-wife's inability to give to him on any level.

Counseling enabled them to be interdependent and to trust each other to accept their needs. It also helped to break through their rigidified communication system that blocked conflict resolution. As Mrs. M became calmer and less frightened, Mr. W became less withdrawn and more eager to express himself. He began to participate in the Rem unit and feel more a part of the household and less a stranger who happened to have been invited to live in her house. He began to see his former request for legal marriage as a premature attempt to feel like a valid member of the household. The 10-session contract was adhered to and counseling terminated. The couple and the therapist agreed that clarification had taken place, that they now were better prepared for marriage, and that each had become aware of his/her contribution to upsetting the family system and had greater control of his/her behavior. The couple married shortly after these sessions concluded.

For the Wessler-Martin family pre-remarital counseling served the important purposes of defining roles and structures within the Rem family system, clarifying distortions from the previous marriages and from families of origin, and delineating long-term characterological problems. Although the short-term counseling did not significantly help in working through primitive fears, since it was not designed to attempt that more time-consuming goal, it did help both partners develop ego control and an understanding of their fears. This aided them in monitoring their interactions and communication so that these fears did not cause a vicious circular dystonic system. Hopefully, with the security of a reasonably good marriage they will eventually feel safe enough to work further on such problems, knowing that additional help would be available for them in the agency if requested.

At different junctures during the 10-session course of pre-Rem counseling, we recognize that by some professionals' standard our work with the couple and Rem family might be considered as treatment. Our differentiation is based on the goals of the process. No attempt was made to produce structural change or to change intrapsychic dynamics. Our objective was to decrease the anxiety level by making simple connections of past and present behavior, and to help each partner accept the other's and his own unique needs. This facilitated understanding and acceptance and diminished defenses of denial and reaction formation.

To Have or Not Have a Child

A successful four-session pre-Rem counseling case involved Marjorie White, age 33, and Charles Thomas, age 34, who had been together for four years. Charles' previous marriage during college had been annulled after one year. He was resolute that he did not want a child, as it would take away his and his companion's mobility. He and Marjorie loved one another and enjoyed successful careers and an active social life. They wanted to marry but came to realize that they probably would have to separate because Charles definitely did not want a child and Marjorie was just as emphatic that she could not be happy unless they did. This had been an issue for the past four years and Marjorie felt that the biological clock was running out and that she could no longer delay the decision.

Past history, family of origin, and life experiences revealed no significant psychopathology. Charles just knew he enjoyed his lifestyle tremendously, and children were a burden and a type of responsibility he did not want. Reluctantly, he stated his willingness to stop seeing Marjorie rather than change his lifestyle. Both agreed that, although separation would be very painful, they would have to split if neither would alter his/her position. Among other interventions, we did guided fantasy work on the feelings and style of life each expected after separation. It was a moving experience for the therapist (who confesses he is a bit of a romantic). Charles emerged as a Peter Pan character. The therapist was aware of the judgmental reaction involved in this diagnosis but reflected on it and did not react to Charles in a negative prejudicial way.

These two individuals elected to separate. A scheduled telephone appointment one month later revealed that they had separated, now lived in separate apartments, and had decided not to see one another for a few months before attempting to see if they could structure a platonic friendship.

Respecting Premarital Anxiety

On a number of occasions we have had couples apply for pre-remarriage counseling at the eleventh hour, i.e., a few days to six weeks before the wedding. They are usually impulsive people with strong abandonment fears. They seek help in a state of heightened anxiety and place unrealistic expectations on the therapist. It is important for the therapist to stay free of the couple's panic so that the "deadline" will not blur therapeutic effectiveness. In an attempt to slow down the couple's process, it is helpful to question whether or not they feel that they have the choice to consider canceling or postponing the wedding. On a conscious level they usually feel that they do not have such a choice since invitations are out, money has been spent, and there is a strong need to save face with children, parents, even an ex-spouse and friends. Discussing (perhaps employing role playing) with the partners how they can effect their change of plans with the significant people in their lives may free them sufficiently enough to elucidate that a choice to cancel the wedding might be a possibility for them and in their best interest. Discussing the similarities of their feelings and actions in their current relationship and their prior marriage can also slow down the process. In the most disturbed situations, partners admit that they are as "stubborn" now about changing their minds in the face of several problems in the relationship as they were before, but, "It is easier to get a divorce than cancel a wedding." In these situations, on a preconscious and unconscious level, abandonment fears, despair about finding a more suitable mate, and doubts about one's own desirability run high.

Whether or not partners decide to go ahead with their plans to marry despite the quantity and severity of problems evident to themselves and to the therapist is the couple's choice. The therapist's job is to be in control of the counseling process, not the couple. In these situations, if they cannot be helped to give themselves more time before getting married, another option is for them to contract for immediate treatment.

Reiss-Balant

The following case example illustrates several of the treatment concepts described above.

Miss Reiss, age 34, a divorced custodial parent of five-year-old twin girls, was engaged to 32-year-old Mr. Balant, a divorced noncustodial parent of a five-year-old daughter. Both Miss R and Mr. B had successful careers in the performing arts. Miss R called to ask for premarriage counseling one month prior to the wedding. She described that her fiancé recently had a nightmare, was having trouble sleeping and seemed depressed. Miss R and Mr. B were seen together for the first session. Mr. B recounted this nightmare: He is walking down the aisle to the huppa (bridal canopy in a Jewish wedding ceremony) and is upset because instead of wearing his new suit he is wearing a formal morning suit (the attire at his previous wedding). When he greets his wife-to-be, he notices she is wearing a white wedding gown and not the pink dress she had bought. The rabbi is talking but he does not hear him and instead says to his bride, "You should not be wearing white, you were married before." She comments, "It was really nothing, stop making such a big deal about my first marriage." At the end of the ceremony, as tradition dictates, Mr. B is to smash a wine glass with his foot. Instead he picks it up with his hand and throws it into the "audience," at his ex-wife who is sitting in the back.

Discussion (not interpretation) of this vivid dream revealed that Mr. B, who had been divorced for ten months, had not sufficiently mourned (morning suit) that relationship and was still emotionally involved with his ex-wife. In addition, he had strong feelings about his fiancée's previous, and more so her present, relationship with her first husband, although they had been divorced for almost three years. Miss R, after initial defensiveness and attempts to triangulate with Mr. B's former wife, was able to express her own reservations about her fiancé. She was worried about his mood swings and questioned his emotional stability.

When the therapist raised the question of whether or not they felt they had the choice of canceling the wedding, both were adamant that "The show must go on." When the therapist challenged this, stating that their wedding was not a performance, both evidenced a helplessness in discussing a change of plans with their children, parents, and former spouses. With the counselor's help they role played how they might effect the cancellation.

A follow-up session one week later explored similarities between the anxieties Miss R and Mr. B felt in the first and in the forthcoming second marriage. These discussions enabled this couple to postpone their wedding and contract for treatment to work through their fears.

Premarriage treatment sessions continued, both conjoint and individual. The Reminder List for Remarriage (see Appendix A) was the springboard for more intensive work. After eight months (one Rem suprasystem meeting and several Rem family subsystem meetings), the couple chose to marry. A month before the wedding Mr. B daydreamed a variation of his earlier nightmare: He is under the wedding canopy, wearing his new suit. This time he smashes the glass with his foot and kisses the bride.

Similar approaches apply to post-Rem and pre-Rem counseling, with the added factor that a commitment had been made. Situations and systems change over time; a well functioning Rem family unit or Rem suprafamily system can develop problems after several years. Here, too, counseling may be the first effort to prevent and/or arrest incipient dysfunction.

The major work in the preventive area lies in the future. It is heartening to see how many remarried people themselves, as well as professionals, are embarking on efforts to fill this obvious need.

APPENDIX A

Marriage Contract
Reminder List—Rem

"Marriage Contract" as the term is used here does not refer to formal contracts or agreements that both mates write out and subscribe to openly. This "contract" consists of conscious and unconscious expectations of the relationship: of what you will give and what you wish to receive from your partner. You each have your own "contract" that probably differs from the other. Do not be surprised if your contract is inconsistent because you simultaneously may have strong contradictory wishes or needs. For example, you may have the desire to be independent and yet at the same time also require your spouse's approval of your actions. Such apparent contradictions are usual for most of us. If one or both of you have children from a previous marriage, you are marrying into a new type of family—you are making a commitment not just to one other person who has no important responsibilities to anyone else.

Each "contract" has three levels of awareness:

1) *Verbalized*—those aspects that are discussed with each other, although not always heard and/or accepted by the receiver.
2) *Conscious but not verbalized*—the parts of your contract that you are aware of but do not verbalize to your spouse because you fear his/her anger, disapproval, you would feel embarrassed, etc.
3) *Beyond awareness or unconscious*—aspects that are beyond your usual awareness. You may have an idea of what some of these are. They are often felt as a warning light in your head or a fleeting feeling of concern that gets pushed away. Do the best you can with these.

Each person acts as if the other knows the terms of the "contract" (which were never really agreed upon) and feels angered, hurt, betrayed, etc. when they believe their spouse did not fulfill their part of the "contract." In each area note down where you feel your needs are being met and are not being met.

"Contractual" terms, i.e., desires, needs and expectations, fall into three general categories. The reminder list that follows consists of these three categories; following under each are listed several common areas that are sources of marital and personal trouble. Some you may have thought of before, others not.

EXPLANATION OF REMINDER LIST FOR
MARRIAGE CONTRACT—REM

The following is a guide to help you respond to the questions. You can each write out your response separately or you can talk them through, noting down where you agree and disagree. You do not have to resolve differences—just be sure of how each feels or wants things to be at this time.

1) Respond to all areas that are meaningful to you.
2) Answer in terms of today. If something is a sore point from the past indicate this.
3) Make your answers as long or as short as you wish but if they are to be useful they must convey your feeling, not just "yes" or "no."
4) Do not try to do all three categories at one time. One at a sitting is recommended.

Name _____ Date _____

This is your (circle)   1st   2nd   3rd Marriage
Your partner's (circle)   1st   2nd   3rd Marriage

Length of current relationship:
    Living together—years _____ months _____
    Married—years _____ months _____

For you: years_____ and months_____since separation.
           years_____ and months_____since divorce.
For mate: years_____ and months_____since separation.
           years_____ and months_____since divorce.

I bring the following child(ren) to this household:
Name_____M F Age_____ Lives with us_____ Visits_____
Name_____M F Age_____ Lives with us_____ Visits_____
Name_____M F Age_____ Lives with us_____ Visits_____

My partner brings the following child(ren):
Name_____M F Age_____ Lives with us_____ Visits_____
Name_____M F Age_____ Lives with us_____ Visits_____
Name_____M F Age_____ Lives with us_____ Visits_____

We have the following child(ren) together:
Name_____M F Age_____
Name_____M F Age_____

1) CATEGORIES BASED ON EXPECTATIONS OF MARRIAGE

Each partner lives with or marries for their own purposes and goals in relation to coupling. The couple system itself generates other purposes of which the individuals may have originally been unaware. Keep in mind that this list is meant only to remind you to consider these possibilities. Others may be important for you, if so, include them.

This area relates to each persons' purposes and goals in relation to the institution of marriage itself or living together and what you are willing to contribute and what you believe your mate's position is. Please write out a summary of what you *want* from your marriage that relates to the above areas and what *in exchange* you will *give*. The most common expectations of marriage, as related to remarriage are:

1) A mate who will be loyal, devoted and exclusive. A relationship with a person that is very like the first mate when "things were good," or that will provide what the first mate didn't. To have romantic love and intimacy.
2) Help in dealing, caring for, disciplining the children.
3) Companionship and insurance against loneliness. A relief from the world of the formerly married, the single parent or the single person.
4) Marriage as a goal in itself. That one will live happily after once married or remarried.
5) To be rescued from responsibilities and burdens. To return to the "order" and "certitude" of marriage and the two-parent family.
6) A relationship till death do us part. There may be a grim determination or pressure to make the marriage work this time.
7) Sanctioned and readily available sex. Escape from the pressures of dating. Sex which is legitimate in the eyes of the children and an example of values you wish to transmit as a parent or stepparent.
8) To have children with your new mate.
9) A relationship that emphasizes parenting and family life.
10) A home and economic unit where possessions and financial resources will or will not be shared.

11) A social unit which lends purpose to one's life.
12) To have an immediate ready-made family.
13) To be taken care of by a strong mother or father person.
14) To prove your desirability and superiority as a spouse to your partner's former mate, and/or your own former mate.
15) To rescue an apparently struggling person and perhaps his or her children.
16) Others—list and discuss.

2) CATEGORIES BASED ON PSYCHOLOGICAL AND BIOLOGICAL NEEDS

These parameters are important because it is here that your mate is expected to fulfill your needs directly. They arise largely from within you and from your interaction with your partner. The needs and desires by which these factors may be expressed often are beyond your awareness, yet you do have some ideas about them. Write out a summary of what you *want* from your mate that relates to the above categories and what *in exchange* you will *give*. The reciprocal nature of these contracts is especially important here. Some of the most common areas that require consideration and awareness are:

1) *Adaptations and ties to your own children.* Do you recognize the need to alter an overclose bond with your child that developed during the single-parent stage? Can your new mate be helpful in understanding your relationship with your child? Does your new mate react by feeling excluded, jealous, angry? Vice versa in reference to your mate's children and what you expect.
2) *Ties to ex-spouse.* Are you aware of residual, appropriate and inappropriate, feelings of affection, hostility or revenge to the ex? Do these feelings and/or actions affect your relationship? Do you do provocative things to arouse jealousy between former and current spouse; or does your present spouse?
3) *Independence-dependence.* What degree and type of independence do you want for yourself and mate?
4) *Closeness-distance.* Communication problems are often related to the ability or inability to tolerate closeness. How much space and time alone do you need? Is there a reaction in this marriage which relates to the past: for example, a fear of risking too much closeness again, or a demand for closeness which wasn't present in the first marriage? To what extent do you or your mate's children and their needs come between you and your mate?
5) *Use-abuse of power.* The distribution of power. How much power and control do you need? How is your need for power different or

similar to your first marriage? Do you or your mate abuse power; can you share power? How does it work for you two?

6) *Decision-making.* How are decisions made?

7) *Guilt.* Does guilt towards your former spouse, children, your parents, ex-in-laws or religious beliefs affect or color what you wish to or feel you can or should give in your new marriage? Does your spouse have problems around guilt or lack of guilt that bother you? Is he or she too feeling/unfeeling or responsible/irresponsible in regard to his/her children, ex-spouse or you?

8) *Roles.* What role expectations do you have of yourself and your mate as stepparent or parent to the visiting and/or custodial children? What does each mate expect from the other in this regard? How do you expect and desire co-parenting to work for the two bioparents and the stepparents?

9) *Fear of loneliness or abandonment.* To what extent does the fear of another loss or abandonment play a role in this marriage? Is this a fear you have always had?

10) *Anxiety:* a) To what extent are you fearful of another failure, repetition of old patterns, and/or the new mate will show evidence of acting like the former? b) Do you tend to react to problems with anxiety or does your spouse? On a scale of 1 to 5 with 1 no anxiety and 5 frequent and overwhelming, where do you rate your *anxiety level* and your spouse's? Circle appropriate number.

You: 1   2   3   4   5
Mate: 1   2   3   4   5

11) *Nurturing/affection.* How would you like affection, love, consideration to be shown to you, and how would you like to express it to your partner? For example, do you like physical affection, thoughtfulness, kind words, gifts, and/or consideration of your sensitivities and idiosyncrasies? Is there anything that you or your partner feel or does that makes expressing affection difficult?

12) Are these problems arising from where you and your spouse are in your life cycles? E.g., does one want children but the other mate does not because he/she has children; or do problems arise because one is ready to cut down on work while the other wants to pursue a career?

13) *Characteristics desired in your partner.* These may include sex, personality, physical appearance, expressiveness, achievement level, giving and receiving love, gender, tenderness, ability to function socially, at work, as family member and many other parameters. These may consciously or unconsciously relate to the characteristics of your first mate directly or indirectly.

14) *Acceptance of self and other.* Do you have the ability to love yourself as well as the other? Is love equated with vulnerability? Did

you or your spouse "love" the first time and now see love as dangerous?

15) *Cognitive style.* This refers to the way in which you and your mate take information in, process it, arrive at decisions and communicate the process and conclusions to the other. Are intelligence and conceptualization levels compatible? Is there a positive complementarity of differences or does it cause dissonance?

16) Are your interests and those of your mate the same? Do you feel that most interests should be similar?

17) Add any other areas not mentioned.

18) Please write out a summary of what you *want* from your mate that relates to the above categories and what *in exchange* you will *give.*

3) EXTERNAL FOCI OF MARITAL PROBLEMS

These are common areas of complaints that many couples have. They may appear to be the core of the marital or family problem; however, more often they are the *external manifestations* of problems that are rooted in the first two categories. Write a summary of what you *want* in regard to the above expectations and what you will *give in exchange.* These most common manifestations are:

1) *Communication.* To what extent can you be open with one another? Can conclusions be reached by talking over disagreements? Are messages sent clearly? Are they heard properly or at all?

2) *Lifestyles.* To what extent are your lifestyles similar? Do you make comparisons to lifestyles of your former marriage and family? To what extent does this cause difficulties?

3) *Families of origin.* Does one partner resent the other's family or the mate's involvement with them? Did your parents or your spouse take a major role before remarriage that causes problems now? Are their financial or business ties to families of origin with strings attached?

4) *Relations with ex-spouse and ex-in-laws.* How involved is each mate with the former spouse, how friendly or hostile? How does that affect the current relationship? What role should each of you have with his/her former spouse and in-laws?

5) *Childrearing.* To what extent do you agree on how to raise the children, how much authority to exercise, how much leniency, and how caretaking should be shared?

6) *Relationship with children.* How does each relate to the other's

and their own children, both living in and visiting? Anything you would like to see changed?

7) *Family myths.* Do partners collaborate in the maintenance of myths, for example that the Rem family is perfect and harmonious? Is anyone idealized?

8) *Money.* How is it controlled? Is it kept separate or combined? Does one partner feel cheated because of the economic obligations to the former family? How are resources from present, former marriage and inherited monies and property allocated in wills? Do older children resent new spouse as "stealing" their inheritance?

9) *Milestones.* What are expectations regarding who in the Rem and other bioparent's household will attend children's celebrations—birthdays, graduations, bar mitzvahs, confirmations, weddings? How are children expected to spend holidays—Christmas, Thanksgiving, summers, etc.?

10) *Sexuality.* Attitudes and predelictions may differ in frequency, forms of pleasuring, fidelity, initiation, openness with children about sexuality, etc. How is this dealt with by the adults and with children?

11) *Values.* Is there general agreement on priorities such as money, culture, ethics, relations with others, religion, use of time together? How are or will be differences of values and cultures between two bioparent households handled?

12) *Friends.* What is the attitude towards the other's friends? Can each tolerate the other's friends from former relationships? Do all friends have to be joint or can each have individual friendships? How much time should be allotted for friends and how much as a couple? Are male friends as acceptable as female or vice-versa?

13) *Housing.* Are there problems arising from continual use of your home or your mate's as your common home? Same for furnishings. Any space problems related to space?

14) Add any subjects you deem significant.

15) FINAL QUESTION—add any additional comments or thoughts about yourself, your mate, the children, your marriage and remarriage that have occurred to you.

APPENDIX B

*Reminder List for Children and Teenagers (Ages 10–17) Whose Parent Has Remarried**

This "contract" is for older children and teenagers who live with or visit a biological parent who has remarried. Now, in addition to your biological parents, you also have one or more stepparents and perhaps stepsiblings.

A "contract" like this is not a formal contract. It is not something written down that everyone signs, like in business. Our "contract" refers to how you would like your family (mother, father, stepmother, stepfather, brother, sister, stepbrother, stepsister) to think, feel, and act toward you and how you expect to think, feel, and act toward them.

Maybe you never thought about your "contract" for your family before. Think about your family for a minute. First, how you would like them to act with you and how you in return will want to act with them.

Try to answer the questions, making the answers as long or short as you want. Attempt to write down your feelings, not just answering "yes" or "no."

Name _____ Date _____
Boy_____   Girl_____
Age_____
Grade in School_____

---

*If the reader wishes to use this reminder list, leave sufficient space for a full response between questions 3 through 16.

Items 1-2 check correct answer

1) My mother is remarried   Yes_____   No_____
2) My father is remarried   Yes_____   No_____
3) Please describe which parent(s) you live with, and which parent you visit. How much time do you spend with each?
4) Who lives in your father's household (stepmother, stepsibs)? Give name and ages and relation to you:

5) Who lives in your mother's household (stepfather, stepsibs)? Give name and ages and relation to you:

6) Describe the kind of family you would like to have (for instance, a family that does many things together; a family that includes many different people like outside friends, a family in which people do things independently).
7) Describe the kind of family member you would be in return (for example, a friend, a leader, a helper).
8) Describe the kind of stepparent you would like to have, and what kind of stepchild you would be in return. Would you like your stepparent to make the rules; to tell you what to do; to spend time with you alone; to act like a parent; to go to with problems, to act like a friend? Would you like to act like a friend in return, or like a relative? What kind?
9) Describe the kind of stepbrother/sister you would like to have and what kind of stepbrother/sister you would be in return (to be close and talk to each other, to share things, to do things together with your parents, to do things without each other, to share friends, to have your own friends).
10) Describe the way you would like your mother or father who you live with to act and how you would act in return (to spend time with you alone, not just together with your stepparent, to make the rules and correct you, to let you be independent). In return, you would act like a friend, a helper, a companion, etc.
11) Describe the way you would like your father or mother who you visit to act and how you would act with them (to see them frequently, to make rules; to go to with your problems, to just be a pal, to share activities). In return how would you be to them?
12) Please add any other thoughts or feelings about yourself, your parents, your stepparents, your siblings or stepsiblings or your family as a whole.
13) What, if anything, would you like to see changed?
14) How do you see your parent's remarriage affecting your life and future? Anything about it particularly advantageous for you, or disadvantageous? How does it work out for you and your needs?
15) In which household do you feel more comfortable? Tell why; be specific.
16) Draw a picture of those you consider to be your family. Label who each one is, including yourself.

APPENDIX C

*A Reappraisal of Marital and/or Long-term Relationships**

Name _____ Date _____

Age: _____ Length of relationship _____

This is to be completed in private by each person to be shared at a later date. Please be as specific as possible and if you need more space for any category use additional paper. (When preparing this form for use the questions should be printed on several pages, leaving four inches between questions for responses.)

1) What are your expectations from this marriage and/or a long-term relationship? As you, your mate or both had a prior marriage, in what ways do your expectations differ because of this fact? Include positive and negative.

2) Which of your expectations do you feel are being met?

3) Which expectations do you feel are *not* being met?

4) What personality traits or behavior would you like to see changed in your partner?

---

*This form is adapted from one by Ilona Sena, M.S.W., Jewish Board of Family and Children's Services.

Note: In the first session the therapist will get clues to significant areas of tension. Specific questions can be added for these couples. Questions we have most commonly added pertain to physical health, expression of affection and sexuality, substance abuse, financial problems.

5) What do you feel you would like to change about yourself?

6) How do you make decisions and resolve differences and arguments?

7) Are there any problems related to you or your mate's previous marriage, former spouse, children or stepchildren?

8) Are there any private hopes or plans that you've always wanted to share with your spouse/partner, but have been reluctant to do so? If so, please indicate.

9) Is there anything else you'd like to add?

APPENDIX D

Guidelines for Divorced and Remarried Parents Whose Children Will Be Visiting for Several Weeks *

Specific Phase	*Emotional Considerations*	*Practical Considerations*
A. *Preparatory Phase* (approximately 6 weeks prior to visit)	*Anxiety* 1) Unfamiliar	1) Time must be given to preparation—include others in your household and the custodial parent.
	2) Separation from parent (How will I make it away from parent? How will parent make it away from me?)	2) More frequent contact with child/specific date and travel plans communicated.
	3) Reunion with parent/ remarried unit.	3) Special needs of child known and provided for, e.g., medication, diet, etc.
	4) Fantasy about how the visit will work out. Exaggerated picture based on child's needs: ideal/terrible. (I'll fit right in.) (I'll never fit in.)	4) Physical space for child set up, e.g., room, closet, drawer.
	5) Budding divided loyalties.	5) Child has input into plans for summer.
	6) Previous history of visits may determine	6) Welcoming gesture: favorite food, period of un-

*Jerry Cohen, M.S.W. and Barbara Zerzan, of the 92nd Street YM-WHA, New York City contributed to the development of this guide for parents.

Specific Phase	Emotional Considerations	Practical Considerations
	positive or negative expectations.	interrupted time together, etc. Thoughtful is more important than elaborate.
B. *Transition Phase* (approximately the first 1–3 weeks)	*Heightened Anxiety* 1) Separation and entry to "new" system. 2) Reunion/new significant others may be introduced for the first time.	1) Frequent telephone calls "home." 2) Not criticism but clear expectations put forth through negotiations with child and limit setting, e.g., "This is the way it is done when you are with me. Your mom (dad) and I are *different* (not better or worse)."
C. *Temporary but Ongoing Visit*	1) Period of relative calm or constant struggle. Perhaps more difficult in remarried families where rivalries and divided loyalties are at issue. 2) The task of adjusting to each other's and family's needs dealt with/not dealt with.	1) Predictable time for telephone calls home. 2) Avoid trying to put a year's activity into two months. Moderation on visits to relatives, sightseeing, and "marathon monopoly." 3) Respite time for parents important. 4) In the remarried family, the biological parent and not stepparent should do the parenting especially around limit setting, clear expectations, money. The more the biological parent can do the "heavy work," the *less* likely the stepparent will be seen as and become "wicked."
D. *Leave-taking Phase* (last 3 weeks)	*Heightened Anxiety* 1) Separation. 2) Loss and reaction to that: denial, anger, sadness.	1) More frequent contact "home"—specific date and travel plans communicated. 2) Specific plans for continued contact with the home and family the child is now leaving.

APPENDIX E

Sample Informational Sheet for Schools Regarding Children of Divorce and Remarriage*

Child's Name _____ Date _____

Who is the custodial parent?
Who is the non-custodial parent?
Date of separation:
Date of divorce:
Which parent(s) are remarried?
Name of stepparent(s):
Date of remarriage:
Composition of household in which child lives (include step-siblings, grandparents, etc.):

Does the child have contact with the noncustodial parent? How much? When? What is the composition of the household the child visits?

When was the school informed of the separation? The remarriage? By whom?

Was the child having school problems before the divorce/separation/remarriage? If so, same or different?

---

*This Informational Sheet is an extension of one developed by Drake (1981) for use by teachers and guidance personnel with children of separation and divorce. We have extended it to include more information concerning remarriage.

Clarify below if different in either degree of problem or type of problem.

What was the child's initial reaction to the separation? To the remarriage? Through your observations in school, any change from prior status in a) school work; b) behavior:

Through child's spontaneous and voluntary report:

Through parents' report:

What instructions have been given the school regarding its contact with (or inclusion or exclusion) of the noncustodial parent? Of the stepparent?

Have any household circumstances changed significantly? Examples: move, finances, parent working, change in household composition, visitation, etc.

Bibliography

ANTHONY, E. J. The reactions to adolescents and their behavior. In: *Adolescent Psychosocial Perspectives*, edited by G. Caplan and S. Lebovici. New York: Basic Books, 1969.

APPELBERG, E. *The Uprooted: The Collected Papers of Esther Appelberg*, edited by H. Feiner. New York: Child Welfare League of America, 1977.

AUERBACH, A. B. *Parents Learn Through Discussion: Principles and Practices of Parent Group Education.* New York: John Wiley and Sons, 1968.

BACH, G. R., and WYDEN, P. *The Intimate Enemy (How to Fight Fair In Love and Marriage).* New York: William Morrow & Co., Inc. 1969.

BAER, J. *The Second Wife: How to Live Happily With a Man Who Has Been Married Before.* New York: Doubleday, 1972.

BEAL, E. W. Separation, divorce and single-parent families. In: *The Family Life Cycle: A Framework for Family Therapy*, edited by E. A. Carter and M. McGoldrick, New York: Gardner Press, 1980.

BERLINER, L. Child abuse: What happens next? *Victimotology*, 2, 2, 1977.

BERMAN, C. *Making It as a Stepparent: New Roles, New Rules.* New York: Doubleday, 1980.

BERMAN, E. M., and LIEF, H. I. Marital therapy from a psychiatric perspective: An overview. *American Journal of Psychiatry*, 132, 6: 583–592, June 1975.

BERMAN, E., LIEF, H., and WILLIAMS, A. M. A model of marital interaction. In: *The Handbook of Marriage and Marital Therapy*, edited by G. P. Sholevar. New York: Spectrum Publications, 1981.

BERNARD, J. *Remarriage: A Study of Marriage*, 2nd Ed. New York: Russell and Russell, 1971.

BERNE, E. *Transactional Analysis in Psychotherapy.* New York: Grove Press, 1961.

BIBRING, E. *The Mechanisms of Depression, Affective Disorders.* New York: International Universities Press, 1953.

BITTERMAN, C. M. The multi-marriage family. *Social Casework*, 49:218–221, April 1968.

Black's Law Dictionary, Revised, 4th Edition. St. Paul: West Publishing Co., 1968.

BLOCH, D. A. The clinical home visit. In: *Techniques of Family Psychotherapy: A Primer*, edited by D. A. Bloch. New York: Grune and Stratton, 1973.

371

BOHANNAN, P. Divorce chains, households of remarriage, and multiple divorcers. In: *Divorce and After: An Analysis of the Emotional and Social Problems of Divorce,* edited by Paul Bohannan. New York: Anchor Books, 1971.

BOHANNAN, P. Stepfathers and the Mental Health of Their Children. Final Report, Western Behavioral Sciences Institute, La Jolla, California, 1975.

BOWEN, M. *Family Therapy in Clinical Practice.* New York: Jason Aronson, 1978.

BOWERMAN, C. E., and IRISH, D. P. Some relationships of stepchildren to their parents. *Marriage and Family Living,* 24: 113–121, 1962.

BOWLBY, J. *Attachment and Loss, Volume I: Attachment.* New York: Basic Books, 1969.

BOWLBY, J. *Attachment and Loss, Volume II: Separation: Anxiety and Anger.* New York: Basic Books, 1973.

BOWLBY, J. *Attachment and Loss, Volume III: Loss: Sadness and Depression.* New York: Basic Books, 1980.

BRADEN, J. A. Adoption in a changing world. *Social Casework,* 51: 8, 1970.

BRADT, J. O. *The Family Diagram.* Washington, D.C.: Groome Center, 1981.

BURGESS, A. W. and HOLSTROM, L. L. *Rape: Victims of Crisis.* Maryland: Robert J. Brady Co., 1975.

BURGESS, A. W., HOLSTROM, L. L., and McCAUSLAND, M. P. Child sexual assault by a family member: Decisions following disclosure. *Victimotology,* 2, 2, 1977.

CALVIN, D. A. Joint custody: A family and social policy. In: *Children of Separation and Divorce: Management and Treatment,* edited by I. R. Stuart and L. E. Abt. New York: Van Nostrand Reinhold, 1981.

CARTER, E. A., and McGOLDRICK, M. (Eds.) *The Family life Cycle: A Framework for Family Therapy.* New York: Gardner Press, 1980.

CROHN, H., SAGER, C. J., RODSTEIN, E., BROWN, H. S., WALKER, L., and BEIR, J. Understanding and treating the child in the remarried family. In: *Children of Separation and Divorce: Management and Treatment,* edited by I. R. Stuart and L. E. Abt. New York: Van Nostrand Reinhold, 1981.

CUMMINGS, E. E. *Poems: 1923–1954.* New York: Harcourt, Brace, 1954.

DeFRANCIS, V. *Protecting the Child Victim of Sex Crimes Committed by Adults.* Denver: American Humane Association, Children's Division, 1969.

DESPERT, L. J. *Children of Divorce.* New York: Doubleday, 1953.

DICKS, H. V. *Marital Tensions: Clinical Studies Towards a Psychological Theory of Interaction.* London: Routledge and Kegan Paul, 1967.

DRAKE, A. Helping children cope with divorce: The role of the school. In: *Children of Separation and Divorce: Management and Treatment,* edited by I. R. Stuart and L. E. Abt. New York: Van Nostrand Reinhold, 1981.

DRAUGHON, M. Stepmother's model identification in relation to mourning in the child. *Psychological Reports,* 36: 183–189, 1975.

DUBERMAN, L. *The Reconstituted Family: A Study of Remarried Couples and Their Children.* Chicago: Nelson-Hall, 1975.

DUBERMAN, L. Step-kin relationships. *Journal of Marriage and the Family,* 35: 283–292, 1973.

DUHL, F. J., KANTOR, D., and DUHL, B. S. Learning, space and action in family therapy: A primer of sculpture. In: *Techniques of Family Psychotherapy: A Primer,* edited by D. A. Bloch. New York: Grune and Stratton, 1973.

EINSTEIN, E. *The Stepfamily: Living, Loving and Learning.* New York: Macmillan, 1982.

EINSTEIN, E. (Ed.) *Stepfamily Bulletin.* A Publication of the Stepfamily Association of America Inc. New York: Human Sciences Press, 1980–82.

EISSLER, R. S., FREUD, A., KRIS, M., and SOLNIT, A. J. (Eds.) *An Anthology of the Psychoanalytic Study of the Child: Psychoanalytic Assessment: The Diagnostic Profile.* New Haven: Yale University Press, 1977.

ERIKSON, E. H. *Identity: Youth and Crisis.* New York: W. W. Norton, 1968.

FAST, I., and CAIN, A. C. The stepparent role: Potential for disturbances in family functioning. *American Journal of Orthopsychiatry,* 36: 485–491, 1966.

FREUD, A. *Normality and Pathology in Childhood: Assessments of Development.* New York: International Universities Press, 1965.

FREUD, S. *Three Essays on the Theory of Sexuality* (1905). New York: Basic Books, 1962.

FROST, R. "The Death of the Hired Man." In: *Chief Modern Poets of England and America. Volume II,* edited by G. Sanders et al. New York: Macmillan Company, 1962.

FURMAN, E. *A Child's Parent Dies: Studies in Childhood Bereavement.* New Haven: Yale University Press, 1974.

GARDNER, R. A. *The Boys and Girls Book About Divorce.* New York: Bantam, 1971.

GARDNER, R. A. *The Parents Book About Divorce.* New York: Doubleday, 1977.

GARDNER, R. A. *Psychotherapy With Children of Divorce.* New York: Aronson, 1976.

GEISER, R. *Hidden Victims.* Boston: Beacon Press, 1979.

GLENN, N., and WEAVER, C. N. The marital happiness of remarried divorced persons. *Journal of Marriage and the Family,* 39: 331–337, 1977.

GOLDSTEIN, H. S. Reconstituted families: The second marriage and its children. *Psychiatric Quarterly,* 48: 433–440, 1974.

GOLDSTEIN, J., FREUD, A., and SOLNIT, A. J. *Beyond the Best Interests of the Child.* New York: Free Press, 1973.

GOLDSTEIN, M. J. (Ed.) *New Developments in Interventions with Families of Schizophrenics.* San Francisco: Jossey-Bass, 1981.

GOULD, R. L. The phases of adult life: A study in developmental psychology. *American Journal of Psychiatry,* 129, 5:521–531, 1972.

GOULD, R. L. *Transformations: Growth and Change in Adult Life.* New York: Touchstone Edition, Simon and Schuster, 1978.

GREEN, P. *A Second Mother for Martha.* New York: Human Sciences Press, 1978.

GREENE, B., LUSTIG, N., and LEE, R. Marital therapy when one spouse has a primary affective disorder. *American Journal of Psychiatry,* 133, 7: 827–830, 1976.

GREENE, B. L. *A Clinical Approach to Marital Problems.* Springfield, IL: C. C. Thomas, 1970.

GUERIN, P. J., and PENDAGAST, E. G. Evaluation of family system and genogram. In: *Family Therapy: Theory and Practice,* edited by P. J. Guerin. New York: Gardner Press, 1976.

HARDING, M. E. *The Way of All Women: A Psychological Interpretation.* New York: Harper Colophon Books, 1975.

HAYNES, J. M. *Divorce Mediation.* New York: Springer, 1981.

HETHERINGTON, E. M., COX, M., and COX, R. The aftermath of divorce. In: *Mother-Child, Father-Child Relations,* edited by J. J. Stephens and A. Matthews. Washington, D.C.: NAEYC, 1977.

HOFFMAN, L. *Foundations of Family Therapy: A Conceptual Framework for Systems Change.* New York: Basic Books, 1981.

HUNT, M., and HUNT, B. *The Divorce Experience.* New York: McGraw-Hill, 1977.

HUNTER, J. E., and SCHUMAN, N. Chronic reconstitution as a family style. *Social Work,* 25: 446–451, 1980.

JACOBSON, D. Stepfamilies: Myths and realities. *Social Work,* 24, 3: 202–208, 1979.

JOLOWICZ, A. R. The hidden parent: Some effects of the parent's life upon the child's use of a foster home. In: *Source Book of Teaching Materials on the Welfare of Children.* New York: Council on Social Work Education, 1969.

KAPLAN, H. S. *Disorders of Sexual Desire.* New York: Brunner/Mazel, 1979.

KAPLAN, S. L. Structural family therapy for children of divorce: Case reports. *Family Process,* 16: 75–83, 1977.

KATZ, S. *When Parents Fail.* Boston: Beacon Press, 1971.

KEATS, J. Letter to George and Thomas Keats (1817). *English Romantic Poetry and Prose,* edited by Russell and Noyes. New York: Oxford University Press, 1956.

KELLY, J. B. The visiting relationship after divorce. In: *Children of Separation and Divorce: Management and Treatment,* edited by I. R. Stuart and L. E. Abt. New York: Van Nostrand Reinhold, 1981.

KELLY, J. B., and WALLERSTEIN, J. S. Brief interventions with children in divorcing families. *American Journal of Orthopsychiatry,* 47: 23–39, 1977.

KELLY, J. B., and WALLERSTEIN, J. S. The effects of parental divorce: Experiences of the child in early latency. *American Journal of Orthopsychiatry,* 46: 20–42, January 1976.

KOHL, R. N. Pathologic reactions of marital partners to improvement of patients. *American Journal of Psychiatry,* 118: 1036–1041, 1962.

KOHUT, H. *The Restoration of the Self.* New York: International Universities Press, 1977.

LAING, R. D. *The Politics of the Family and Other Essays.* London: Tavistock Publications, 1971.

LAMB, M. E. The effects of divorce on children's personality development. *Journal of Divorce,* 1(2): 163–174, 1977.

LANGNER, T. S., and MICHAEL, S. T. *Life Stress and Mental Health.* New York: Free Press, 1963.

LAQUEUR, P. Mechanisms of change in multiple family therapy. In: *Progress in Group and Family Therapy,* edited by C. J. Sager and H. S. Kaplan. New York: Brunner/Mazel, 1972.

LATHANS-JAFFE. *I'm My Own Grandpa.* Performed by Lonzo & Oscar in 1946. Stars of the Grand Old Opry, 1926–1974. RCA 2 Record Set. CPL2-04661.

LEVINSON, D. J., with DARROW, C. N., KLEIN, E. B., LEVINSON, M. H., and McKEE, B. *The Seasons of a Man's Life.* New York: Ballantine Books, 1978.

LEVINSON, D. J., DARROW, C. M., KLEIN, E. B., LEVINSON, M. H., and McKEE, B. The psychosocial development of men in early adulthood and the mid-life transition. In: *Life History Research in Psychopathology, Vol. 3.,* edited by D. R. Ricks, A. Thomas and M. Roff. Minneapolis: University of Minnesota Press, 1974.

LEWIS, H. C. *All About Families, The Second Time Around.* Atlanta: Peachtree Publishers, 1980.

LEWIS, J. M., BEAVERS, W. R., GOSSETT, J. T., PHILLIPS, V. A. *No Single Thread: Psychological Health in Family Systems.* New York: Brunner/Mazel, 1976.

LOVE, N. A wedding with some relative problems. *New York Times.* June 24, 1981.

LURIE, A., and HAROLD, R. Multiple group counseling with discharged schizophrenic adolescents and their parents. Paper presented at American Group Psychotherapy Association Conference, Chicago, January 1968.

LUSTIG, N., DRESSER, J. W., SPELLMAN, S. W., and MURRAY, T. B. Incest: A family group survival pattern. *Archives of General Psychology,* 14: 31–40, 1966.

MacGREGOR, R., RITCHIE, A. M., SERRANO, A. C., SCHUSTER, F. P. *Multiple Impact Therapy with Families.* New York: McGraw-Hill, 1964.

MacNeill/Lehrer Report: *Gang Violence.* (Television Program) Public Broadcasting System, Dec. 8, 1981. Script available. Channel 13, N.Y.C.

McGOLDRICK, M., and CARTER, E. A. Forming a remarried family. In: *The Family Life Cycle: A Framework for Family Therapy,* edited by E. A. Carter and M. McGoldrick. New York: Gardner Press, 1980.

MADDOX, B. *The Half-parent: Living With Other People's Children.* New York: Signet, 1975.

MAHLER, M. S., PINE, F., and BERGMAN, A. *The Psychological Birth of the Human Infant.* New York: Basic Books, 1975.

MAYLEAS, D. *Rewedded Bliss: Love, Alimony, Incest, Ex-Spouses and Other Domestic Blessings.* New York: Basic Books, 1977.

MECHANIC, D. *Mental Health and Social Policy:* Englewood Cliffs, N.J.: Prentice-Hall, 1969.

MESSINGER, L., WALKER, K. N., and FREEMAN, S. J. Preparation for remarriage following divorce. *American Journal of Orthopsychiatry,* 48, 2: 263–272, April 1978.

MESSINGER, L. Remarriage between divorced people with children from previous marriages: A proposal for preparation for remarriage. *Journal of Marriage and Family Counseling*, 2: 193–200, 1976.

MISHLER, E., and WAXLER, N. (Eds.) *Family Process and Schizophrenia.* New York: Science House, 1968.

MNOOKIN, R. H. Child custody adjudication: Judicial functions in the face of indeterminancy. *Law and Contemporary Problems*, 39: 276–293, Summer, 1975.

MONAHAN, T. P. The changing nature and instability of remarriages. *Eugenics Quarterly*, 5: 73–85, June 1958.

MONAHAN, T. P. How stable are remarriages? *The American Journal of Sociology*, 58: 280–288, November 1952.

MOSKOWITZ, F. I left it at my father's/mother's house. *New York Times.* November 12, 1981.

MOWATT, M. Group psychotherapy for stepfathers and their wives. *Psychotherapy: Theory, Research and Practice*, 9: 328–331, 1972.

National Analysis of Official Child Neglect and Abuse Report. Englewood, CO: The American Humane Association, November 1979.

NEUGARTEN, B. L. Adult personality: Toward a psychology of the life cycle. In: *Middle Age and Aging: A Reader in Social Psychology*, edited by B. L. Neugarten. Chicago: University of Chicago Press, 1968.

NICHOLS, W. Divorce and remarriage education. *Journal of Divorce*, 1, 2: 153–161, Winter 1977.

OKPAKU, S. R. Psychology: Impediment or aid in child custody cases? *Rutgers Law Review*, 29: 117–153, Summer 1976.

PALAZZOLI, M. S., BOSCOLO, L., CECCHIN, G., and PRATA, G. *Paradox and Counterparadox: A New Model in the Therapy of the Family in Schizophrenic Transaction.* New York: Jason Aronson, 1978.

PAPP, P. Family choreography. In: *Family Therapy: Theory and Practice*, edited by P. J. Guerin. New York: Gardner Press, 1976.

PATTISON, M. E. Foreword. In: *Family Therapy of Drug and Alcohol Abuse*, edited by E. Kaufman and P. Kaufman. New York: Gardner Press, 1979.

PECK, B. B. *A Family Therapy Notebook: Experiential Techniques of Family and Couples Psychotherapy.* New York: Libra Publishers, 1974.

PEYSER, H. Lecture given at Jewish Federation of Philanthropies, New York, 1980.

POST, E. L. *The New Emily Post's Etiquette.* New York: Funk and Wagnall, 1975.

RANSOM, J. W., SCHLESINGER, S., and DERDEYN, A. A stepfamily in formation. *American Journal of Orthopsychiatry*, 49: 36–43, January 1979.

RHODES, S. L. A developmental approach to the life cycle of the family. *Social Casework*, 301–311, May 1977.

RHODES, S. L. *Surviving Family Life.* New York: G. P. Putnam, 1981.

RICCI, I. Divorce, remarriage and the schools. *Stepfamily Bulletin: Newsletter of the Stepfamily Association of America.* 2–3, Fall 1980.

ROFES, E. E. (Ed.). *The Kids' Book of Divorce: By, For and About Kids, by the Unit at Fayerweather Street School.* Massachusetts: Lewis Publishing Co., 1981.

ROSENBERG, M. *Society and the Adolescent Self-Image.* Princeton, N.J.: Princeton University Press, 1965.

ROSENFELD, A. A. Sexual misuse and the family. *Victimology*, 2, 2, 1977.

ROSENTHAL, D. Genetic research in the schizophrenic syndrome. In: *The Schizophrenic Reactions*, edited by R. Cancro. New York: Brunner/Mazel, 1970.

ROSENTHAL, D., WENDER, P., KETY, S., SCHULSINGER, F., WELNER, J., and OSTERGAARD, L. Schizophrenics' offspring reared in adoptive homes. *Journal of Psychiatric Research*, 6 (Supp. 1), 1972.

SAGER, C. J. From a survey of private patients. Unpublished, 1981.

SAGER, C. J., WALKER, E., BROWN, H. S., CROHN, H., and RODSTEIN, E. Improving functioning of the remarried family system. *Journal of Marital and Family Therapy*, 3–13, January 1981.

SAGER, C. J., BROWN, H., CROHN, H., RODSTEIN, E., and WALKER, E. Remarriage revisited. *Family and Child Mental Health Journal,* 6: 19–33, 1980.

SAGER, C. J. A Typology of Intimate Relationships. *Journal of Sex and Marital Therapy,* 3: 83–112, 1977.

SAGER, C. J. *Marriage Contracts and Couple Therapy: Hidden Forces in Intimate Relationships.* New York: Brunner/Mazel, 1976.

SAGER, C. J. Sexual dysfunctions and marital discord. In: *The New Sex Therapy,* by H. S. Kaplan. New York: Brunner/Mazel, 1974.

SAGER, C. J., and KAPLAN, H. S. (Eds.) *Progress in Group and Family Therapy.* New York: Brunner/Mazel, 1972.

SAGER, C. J., KAPLAN, H. S., GUNDLACH, R., KREMER, M., LENZ, R., and ROYCE, J. The marriage contract. *Family Process,* 10: 311, 1971.

SAGER, C. J. Transference in conjoint treatment of marital couples. *Archives of General Psychiatry,* 16: 185–193, 1967.

SCARF, M. *Unfinished Business: Pressure Points in the Lives of Women.* New York: Doubleday, 1980.

SCHEFLEN, A. E. *Levels of Schizophrenia.* New York: Brunner/Mazel, 1981.

SCHWARTZ, M. Situational/transitional groups: A conceptualization and review. *American Journal of Orthopsychiatry,* 45: 744–755, 1975.

SCHULMAN, G. L. Myths that intrude on the adaptation of the stepfamily. *Social Casework,* 53: 131–139, 1972.

SCHULTZ, L. G. The child sex victim: Social, psychological and legal perspectives. *Child Welfare,* 11, 3, 1973.

SEAGRAVE, R. T. Marriage and mental health. *Journal of Sex and Marital Therapy,* 6: 187–198, 1980.

SEARLES, H. F. The effort to drive the other person crazy—An element in the aetiology and psychotherapy of schizophrenia. *British Journal of Medical Psychology,* 32: 1–18, 1959.

SGROI, S. M. Sexual molestation of children: The last frontier in child abuse. *Children Today,* 1975.

SINGER, L. *Stages: The Crises that Shape Your Marriage.* New York: Grosset and Dunlap, 1980.

SPECK, R. V., and ATTNEAVE, C. L. *Family Networks.* New York: Pantheon Books, 1973.

SPIRO, H. Prevention in psychiatry: Primary, secondary and tertiary. In: *Comprehensive Textbook of Psychiatry, III,* edited by H. I. Kaplan et al. Baltimore: Williams and Wilkins, 1980.

SPITZ, R. A. *The First Year of Life.* New York: International Universities Press, 1965.

SPITZ, R. A. *A Genetic Field Theory of Ego Formation.* New York: International Universities Press, 1959.

STACK, C. Who owns the child: Divorce and child custody decisions in middle-class families. *Social Problems,* 4: 505–515, April 1976.

STEINBERG, J. L. The therapeutic potential of the divorce process. *American Bar Association Journal,* 62: 617–620, May 1976.

STIERLIN, H. *Separating Parents and Adolescents: A Perspective on Running Away, Schizophrenia and Waywardness.* New York: Quadrangle, 1979.

STUART, I. R., and ABT, L. E. (Eds.) *Children of Separation and Divorce: Management and Treatment.* New York: Van Nostrand Reinhold, 1981.

SUGAR, M. (Ed.) *The Adolescent in Group and Family Therapy.* New York: Brunner/Mazel, 1975.

SUZUKI, S. *Zen Mind, Beginner's Mind.* New York: Weatherhill, 1970.

TERKELSEN, K. G. Toward a theory of the family life cycle. In: *The Family Life Cycle: A Framework for Family Therapy,* edited by E. A. Carter and M. McGoldrick. New York: Gardner Press, 1980.

TESSMAN, L. H. *Children of Parting Parents.* New York: Aronson, 1978.

THOMAS, A., and CHESS, S. *Temperament and Development.* New York: Brunner/Mazel, 1977.

Bibliography

Bibliography

Bibliography 377

Bibliography

Bibliography

Bibliography 377

Bibliography

THOMSEN, R. *Bill W.* New York: Popular Library, 1975.
TIGER, L., and FOX, R. *The Imperial Animal.* New York: Holt, Rinehart and Winston, 1971.
VISHER, E. B., and VISHER, J. S. Common problems of stepparents and their spouses. *American Journal of Orthopsychiatry,* 48: 252-262, 1978.
VISHER, E. B., and VISHER, J. S. *Stepfamilies: A Guide to Working with Stepparents and Stepchildren.* New York: Brunner/Mazel, 1979.
VISHER, E. B., and VISHER, J. S. *A Stepfamily Workshop Manual.* California: Stepfamily Association of America, 1980.
WALD, E. *The Remarried Family: Challenge and Promise.* New York: Family Service Association of America, 1981.
WALKER, K. N., and MESSINGER, L. Remarriage after divorce: Dissolution and reconstitution of family boundaries. *Family Process,* 18, 185-192, June 1979.
WALKER, K. N., ROGERS, J., and MESSINGER, L. Remarriage after a divorce: A review. *Social Casework,* 58: 276-285, 1977.
WALKER, L., BROWN, H., CROHN, H., RODSTEIN, E., ZEISEL, E., and SAGER, C. J. An annotated bibliography of the remarried, the living together and their children. *Family Process,* 18: 193-212, 1979.
WALLERSTEIN, J. S. Talk given at Jewish Family Service, New York. Unpublished, 1976.
WALLERSTEIN, J. S., and KELLY, J. B. California's children of divorce. *Psychology Today,* 13, 1, 1980a.
WALLERSTEIN, J. S. and KELLY, J. B. *Surviving the Breakup: How Children and Parents Cope With Divorce.* New York: Basic Books, 1980b.
WALLERSTEIN, J. S., and KELLY, J. B. The effects of parental divorce: Experiences of the child in later latency. *American Journal of Orthopsychiatry,* 46: 256-269, April 1976.
WALLERSTEIN, J. S., and KELLY, J. B. The effects of parental divorce: Experiences of the preschool child. *Journal of the American Academy of Child Psychiatry,* 14: 600-616, Autumn 1974a.
WALLERSTEIN, J. S., and KELLY, J. B. The effects of parental divorce: The adolescent experience. In: *The Child in His Family,* edited by A. Koupernik. New York: John Wiley and Sons, 1974b.
WESTOFF, L. A. *The Second Time Around: Remarriage in America.* New York: Viking Press, 1975.
WILSON, K. L., ZUCHER, L., McADAMS. D. C., and CURTIS, R. L. Stepfathers and stepchildren: An exploratory analysis from two national surveys. *Journal of Marriage and the Family,* 35: 526-536, 1975.
WINNICOTT, D. W. *The Maturational Processes and the Facilitating Environment: Studies in the Theory of Emotional Development.* New York: International Universities Press, 1965.
WISEMAN, J. M., and FISKE, J. A lawyer therapist team as mediator in a martial crisis. *Social Work,* 25, 6: 442-446, November 1980.
WYNNE, L., RYCOFF, I., DAY, J., and HIRSCH, S. Pseudomutuality in the family relations of schizophrenics. *Psychiatry,* 21: 205-220, 1958.
ZINNER, J. The implications of projective identification for marital interaction. In: *Contemporary Marriage: Structure, Dynamics and Therapy,* edited by H. Grunebaum and J. Christ. Boston: Little, Brown, 1976.

FILMS

Stepparenting. 16 mm, color. Polymorph Films, 331 Newberry Street, Boston.

Index

Unconscious:
  and adoption, 312
  and divorce, 165–66
  and family of origin replay, 278
  and marital contract, 67, 355
  and marital therapy, 196, 198
  and sabotage of treatment, 244, 348–
    49
  and sexuality, 219–20
Unemployment, 201
United States Census, 21

Values, 76
  and marital contracts, 72
  in reminder list, 361
  and therapists, 86–88
Vermont State Hospital, 319
Visher, E. B., 340, 377*n.*
Visher, J. S., 340, 377*n.*
Visitation rights, 29, 35, 56, 203, 269
Vocational training, 111

Wald, E., 233, 258, 293, 299, 312, 313,
    318, 377*n.*
Walker, E., xiii
Walker, K. N., 5, 277, 377*n.*
Walker, L., 90, 372*n.*
Wallerstein, J. S., 22, 90, 106, 225, 226,
    230, 249, 254, 374*n.*, 377*n.*
Weaver, C. N., 63, 373*n.*
Weddings, 275, 279, 352
Weight Watchers, 19
Widowhood, 65
Winnicott, D. W., 40, 44, 229, 377*n.*
Withdrawal, 149, 191
Withholding, 288
Working-through, 86
Wynne, L., 194, 377*n.*

Young Men and Women's Association,
    335

Zinner, J., 174, 377*n.*